Reimagining Art History with Artificial Intelligence

Leda Cempellin • Melissa Geiger
Editors

Reimagining Art History with Artificial Intelligence

Navigating Limitations and Pioneering New Paths for Innovation

palgrave
macmillan

Editors
Leda Cempellin
South Dakota State University
Brookings, SD, USA

Melissa Geiger
East Stroudsburg University
East Stroudsburg, PA, USA

ISBN 978-3-032-21684-7 ISBN 978-3-032-21685-4 (eBook)
https://doi.org/10.1007/978-3-032-21685-4

This Palgrave Macmillan imprint is published by the registered company Springer Nature Switzerland AG
The registered company address is: Gewerbestrasse 11, 6330 Cham, Switzerland

Preface

This anthology originated from the virtual Colloquium on *Art History & Artificial Intelligence* hosted by Dr Leda Cempellin (South Dakota State University) and Dr Melissa Geiger (East Stroudsburg University) on February 19, 2024. Broadcast via zoom from South Dakota State University (Fig. 1.1),[1] the event brought together scholars and artists from across continents who were already engaged in active experimentation with AI in their work. To spark dialogue at its early stage, the programme featured diverse formats—individual presentations, interdisciplinary round tables, and spontaneous conversations. Conceived as a broad event to capture a pivotal moment of transition for the discipline, the colloquium balanced wide-ranging theoretical questions with concrete examples of change, both recent and ongoing.

As scholars gathered and conversations unfolded during the colloquium, some key questions emerged about ethics, pedagogy, agency, and the future of creative practice. These questions revealed common threads across diverse perspectives. The colloquium became the main catalyst for the efforts that led to this anthology, supported by a grant from The Gladys Krieble Delmas Foundation awarded to South Dakota State University in September 2024.

[1] The initial strategy for recruiting authors for this anthology extended beyond the Feb. 19, 2024, Colloquium. It included sessions at SECAC in October 2024 (*Teaching Art History with Artificial Intelligence*) and CAA in February 2025 (*Contemporary Artists using AI: A Paradigm Shift for Art Historians*). Both sessions were co-chaired by Leda Cempellin and Melissa Geiger.

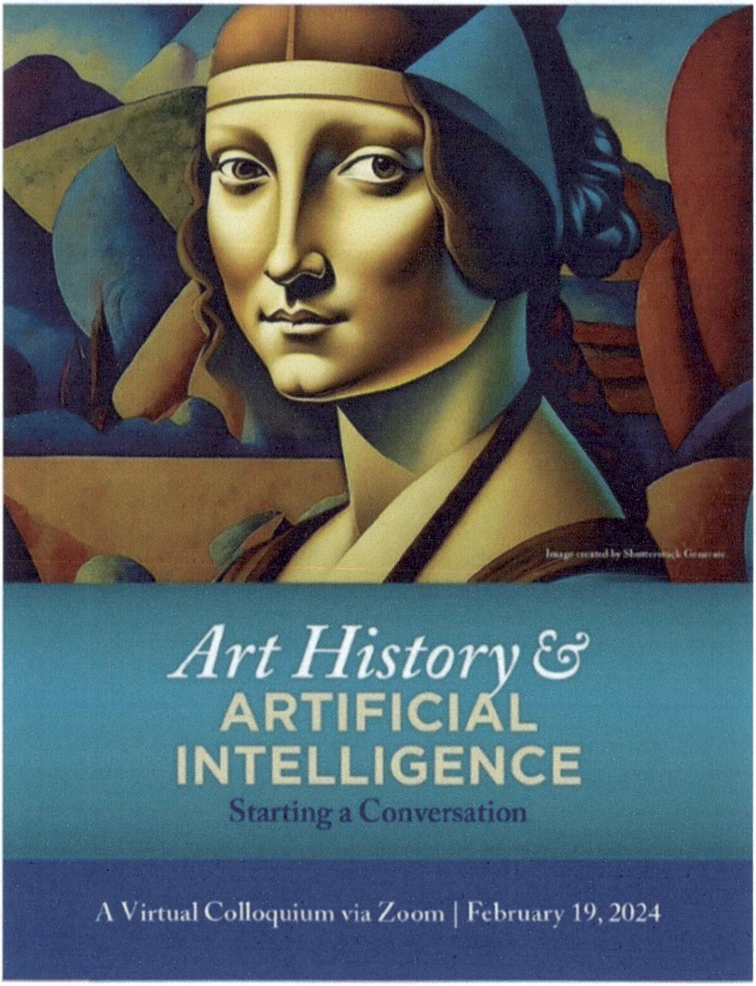

Fig. 1.1 *Art History & Artificial Intelligence: Starting a Conversation*, Colloquium hosted at South Dakota State University, February 19, 2024. Cover of the programme. Image generated with Shutterstock AI powered by DALL·E. Courtesy Professor Marisa Ten Brink, Graphic Design, School of Design, SDSU

As the work on this anthology progressed with the authors, a unifying vision gradually crystallised: AI is not a passing set of tools but a catalyst for rethinking art history's professional ecosystem across research, museums, pedagogy, and global contexts. Amid uncertainty and diverse attitudes towards AI, this volume avoids imposing a single position. Instead, it offers a rich and nuanced dialogue, providing both the foundations for a multi-pronged theoretical debate and insights into how changes are beginning to take shape across the art history field. Through this approach, the anthology seeks to foster a thoughtful relationship with AI that balances curiosity with care, and possibility with responsibility.

Brookings, SD, USA — Leda Cempellin
East Stroudsburg, PA, USA — Melissa Geiger

Acknowledgements

This anthology was supported by the Gladys Krieble Delmas Foundation. Special thanks to Dr Pat Crawford, School of Design, whose support enabled the corresponding editor to devote time and focus to completing this project. For institutional assistance, we thank SDSU Division of Research and Economic Development and the Academic Shared Service Center, with particular gratitude to Dr Dianne Nagy and Chris Francis. We appreciate Dissertation Editor, notably Dr Joseph Hurtgen, for developmental review made possible by Delmas funding, as well as the AI platforms' policies that support scholarly dissemination. We also thank Santharine I at Straive and Danilo Restiotto. The assistance our authors received from their institutions and colleagues is noted in the respective chapters. Above all, we thank our contributing authors for their commitment and rigour, and Camille Davies and Uma Vinesh at Palgrave and Springer Nature for their guidance throughout this project.

Contents

Notes on Contributors

Leda Cempellin, PhD University of Parma (Italy), is a professor of Art History at South Dakota State University. Her interdisciplinary individual and collaborative research spans late modernism, art history SoTL, and museum studies, focusing on collaborative practices, teamwork, metacognition, wayfinding, artificial intelligence, and critical thinking. She has published in various peer-reviewed journals including *AHPP*, *International Journal of Education & The Arts*, *Educational Research and Evaluation*, *Nierika*, *Nuova Museologia*, the *Interdisciplinary Journal of Signage and Wayfinding*, and soon *Teaching & Learning Inquiry*. Her single-authored books include *L'Iperrealismo 'Fotografico' Americano in Pittura* (Cleup, 2004) and *The Idea, Identity and Art of Daniel Spoerri* (Vernon Press, 2017). From 2021 to 2024, she served as the inaugural Associate Director of the School of Design at South Dakota State University and earned five non-degree professional development credentials from the University of Cape Town and at the University of Toronto to hone her skills in project management and leadership. Cempellin's research has evolved into leadership roles in large-scale collaborative projects focused on capturing broad phases of cultural transition: before leading the efforts of this anthology, she co-edited with Dr Pat Crawford the anthology *Museum Studies for a Post-Pandemic World: Mentoring, Collaborations, and Interactive Knowledge Transfer in Times of Transformation* (Routledge, 2024). Cempellin's research has been supported by the FUNd for Museum Studies, the EFG Foundation, the Gladys Krieble Delmas Foundation, and the National Endowment for the Arts. She has been serving in governance roles at the College Art Association since 2013.

Bárbara Romero Ferrón is a research associate at the Provenance Lab, Leuphana University, and a senior researcher at iArtHis_Lab, University of Málaga. She holds a BA and MA in Art History from the University of Málaga and completed a fully funded PhD at the CulturePlex Lab, Western University (Canada), with a focus on computational analysis. Her current work centres on knowledge graphs and complex network analysis applied to cultural phenomena, particularly in the areas of exhibition and provenance studies. She is finalising a monograph on exhibitions and network analysis and collaborates with institutions such as the Getty Research Institute, the Rijksmuseum, and Spain's National Research Council. Since 2019, she has taught computational methods in art history in various academic settings and languages. She also serves as Associate Director of the Digital Art History Summer School (DAHSS), organised by the University of Málaga.

Melissa Geiger is Associate Professor of Art History in the Art + Media + Design department at East Stroudsburg University of Pennsylvania. She earned both her MA and PhD in Art History at Pennsylvania State University, after earning degrees in music performance and arts and music management from Manhattanville College. Her scholarly contributions demonstrate breadth and scope—one particular area of focus is paradigm shifts throughout art's history, often focusing on emerging technologies and how they shape and/or deconstruct traditional concepts in the arts, be it the invention of photography, Rauschenberg's pioneering Experiments in Art and Technology or today's emergence of AI. Her interdisciplinary approach to art history led to her oversight and leadership in co-founding the academic art history association, the Paragone Society, and co-designing its inaugural conference in collaboration with the University of Michigan, Flint Art Department, and the Flint Museum of Art. In the spirit of Rauschenberg's Overseas Cultural Interchange Project, Geiger has curated exhibitions and partnered with multiple community initiatives fostering community support and engagement in the arts.

Jennifer L. Karson is an artist who uses scientific processes and technologies as creative catalysts. She earned a full fellowship to attend the San Francisco Art Institute, where she completed an MFA in Design + Technology. A senior lecturer at the University of Vermont, where she also earned her BA, her current research and practice employs studio-sourced datasets and speculative design frameworks that imagine symbiotic plant and machine relationships. Bridging the worlds of art and engineering, she founded the art/science collective Vermont Makers and, as director of the UVM FabLab for a decade, oversaw the significant expansion of its footprint and interdisciplinary reach. Karson teaches digital fabrication and generative design, and in 2020 she founded and has since led the art and AI research project, Plant Machine Design. Karson exhibits her work nationally and internationally and has secured funding from the National Endowment for the Arts and the National Science Foundation. Recent solo exhibitions include *The Generative Tree* and *Liquid Architectures.* She's created numerous site-specific sound installations and released four musical recordings including the solo album *Bad Ju Ju*.

Kay Kim is a media scholar with a master's degree in Humanities from the University of Chicago. She presented her MA thesis *Machine-Aided Creativity in the Age with Artificial Intelligence* at the 2025 Society for Cinema and Media Studies Annual Conference. As part of her research methodology, she practises prompt engineering with diffusion models to create digital images. Her research interests are media aesthetics, visual culture, and philosophy of media. She is currently a lector in the "Little Red Schoolhouse" Writing Program at the University of Chicago.

Monica Lanaro holds an MA in Arts and Cultural Management from Ca' Foscari University of Venice and has over a decade of experience developing programmes at the intersection of culture, technology, and digital engagement. She is currently Head of News for Southern Europe at TikTok, and previously coordinated cultural partnerships for the region at Google Arts & Culture. Her work focuses on digital cultural mediation, institutional collaboration, and the design of technologically driven cultural experiences. She has received recognition from ByteDance and the Tate/Microsoft IK Prize.

Emily Leifer is an adjunct professor at Seton Hall University and Montclair State University. She earned her PhD in the History of Art from Bryn Mawr College. Her work examines the connections between ecology and abstraction in twentieth-century American art. Her research has been published in the *Journal of the Archives of American Art* and supported by the Getty Research Institute.

Adriel Luis is a writer, artist, and curator who is interested in the ways that technology informs human connections and community organising. His life's work is focused on highlighting the mutual thriving of artistic integrity and social vigilance. He is a part of the iLL-Literacy arts collective, which creates music and media to strengthen Black and Asian coalitions, and he is creative director of Bombshelltoe, a collaborative of artists and leaders from frontline communities responding to nuclear histories. From 2013 to 2026, Luis was the Curator of Digital and Emerging Practice at the Smithsonian Asian Pacific American Center, where he curated projects in a range of venues including the Smithsonian American Art Museum in Washington DC; MoMA and Pearl River Mart in New York City; Queensland Art Gallery in Brisbane, Australia; Silo Park in Auckland, Aotearoa; Atom Bar in Buenos Aires, Argentina; and an abandoned Foodland in Honolulu, Hawai'i. His writing has appeared in *Poetry Magazine*, the *Asian American Literary Review*, and *Smithsonian Magazine*. He has spoken at the Tate Modern, Yale University, the National Museum of African American History and Culture, and the China Academy of Fine Arts. He has a degree from the University of California, Davis in Community and Regional Development and a minor in Asian American Studies. He is the author of *Going Pop*, an online periodical about fatherhood as an artistic experience. His ancestors are rooted in Toisan, China, and migrated through Hong Kong, Mexico, and the United States. Luis was born and raised on Ohlone land.

Arvin Maghsoudlou received his PhD in Art History from Southern Methodist University (2025) and is now the Gramian-Emrani Family Curatorial Fellow in Ancient Iranian Art at the Los Angeles County Museum of Art. He specialises in the art of late antique West Asia, with a particular interest in materiality, sensory studies, and technical art history. Maghsoudlou was previously the Andrew W. Mellon Fellow at the Metropolitan Museum of Art, where he advanced his research on late antique Iranian silver. He has taught multiple courses on the art of Iran, ancient West Asia, and the Islamic world, and his recent and forthcoming publications address a range of topics, including silver vessels, Sasanian rock reliefs, and sensory experiences in late antique Iran.

Kimiko Matsumura is an assistant professor of Art History at Lake Forest College specialising in modern and contemporary art. Her research addresses intersections of art and science, the role of visual culture in shaping knowledge and knowledge-making practices, and inclusive pedagogy. She holds a PhD in Art History from Rutgers University.

Andrew Murray lectures on the History of Art at the Open University, UK, specialising in the art and ceremony of late medieval France and

Valois Burgundy (c. 1350–1520). He investigates how authority—cultural, legal, and political—is manifested in visual culture, paying particular attention to the representation and performance of emotions and virtues. He has published on tomb sculpture, funerary ceremony, Jan van Eyck, political rhetoric, and Johan Huizinga. Some of these ideas have spilled out into discussions of contemporary issues in visual culture, finding their way into Andrew's published articles on digital painting, the concept of spectacle, and AI-generated images.

Nuria Rodríguez Ortega is Professor of Art History at the University of Málaga and Director of iArtHis_Lab, a research group focused on the digital, computational, and techno-critical study of artistic culture. She holds a PhD in Art History, a Master's in Cognitive Science, and a Specialist Certificate in Digital Humanities. Her research explores the application of data analytics, natural language processing, and computer vision to the analysis of complex cultural systems, as well as the impact of artificial intelligence on the classification and interpretation of cultural objects. She has published widely on critical and post-critical museology within the framework of digital culture and curatorial practice. In addition to her academic work, she directs the Telefónica-UMA Chair, is Honorary President of the Society for Hispanic Digital Humanities, and founded the ReArte.Dix. network. Since 2016, she has served as Academic Director of the Digital Art History Summer School (DAHSS), where she fosters transdisciplinary approaches that combine technological literacy with critical thinking.

Kurt Ralske is Professor of the Practice in Digital Media at the School of the Museum of Fine Arts at Tufts University, Boston. Ralske's video installations and performances have been showcased internationally, including at the Guggenheim Bilbao, the Los Angeles Museum of Contemporary Art, and the Venice Biennale (2009, 2015, 2017, 2019). His artwork, created with custom software, uses digital techniques to reinterpret the archive, proposing new relationships between past and future. Ralske is the recipient of a Rockefeller Foundation Media Arts Fellowship and received First Prize at the Transmediale International Media Art Festival in Berlin in 2003. He is also the developer of AUVI, a real-time video software environment used by artists in over 22 countries for creating and manipulating video art. A book of Ralske's images and texts, *Rediscovering German Futurism 1920–1929*, co-authored with Miriam Atkin, was published by Noncept.

Meghan Rubenstein, PhD is the Curator of Visual Resources and a lecturer in the Art Department at Colorado College. She presents and publishes on a wide range of interconnected topics including visual literacy, documentation practices, information management, and Mesoamerican art. Her current collaboration on a Maya fibre arts project with Dr Astrid Runggaldier has sparked a new interest in AI literacy. Rubenstein is always looking for ways to bring literacy training and explorations of technology into the classroom, where she works primarily with undergraduate liberal arts students. In 2024, Rubenstein was recognised with the Visual Resources Association's Distinguished Service Award.

Astrid Runggaldier, PhD is an associate professor of Instruction in the Department of Art and Art History and the Assistant Director for the Mesoamerica Center at the University of Texas, Austin. Trained in anthropological archaeology and art history, Runggaldier contributes to the undergraduate curriculum of the Department of Art and Art History, the Lozano Long Institute for Latin American Studies, the Native American and Indigenous Studies programme, and the Bridging Disciplines Program in Museum Studies. As the curator for UT's Art and Art History Collection of pre-Columbian artefacts and ethnographic textiles from the Americas, she has been exploring AI's potential and limitations in museum label descriptions and object-based essays.

Brenda Segone is an art historian and a creative writer. She holds a PhD in Art History from Sorbonne University-Paris I, an MA in General and Comparative Literature from the University Sorbonne-Nouvelle Paris 3, and an MFA in Film Directing from ALBA, Beirut. She is currently an assistant professor at the American University in Cairo. Her interests include transcultural theory, epistemologies, and modernisms. She explores topics related to representation, discourse, human perception, and the intersection of Eastern and Western visual cultures through a multidisciplinary lens. Her interdisciplinary work has been recognised by multiple fellowships, awards, and grants. Fluent in five languages, her research is nourished by diverse cultures and artistic traditions.

Giulia Taurino, PhD is a research scientist specialised in AI for the management and preservation of cultural heritage collections. Her work focuses on forms of content organisation in online repositories and digital archives, cultural implications of algorithmic technologies, and applications of AI in the arts, heritage, and museum sectors. Her latest projects include the development of textual corpora for AI research, metadata enrichment in photo-archives, and the design of computational tools for the study of art provenance. Past and present affiliations include Northeastern University, The Alan Turing AI & Arts Interest Group, Getty Research Institute, metalab (at) Harvard, MIT Data, + Feminism Lab. Taurino holds a doctoral degree in Media Studies and Visual Arts from the University of Bologna and the University of Montreal.

Karl van Heerden has been a scholar and lecturer in the fields of Visual Culture and Digital Media for the past 12 years and has a keen interest in the evolution of sexual identity formation and expression in virtual communities. van Heerden's professional history includes a prodigious background in commercial photography. For over a decade, he has established a broad portfolio of commercial clients, as well as appearing in several gallery exhibitions. A synergy of academic and commercial interests enriches van Heerden's academic investigations into Internet culture and virtual communities through an exploration of the role photography plays in online identity formation. Conversely, his simultaneous exposure to the commercial and academic worlds has resulted in an artistic style that is both philosophically and conceptually grounded while remaining commercially appealing.

Amanda Wasielewski is an Associate Senior Lecturer of Digital Humanities and Associate Professor of Art History in the Department of ALM (Archives, Libraries, Museums) at Uppsala University. Her research investigates the use of digital technology in relation to art, visual culture, and spatial practice. Her recent focus has been on the use of artificial intelligence techniques for the analysis and creation of art and other visual media. Wasielewski is the author of four monographs: *Made in Brooklyn: Artists, Hipsters, Makers, Gentrifiers* (Zero, 2018), *From City Space to Cyberspace: Art, Squatting, and Internet Culture in the Netherlands* (Amsterdam University Press, 2021), *Computational Formalism: Art History and Machine Learning* (MIT Press, 2023), and *Digital Photography After AI: Continuity and Rupture in the Age of Automated Images* (MIT Press, 2026). She also co-edited the volume *Critical Digital Art History: Interface and Data Politics in the Post-Digital Era* (Intellect, 2024). In 2023 she was awarded a grant from Google's Artists + Machine Intelligence programme for her work on photography and AI. Wasielewski has recently served as an advisor to the Swedish parliament and collaborated with the European Commission's Joint Research Centre on cultural policy and AI. She has previously worked as a researcher and lecturer in Art History at Stockholm University, Media Studies at the University of Amsterdam, Architectural History at the Spitzer School of Architecture, CCNY, and Art History at Lehman College in New York. Wasielewski has a background as a practising artist and has exhibited her work internationally.

List of Figures

List of Tables

CHAPTER 1

Introduction: Towards an Integrated Ecosystem—AI and Art History as a Synergic Professional Landscape Across Research, Museums, Pedagogy, and Global Perspectives

Leda Cempellin

Art History and AI: Orienting the Epistemological Landscape

Art history, rooted in the humanities, treats artworks as "historical documents" (Preziosi 2009, 7)—emblems of their time and context—through methods that, characteristic of the humanities, value ambiguity, contradiction, and cultural nuance. What Laurent Dubreuil (2025) calls the "attribution of signification" arises from the the interaction between text and an individual's imagination shaped by lived experience, rather than from prediction; as such, it is beyond the current capacities of AI (Dubreuil 2025, 24). By contrast, artificial intelligence (AI) relies on logic, algorithms, and probabilistic models, often in multimodal architectures that integrate text, vision, and other data streams. Large language models (LLMs) excel at generating and interpreting text that mimics human language, while

L. Cempellin (✉)
South Dakota State University, Brookings, SD, USA
e-mail: Leda.Cempellin@sdstate.edu;

L. Cempellin, M. Geiger (eds.), *Reimagining Art History with Artificial Intelligence*,
https://doi.org/10.1007/978-3-032-21685-4_1

computer vision systems process visual data for tasks like identifying objects and distinguishing elements within an image (Dang et al. 2024). As these technologies continue to converge, multimodal large language models (MLLMs) increasingly combine and improve these capabilities, enabling cross-modal reasoning, such as linking image and text for visual question answering that supports art and art history faculty in testing visual analysis assignments (Bayer 2024; Hutson 2024; Smith 2025).

Yet, interpretability in multimodal large language models (MLLMs) that involves "the alignment and decomposition of different modalities" (Dang et al. 2024, 2) is a complex matter, as it operates at the model-development level through techniques aiming at clarifying how internal architectures shape AI models' decision-making, and also at the training and user levels, which involves understanding how learning processes influence outputs (Dang et al. 2024). These distinctions carry practical implications for the humanities in general and art history in particular, because they shape how explanation and interpretation are negotiated when technology mediates cultural meaning. In *Computational Formalism: Art History and Machine Learning*, Amanda Wasielewski (2023) underscores that machine learning relies on dataset compilations shaped by particular cultural actors' priorities—embedding biases at inception and raising crucial questions about "who digitizes artworks and why certain artworks are chosen for digitization" (3). This calls for heightened model literacy in the humanities: interpretive vigilance towards sources, selection, and the effects of algorithmic generalization and interpretability constraints on representation and meaning. The overarching question—"Can AI truly 'understand' human culture?" (Abbood 2025, 192)—clarifies that proactive partnership, rather than delegation, should guide methodological experimentation, involving close human monitoring in what Romero Ferrón and Rodríguez Ortega call "supervised collaboration" (Chap. 8).

This volume presents a coherent synthesis of perspectives on AI by framing it not as a transient collection of tools—though some case studies reference specific platforms to illustrate processes and limitations—but as a catalyst for rethinking how technological shifts intersect with art history's professional ecosystem. These transformations prompt art history to adapt and thrive within an environment where data-driven and probabilistic reasoning introduce new interpretive challenges and opportunities for the humanities. At the same time, AI-driven changes reshape the ways meaning is imagined and negotiated in a digitally mediated world. The chosen approach privileges the interpretive rigour that defines the discipline while engaging AI as a means to generate new questions and problem-solving strategies across research, museums, pedagogy, and global contexts. What matters for this anthology is not which specific platform version an author used—since choices in practical chapters reflect experimental design—but more generally how AI capabilities intersect with creativity, authorship, transparency, interpretation, and cultural responsibility. By foregrounding dataset provenance and interpretive accountability, this volume aims to shape a resilient professional ecosystem that remains relevant even as technologies continue to evolve.

Leaving detailed discussions to the individual chapters, the following overview provides the context neeeded to understand how the four interconnected parts that constitute this volume work together. Part I lays out the theoretical and aesthetic foundations for understanding AI in art history research; Part II shows how these ideas translate into museum practices; Part III explores pedagogical innovations that integrate AI into teaching and learning; and Part IV situates these transformations within global perspectives, addressing cultural bias and representation. This structures helps guide readers in identifying the shared themes and methodological challenges that appear throughout the volume.

Conceptual Foundations for Art History in Computational Culture

Part I establishes the conceptual scaffolding for the entire volume by examining how generative AI is reshaping notions of representation, creativity, and authorship within art history, treating AI not as a transient toolkit but as a probabilistic system of modelling and prediction that both expands generative possibilities (Wasielewski, Karson) and introduces unique tensions with humanistic values of ambiguity, exception, and cultural nuance (Segone, Murray, Ralske).

Amanda Wasielewski (Chap. 2) discusses AI models at the macro level, arguing that generative models function not merely as content generators but as conceptual models that synthesise vast datasets into generalizable forms. This perspective places AI within a broader lineage of modelling practices, emphasizing that its creative logic relies on probabilistic prediction rather than on the embodied human experience that informs interpretation. Such reliance on statistical generalization introduces a challenge to art history's commitment to singularity and ambiguity, even as it enables novel synthesis. However, as Wasielewski wrote in 2023, "A computational technique can determine whether certain images match one another, but it cannot tell you why they match or whether the fact that they match is relevant information. There are plenty of ways that images can be compared to one another that, one could argue, are not meaningful, but the machine learning system does not know this (and sometimes the computer science researcher does not recognize this either, if the researcher is not familiar with issues of art-historical context)" (Wasielewski 2023, 19). This insight underscores the epistemic gap between algorithmic pattern recognition and the interpretive depth essential to art history, highlighting that computational matching may assist interpretation but cannot replicate the contextual and nuanced understanding that only human judgement, informed by disciplinary expertise, can provide.

Brenda Segone (Chap. 3) shifts the discussion to the technical substrate of generative AI, focusing on the latent space—a compressed mathematical structure where generative models encode and organise data into semantically meaningful directions. This mechanism enables the model to synthesise new outputs guided by learned probability patterns among data, rather than drawing on human sensory experience. Segone's discussion highlights a parallel tension: latent-space compression not only drives generative creativity but also risks cultural flattening, reminding us that technical innovation must be paired with ethical vigilance to preserve nuance and interpretive depth. Lev Manovich (2023) has described "prediction" as the process by which models trained on large datasets translate inputs across media to generate new images by trying "to predict the images that correspond best to your text input" (Manovich 2023, 36). Yet predictive modelling privileges recurrence over exception, potentially rubbing against the humanities' commitment to singularity and ambiguity (Dubreuil 2025).

Contemporary practice makes these tensions visible: Refik Anadol's *Unsupervised* (MoMA, 2022–2023) and the planned Dataland museum dedicated to AI art under Refik Anadol Studio's direction (Gelt 2024) will contribute to institutionalizing AI-generated art while raising questions of authorship, authenticity, and ethics. At the opposite end of the unsupervised–supervised spectrum, Jennifer L. Karson and her team (Chap. 6) train models on artist-owned datasets, converting the hidden probabilistic substrate of AI-generated creativity into a transparent and ethically accountable process by modelling a form of highly supervised collaboration.

Alongside these technical contrasts, aesthetic and interpretive concerns surface in the ways viewers experience AI-generated images. Kurt Ralske (Chap. 5) examines how viewers often misattribute sentience to AI, especially when AI-generated images are perceived as "untouched," echoing the theological status of acheiropoieta icons. Andrew Murray (Chap. 4) critiques how AI unsettles aesthetic categories and blurs the distinction between producing and consuming images, reframing creative labour in ways that contribute to its deskilling.

These multiple approaches, each offering a different lens, invite ongoing debates over authorship, accountability, and cultural responsibility. Recent studies highlight the tension between enhanced creative productivity and the risk of eroding originality and cultural specificity. On one hand, van Hees et al. (2025) report that, when authorship is undisclosed, participants often showed a significantly stronger preference for AI-generated artworks than for human-made ones (van Hees et al. 2025, 05). On the other hand, Zhou and Lee (2024) identify a paradox: AI boosts creative productivity but may erode originality over time (Zhou and Lee 2024, 6). Seli et al. (2025) found that AI-generated visuals created without human input outperform those produced by inexperienced users working with AI, yet they still fall short of the creativity achieved by professional artists using AI. Taken together, these findings reveal both promise and friction: while AI expands generative possibilities, latent-space distortions risk homogenizing creativity by operating through compressed representations that flatten cultural nuance and privilege recurrence over exception. These perspectives also underscore that probabilistic creativity is not merely a technical phenomenon but a cultural one as well, requiring interpretive guardrails and ethical oversight.

Museums: Innovation Anchored by Responsibility

These theoretical frameworks directly inform Part II, where museum practices—such as digital cataloguing, algorithmic curation, and visitor experience—translate theory into institutional strategies. AI now contributes by helping researchers filter collections for analytical review and by surfacing insights (e.g colour, patterns) that aid visitor engagement and enhance their experience. It also supports exhibition planning by collecting interaction data and the design of customized visits via voice assistants (Derda and Predescu 2025, 536). At this early stage, evidence of AI adoption in museums remains mixed: Kiourexidou and Stamou (2025) surveyed self-disclosed and publicly available information from nineteen major European museums and found low self-reported use of AI, concluding that AI does not significantly influence overall attendance (Kiourexidou and Stamou 2025, 4–7). Avlonitou et al. (2025) propose a "Human–AI Compass" for sustainable museum practice, mapping intervention domains across operations, digital collections management, and visitor experience, while emphasizing the need for museum-specific ethical frameworks to govern AI's "self-learning and self-improving" capacities, particularly in museum settings, "...where continuous performance improvement and responsiveness to user needs are essential" (Avlonitou et al. 2025, 2).

These institutional trends provide a framework for the case studies that follow, each illustrating the tension between technological innovation and interpretive responsibility.

Giulia Taurino (Chap. 7) presents a compelling chapter that surveys traditional and emerging methods for compiling catalogues raisonnés—now often inplemented as dynamic digital databases that comprehensively document an artist's body of known work. She bridges past and present by highlighting how pre-digital catalogues often reflected culturally specific values and lacked flexibility for updates or reparative scholarship. Taurino underscores a critical tension: while AI-enhanced catalogues offer unprecedented flexibility for reparative description—enabling updates that can correct historical omissions—they simultaneously risk perpetuating stereotypes and cultural bias when large language models rely on statistical pattern recognition. In contexts with limited documentation, such as underrepresented cultures, this reliance can flatten nuance and reinforce dominant narratives rather than dismantling them. This is a concern that echoes Part I's discussion of latent-space distortions and Part IV's broader analysis of cultural homogeization. To illustrate this concern, Taurino conducted an exptertiment using Claude Opus 4.1 to test the model's ability to generate rigorous catalogue-style entries for Claude Monet, assessing performance in terms of citation accuracy, content completeness, and use of art historical terminology. She concludes that AI will not replace art historians; rather, their expertise is ethically essential in guiding AI-generated content.

Bárbara Romero Ferrón and Nuria Rodríguez Ortega (Chap. 8) explore how generative AI can reshape curatorial practice when approached as a collaborative partner rather than a substitute for human expertise. Through their experimental workshop, *Picasso and AI: Analysing and Questioning the Technology That Overwhelms Us*, they contextualize AI use across the fields of digital humanities, art historical inquiry, teaching practice, and curatorial theories. Using a custom-built interface (*PicassoAI*) that integrates OpenAI's GPT-3.5 for narrative generation and CLIP for image selection, the workshop invited students and professionals to interrogate algorithmic processes. Rather than promoting automated curation, the authors advocate for a collaborative model in which generative AI disrupts linear storytelling and reveals surprising thematic connections by identifying patterns across large datasets. This approach enhances, rather than replaces, the human curator's contextual knowledge and interpretive expertise.

Monica Lanaro (Chap. 9) examines *Recognition*—the award-winning 2016 project developed with Coralie Gourguechon and Angelo Semeraro at the Benetton Group's Fabrica— as an early example of AI-driven visitor engagement that prioritises transparency and interpretive depth. The AI-powered system paired contemporary Reuters photojournalism with Tate Britain's collection, matching images by formal criteria such as composition and colour while also displaying the algorithm's decision-making logic through visible matching percentages. Lanaro argues that while the algorithm effectively identifies visual similarities, it often overlooks symbolic nuance and cultural context—revealing the epistemic limits of machine vision. Rather than treating these gaps as failures, she frames them as productive sites for critical inquiry, where algorithmic "errors" can spark meaningful conversations about interpretation that challenge entrenched interpretive hierarchies and expand opportunities for visitor discovery and engagement.

Pedagogical Experiments: Promise, Pitfalls, and Critical Engagement

Early classroom experiments with AI reveal both opportunities and challenges, reflecting the pedagogical tensions many educators encounter when integrating new technologies into the humanities classroom. In Scholarship of Teaching and Learning (SoTL) traditions—especially in the humanities—classroom inquiry is context-specific and exploratory, often beginning with a specific teaching issue experienced in the classroom or student misunderstanding of disciplinary concepts (Felten 2013, 121).

Most teachers-scholars focus on finding "what works" in the classroom (Hutchings 2000, 4) and less often on developing broader interpretive frameworks to guide pedagogical thinking (5). Drawing on theories of posthumanism, Adams et al. argue that AI technologies are becoming active participants in shaping educational practices by entangling themselves with human cognition, ethics, and agency and forming "complex human-technology hybrids that mobilise new actions, transform knowledge frameworks and inaugurate novel ways of being in the world" (Adams et al. 2022, 3). When AI becomes part of the learning environment, the traditional teacher–student co-partnership that Felten (2013) identifies as central to SoTL (123) expands into a triadic relationship. AI introduces an additional layer of algorithmic mediation, creating new dimensions of interactions that can unsettle trust and need to be addressed. Students' undisclosed use of AI for their assignments mirrors the opacity of training data; yet, while educators often worry about academic misconduct, such misuse is frequently unintentional. At the same time, these technologies can be harnessed to design innovative strategies that position AI as an active participant rather than a neutral tool, helping students develop responsible and reflective practices. This is the context in which AI enters the classroom, engaging educators already attuned to experimentation and problem-based learning, as illustrated by Kimiko Matsumura's experience (Chap. 11).

As Karl van Heerden's structured simulations show (Chap. 12), AI can act as that third voice, reshaping dialogue and stimulating critical thinking through active engagement. In this delicate balance, AI-generated outputs become catalysts for identifying gaps, unsupported claims, and hidden biases—deepening disciplinary inquiry. The tension produced by this paradoxical encounter between SoTL's context-specific, exploratory nature (which mirrors the humanities) and AI's probabilistic convergence (more aligned with STEM and its statistical foundations) complicates pedagogical integration. At the same time, it opens productive gaps that create opportunities for SoTL-driven experimentation and systematic approaches that position art history, as an intrinsically interdisciplinary field, to embrace collaborative, empirical, and mixed-method strategies. Indeed, AI's ability to test hypotheses across large datasets, as noted by Mathkunti et al. (2023), introduces new possibilities for integrating empirical methods into art history. This unique convergence between interpretive approaches and quantitative techniques has significant implications for pedagogy, demanding strategies that preserve critical depth while embracing technological fluency. Part III addresses this challenge by showcasing course designs that foreground reflection, transparency, and epistemological awareness. Guo (2024) demonstrated that students without coding experience could use AI to analyze the MoMA database in Python, creating pathways for computational engagement while maintaining humanistic interpretation (Guo 2024, 59). Other interdisciplinary pilots have explored reverse prompt engineering to recreate canonical artworks, leveraging visual analysis skills to boost engagement (Smith 2025). Yet concerns about accuracy and academic integrity persist, underscoring the need for model literacy and ethical guardrails to prevent overreliance on automated output.

Emily Leifer's opening review (Chap. 10) situates AI within the trajectory of digital art history, highlighting both continuity and disruption. She notes that while large-scale digitization can reveal alternative narratives and connections across vast datasets, image-analysis models often reflect Western-centric frameworks, which risk obfuscating the fuller cultural contexts central to art history inquiry and undermine the profession's ongoing work. Her argument reinforces a central theme running through this anthology: AI can augment interpretive processes but continues to fall short on the nuanced understanding that remains essential to the discipline.

Kimiko Matsumura (Chap. 11) offers a personal account of adaptative pedagogy amid the rapid rise of AI. Confronting the limitations of traditional art history assignments and growing concerns about potential students' undisclosed AI use, she redesigned an introductory course to teach students how to critique AI-generated essays. Through colour-coded analysis and guided reflection, students learned to identify unsupported claims and gaps in reasoning, developing critical awareness of AI's shortcomings while strengthening essential writing skills in the discipline. Matsumura frames this approach as part of a broader adaptative educational shift from knowledge transmission to skills development, positioning art history as a vital site for cultivating critical thinking in an AI-saturated world.

Karl van Heerden (Chap. 12) demonstrates how art history pedagogy can leverage AI's empirical affordances without compromising interpretive depth. Using Tree-of-Thought (ToT) prompting—a sophisticated technique that structures AI reasoning into multi-step processes—he scaffolds students' metacognitive engagement in writing. By pairing AI-generated feedback with structured reflection, van Heerden turns what might otherwise be a passive interaction into an active learning experience. This pedagogical experiment shows that, when grounded in human-centred assignment design, algorithmic pattern recognition can become a catalyst for deeper critical thinking. Data collected over two semesters revealed that ToT-supported assignments improved students' ability to identify weaknesses in their arguments and articulate revision strategies, underscoring the potential for structured AI integration to advance both teaching practice and scholarly inquiry into art history education.

Global Perspectives: Canon, Bias, and Ethical Horizons

In a redesign of a non-Western survey assignment presented in this anthology (Chap. 15), Arvin Maghsoudlou used text-to-image prompting to expose cultural misalignments—such as Islamic art rendered with Renaissance perspective—turning algorithmic error into a teaching tool for interrogating embedded assumptions and Western/non-Western imbalances. The "canon," shaped by systematic selections "to arrive at a grand narrative that fits in with the western notion of evolution" (Mast 2019, 45) and defined by Gregor Langfeld (2018) as a process that produces a sanitised and reconciled narrative in which "Works of art that in their day were locked in an irreconcilable struggle with one another exist harmoniously side by side in the neutralised state of the canon and enter history," reminds us that inclusion inevitably entails exclusion (Langfeld 2018, 1).

Generative AI risks reinforcing existing cultural hierarchies by reproducing and even intensifying biases and stereotypes embedded in its training data and circulating online. Consequently, its outputs may marginalise non-Western cultural traditions or distort how they are portrayed (Said et al. 2025). Yet, its critical use can paradoxically help uncover such imbalances and open new avenues of inquiry. Similar to the opacity of AI training datasets, the power struggles at the heart of canon formation often remain concealed (Langfeld 2018, 8). To confront these inequities, the final section of this anthology addresses cultural bias across collections (Runggaldier & Rubenstein), pedagogy (Maghsoudlou), and artistic experimentation (Luis; Kim), incorporating perspectives from the Pacific Islands, East Asia, the Near East, and the Indigenous Americas. Closing with advocacy helps define the ethical horizon to ensure that AI supports globally responsive reparative practices, rather than perpetuating systemic imbalance.

Part IV of this anthology situates these innovations within global contexts, examining cultural bias, the colonial gaze, and ethical responsibility in AI-generated imagery. Chapters explore AI-assisted art making, pedagogy, and intersections of classroom and museum practice, each centring on a distinct non-Western cultural tradition to broaden the art historical conversation. Art history's sensitivity to the perspective from which a narrative is constructed becomes crucial in interrogating how AI mediates meaning.

The section opens with an interdisciplinary chapter by Adriel Luis (Chap. 13), who traces a "lineage of misinformation" from colonial explorers to museums, film, and AI systems. Using Paul Gauguin as a case study, Luis demonstrates how misrepresentations of Pacific Islanders persist in AI outputs, exposing the risks of uncritically reproducing problematic imagery. By testing three AI models and comparing outputs, Luis reveals AI's inability to recognise or correct these biases, showing how Gauguin's colonial perspective continues to shape algorithmic interpretations.

Kay Kim (Chap. 14) closely examines how linguistic bias shapes AI-generated imagery. Kim explains that AI-powered image generators, which rely on large language models to interpret user prompts, are deeply influenced by the dominance of English in training data, producing a systemic imbalance that affects multilingual representation. To illustrate this, Kim conducted an experiment using a culturally neutral prompt in both English and Korean. English prompts produced significantly more accurate and relevant images, while the Korean prompts yielded largely irrelevant results. These discrepancies reveal how AI "hallucinates" in the gaps between language and image, exposing structural inequities in dataset composition and the illusion of neutrality in generative systems. Kim's findings underscore the need for greater transparency in AI development, as linguistic hierarchies risk perpetuating cultural marginalization in digital visual culture.

Arvin Maghsoudlou (Chap. 15) adopts an exploratory approach to AI in course assignment design, integrating text-to-image tools like DALL·E into a foundational non-Western art history course. Preliminary testing revealed striking distortions, such as AI-generated Islamic art incorporating Western tropes like Renaissance perspective. These shortcomings can serve as productive teaching moments, sparking reflective discussions about the assumptions embedded in visual technologies and the narratives that shape digital visual culture.

Astrid Runggaldier and Meghan Rubenstein (Chap. 16) present a collaborative teaching model that integrates Indigenous fibre art into art history pedagogy, bridging curatorial practice with academic research. Their cross-institutional project connects courses at Colorado College and University of Texas at Austin through a multi-phase assignment combining traditional formal analysis with AI-based computer vision, comparing their findings across methods. During the assignment design phase, the authors rigorously tested AI's ability to interpret the visual, material, and cultural complexity of Mayan fibre artefacts—including composition, colour, pattern, and weaving techniques—and found significant limitations that reaffirm the necessity of involving human insight and expertise. This initiative cultivates transferable skills in museum practice while broadening art historical education, promoting a thoughtful and responsible integration of AI to enhance non-Western representation.

Towards an Integrated Professional Terrain in Art History: Contextual Foundations and Intersecting Practices Across Research, Curation, Pedagogy, and Advocacy

It is appropriate to conclude this introduction by stepping back to synthesise Parts I–IV and to highlight how the chapters intersect and collectively articulate the volume's overarching aims. Each section examines how AI is reshaping the core responsibilities of art historians: researching and interpreting artworks, curating collections and exhibitions, educating future scholars, and engaging with global cultural narratives. Common threads such as authorship and creativity, data literacy, interpretation, representation and bias, and ethical responsibility weave these individual chapters into a unified vision of a profession that is technologically engaged and globally responsive.

Part I establishes the conceptual foundations, interrogating how generative models, latent-space dynamics, and algorithmic opacity challenge art history's commitments to singularity, ambiguity, and cultural nuance. The chapters by Wasielewski, Segone, Murray, Ralske, and Karson articulate tensions between probabilistic creativity and humanistic interpretation, setting the theoretical stage for the volume. Part II translates these debates into institutional contexts. Taurino's analysis of catalogue raisonnés, Romero Ferrón and Rodríguez Ortega's co-curatorial approach, and Lanaro's study of AI-driven visitor engagement reveal how museums navigate the balance between innovation and responsibility. Each case study underscores the need for transparency, interpretive oversight, and cultural sensitivity when integrating AI into museum practice. Part III turns to pedagogy, where epistemic tensions between AI's pattern recognition and the humanities' interpretive depth become most pronounced. Leifer's review situates AI within the trajectory of digital art history, while Matsumura and van Heerden demonstrate how reflective course design and structured prompting can strenghten disciplinary literacy and metacognitive engagement. Part IV expands the lens globally, confronting cultural bias and the colonial gaze embedded in AI-generated imagery. Chapters by Luis, Kim, Maghsoudlou, and Runggaldier and Rubenstein unearth various forms of cultural imbalance, helping to illuminate where more informed, thoughtful, and reparative methodological responses will be needed.

Across these contexts, the contributors to this anthology chart an integrated professional terrain in which art historians research, curate, teach, and advocate for engagements with AI that foreground human expertise and cultural sensitivity, advancing methodological transparency, interpretive adaptability, and globally attuned practice.

In an era where misinformation proliferates and visual narratives often detach from their original contexts, these professional competencies become essential. By positioning AI not as a replacement but as a catalyst for rethinking art history's methods, ethics, and scope, this volume invites readers to imagine a future in which technological innovation and humanistic inquiry converge in dynamic and productive dialogue.

References

Adams, Catherine, Patti Pente, Gillian Lemermeyer, Joni Turville, and Geoffrey Rockwell. 2022. Artificial Intelligence and Teachers' New Ethical Obligations. *IRIE: International Review of Information Ethics* 31 (1): 1–18. https://doi.org/10.29173/irie483.

Avlonitou, Charis, Eirini Papadaki, and Alexandros Apostolakis. 2025. A Human–AI Compass for Sustainable Art Museums: Navigating Opportunities and Challenges in Operations, Collections Management, and Visitor Engagement. *Heritage* 8 (422): 1–59. https://doi.org/10.3390/heritage8100422.

Bayer, Zehra Canan. 2024. Artificial Intelligence in Pedagogical Processes: A Transformative Perspective on Teaching Art History. *Necmettin Erbakan Üniversitesi Ereğli Eğitim Fakültesi Dergisi* 6 (2): 914–939. https://doi.org/10.51119/ereegf.2024.114.

Dang, Yunkai, Kaichen Huang, Jiahao Huo, Yibo Yan, Sirui Huang, Dongrui Liu, Mengxi Gao, Jie Zhang, Chen Qian, Kun Wang, Yong Liu, Jing Shao, Hui Xiong, and Xuming Hu. 2024. Explainable and Interpretable Multimodal Large Language Models: A Comprehensive Survey. *arXiv preprint*. https://doi.org/10.48550/arXiv.2412.02104.

Derda, Izabela, and Domnica Predescu. 2025. Towards Human-Centric AI in Museums: Practitioners' Perspectives and Technology Acceptance of Visitor-Centered AI for Value (Co-)creation. *Museum Management and Curatorship* 40 (4): 532–554. https://doi.org/10.1080/09647775.2025.2467703.

Dubreuil, Laurent. 2025. *Humanities in the Time of AI*. Minneapolis: University of Minnesota Press.

Felten, Peter. 2013. Principles of Good Practice in SoTL. *Teaching & Learning Inquiry* 1 (1): 121–125. https://doi.org/10.2979/teachlearninqu.1.1.121.

Gelt, Jessica. 2024. Dataland, the World's First AI Arts Museum, Will Anchor the Grand Complex in Downtown L.A. *Los Angeles Times*, September 24, 2024. https://www.latimes.com/entertainment-arts/story/2024-09-24/refik-anadol-dataland-ai-art-museum-the-grand-dtla.

Guo, Qiuzi. 2024. Prompting Change: ChatGPT's Impact on Digital Humanities Pedagogy—A Case Study in Art History. *International Journal of Humanities and Arts Computing* 18 (1): 58–78. https://doi.org/10.3366/ijhac.2024.0321.

Hutchings, Pat. 2000. Approaching the Scholarship of Teaching and Learning. In *Opening Lines. Approaches to the Scholarship of Teaching and Learning*, ed. Pat Hutchings, 1–10. Menlo Park, CA: The Carnegie Foundation for the Advancement of Teaching. https://files.eric.ed.gov/fulltext/ED449157.pdf.

Hutson, James. 2024. Integrating Art and AI: Evaluating the Educational Impact of AI Tools in Digital Art History Learning. *Faculty Scholarship* 578. https://digitalcommons.lindenwood.edu/faculty-research-papers/578/.

Kiourexidou, Matina, and Sofia Stamou. 2025. Interactive Heritage: The Role of Artificial Intelligence in Digital Museums. *Electronics* 14:1–12. https://doi.org/10.3390/electronics14091884.

Langfeld, Gregor. 2018. The Canon in Art History: Concepts and Approaches. *Journal of Art Historiography* 19:1–18. https://arthistoriography.wordpress.com/wp-content/uploads/2018/11/langfeld.pdf.

Manovich, Lev. 2023. AI Image Media Through the Lens of Art and Media History. *IMAGE: The Interdisciplinary Journal of Image Sciences* 37 (1): 34–41. https://doi.org/10.1453/1614-0885-1-2023-15448.

Mast, Kimberly. 2019. The Art History Canon and the Art History Survey Course: Subverting the Western Narrative. *The Journal of Social Theory in Art Education* 39:40–51. https://scholarscompass.vcu.edu/cgi/viewcontent.cgi?article=1548&context=jstae.

Mathkunti, Nivedita Manohar, U. Ananthanagu, and Satish Menon. 2023. AI in Humanities: Review. *Tuijin Jishu/Journal of Propulsion Technology* 44 (5): 3674–3678. https://www.propulsiontechjournal.com/index.php/journal/article/view/3431.

Preziosi, Donald. 2009. *The Art of Art History: A Critical Anthology*. Oxford and New York: Oxford University Press.

Said, Muna Numan, Aarib Zaidi, Rabia Usman, Sonia Okon, Praneeth Medepalli, Kevin Zhu, Vasu Sharma, and Sean O'Brien. 2025. Deconstructing Bias: A Multifaceted Framework for Diagnosing Cultural and Compositional Inequities in Text-to-Image Generative Models. *arXiv preprint* 1–9. arXiv:2505.01430v1.

Seli, Paul, Anya Ragnhildstveit, William Orwig, Lucas Bellaiche, Sarah Spooner, and Nathaniel Barr. 2025. Beyond the Brush: Human Versus Artificial Intelligence Creativity in the Realm of Generative Art. *Psychology of Aesthetics, Creativity, and the Arts*. Advance online publication: 1–9. https://doi.org/10.1037/aca0000743.

Smith, Caitlan. 2025. AI Applications for Ancient Art History Education. *AI & Antiquity: Journal of Teaching and Technology in Ancient Studies* 1 (1): 67–92. https://doi.org/10.64946/aiantiquity.v1i1.004.

van Hees, Jules, Tijl Grootswagers, Genevieve L. Quek, and Manuel Varlet. 2025. Human Perception of Art in the Age of Artificial Intelligence. *Frontiers in Psychology* 15:1–8. https://doi.org/10.3389/fpsyg.2024.1497469.

Abbood, Mohammed Wahhab. 2025. AI in Humanities Research: Envisioning New Scientific Paradigms. *Al-Noor Journal for Digital Media Studies* 1 (1): 190–212. https://doi.org/10.69513/jnfdms.v1.i1.en14.

Wasielewski, Amanda. 2023. *Computational Formalism. Art History and Machine Learning*. Cambridge, MA: The MIT Press.

Zhou, Eric, and Dokyun Lee. 2024. Generative Artificial Intelligence, Human Creativity, and Art. *PNAS Nexus* 3 (3): 1–8. https://doi.org/10.1093/pnasnexus/pgae052.

PART I

Reframing Art History: Theoretical and Aesthetic Foundations in the Age of AI

CHAPTER 2

New Models for Art: AI as Representational Tool

Amanda Wasielewski

The term model is widely used in both the tech industry and media coverage of artificial intelligence (AI). Tech companies today not only make hardware, software, and platforms but also something called models. But what exactly do contemporary AI tools *model* or what are they models *of*? Many of these models are so-called generative models, meaning that they can be used to create new text, images, video, or other media. The advent of such tools has serious implications for creative practice and, therefore, art history. As was the case with automated technologies of the past, recent commentary on generative AI has expressed fear of displacement or replacement of creative labour, particularly when it comes to unlawful use of copyrighted work (Vincent 2023; Davis 2023; Karamolegkou et al. 2023; Lemley 2024). However, there are many contemporary artists experimenting with generative AI models today who rely on the long-standing emphasis on concept rather than craft in contemporary art. This means that concerns about copyright may be less of an issue for the

A. Wasielewski (✉)
Uppsala University, Sollentuna, Sweden
e-mail: amanda.wasielewski@abm.uu.se

L. Cempellin, M. Geiger (eds.), *Reimagining Art History with Artificial Intelligence*,
https://doi.org/10.1007/978-3-032-21685-4_2

contemporary fine art world, even though they represent an existential crisis for creative labour more generally (Wasielewski 2026).

Given the potential of generative AI to aid artists in their work, this chapter takes a closer look at the concept of models from the perspective of art history and practice. How do AI models serve as new models for art? They are composed of data and this data is often collected through large-scale web-scraping. As such, they not only utilise vast quantities of image, text, and video without explicit permission but they also represent a largely unknown or uncurated body of material, given the scale. The contemporary AI model thus provides both a resource for generating content and also a unique way of understanding and representing the world.

What Is a Model?

Depending on the field, one might define a model as an object, a sketch, a maquette, an explanation, a way to work out ideas through materials, or a smaller-scale or simplified version of a larger phenomenon. Models can range from mathematical models to architectural models to fashion models. In fine art, the artist's model was traditionally a *person* posing in an artist's studio. In western art history, the artist's model was a close collaborator, serving as both inspiration and as a direct aid in representation (Fig. 2.1). They serve a functional role in helping the artist to replicate the form of the human body but they also embody larger concepts via allegory and narrative. This means that the model is not just a mimetic aid but also a representational one.

What, then, is an artificial intelligence model? AI models are a specialised type of machine learning that makes use of artificial neural networks. Designed to function like the neural structures of biological brains, artificial neural networks were first conceptualised in the late 1950s with Rosenblatt's perceptron (Rosenblatt 1958; Dobson 2023) and continued to be developed in the 1980s and 1990s (Fukushima 1980; Lecun et al. 1998). However, thanks to recent increases in computational processing power and the availability of massive datasets, the field saw significant advancements in the 2010s (Krizhevsky et al. 2017). Researchers are now able to train and implement robust neural networks to create 'models' capable of learning complex tasks such as language or image creation. These models are thus complex *mathematical* models that perform algorithmic data processing.

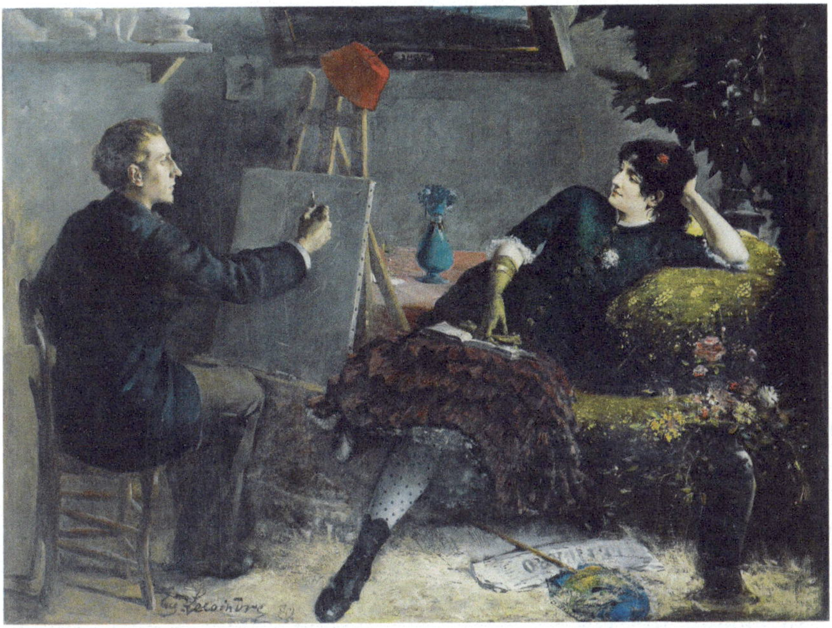

Fig. 2.1 Eugène Lecoindre, *In the Atelier*, 1882. Oil on canvas. 149.9 × 200 cm. Private collection. Source: Wikimedia Commons, public domain

The most talked about and fastest-growing area of AI model-making is generative AI, which is a term for AI models that create text, images, and other media. In 2021 researchers at Stanford University published a book-length report that characterises the largest generative AI models, such as GPT-3/4, DALL·E, and BERT, as foundation models. They define foundation models as models that have been trained on "broad data" collected automatically at scale (typically through web-scraping) that can then be applied to a variety of "downstream tasks" (Bommasani et al. 2021). In other words, foundation models are trained on some of the largest and most diverse data collection efforts ever performed and, as a result, are meant to be useful for many different applications. This data is the fodder that allows these models to function. So, it does not matter how sophisticated the architecture of an artificial neural network is because, without this mountain of 'big data', there is no model.

Over the past twenty years, the number of digital images in existence has rapidly grown. These images are both consciously produced by humans and created automatically by machines (Zylinska 2017). Many of these images are made by individuals identifying as artists and designers. The advent of social media in the mid-2000s offered users a place to share their pictures (including artwork) but, at the same time, encouraged production of ever more images with the reward of likes and followers (Hand 2020). The mass data collection efforts that companies like Google and social media giants like Facebook pioneered led to a number of different threads of critique.

During the mid-2010s, critical data studies (CDS) introduced a framework for engaging with the era of social media data collection (Dalton and Thatcher 2014; Kitchin and Lauriault 2014; Iliadis and Russo 2016; Richterich 2018). The primary point of departure for CDS is that data is not neutral and that the collection and implementation of data is a reflection of competing power dynamics rather than an empirical reality (Dalton and Thatcher 2014). These issues have become even more relevant for generative AI implementations, which create new content from the existing mass of large data collections.

In addition to CDS, theories of big data and critique of mass digitisation emerged in the 2010s to not only problematise the use of data but also the underlying conditions and motivations of the collection itself, even when intended for open and non-proprietary distribution (Kitchin 2014; Crawford et al. 2014; Beer 2016; Thylstrup 2019; Fuchs 2021). At the time, these critiques were somewhat abstract for the general public and often focused on data accumulation as a form of surveillance (Boellstorff 2013; Andrejevic and Gates 2014; Klauser and Albrechtslund 2014). Today, those critiques have grown more concrete as visual artists can see images generated to look like their own work or writers see models trained on their writing to generate output in their personal style. In essence, the era of generative AI has made these data collection efforts and their critiques much more visible.

This critical research on data collection and use, in other words, emerged to address the collection of big data before it was instrumentalised by foundation models. Whereas once mass data collection was designed for targeted marketing and advertising, it now has more ambiguous potential applications in creative fields, that is, in art and design or, as many fear, as a replacement for trained artists and designers. The flaws of data collection and its assumed objectivity have been critiqued extensively since the mid-2000s. Early writing by danah boyd and Kate Crawford (2012), for example, sought to define the term 'big data' as the product of three factors: the technology that creates it, the computational analysis that orders and deploys it, and the mythology around its power, objectivity, and representativeness. Crawford has continued to lead the way in critical engagement with these issues in the era of AI (Crawford and Paglen 2021; Crawford 2021). Essential to such critiques are a conception of AI models as loci of power, thanks to the data contained in them, and expressions of the bias and stereotypes that can result from automating large-scale human-produced datasets.

Given these critiques and the ethical quandaries inherent in using generative AI, some artists have chosen to reject these tools outright. For example, an open letter written by artist/illustrator Molly Crabapple for the Center for Artistic Inquiry and Reporting (CAIR) in May 2023 had over 4000 co-signers, the majority of which identify as artists or creative practitioners. The letter specifically calls the use of generative AI theft and copyright infringement (Crabapple 2023). Another petition that attracted high-profile artists and musicians was launched in 2024 by Ed Newton-Rex, a composer and former AI executive who became worried about the unlicensed use of copyrighted material in training AI (Milmo 2024). The statement from this petition was short and to the point: "The unlicensed use of creative works for training generative AI is a major, unjust threat to the livelihoods of the people behind those works, and must not be permitted" ("Statement on AI Training" 2024).

Nevertheless, there are artists who continue to use AI models in their work. Not only are high-profile newcomers to the mainstream art world like Refik Anadol and long-established media art figures like Mario Klingemann gaining wider attention for their artwork using artificial neural networks but older, blue-chip contemporary artists like Cindy Sherman and Paul McCarthy are also using AI tools to make their work (Growcoot 2023; Griffin 2025). Sometimes the use of fine-tuned (i.e., custom-trained) implementations offsets concerns about copyright infringement. Prior to 2022 and the release of commercial text-to-image models like DALL-E, Midjourney, and Stable Diffusion, most of the artists working with visual AI models were using GAN-based models (generative adversarial networks) trained on smaller, curated image datasets rather than web-scraped data (Wasielewski 2025). However, most fine-tuning of post-2022 text-to-image models still may access copyrighted material given that pre-trained foundational models are used.

In other cases, artists can appeal to the history of appropriation and remix in art practice. The successors of Marcel Duchamp and his ready-mades, which designated common mass-produced objects as works of art, have long disregarded copyright in the making of their work. For example, Andy Warhol appropriated photographs and logos during the pop art era, such as a Lynn Goldsmith photograph of the musician Prince that was later subject to a posthumous copyright infringement case (Veltman 2023), and Sherrie Levine copied the work of photographers like Walker Evans and presented the copies as her own work (*After Walker Evans*, 1981). Artists working with visual generative AI tools, particularly commercial models like DALL-E, Midjourney, and Stable Diffusion, which are thought to contain copyrighted art in their datasets, can thus appeal to this history in defence of their use of other artists' material, rightly or wrongly.

Model-Making in Art and Science

Despite these pressing ethical issues, it is safe to assume that artists will continue to use AI tools, in whatever form they may take over the coming years. The current trend, at time of writing, of using multimodal artificial neural networks will likely continue into the near future, as these are the most user-friendly and flexible image generators developed to date. The question, then, is: What kind of model or form of model-making do AI models provide for artists?

Across the arts and sciences, there is a long history of modelling. Most of the in-depth studies of the concept of modelling and model-making are domain specific rather than interdisciplinary and therefore address a very particular purpose for a given type of model. For example, in architectural history, Matthew Mindrup (2019) and David Lund (2023) trace the use of architectural models from ancient times to modern times to highlight the ways in which a small-scale model becomes or instantiates the built environment. In the history of science, contributors to the volume *Models: The Third Dimension of Science* (de Chadarevian and Hopwood 2004) write about models from the molecular level to animal specimens and mathematical modelling, detailing primarily how models are used in the natural sciences to help explain or predict natural phenomena. Rachel A. Ankeny and Sabrina Leonelli (2021), in a similar vein, investigate the philosophical implications of the concept of the 'model organism' in biology. In archaeology, on the other hand, Loes Opgenhaffen (2021) discusses the use of models and visualisation as a knowledge creation tool.

In the field of art history and visual studies, the idea of the model has been more elastic in the sense that art models can serve all of the purposes described above: they provide a guide or testing ground, help explain the world, serve as an emblem, and are a mode of visualisation. However, the most common way that an artist's model is defined is as a human being who poses for representative art forms. There have been several studies that focus on the use of models in artistic practice that try to highlight the humans, particular the women, behind the representations. Susan Waller (2017) and Marie Lathers (2001), for example, write about the importance of female models in nineteenth-century France. *The Dictionary of Artists' Models* (Jiminez 2013) and accompanying essays highlight the contribution of models to the works of art that were created in western art history. Wendy Steiner (2010), on the other hand, conceptualises the artist's model more widely in the transition towards abstraction in art in the twentieth century. These studies, however, do not reflect contemporary art practice, which has largely moved away from the western academic tradition of the artist's model.

Presenting a different perspective on how artists use models, Susan Küchler (2010) frames the use of models in modern art in relation to science and technology, drawing on the concept of the prototype. Küchler argues that, in the twentieth century, artists no longer treated object-based models as preparatory exercises, as they had previously. Whereas previously artists might make a smaller maquette out of wax or clay for a larger sculpture in metal or stone, object-based models served a different purpose for modern art. Instead, artists began using models as prototypes, in the way that a prototype is a precursor for mass-produced factory products. The prototype is, in other words, the first or the model of an expected multitude of identical replicas (Cempellin 2015, 70).

This framing of the model as prototype in modern art draws from the arguments of Walter Benjamin (2008) and Rosalind Krauss (1981) in the move from thinking of art as singular and original to something multiple and reproducible. Indeed, it is copies and rapid reproducibility that dominate the mode of production, from the mechanical means of the nineteenth and early twentieth centuries to the digital means of production from the latter half of the twentieth century to today. This, of course, is reflected in the art movements of the twentieth century that drew inspiration from mass media, industrial production, and the prevalence of concept over unique object: pop art, conceptual art, and appropriation art, to name a few.

All models, including artists' models, serve a representative function. These representations help tell a story or make something that is complex clearer. For some mathematical models, they even represent future scenarios rather than the current situation. Models are aids in representative communication, making the abstract visible. So, what kind of model is an AI model in the context of creating art and imagery? How does it fit into a trajectory of artists models from human model and maquette to prototype? Whereas critics of AI argue that AI models are theft and copyright infringement, these models do not in fact reproduce existing works like traditional mechanical or digital copies do. Statistical iterations—the automated output of visual generative AI models—represent a generalisation *based on* but not *identical to* the training data that is run in an automated way. In other words, the output is derivative but not identical. This is a significant departure from mechanical and even much of the earlier digital modes of reproduction.

AI Models: Chance and Generalisation

While any given model can be specially designed for an intended use, it is not dependent on the outcome of that use and doesn't need to bear any particular relationship to that outcome. For instance, a maquette need not be turned into a large-scale sculpture and an architectural model need not be turned into a building. Some models can be used for many things and some only serve one function. So, what does this mean in practice for AI models?

Generative AI models are highly flexible and can be used for a wide variety of outcomes within a particular media form like image or video. Unlike other types of artists' models, there is no unified formal or visual correspondence between the model itself and the outcome. The correspondence is a mathematical process rather than a visual or material one. No matter how adept one is at directing a visual generative AI model, there is always an element of chance inherent in the procedure. For example, using CLIP-based (Radford et al. 2021) text-to-image multimodal models like DALL-E, Midjourney, or Stable Diffusion requires one to input a text prompt in order to generate an image. Even though, from the user perspective, it seems like the input text is similar to, for example, searching for a string of text in a document, the text is not merely searching and delivering something concrete that already exists in the data. Instead, the text initiates a complex automated process where the section of the model trained with the given words and associated image data is tapped into in order to produce coherent visual content and also undergoes some eventual post-processing.

This can be illustrated with a simple example. Figure 2.1, referenced above, is a nineteenth-century painting of an artist drawing from a life model in the studio. I found this painting by searching Wikimedia Commons using the simple input: 'art studio model.' These search words called up existing images of photographs and artworks from the database that were tagged with those words, and, even given the simplicity of the input and the depth of the Wikimedia image collection, the results showed many options that were exactly what I was looking for. This is not how generative AI works, however. Using Midjourney, I generated a series of images with the prompt 'art studio model' (Fig. 2.2). The images produced primarily depicted smaller-scale architectural-type models of artists' studios, which was surprising because it was not what I was expecting, but of course it made sense when I saw them.

Whereas the combination of art + studio + model in a search calls up existing images tagged with those words, the vast majority of them

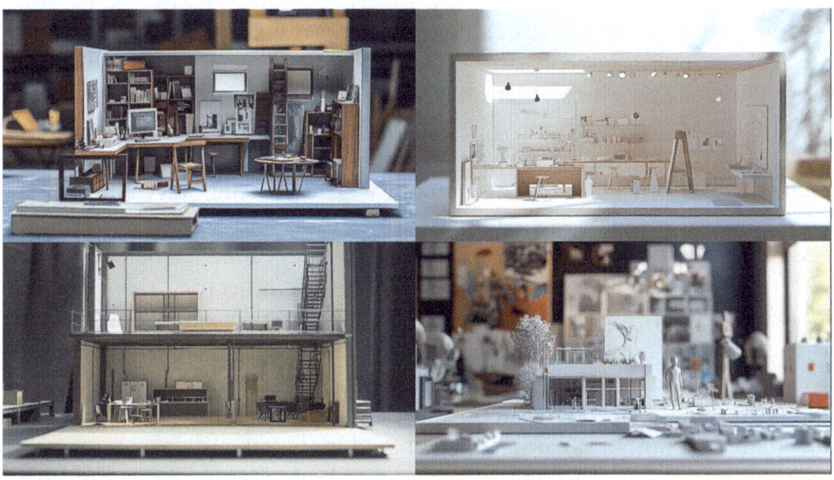

Fig. 2.2 Images generated with Midjourney using the prompt 'art studio model --ar 16:9 --style raw' Source: Author/Midjourney

depicting artists and models in a studio setting, the AI model performs a synthesis and generalisation of these terms in combination. It does not parse them as individual tags but, rather, a cohesive and holistic encapsulation of the many trained images associated with those words. There is no 'command' here because there are no existing images to be called up. Instead, something much more interesting is happening: a semantic generalisation. Of course, this was the *wrong* image, i.e., it was not the image I had in mind, but this kind of programmed interpretation is what produces strange, unexpected, and, often, very revealing imagery from AI models. There are, I would imagine, no images of architectural models of artists' studios on Wikimedia Commons, so this is not an image that I could find in an image repository. Instead, it is a synthetic image in the truest sense of the word.

Mechanical or traditional digital reproduction is quick and automated, creating exact or nearly exact copies of a particular visual or material form. Generative AI models, on the other hand, are not exact, and it is precisely this quality that makes them interesting for contemporary artists to use as models for representation. They are a means by which to set up a scenario with an unknown outcome. They are creative in the sense that they produce something new in the act of making. The making of any kind of model, indeed, contains this kind of practice-based knowledge or the knowledge inherent in process and processing. However, visual generative AI introduces an even greater degree of the unplanned or unexpected through synthetic generalisation. It allows the artist to relinquish even more control over the formation of the work but discover new semantic possibilities in the process.

This is the power of generative artmaking practices, which are not exclusive to recent advances in generative AI. Contemporary commentators trace the genealogy of AI art to early digital and generative art practices from the 1960s (Krewani 2022; Schubbach 2023). Philip Galanter (2016) places generative art in an even longer trajectory that predates modern digital computing, isolating the idea of chance and ceding control as the essential quality of such works. In 1971, Max Bense (p. 57) proposed a definition for a generative aesthetics that combined both 'free' and 'determined' formal structures created by artists through the use of automated techniques, namely those based in digital computing.

The logic of systems and programmatic thinking spread through society in the 1960s (Corris 2009). The aesthetics of generation and automation were thus prevalent in the wider contemporary art world during that era, even in work that did not directly use computers. Artists like John Cage, Robert Rauschenberg, and others associated with E.A.T. (Experiments in Art and Technology) made work that embodied the cybernetics era and its statistical machines in both explicit and implicit ways (Battista et al. 2016). These artists built off of the interest in chance and automation found in Dada and Surrealism, which responded to an earlier machine age (Foster 1995, 125–153). The element of chance continues to be present in generative art today, namely in contemporary visual generative AI.

Artists are often some of the earliest adopters of new technologies and AI tools have been no different. To conclude this chapter on the use of AI models in artmaking, therefore, I return to the opening question: How do AI models serve as new models for art? Essentially, they provide a way for artists to process the immense information overload one experiences through, for example, social media into a generalised or crystallised form. Rather than a copy of a singular image, piece of text, or video, generative AI gives a synthetic generalisation in a singular form of a multitude of data. It is a data visualisation that creates something specific from the near-incomprehensible data deluge that we have created via the Internet and that was subsequently web-scraped as training data. Acting as a model, therefore, to help represent and understand society and culture today.

References

Andrejevic, Mark, and Kelly Gates. 2014. Big Data Surveillance: Introduction. *Surveillance & Society* 12 (2): 185–196.

Ankeny, Rachel A., and Sabina Leonelli. 2021. *Model Organisms. Elements in the Philosophy of Biology*. Cambridge: Cambridge University Press.

Battista, Kathy, Simone Forti, Billy Klüver, Michelle Kuo, Catherine Morris, Zabet Patterson, John Tain, and Sabine Breit. 2016. In *E.A.T.: Experiments in Arts and Technology*, ed. Sabine Breitwieser. Köln: Walther König.

Beer, David. 2016. How Should We Do the History of Big Data? *Big Data & Society* 3 (1).

Benjamin, Walter. 2008. The Work of Art in the Age of Its Technological Reproducibility. In *The Work of Art in the Age of its Technological Reproducibility, and Other Writings on Media*, ed. Michael William Jennings, Brigid Doherty, and Thomas Y. Levin, Translated by Edmund Jephcott, Rodney Livingstone, and Howard Eiland, 19–55. Cambridge, MA: Belknap Press of Harvard University Press.

Boellstorff, Tom. 2013. Making Big Data, in Theory. *First Monday*, September. https://firstmonday.org/ojs/index.php/fm/article/view/4869.

Bommasani, Rishi, Drew A. Hudson, Ehsan Adeli, Russ Altman, Simran Arora, Sydney von Arx, Michael S. Bernstein, et al. 2021. On the Opportunities and Risks of Foundation Models. *arXiv*. http://arxiv.org/abs/2108.07258.

boyd, danah, and Kate Crawford. 2012. Critical Questions for Big Data: Provocations for a Cultural, Technological, and Scholarly Phenomenon. *Information, Communication & Society* 15 (5): 662–679.

Cempellin, Leda. 2015. Multiples in Late Modern Sculpture: Influences Within and Beyond Daniel Spoerri's 1959 Edition MAT. *Nierika: Revista de Arte Iberoamericana* 7:58–73.

Corris, Michael. 2009. Systems Upgrade: Conceptual Art and the Recoding of Information, Knowledge and Technology. In *Proud to Be Flesh: A Mute Magazine Anthology of Cultural Politics after the Net*, ed. Josephine Berry Slater and Pauline van Mourik Broekman, 107–120. London: Mute Publishing.

Crabapple, Molly. 2023. Restrict AI Illustration from Publishing: An Open Letter. May 2, 2023. https://artisticinquiry.org/AI-Open-Letter.

Crawford, Kate. 2021. *Atlas of AI: Power, Politics, and the Planetary Costs of Artificial Intelligence*. New Haven: Yale University Press.

Crawford, Kate, and Trevor Paglen. 2021. Excavating AI: The Politics of Images in Machine Learning Training Sets. *AI & SOCIETY* 36 (4): 1105–1116. https://doi.org/10.1007/s00146-021-01162-8.

Crawford, Kate, Mary L. Gray, and Kate Miltner. 2014. Critiquing Big Data: Politics, Ethics, Epistemology. *International Journal of Communication* 8:10.

Dalton, Craig, and Jim Thatcher. 2014. What Does A Critical Data Studies Look Like, And Why Do We Care? *Society and Space*, May 12, 2014. https://www.societyandspace.org/articles/what-does-a-critical-data-studies-look-like-and-why-do-we-care.

Davis, Wes. 2023. Sarah Silverman Is Suing OpenAI and Meta for Copyright Infringement. *The Verge*, July 9, 2023. https://www.theverge.com/2023/7/9/23788741/sarah-silverman-openai-meta-chatgpt-llama-copyright-infringement-chatbots-artificial-intelligence-ai.

de Chadarevian, Soraya, and Nick Hopwood. 2004. *Models: The Third Dimension of Science*. Stanford: Stanford University Press.

Dobson, James E. 2023. *The Birth of Computer Vision*. Minneapolis: University of Minnesota Press.

Foster, Hal. 1995. *Compulsive Beauty*. Cambridge, MA: MIT Press.

Fuchs, Christian. 2021. From Digital Positivism and Administrative Big Data Analytics Towards Critical Digital and Social Media Research. In *Digital Capitalism*. London: Routledge.

Fukushima, Kunihiko. 1980. Neocognitron: A Self-Organizing Neural Network Model for a Mechanism of Pattern Recognition Unaffected by Shift in Position. *Biological Cybernetics* 36 (4): 193–202. https://doi.org/10.1007/BF00344251.

Galanter, Philip. 2016. Generative Art Theory. In *A Companion to Digital Art*, 146–180. Chichester: Wiley. https://doi.org/10.1002/9781118475249.ch5.

Griffin, Jonathan. 2025. 'Who Made This Mess?': Paul McCarthy's Gross-Out AI. *Frieze*, January 8, 2025. https://www.frieze.com/article/paul-mccarthy-one-take-248.

Growcoot, Matt. 2023. Cindy Sherman Is 'Experimenting' With AI and Not Everyone's Happy. *PetaPixel*, August 23, 2023. https://petapixel.com/2023/08/23/cindy-sherman-is-experimenting-with-ai-and-not-everyones-happy/.

Hand, Martin. 2020. Photography Meets Social Media: Image Making and Sharing in a Continually Networked Present. In *The Handbook of Photography Studies*. Routledge.

Iliadis, Andrew, and Federica Russo. 2016. Critical Data Studies: An Introduction. *Big Data & Society* 3 (2).

Jiminez, Jill Berk, ed. 2013. *Dictionary of Artists' Models*. New York: Routledge.

Karamolegkou, Antonia, Jiaang Li, Li Zhou, and Anders Søgaard. 2023. Copyright Violations and Large Language Models. *arXiv*. https://doi.org/10.48550/arXiv.2310.13771.

Kitchin, Rob. 2014. *The Data Revolution: Big Data, Open Data, Data Infrastructures & Their Consequences*. London: SAGE Publications Ltd.

Kitchin, Rob, and Tracey Lauriault. 2014. Towards Critical Data Studies: Charting and Unpacking Data Assemblages and Their Work. SSRN Scholarly Paper. Rochester, NY. https://papers.ssrn.com/abstract=2474112.

Klauser, Francisco R., and Anders Albrechtslund. 2014. From Self-Tracking to Smart Urban Infrastructures: Towards an Interdisciplinary Research Agenda on Big Data. *Surveillance & Society* 12 (2): 273–286.

Krauss, Rosalind. 1981. The Originality of the Avant-Garde: A Postmodernist Repetition. *October* 18:47–66.

Krewani, Angela. 2022. Cybernetics and the Early Experiments in Computer Art. *Digital Culture & Society* 8 (2): 107–122. https://doi.org/10.14361/dcs-2022-0208.

Krizhevsky, Alex, Ilya Sutskever, and Geoffrey E. Hinton. 2017. ImageNet Classification with Deep Convolutional Neural Networks. *Communications of the ACM* 60 (6): 84–90.

Küchler, Susanne. 2010. The Prototype in 20th-Century Art. *Visual Communication* 9 (3): 301–312.

Lathers, Marie. 2001. *Bodies of Art: French Literary Realism and the Artist's Model*. Lincoln: University of Nebraska Press.

Lecun, Y., L. Bottou, Y. Bengio, and P. Haffner. 1998. Gradient-Based Learning Applied to Document Recognition. *Proceedings of the IEEE* 86 (11): 2278–2324. https://doi.org/10.1109/5.726791.

Lemley, Mark. 2024. How Generative AI Turns Copyright Law Upside Down. *Science and Technology Law Review* 25 (2). https://doi.org/10.52214/stlr.v25i2.12761.

Lund, David. 2023. *A History of Architectural Modelmaking in Britain: The Unseen Masters of Scale and Vision*. London: Routledge.

Milmo, Dan. 2024. Thom Yorke and Julianne Moore Join Thousands of Creatives in AI Warning. *The Guardian*, October 22, 2024, sec. Technology. https://www.theguardian.com/film/2024/oct/22/thom-yorke-and-julianne-moore-join-thousands-of-creatives-in-ai-warning.

Mindrup, Matthew. 2019. *The Architectural Model: Histories of the Miniature and the Prototype, the Exemplar and the Muse*. MIT Press.

Opgenhaffen, Loes. 2021. Visualizing Archaeologists: A Reflexive History of Visualization Practice in Archaeology. *Open Archaeology* 7 (1): 353–377.

Radford, Alec, Jong Wook Kim, Chris Hallacy, Aditya Ramesh, Gabriel Goh, Sandhini Agarwal, Girish Sastry, et al. 2021. Learning Transferable Visual Models From Natural Language Supervision. In *Proceedings of the 38th International Conference on Machine Learning*, 8748–8763. PMLR.

Richterich, Annika. 2018. *The Big Data Agenda: Data Ethics and Critical Data Studies*. London: University of Westminster Press. https://doi.org/10.16997/book14.

Rosenblatt, F. 1958. The Perceptron: A Probabilistic Model for Information Storage and Organization in the Brain. *Psychological Review* 65 (6): 386–408. https://doi.org/10.1037/h0042519.

Schubbach, Arno. 2023. AI and Art: Arguments for Practice. In *AI and Art: Arguments for Practice*, 41–56. transcript Verlag. https://doi.org/10.1515/9783839467107-005.

"Statement on AI Training." 2024. Statement on AI Training. https://www.aitrainingstatement.org. Accessed 23 January 2025.

Steiner, Wendy. 2010. *The Real Real Thing: The Model in the Mirror of Art*. Chicago: University of Chicago Press.

Thylstrup, Nanna Bonde. 2019. *The Politics of Mass Digitization*. Cambridge: MIT Press.

Veltman, Chloe. 2023. Supreme Court Sides against Andy Warhol Foundation in Copyright Infringement Case. *NPR*, May 18, 2023, sec. Culture. https://www.npr.org/2023/05/18/1176881182/supreme-court-sides-against-andy-warhol-foundation-in-copyright-infringement-cas.

Vincent, James. 2023. AI Art Tools Stable Diffusion and Midjourney Targeted with Copyright Lawsuit. *The Verge*, January 16, 2023. https://www.theverge.com/2023/1/16/23557098/generative-ai-art-copyright-legal-lawsuit-stable-diffusion-midjourney-deviantart.

Waller, Susan. 2017. *The Invention of the Model: Artists and Models in Paris, 1830–1870.* London: Routledge.

Wasielewski, Amanda. 2025. Abundance and Absence in AI: A Review of 'Missing Mirror: Photography through the Lens of AI'. *Photography and Culture* 18 (1): 1–10. https://doi.org/10.1080/17514517.2025.2478753.

Wasielewski, Amanda. 2026, forthcoming. *Digital Photography After AI: Continuity and Rupture in the Age of Automated Images.* Cambridge MA: MIT Press.

Zylinska, Joanna. 2017. *Nonhuman Photography.* Cambridge, MA: MIT Press.

CHAPTER 3

The Human Glitch or Artificialism

Brenda Segone

As a global civilisation, we excel at conceiving products embedded in an epistemological ambiguity: coffee without caffeine, cheese without dairy, vegan meat, beer without alcohol. The latest in this line of products is the artwork without the artist, produced by a text-to-image algorithm. This algorithm, even though it is deprived of senses, can deliver in a fraction of seconds what unmistakably can be called, by everyone, an image. I prompted this artificial intelligence (AI) to create an image of the famous Tahrir Square in downtown Cairo, capital of Egypt, the stage of a massive revolution that ousted Egyptian President Hosni Mubarak in 2011. The image created was original in that it did not imitate any other image (see Fig. 3.1).

The achievement is not small. Realising AI's ability has taken billions of dollars of investment with top scientists and researchers dedicated to producing *intelligent* machines capable of competing with humans in the sciences and humanities.

The progress is such that the conundrums it poses today are no longer limited to "intelligence" alone, but challenge the very notions of

B. Segone (✉)
AUC, American University in Cairo, Cairo Governorate, Cairo, Egypt
e-mail: brendasegone@aucegypt.edu

L. Cempellin, M. Geiger (eds.), *Reimagining Art History with Artificial Intelligence*,
https://doi.org/10.1007/978-3-032-21685-4_3

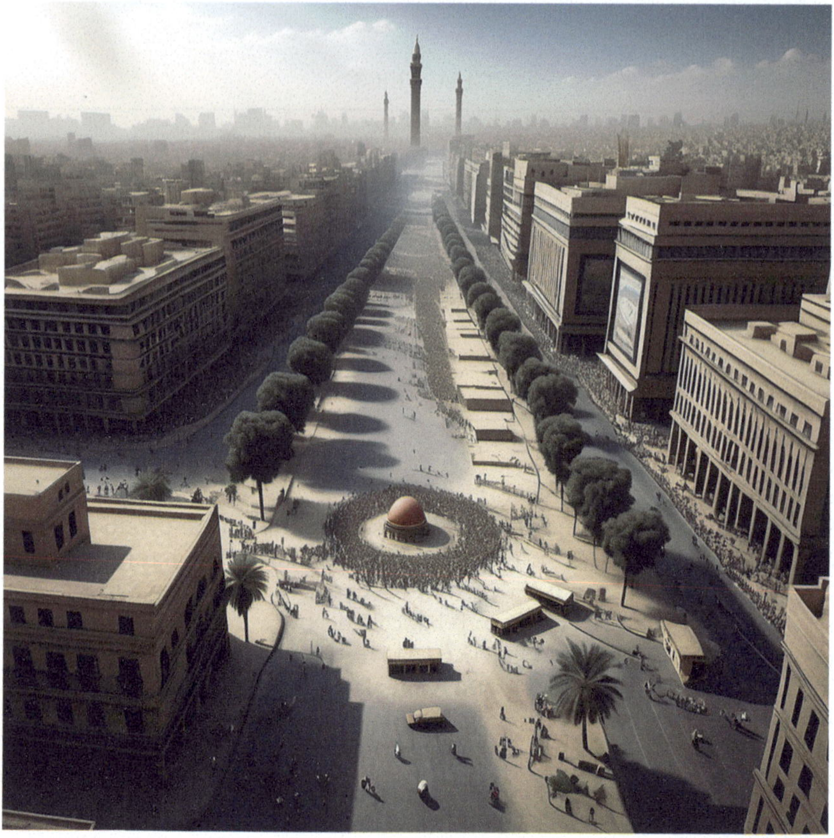

Fig. 3.1 Midjourney. Prompt: "A photorealistic bird's eye view of Tahrir Square, in Downtown Cairo, capital of Egypt, in 2011, with massive crowd protesting." November 5, 2024

"sentience" (Birch 2024), "creativity," or, put simply, of "what is us at our most human" (Avishai 2025), triggering in the public opinion epidermal reactions of exaggerated fear or enthusiasm. Philosophers, for their part, attempt to explore the question through an analysis of the different forms of sentience and even the various definitions of consciousness (Kalita 2025). From the perspective of sentience and agency in creative works, AI can be placed within the larger dialectic of creator and creation. The concept of a man-made entity developing a consciousness of its own has regularly fed mankind with some of its best fictions, belonging, for the most part to the horror genre and to dystopian science-fiction, for it seems embedded in the collective unconscious that this self-aware entity will have no good intentions towards its creators. Some good examples are Mary Shelley's novel *Frankenstein* (1818) and Ridley Scott's science-fiction film *Blade Runner* (1982). But AI is no fiction. Even though, since the pioneering book *The Animal Mind* (Washburn 1908), studies on animal cognition for over a century continue providing evidence for thinking and problem-solving in different species of animals such as rats, crows, or dolphins, *deep reasoning*, through language and symbolic mental representations, was believed to be intrinsically reserved to humans and a highly challenging cognitive task (Matlin 2009). Furthermore, art making was perceived as the highest manifestation of the unparalleled human *genius*, a concept articulated during the humanistic philosophy of the Renaissance period and relevant today. AI, with its current capacity to write, to dialogue, and to produce imagery, implies our species is not so special, and our rule over the other species might end soon. Worse: we, as a species, might become subservient to AI, should AGI or Artificial General Intelligence be developed as Sam Altman, the CEO of ChatGPT, is striving to.

Regarding the fields of art and art history, AI raises the following problematics: Can a machine emulate art? Is the text-to-image generation of visuals really *art*? Is it the end of art and art history as we know it? Or a new beginning that will democratise everything, including art making? Slogans marketing text-to-image generators such as "Easy Creation" or "Anyone can create a new art in a matter of seconds" certainly seem to imply that.

This chapter offers a qualitative, multi-disciplinary exploration of AI in relation to art history and text-to-image generators through a comparative overview of the literature from computer sciences, neurosciences, and the humanities. While providing answers to the stated issues seems like a utopian enterprise, the attempt to do so will hopefully lead to a better understanding of the opportunities and challenges AI can bring to art history and will provide a greater insight into the directions in which art history should evolve.

AI Technology

AI technology is paradoxical. On the one hand, it can beat the 9 dan Korean world champion of Go, Lee Sedol, filling humanity with awe towards AlphaGo, Google's deep learning machine, and with utter despair for mankind's "defeat." On the other, it struggled to solve a Captcha puzzle that a two-year-old would decipher in seconds. In fact, the paradox is only valid if it is applied to a human, but in the case of a machine, it is quite normal since these machines are trained asynchronously to achieve only one specific goal, such as finding patterns in visual datasets, or predicting the next sequence of words by analysing a huge digital library of possibilities, or, in this case, predicting the next *move* which is one very specific objective. It succeeded thanks to complex calculations built on top high-level games (policy network), coupled with a probability calculation of winning in a particular position (value network), multiplied by the different variations of the game to figure out the outcome (tree search). What is fascinating is the fact that Sedol beat the machine, even if in one round only, and his decisive move, the "*only one that came to his mind*" (Kohs 2017), had a 1/10,000 probability rate according to AlphaGo! This says a lot about the human brain or "glitch." Sedol was told he would be playing against *a* machine, in the singular. The truth is he was not. He played against a superstructure composed of a technological apparatus and human resource, as well as against the whole legacy of Go champion players. All hidden behind the guise of "*one* machine." What is captivating about text-to-image generators that are supported by a similar superstructure?

Unlike the game of Go example, in art and art history, machines and humans are not competing against one another but rather emulating each other. As we are currently witnessing the enormous progress of AI due partially to the capacity of computer scientists to emulate a network of artificial neurons after the biological neural network of the human brain (Kamath 2025), we are also receiving evidence from neurosciences about the specificity, uniqueness, and greatness of the complex human brain and mind. This evidence will further enhance AI systems. In fact, the mere existence of AI is shaping the research questions of the field. What defines creativity from an algorithm's perspective? Is it a variation based on tradition or is it a totally new path? Can creativity be predicted? Does art making require strong sensory emotions to exist such as pain? How does human perception function? Are there similar patterns that make certain cities in history, such as Florence, Paris, New York, and Beirut, centres of inventiveness and the avant-garde?

The Brain Is Not an Algorithm

Specialists in neuroeducation and computer scientists highlight the major difference between a human brain and an algorithm by showing evidence that 50% of the neurons in a human brain have as their objective to inhibit certain automated responses in order to activate a certain algorithm. This leads to the argument that "human intelligence is not an algorithm: the brain is a fine strategist" (Houdé 2019).

Other differences, according to Yann LeCun (2024), ex-chief AI scientist at Meta and Turing award laureate, include the ability of humans to function in a complex world with minimal resources. He provides the example of clearing a dinner table, which is a sequence of actions that a 10 year old would master after a few repetitions while an AI model would require countless hours of training. Researchers are continually stumped by this contrast, called the Moravec paradox. In the late 1990s, computer scientist Hans Peter Moravec explained that what is considered difficult for humans, such as high-level reasoning like chess playing or writing, requires little computation and is hence *easy* for an AI. On the contrary, what is so automatic for humans, such as walking or recognising faces, requires "enormous computational resources" (Rotenberg 2013, 108) and is thus *very challenging* for an AI model.

According to LeCun (2024), to date, we are far from a human-level AI since at four years, a human child has seen more visual data than the best LLM. The area in a human brain that corresponds to our capacity for language treatment similar to an LLM is called the Broca area and is only a fraction of the human brain in size. Therefore, for LeCun the future of AI lies in the capacity to mobilise the equivalent of our prefrontal cortex that is equivalent to one third of the cerebral cortex and to develop "systems that learn world models from sensory inputs" (LeCun 2024). The prefrontal cortex is at the basis of humans' capacity to develop mental representations in the absence of sensory stimuli and abstract thought.

Cedric Villani, a mathematician, winner of the Fields Medal in 2010 and currently professor at the Claude Bernard Lyon I University, reminds us that the machines do not possess "intelligence" (Villani 2025). The LLMs use System 1 thinking which is fast, spontaneous and can lead to erroneous sentences but packaged neatly into an eloquent speech such as in the following example generated by ChatGPT in 2024: "I didn't find any information about the place of burial of the survivors, but it is probable that they are buried in the country of origin according to their wish or that of their families." Pronouncing the very words "burial of the survivors" doesn't bother the LLM.

In addition, despite the similarities between human brains, recent studies in neurosciences attest to the differences between individuals at multiple levels: at the molecular level (Changeux 2015), at the level of the brain structure (Gu and Kanai 2014), and as per the visual and colour scientists, at the level of optical, neural, and cognitive processes we are concerned with in this chapter (Mollon et al. 2017). The variabilities at the micro level, invisible to the human eye, enduce behavioural, cognitive, and perceptual differences that are visible and measurable. A popular example of variation in colour perception is that of "the dress," an image of a dress that went viral in 2015. Some perceived it as blue and black while others saw it as white and gold (Brainard and Hurlbert 2015). We can cite as another noteworthy example the "unique hues" whereby one's unique blue can be another's unique green (Kuehni 2004, 161). Even identical twins have a different connectivity at the neural level, a unique one. Besides these studies that suggest that human beings perceive differently, further research stresses the fact that cognition is not only rational but also social, with empathy at the core of what our societies are built on (Changeux 2015[1]).

Finally, the neuropsychologist Francis Eustache's research on human memory highlights the complex interplay in any human being of different types of memories such as semantic memory, episodic memory, and emotional memory (2019), in the meaning-making process of each individual in our society. The big insight his research provides is that it is through emotions that certain memories come to exist and stabilise. And emotions cannot yet be easily felt upon command through a prompt or predicted based on extracted datasets of emotions.

The Grid-Based Structure of Digitally Generated Images

Antonio Somaini, a visiting professor of Art, Film and Visual Studies at Harvard in 2024, traces the genealogy of generative AI to the invention of the linear perspective (2024). Briefly, by enabling the drawing of a 3D object on a two-dimensional plane in a mathematically accurate way, linear perspective birthed a whole culture of visuals called "realistic" that the

[1] Changeux is also interested in the neuronal basis for the good, the true, and the beautiful, the foundation of aesthetics in Western art (2012).

camera's invention extended further. Linear perspective was defined as a symbolic form by art historian Erwin Panofsky in the 1920s (Panofsky [1924] 1991). Rather than considering linear perspective as just an artificial mathematical matter, or one of style, he saw in it a cultural phenomenon that symbolised a culture's ability to transform psychophysiological space into mathematical space, a living experience into a drawing. According to Somaini, the grid-based structure of digitally generated images and the mathematical space of linear perspective are one. This is why images generated artificially are recognised as such. The geometric perspective seems correct (Stork 2023b). They have other characteristics the history of art has made us familiar with. To name a few: the images are delineated by a frame that is vertical, horizontal, circular, or square; this frame appears on the application's desktop that contains a different set of information; the frame may contain figurative objects, figures, abstract shapes, colours, graphic elements, and text; the content responds to the prompt the user enters but in varying degrees of satisfaction, accuracy, and artistry.

A text-to-image AI such as Dall.e or Midjourney mostly relies on massive quantities of images that have been labelled, classified, and encoded in a certain way. It feeds off datasets of images each digitised and rasterised for processing by an AI algorithm. Images are broken down into small units of information and organised into grids of pixels. At the core of machine learning exists what is called a *latent space*, a space where the original data is represented mathematically and compressed, and where each dimension or similar items group corresponds to a specific characteristic of the data. Latent spaces are used in Analytic AI systems and Generative AI systems such as DALL·E or Midjourney.

Somaini suggests that the latent space should be considered as the new symbolic form of our era (2024). He claims that AI-generated images are "latent space visualisations" of digitised cultural memory and digitised knowledge that show multiple points of view rather than one subjective point of view. They allow the prompter to "see" those latent spaces that are redefining humanity. The latent spaces form what could be called the *datatype* of the machine. Instead of a palette, an algorithm uses this datatype to reconstruct what we identify as an image. We can therefore anticipate the infinite manipulations this datatype can allow from a finite set of image datasets.

Comparison of Two Squares

Based on the above, if we compare two images, one produced by Midjourney and one by the contemporary Egyptian artist Lara Baladi, we immediately sense that they originate from different places. In Midjourney's "creation," we notice how "wrong" it is. Tahrir Square is not located in a perfectly linear boulevard; the monument at its centre is fictitious, as are all the buildings around it; and the Cairo Tower that looks like a gigantic minaret, is not there in reality. More importantly, unlike some artists who deliberately introduce errors in perspective, content, or size, such as the seven fingers in Marc Chagall's *Self-Portrait with Seven Fingers*, Midjourney's "mistakes" were not intentional but rather a manifestation of its limitations due to the fact that it is an algorithm, albeit a powerful one. Midjourney decoded the prompt and responded to it as best as it could by using its dataset that decomposes and aggregates multiple sources, multiple memories, and multiple subjectivities. Chagall's example is interesting since users of AI models often complain about the figures of the generated AI images having only three fingers or six and thus *betraying* their artificial essence.

By contrast, Lara Baladi's experience of the Friday of Victory (see Fig. 3.2) is real and imprinted in all her being in a permanent way. Her image is not simply a click on a camera: "photographing was a political act, equal in importance to demonstrating" (Baladi 2013). It is the incarnation of a specific time (2011) and space (Tahrir Square in Egypt), in a specific moment (revolt against President Mubarak's 30-year-old regime), in her own body and mind. It meant belonging. Thousands of protesters witnessed this moment physically and emotionally. The unique perspective, with the enormous Egyptian flag cutting across Tahrir Square, is absent from Midjourney's proposition, which could not care less about the Friday of Victory, so to speak.

Following Somaini's suggestion, we see the stereotypical "cultural memory" associated with Egypt: a country with little greenery, brown buildings, and minarets. What is more striking is the hybridity of time and space. Midjourney's image has medieval and modern features. Time and space are combined in an unreal, artificial way. It is a simulacra of Tahrir Square and of Tahririan experience, to borrow Baudrillard's terminology (1981). If prompted, Midjourney could generate in a few seconds new variations of Tahrir Square, with a different central monument in each, feeding in the process the datatype with artificially generated images rather

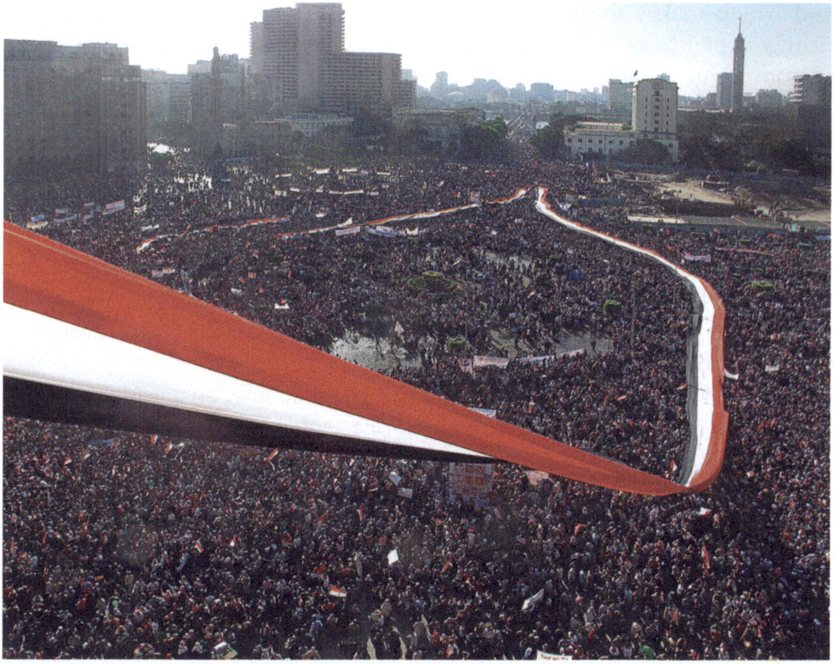

Fig. 3.2 "Friday of Victory." A week after President Hosni Mubarak was unseated. Tahrir Square, Cairo, Egypt. Photo by Lara Baladi, February 18, 2011

than digitised originals. Lara Baladi, on the other hand, has developed a whole series of works on the revolution for the past decade (2024) and is not ready to forget.

The Artwork as an Act of Resistance

At all levels, experiencing a multisensorial event and expressing it is inimitable for a machine deprived of the notions of time and space. Its core is made of computer bytes. As the French philosopher Jacques Derrida ([2002] 2013) explains, the artist does not see with his eyes alone but also with his mind, with his hand, with the other's vision of himself and the world, with that which eludes his reach, in a given time and space. An artist's image is more than meets the eye. It is evidence of "visibility" (71), a holistic and complex condition that affects all things visible and invisible and which makes these things irreducible to the kind of labelling algorithms depend upon. Indeed, an artist's image is not merely information or communication; it is an act of resistance.

Deleuze defines the act of creation as an act of resistance: "There is a fundamental affinity between the artwork and the act of resistance" (1987). Deleuze asks what the relation is between the artwork and the act of resistance. The context he is addressing is that of the late 1980s, when, according to his viewpoint and borrowing from Burroughs (1959), we were entering the era of the societies of control. As the real objectives of how AI technologies will be used in politics are still unspoken, a number of thinkers express concerns of entering an era of fascism through perpetual tracking of citizens.

The true artwork is a glitch in the societal machine, an act of resistance to an order that has become inhumane or to what is inhuman in an order. The artist is the individual who watches society, critiques it, contests it, like the figure of the Greek philosopher Diogenes, and initiates change. Lara Baladi's photograph is doubly an act of resistance, through its status as a work of art witnessing an event, and through what we see in the image: a massive crowd of protesters rising up against Mubarak's dictatorial regime. "Revolting was archiving" says the artist (2016). In short, the artist is the one who dares to break a pattern and by doing so, shows a new possibility, a new horizon. Similarly, an art historian who shapes his era is one who brings a new understanding to his subject, breaking with previous interpretations.

If we consider true art to be that which breaks from the usual pattern, whether iconographic, formal, conceptual, or aesthetic, we see that text-to-image algorithms which function on pattern prediction cannot currently produce this kind of art. Artificially generated art is, therefore, equally locked in an epistemological ambiguity. As such, it is the perfect product of the global era.

I argue that rather than a multiplicity of points of view, latent spaces perform a dissolution of points of view, a dissolution of the united fabric of space and time. The Friday of Victory is now reduced to feeding the datatype of AIs.

Digital Art History

Does this mean that text-to-image generators are mere technological deceptions sold as original creations to generate profit for tech companies? Are they neither *intelligent* nor *artificial*, as AI researchers who express concerns about their underlying superstructure claim (Crawford 2021; Estampa 2024)? Rather than stating that AI systems are neither artificial nor intelligent, we can say that it is a *different* epistemology at stake, a different form of intelligence, yet very powerful. However, this difference, rather than being highlighted and protected, is cancelled out in the media. The marketing of all AI products relies on their "humanness" and their ability to emulate human capabilities.

According to computer scientist David Stork (2023a), AI-driven tools can empower art scholars in diverse ways. Indeed, the machine-driven analyses of datasets of artworks push us to look at creativity and style in novel ways, in ways that are measurable or observable. Trained on thousands of natural portrait photographs, the algorithms could analyse in theory a vast number of artworks in seconds. The results offer insights on trends across major art movements relevant to composition, lighting, or colour scheme. For example, the evolution in trends in composition from the sixteenth to the twentieth century has been measured through the notion of "entropy reduction" (Stork 2023b, 501) and highlights a bigger variability in compositional styles with time, and hence more artistic freedom. Another example is that of the change in Van Gogh's colour palette across different stages of his career. Individual preferences can also be revealed, as well as the dominant hand of the artist or the lateral gender bias in portraiture: the leftward-looking portraits are those of female figures and vice versa. In the past decade, computer scientists have strived to reach similar insights to art historians, as an evidence of the reliability of algorithms, in order to persuade the scientific and intellectual communities (Elgammal and Babak 2015). When performing on an automated mode, the machines tend to analyse questions that might not seem relevant to an art historian such as the yaw, roll, and pitch of a head pose in a portrait (Chou and StorkStork 2023). The next phase is to have the algorithms detect patterns in an automated fashion to which art historians can assign relevant meanings. Stork emphasises the fact that the models function best when an art historian's knowledge is incorporated: "The models are most accurate when they incorporate an art historian's knowledge of factors such as social norms, costumes, and artistic styles" (Stork 2023a,

686). These initial experiments might lead to a special software catered to art historians.

To date, the limitations are visible. As examples, consider portrait paintings that are not realistic and cannot be easily "read" by a machine. Another example is the condition of model training, which is the digitisation of the artworks that in itself is questionable. The screen (of smartphones or computers) acts as a mediator between the artist and the user, distorting the effects of dimension, texture, and level of detail, not to mention the plethora of artworks that cannot be digitised, such as installations and performances.

Nevertheless, the integration of computer-assisted connoisseurship into the toolbox of an art historian opens up the field of art history to scientific inquiry. It seems that, as some researchers prove, human perception as witnessed in artworks is not mathematically correct. To give an example: while figures are represented "accurately" (meaning following the drawing rules of linear perspective), the scientific study of the treatment of light in pictorial spaces reveals another reality: the rendition of shadows is often physically impossible (Wijntjes 2021) and the resulting cast shadows are inaccurate. These deviations from the laws of physics do not prevent artists and observers alike from making sense of art. Visual perception is not about accuracy. Maarten Wijntjes, from the Perceptual Intelligence Lab of Delft University of Technology, claims that "One may actually wonder how much knowledge about perception is latently present in art history, waiting to be discovered by neuroscientists" (68). Further data shows, for instance, that the size of human figures in comparison to their surroundings deviates from the rules of drawing: the figures are huge. It is not just a matter of artistic license but a revelation about the fact that "our visual brain uses a simpler, reduced physics to understand the world" (Cavanagh 2005, 301). In fact, the terms "naive physics" and "alternative physics" are being used to describe the functioning of human perception that seems to disregard physical and mathematical laws, when it comes to reading artworks but also when it comes to making sense of reality, according to a process that remains mysterious.

As Wijntjes reminds us, a "human in the loop" (2021) of this emerging digital field invested with AI-driven tools is an absolute necessity to uncover insights that would otherwise go unnoticed by an automated technique.

The Mystery of Perception

Science and art philosophy agree that perception and visual perception as shown in artworks obey laws not limited to those of physics. One could view the history of modern art movements from the Realism movement onward as an attempt to reclaim the mystery of human perception through an intentional deviation from accurate realistic representation whose objective was to create the perfection of illusion (Gombrich [1960] 2001). Each avant-garde movement explores this mystery through a novel angle. Impressionism focuses on the transient effects of light, shade, and colour theory; cubism creates an analogy between the senses of touch and sight; fauvism inquires into unnatural colours and surrealism into the subconscious; abstraction proposes a new universal language made of geometric shapes and colours; abstract expressionism reclaims the gesture of painting itself, etc.

Despite these attempts, the mystery remains largely intact and many questions have yet to be answered. Is the distance that separates the artist's representation from reality similar to the distance that separates a text-to-image algorithm's generation and art?

Conclusion

The interactive process of working with AI algorithms back and forth is modifiying the field of art history and art making, for in addition to our perception of things, we are internalising a machine's way of looking, seeing, and talking, which is further affecting art practice and art history as well as the programming of AI systems in a never-ending reciprocal loop.

Even if an AI system is able to mimic an artwork, what is engaged in the process of producing the artwork is *different*, at least today, but nonetheless fascinating. Conceivably, in the future, AI models will have diverse types of memories in addition to System 2 thinking, and a type of sentience in our own image. What matters is that in the process we do not become in its image *artificial* humans without senses, biological machines without desires or free will. For the moment, the artwork without the artist is the new mass-produced product that does away with the biographies of artists and nations, perhaps for a future without resistance.

References

Avishai, Tamar. 2025. Art Versus AI: The Salon—Podcast Series 4, episode 8. *Knowing Machine*. https://knowingmachines.org/podcast. Accessed 20 January 2025.

Baladi, Lara. 2013. When Seeing is Belonging: The Photography of Tahrir Square. *Creative Time Reports*, September 16. https://creativetime.org/reports/2013/09/16/larabaladi-photography-of-tahrir-square/.

Baladi, Lara. 2016. Archiving a Revolution in the Digital Age, Archiving as an Act of Resistance. *Ibraaz* 010_03 / 28 July 2016.

Baladi, Lara. 2024. *Anatomy of a Revolution, an ABC and Archive or Revolts and Revolutions*, talk at AUC, May 9.

Baudrillard, Jean. 1981. *Simulacres et Simulation*. Paris: Éditions Galilée.

Brainard, David. H., & Hurlbert, Anya C. 2015. *Colour vision: understanding #thedress. Current Biology, 25*(13). R551–R554.

Birch, Jonathan. 2024. *The Edge of Sentience: Risk and Precaution in Humans, Other Animals, and AI.* Oxford University Press.

Burroughs, William S. 1959. *The Naked Lunch.* New York: Grove Press.

Cavanagh, Patrick. 2005. The Artist as Neuroscientist. *Nature* 434 (7031): 301–307. https://doi.org/10.1038/434301a.

Changeux, Jean-Pierre. 2015. Workshop: East-West Connections. https://www.youtube.com/watch?v=68WcH1hWkas.

Changeux, Jean-Pierre, and Laurence Garey. 2012. *The Good, the True, and the Beautiful: A Neuronal Approach.* Yale University Press. https://www.jstor.org/stable/j.ctt1npn3q.

Chou, Jean-Peïc, and David G. Stork. 2023. Computational Tracking of Head Pose through 500 years of Fine-Art Portraiture. In *Electronic Imaging*, 211–213. https://doi.org/10.2352/EI.2023.35.13.CVAA-211.

Crawford, Kate. 2021. *The Atlas of AI: Power, Politics, and the Planetary Costs of Artificial Intelligence.* Yale University Press. https://doi.org/10.2307/j.ctv1ghv45t.

Damasio, Antonio. 2021. *Sentir et Savoir: Une Nouvelle Théorie de la Conscience.* Paris: Odile Jacob.

Deleuze, Gilles. 1987. *Qu'est-Ce Que l'acte de Création?* Lecture given as part of the *Mardis de la Fondation* series, March 19. https://www.youtube.com/watch?v=2OyuMJMrCRw.

Derrida, Jacques, Ginette Michaud, Joana Maso, and Javier Bassas. 2013. Penser à ne pas Voir. In *Penser à ne pas Voir: Ecrits sur les arts du visible 1979–2004*, 56–78. Paris: Editions de la Difference.

Elgammal, Ahmed, and Saleh Babak. 2015. Quantifying Creativity in Art Networks. *arXiv*, June 2. https://doi.org/10.48550/arXiv.1506.00711.

Estampa, Artistic Collective. 2024. Cartography of Generative AI. http://cartography-of-generative-ai.net/. Accessed 15 November 2024.

Eustache, Francis. 2019. La Mémoire Modulée, Bousculée, Agressée: Épisode 3/4 du podcast Apprentissages et troubles du cerveau. *France Culture*. https://www.radiofrance.fr/franceculture/podcasts/matieres-a-penser/la-memoire-modulee-bousculee-agressee-2875339.

Gombrich, Ernst Hans. 2001. *Art and Illusion: A Study in the Psychology of Pictorial Representation*. Princeton: Princeton University Press.

Gu, Jenny, and Ryota Kanai. 2014. What Contributes to Individual Differences in Brain Structure? *Frontiers in Human Neuroscience* 8:262. https://doi.org/10.3389/fnhum.2014.00262.

Houdé, Olivier. 2019. *L'intelligence Humaine n'est pas un Algorithme: le Cerveau, fin Stratège*. Paris: Odile Jacob.

Kalita, Sunu. 2025. The Metaphysics of AI Consciousness: A Philosophical Inquiry into Subjective Experience in Artificial Systems. *IJCSPUB* 15 (2): 49–47.

Kamath, Nikhil. 2025. *Nikhil Kamath Ft. Perplexity CEO, Aravind Srinivas | WTF Online Ep 1*. 2:16:30. https://www.youtube.com/watch?v=y5Ewu8wYgqM.

Kohs, Greg, director. 2017. *AlphaGo*. United States: Google DeepMind.

Kuehni, Rolf G. 2004. Variability in Unique Hue Selection: A Surprising Phenomenon. *Color Research & Application* 29 (2): 158–162. https://doi.org/10.1002/col.10237.

LeCun, Yann. 2024. Human-Level AI. Keynote Speech at the Hudson Forum 2024: The Future of Science.

Matlin, Margaret W. 2009. *Cognitive Psychology*. Wiley.

Mollon, John D., Jenny M. Bosten, David H. Peterzell, and Michael A. Webster. 2017. Individual Differences in Visual Science: What Can Be Learned and What Is Good Experimental Practice? *Vision Research* 141:4–15. https://doi.org/10.1016/j.visres.2017.11.001.

Panofsky, Erwin. [1924–1925] 1991. *Perspective as Symbolic Form*. 1st ed. Cambridge, MA: Zone Books.

Rotenberg, Vadim S. 2013. Moravec's Paradox: Consideration in The Context of Two Brain Hemisphere Functions. *Activitas Nervosa Superior* 55 (3): 108–111.

Somaini, Antonio. 2024. Perspective and the Genealogy of Generative Artificial Intelligence (The keynote speech by Antonio Somaini, presented online as part of "Histories of Perspectives," International Symposium, Thursday 17 and Friday 18 October. Co-organised by HiCSA (Université Paris 1 Panthéon-Sorbonne) and the Department of Art History at Yale University, in partnership with the German Center for Art History in Paris and the Centre Pompidou).

Stork, David G. 2023a. How AI is Expanding Art History. *Nature* 623 (7988): 685–687. https://doi.org/10.1038/d41586-023-03604-3.

Stork, David G. 2023b. *Pixels & Paintings: Foundations of Computer-Assisted Connoisseurship*. Wiley.

Villani, Cédric. 2025. L'agent Conversationnel par qui le Chaos Arriva: Épisode 4/4 du podcast L'Intelligence Artificielle: Utopie dystopique. *France Culture*, January 17. https://www.radiofrance.fr/franceculture/podcasts/serie-l-intelligence-artificielle-utopie-dystopique.

Washburn, Margaret Floy. 1908. *The Animal Mind: A Text-Book of Comparative Psychology*. New York: Macmillan.

Wijntjes, M. W. A. 2021. Shadows, Highlights and Faces: The Contribution of a 'Human in the Loop' to Digital Art History. *Art & Perception* 9 (1): 66–89. https://doi.org/10.1163/22134913-bja10022.

CHAPTER 4

AI Art, Deskilling and Prosumption

Andrew Murray

Prosumptive Deskilling

According to one modern observer, AI images have become "the refuge of every would-be painter, every painter too ill-endowed or too lazy to complete his studies, this universal infatuation bore not only the mark of a blindness, an imbecility, but had also the air of a vengeance." I lie, the quotation is from Charles Baudelaire (1955 [1859], 230), writing on photography. Yet scholars have likened text-to-image models to how photography in the nineteenth century disrupted and replaced artistic work (Bueno et al. 2025; Hertzmann 2020, 45–46, 2018, 2–6; Zylinska 2020). If alive today, Baudelaire, who damned photography for stepping into the spaces he thought belonged to trained artists, would have bemoaned a report from the World Economic Forum (2025) that charts how skills in graphic design are threatened by AI. Unsurprisingly, artists' reactions to AI include protests on ArtStation with artists displaying an image wishing to ban AI-generated images (Xiang 2022), protests against Magic the Gathering for using AI art (advertently or not; Heckman 2024), copyright

A. Murray (✉)
The Open University, London, UK
e-mail: andrew.murray@open.ac.uk

L. Cempellin, M. Geiger (eds.), *Reimagining Art History with Artificial Intelligence*,
https://doi.org/10.1007/978-3-032-21685-4_4

claims against specific artists who have used AI art, as well as against the owners of the models generating such images, and a petition urging Christie's to cancel its AI-art auction (Thomas 2025).

Baudelaire's invective against photography, along with other observations of this poet, has recently been discussed in a paper co-authored by Claudio Celis Bueno, Steve Jankowski and Jakko Kemper as an example of a reaction against the capacity of technology to reduce the "friction" of artistic production, the effort and skill that goes into its production, and with that the supposed artistry of overcoming such obstacles (2025, 8). Here, Bueno, Jankowski and Kemper borrow the concept of "frictionlessness" from Kemper's use of this term as a critical characterisation of the philosophy and objectives of Silicon Valley's tech companies (2024). Also drawing on Erkki Huhtamo's concept of recurring media "topoi," Bueno et al. argue that the pursuit of frictionlessness underlies repeated discursive patterns that accompany technological disruptions, including questions and debates concerning the actual nature of art, skill, authorship, and the proper relationship between art and industry. For Bueno et al., these topoi appear both in nineteenth-century debates around photography and in twentieth-century responses to AI (Bueno et al. 2025, 2–4).

But if similar topoi shaped responses to the respective emergences of photography and AI, each technology transformed the conditions of artistic practice in different ways. Focusing on how AI reshapes the artistic labour market, this chapter discusses how this technology has prompted reconceptions of art and artistic skill that exceed reactions to technological "frictionlessness." To explain how "frictionlessness" shapes the market for skilled labour, Bueno et al. use the concept of "democratisation" (2025, 2, 6, 8–9, 13), arguing that lowering the skill threshold for image production broadens access to the practice. But democratisation does not account for the social distribution of these newly accessible artistic skills. A tradition for thinking about such distribution stems from Marx, who Kemper does consider through Derrida's account of hauntology (2024, 26–27), but not through Marx's own writings. In one respect, Marx's description of the impact of capital investment on skilled labour is compatible with the concept of "frictionlessness," in that systematised and mechanised labour effect "the separation of the intellectual powers of production from manual labour" (Marx 1976, 548).[1] But crucially, for Marx, such reduc-

[1] Harry Braverman discusses this passage in [1974] 1998, 158.

tion in the requirement for "intellectual power" extends across the labour market as a whole and not only in the immediate process of production. In his earlier "Fragment on Machines" in the *Grundrisse*, he argued that capital would increasingly invest machines with the "social brain," reducing the need for skilled labour embedded within social networks (Marx [1939] 1973, 694).[2] This argument was later developed by the sociologist Harry Braverman, who contended that the expansion of capital in the United States produced an overall reduction and polarisation of skill in the labour market. While automation and the systematisation of work created new, highly skilled roles for university-educated managers and engineers, it simultaneously decreased the total amount of skill needed across the workforce to maintain the same level of output (Braverman 1998 [1974], 294–295).

This Marxist tradition offers a different perspective on how technological disruption shapes debates about the nature of art and artistic skill. For Bueno et al., although AI differs from photography in that it "seeks automation of the imagination itself" rather than "the mechanical imitation of nature," both raise the same underlying question: "…which frictions can be productively erased by technology and which frictions are indispensable to a fulfilling creative life?" (Bueno et al. 2025, 13). But from the perspective of Marx and Braverman, the automation of "imagination" (AI) and of "mechanical imitation" (photography) may produce different labour-market effects and therefore distinctly influence how artists conceptualise their work. To develop this point, it is necessary to clarify the distinction Bueno et al. draw between AI's automation of "imagination" and photography's automation of "mechanical imitation." The distinction, I argue, separates the automation of image production on the one hand (achieved by photography and AI), and the transformation of such production into a type of "prosumption" on the other. The term "prosumption" has been coined to refer to an act of instantaneous production and consumption (see Ritzer 2015, 1–17). No clear boundary exists between acts of production and consumption when generating AI images. While the user of a text-to-image model is the producer of a prompt, that same prompt is not a desired product, but rather a description of the service the consumer requires from the text-to-image model, which seems to interpret and attempt to meet those demands. By contrast, a camera might produce

[2] Marx's "Fragment on Machines" is also discussed in the context of artificial intelligence in Pasquinelli (2023, 100–103). See also Tomba (2012, 79–81).

results not predicted or anticipated, but it does not process and interpret its user's stated desires. AI therefore deskills labour not only by lowering the friction to image production (thereby "democraticising it"), but also by eroding the distinction between the producers and consumers of images.

My characterisation of AI art as prosumptive may not capture the full range of practices artists engage in when using this technology. For instance, below I discuss artists that engineer text-to-image models, while others will integrate their use of AI in what might be a complex and personal production process. But my argument concerns less such granularity of practices, and instead hinges on the fact that AI-driven prosumption reshapes the labour market much as earlier waves of automation did in the nineteenth and twentieth centuries. As Harry Braverman observed, automation tends to monopolisation, favouring capital-intensive firms over smaller, highly skilled enterprises (Braverman 1998 [1974], 175–178). Text-to-image models follow a similar pattern: they are developed and deployed by large tech companies that can outcompete freelance artists by replacing skilled labour with scalable automated systems. Ritzer's account of prosumption further clarifies this dynamic. He shows how many digital platforms use prosumption to reduce labour costs: social media users generate the data that sustains the platform, and consumers on Amazon or Expedia perform tasks once handled by paid employees, such as searching for products or completing checkout processes (Ritzer 2015, 5–6). Because prosumption transfers work from employees to consumers, it eliminates skilled jobs required by competing, smaller firms lacking the capital resources to allocate such tasks to "consumers" (Ritzer 2015, 7). Prosumption therefore co-extends with deskilling and monopoly tendencies within contemporary capitalism. The same logic applies to AI art. When users employ text-to-image models, they effectively contract capital-intensive tech companies to produce images at speed and scale, bypassing the skilled workers who previously interpreted, reframed, and executed such requests.

In sum: while the automation and industrialisation of image-making through technology is nothing new, evident in both the history of photography and AI, what is new with AI is the automation of image-making through a prosumptive process. A consideration of AI art within the history of labour markets and monopoly capitalism could therefore clarify how and why current arguments among artists and critics echo older concerns (or "topoi," in Bueno et al.'s terms) while simultaneously confronting this novel problem of prosumption. A key term that has featured in such historical accounts of art's relation to labour markets is "deskilling." Although Braverman did not use the term "deskilling," art historians have developed the term through a reading of his work to address how avant-garde art practices increasingly disavowed artistic skills that had been taught in the European academies since the sixteenth century (Charnley 2025a, 174–195; Beech 2025, 136–137). Without referencing this art scholarship, some researchers have nevertheless tried to situate AI art within this history of "deskilling" by comparing it to conceptual art, since both supposedly replace the skill of craft labour with the generation of an idea (a prompt in the case of AI art) or a set of instructions (Stephensen 2024, 125–138). Such comparisons do not stand up to the contemporary scholarship on conceptual art, which emphasise the range of material practices this broad field of art explored, as well as the internal debates and differences between its practitioners on what constitutes conceptual art (Parvu 2025). But rather than compare conceptual art and AI art as a type of linguistic or creative procedure, I will argue that one can instead consider how they both emerged from and responded to the reduction of skill within the labour market.

I cannot here provide comprehensive histories of conceptual and AI art. But I can outline how two art historians, John Roberts and Marina Vishmidt, respectively analyse how conceptual art responded to deskilling in the twentieth century, and consider how AI artists address comparable issues. Current academic debates and protests regarding AI art tend to focus on whether a machine can be an author (Manovich 2024, 60–65; Auer 2024, 139–150; Zylinska 2020, 49–55; Hertzmann 2018, 2020). But the process of deskilling reveals that the challenge it poses to the concept of authorship concerns not only the legal and conceptual differentiation between subjects and objects, i.e., people and machines, but also the relationship between the owners of AI models and their deskilled prosumers, the former having appropriated the critical and creative skills—those skills of authorship—of the latter, to sell them back to them as a service. I consider the work of two very different artists, Pindar Van Arman and Simon Stålenhag, each of whom presents AI art as a form of technologically induced dreaming. I argue that these artists think of dreaming and the unconscious as suitable metaphors for AI art because prosumption is a state in which images, like dreams, are seemingly made by and for the prosumer, but without their autonomy in designing or making them. Whereas Van Arman's work posits the possibility of computers developing such creative autonomy, Stålenhag reads such a project as inherently dystopian. These reflections on dreaming are ones that take topoi articulated by Baudelaire and identified by Bueno et al.—that technology might threaten skill, the idea of the artist, or the distinction between imagination and automation—and reformulate them within a new concern, or "topos", for prosumption.

Comparing AI With Conceptual Art

Mikel Arbiza Goenaga (2020) has pointed out that any direct comparison between AI art and conceptual practices is spurious, because text-to-image models are "not just creating a new thought for an object, but apparently creating an artefact capable of doing the 'thinking' and 'painting' for us" (57). Just as significantly, such comparisons also overlook how conceptual art was not simply a deskilled practice but a diverse set of responses to the deskilling of labour in the twentieth century. For instance, consider Marian Mazzone and Ahmed Elgammal's (2019) statement that: "AI and conceptual art coincide in locating the art act in the system network of the brain, rather than in the physical output. The physical act of an artist, either applying paint or carving marble, becomes optional" (Mazzone and Elgammal 2019, 7). This is a narrative of "dematerialisation," one whereby conceptual art was concerned with ideas over physical making. Kim Charnley, revising this position, points to how the art group, *Art and Language*, whose members often radically asserted the dematerialisation of art, also included members with divergent views on the nature of conceptual art, some of whom explored deskilling through processes of making, and believed art was not reducible to art criticism and theory (Charnley 2025b, 151–152). Charnley shows how from the perspective of artists like Ian Burn art was not the formulation of ideas as a dematerialised practice, but rather as the material of a "reskilled" one, effectively appropriating the skills of critics and historians who had, in effect, "deskilled" painting by theorising the programme of modernism (Charnley 2025a, 170). Therefore, if AI art were to be compared with conceptual art, one would have to find practices that demonstrate artists appropriating it for their own reskilled practice.

Finding those "reskilled" AI practices will be one thing; interpreting them would be another. While such processes of "reskilling" have been theorised as conceptual art's response to a changing labour market, art historians have various interpretation of such responses. Roberts (2007) and Vishmidt (2019) both explore how conceptual art practices that developed in the twentieth century redefined artistic skills in contradistinction to those based in craft labour, that is, labour processes that were increasingly being deskilled by industry and technology (Roberts 2007, 2024; Vishmidt 2019). However, they take different positions on how conceptual art repositioned its practitioners within society and the economy. Consistently, Roberts sees emancipatory potential in such conceptual art practices in that they reimagine the relationship between art, society and labour (Roberts 2024, 43–44, 54–63, 99–100; 2007, 4, 35–36, 85–87, 192–194, 209). For Roberts, deskilling proceeds dialectically, for innovative artistic practices may be "reskilled" for new economic and social landscapes (Roberts 2007, 103–104; 120–121; 2024, 84–85). But this position opens a door to Vishmidt's, who claims that conceptual art often capitulates to the demands of capital by reskilling artists to respond to, and fit within, the precarious labour market of a financialised and deindustrialised economy. For Vishmidt, the "skill" of conceptually informed artists lies in reimagining themselves as human capital—bearers of credentials and networks—while reframing the conservative notion of artistic "genius" by presenting art as the product of an ineffable mental faculty rather than manual labour (Vishmidt 2019, 171–174, 192–199, 225–226).

In sum, Roberts's and Vishmidt's perspectives show how "deskilled" conceptual practices can be read either as critical of or compliant to industry. Adopting Adorno's terms (a key referent for both Roberts and Vishmidt), conceptual art possesses the potential for "autonomy," resisting and critiquing commodification and instrumentalisation, but it also often slides into "heteronomy," one whereby the artists' work becomes embedded within a deindustrialised economy. I argue that some artists' engagement with AI can be compared to conceptual art not because of any formal or procedural resemblance to it, but because they adapt their practice to critically reflect on their work's autonomy and heteronomy in response to monopoly capital and deskilling. This reflection emerges when AI artists interrogate the extent to which autonomous authorship can emerge from the prosumption of AI art.

Referring back to Bueno et al.'s observations, one could object that AI does not raise distinctive problems regarding authorship because the deskilling of artistic production in the nineteenth and twentieth centuries raised "topoi" not just about the nature of art, but also its makers: who is an artist? (Bueno et al. 2025, 11). As Molly Nesbit has shown (1987, 235–237), in the nineteenth century, photography forced a legal re-evaluation on the legal nature of authorship. Comparable to current debates on AI, it centered around questions of copyright law: whether a photographer can claim to be an author of their work like a painter (see Manovich 2024, 60–65; Auer 2024, 139–150; Zylinska 2020, 49–55; Hertzmann 2018, 2020). Similarly, artists engaged with computers and cybernetics from the 1960s to explore authorship and creativity (Schröter 2024, 36–38; Hertzmann 2018, 8–9). A notable example is Frieder Nake, who produced artworks using a pen-plotter informed by algorithms he designed.[3] His *Hommage à Paul Klee* (1965) was inspired by Klee's painting *Highways and Byways* (1929; Fig. 4.1). Nake's work anticipates AI art in how it uses algorithms to attribute creativity to machines, and how it questions the distribution of authorship between that machine, its maker and the original model (Caplan 2024).[4]

However, the example of Nake highlights the difference between producing an image with a machine and the prosumptive process of AI art. Nake's creative process is distinct from that of contemporary text-to-image models, in that he neither trains his algorithms on Klee's paintings nor simply prompts a pre-existing model, but instead writes his own code to produce works inspired by Klee. A recent controversy generated by the contemporary art collective, Obvious, centred around this connection between authorship and algorithm design. As if it were an artist's signature, this group put the algorithm of a generative adversarial network (GAN) onto the lower right corner of an AI-generated image they had it make, the *Portrait of Edmond de Belamy*, a work they sold for $432,500 at a Christie's auction in 2018.[5] However, the attribution of either the algorithm or Obvious as the author has raised controversy, for Obvious trained that algorithm on images of artworks found in the public domain, and took it from another artist, Robbie Barrat, who himself relied on DCGAN architecture developed by Alec Radford, Luke Metz, and Soumith Chintala (Epstein et al. 2020; Rani et al. 2024). Leaving aside the question on whether Obvious have a valid claim to authorship, the *Portrait of Edmond de Belamy* raised a dispute, in a way that, for instance, Nake's authorship

[3] On Nake's practice see Caplan (2022, 136–137).

[4] This conference paper I am citing here by Caplan is a work in progress, so please consult and cite her forthcoming work as well as her *Arte Programmata* (2022), and cite her ideas on Nake instead of this current chapter.

[5] Obvious, Portrait of Edmond de Belamy, GAN-generated image, print, 2018. See Rani et al. (2024).

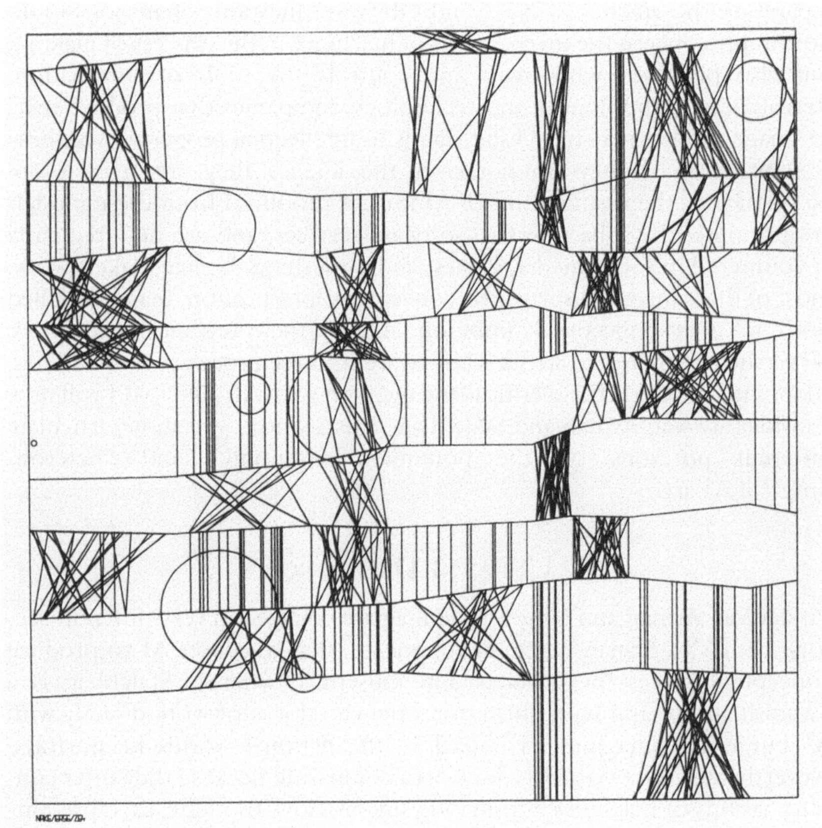

Fig. 4.1 Frieder Nake, *Hommage à Paul Klee*, 13/9/65 Nr.2, 1965, print. © Frieder Nake/Victoria and Albert Museum, London

over *Highways and Byways* could not, because Obvious acted as prosumers. Whereas Nake wrote his own algorithms, Obvious used an existing one and training data they found online to generate an image, thereby acting as the consumers of others work in their apparent production of an image.

Comparisons between AI and conceptual art on the basis that both seemingly rely on ideas rather than craft overlook the distinction separating the practice of Nake and Obvious: questions of authorship do not simply concern the involvement of machines in the process of making, but also pivot on who owns and controls the tools of automation. Researchers, technologists and technology companies that produce text-to-image models may have valid claims to intellectual property over these systems, even if they do not over the images they are trained on. Nevertheless, the vast amount of AI images produced from these models are prompted by subscribers to software services, and are now regularly encountered in social media, games, and publishing. Unlike Nake's work, most of these images display little conceptuasophistication, being deskilled both in their conceptual ambition and in their technical execution. Nevertheless, there are artists who, aware of these processes of deskilling, adapt into their practice a critical engagement with AI. The two I will now consider are Van Arman and Stålenhag, artists who, I will show, articulate different positions on the potential "autonomy" and "heteronomy" of AI art.

Uncanny Dreaming

Pindar Van Arman and Simon Stålenhag are engaged in very different sectors, with Van Arman being an American artist who uses AI to produce conceptual pieces for galleries and museums, whereas Stålenhag is a Swedish author and sci-fi illustrator, one who does not work directly with AI but rather imagines its impact in the fictional worlds he portrays. Nevertheless, the two artists are worth comparing because they offer contrary visions of machines automating unconscious thought, each presenting AI art as an uncanny form of dreaming, uncanny because these dreams are not natural, but technologically induced. These artists think of dreaming as a suitable metaphor for AI art because prosumption is a state in which images, like dreams, seem made by and for the prosumer, but without their conscious work in designing or making them. However, whereas Van Arman is a technologist who imagines the possibility of creative autonomy emerging through such a dreamlike state, Stålenhag imagines this same condition to be one of radical heteronomy, one whereby the consciousness of humans, as prosumers, becomes commodified. These alternative positions are extensions of the rival conceptions of authorship discussed in the previous section: one the one hand, one which sees human creativity as automatable through AI; and on the other, one which defines autonomy as an artist's ability to resist corporate appropriation.

The concept of dreaming, and the related idea of hallucination (used when the text or image is considered faulty), has often been used as a metaphor for the products of AI in both academic literature and popular culture.[6] AI artworks are not literally dream imagery: they are experienced during waking hours and in the outside world. Yet the metaphor strikes a chord with people discussing AI because dreaming shares some qualities with prosumption. A dream image, like AI made by a prompt, is experienced by its producer as one the producer consumes, because it has been generated without the conscious, deliberate and effortful process one sees in the manual and mechanised production of images. This dreamlike quality is not simply commodity fetishism, one whereby the basis of the image's value in labour has been obscured by the market, although certainly AI presents a sophisticated type of fetishisation.[7] AI images resemble dream images in a way that commodities do not because their prosumers become witnesses to the conjuration of these images that define and realise their desires for them.

Given that AI art is not a literal dreaming, but one seemingly generated by machines, it is unsurprising that many artists over the last decade have explored its uncanniness, a trend surveyed by Dejan Grba (2022). The uncanny, as defined by Freud, is the eerie feeling that something familiar suddenly seems strange, or something strange feels familiar, when thoughts or feelings that had been repressed from conscious awareness resurface, whether in dreams or while awake (2003). From a Freudian perspective, AI's dreamlike images appear uncanny because, despite being machine-made, they seem to answer our wishes as if they were living, thereby reviving childhood fantasies that inanimate things are alive (2003).

Van Armam's *Emerging Faces* (Fig. 4.2, 2017) feels uncanny. The painting is made through the interaction of two robotic agents. The first applies paint to the canvas using a GAN trained on 10,000 celebrities' faces.[8] The second agent acts like a GAN discriminator, except rather than accept the image when it reads it as authentic, it instead stops the painting

[6] The literature on AI, dreams and hallucinations is extensive. For recent general discussions, see Adiodun and Nickel (2024) and Halperin and Lukin (2024).

[7] While parallels exist between commodity fetishism and Freudian theory, the precise nature of these homologies is unclear. See Murray and Bradshaw (2024, 280). Slavoj Žižek (2008, 3–9) makes a case for the similarity between the commodity and dreamwork in *The Sublime Object of Ideology*.

[8] Van Arman (2025) "Thanks, I find that simplifying the explanation is preferred," *X.com*, https://x.com/VanArman/status/1888902862521978960 (accessed 5 March 2025).

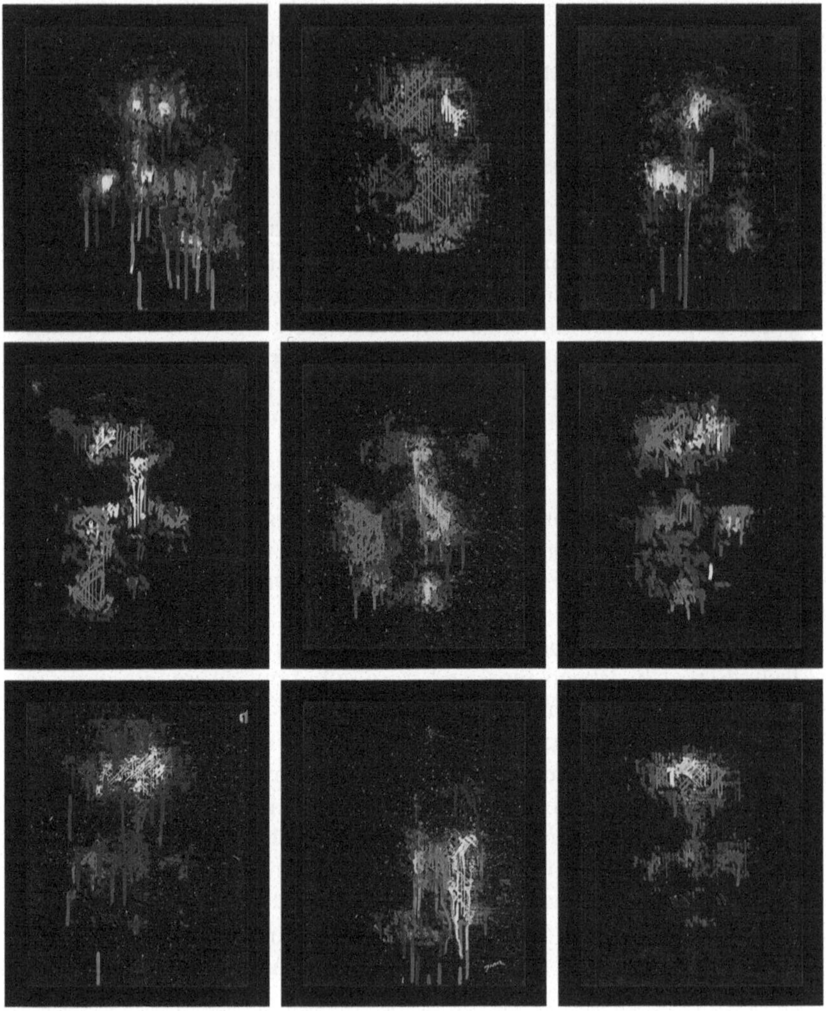

Fig. 4.2 Pindar Van Arman, *Emerging Faces*, acrylic on canvas, 93.9 × 116.8 cm, 2017. Image courtesy of the artist

as soon as it recognises a face. Consequently, rather than generate an experience of the uncanny valley by closely simulating a real human face,[9] the uncanniness of these images is in their play with the threshold of pareidolia, the threshold between abstraction and figuration when shapes suddenly resolve into a face, like apparitions glimpsed in phosphenes. Just as our experience of the uncanny valley occurs when we cannot determine whether a being is a machine or a person, here we have ghostly presences, ones poised between appearing like a person or just a random series of marks.

The serial repetition of Van Arman's paintings underlines their uncanniness. For Freud (2003), the involuntary repetition of experiences that could, individually, be seen as coincidental produces a haunting sense of an inescapable and primal force, one rooted in the repressed repetition-compulsion of the unconscious. While perceiving a face in one of these images could be deemed coincidental, the repetition of the experience brings the unconscious process of pareidolic vision into the viewer's awareness, but as a presence seemingly in their unconscious perception and outside their conscious control. Van Arman may be aware of these resonances between repetition and the unconscious, for the portrait series seemingly quotes Andy Warhol's repeated portraits of Marilyn Monroe, a repetition that has been read in psychoanalytic terms as evoking a trauma response (Foster 1996, 131–144).[10]

In deploying two robotic agents as producer and "discriminator," Van Arman's *Emerging Faces* positions the AI as both creator and built-in viewer, radically automating prosumption by removing humans from the loop of production and consumption. While the resulting uncanniness might suggest a critique of fully automated image-making, Van Arman instead embraces such automation. He believes that AI could eventually be creative like humans, and part of that creative experience in humans is rooted in psychological experiences like the uncanny. He has stated that "[i]t's in the uncanny valley that I am trying to replicate human creativity. It does make some people uneasy" (Reeve 2017). *Emerging Faces* thus shows how an artist rooted in the conceptual-art tradition—one that

[9] A discussion of the "uncanny valley" as found in AI art within the longer context of Freudian psychanalysis can be found in Broad, Grierson and Leymarie (2020, 36–37). URL. See also Raveto-Biagioli (2016, 149–150).

[10] A more recent reading of Warhol in psychoanalytic terms is Solano and Quagelli (2020, 257–276).

challenges craft-based notions of art and authorship and inherits serial strategies from the neo-avant-garde—can produce work heteronomous with the emergent AI industry. Van Arman's "reskilled" artistic practice thereby lies in advancing the automation, systematisation and monopolisations of art-making, and as a technologist these are his explicitly theorised objectives.

In his book *The Electric State* (2018), Stålenhag envisions the full realisation of a project like Van Arman's, the automation of the human unconscious. This graphic novel, composed largely of digital paintings, has been adapted for television and film. It depicts a United States whose population is "neuro-linked," addicted to headsets that connect its citizens to a hive mind: an AI entity built from humanity's collective thoughts. Although Stålenhag's book appeared just before the public availability of text-to-image models around 2020, its fictional technology may have been influenced by research using artificial neural networks to reconstruct images from neuro-physiological data.[11]

In Stålenhag's world, prosumption becomes dystopian. He speculates that the domination of virtual reality will be so complete it will take control of people's unconscious thoughts. One image illustrates well this tyranny of the dream world: the protagonist, Michelle, witnesses a monstrous cartoon robot, built by the headset-wearing people surrounding it, with cables extending from its body like tentacles. The cables enter a car where they sexually engage a woman, the sexual act being unseen in the image, but referred to in the accompanying text (Fig. 4.3; Stålenhag 2018, 89). This perverse reversal of online pornography, with the headset-wearing viewers here being digital and the woman real, exemplifies Freud's account of the uncanniness of ambiguous beings situated between persons or objects, living or dead, an ambiguity felt most keenly in sexual fetishisation. Freud's (2003) own example is the character Olympia in E. T. A. Hoffmann's story "The Sandman" (1816), the protagonist's love interest and a clockwork-automaton. Such fetishisation and ambiguities between objecthood and personhood are evident in Stålenhag's image, in which the sexual robot is also a cartoonish figure, as if out of a kid's TV show, its developed sexuality blurring the distinction between adulthood and childhood. For Freud, "[a]n uncanny experience occurs either when

[11] See Takagi and Nishimoto (2023). As well as describing their own paper on using Stable Diffusion models to decipher brain activity, Takagi and Nishimoto describe a literature into brain encoding and decoding that extends into the first decade of the 2000s.

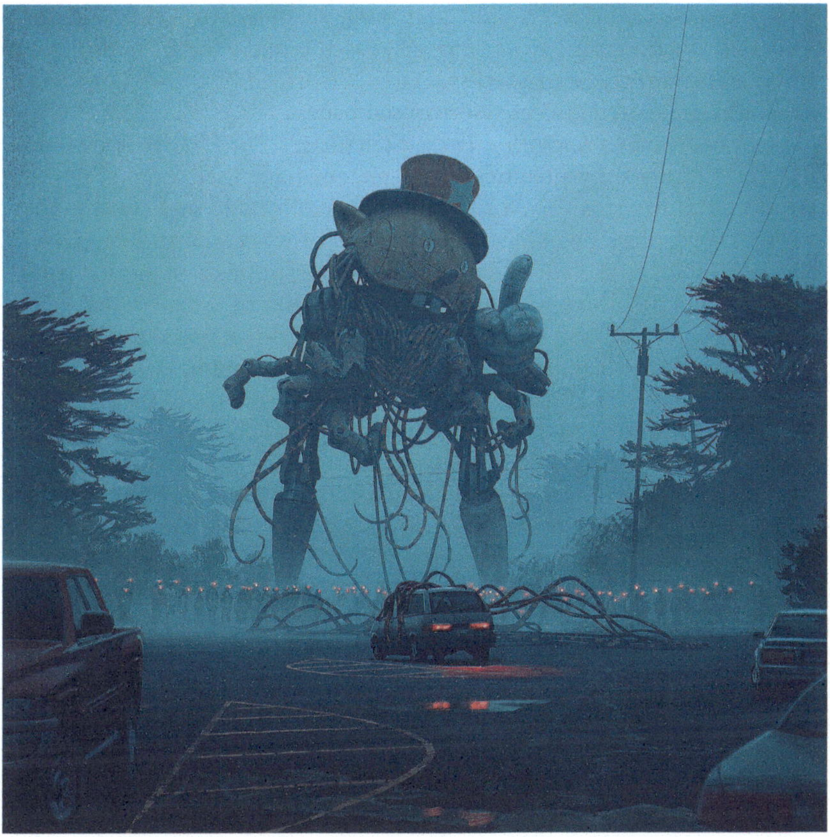

Fig. 4.3 Simon Stålenhag, *The Electric State*, New York: Skybound Books, 2018. Copyright © Simon Stålenhag 2017. Image courtesy of Simon Stålenhag Produktion AB

repressed infantile complexes have been revived by some impression, or when the primitive beliefs we have surmounted seem once more to be confirmed" (155). Stålenhag's monster, with its cartoon face and Mickey Mouse gloves, becomes the double of such "infantile complexes," comparable to Freud's example of childhood dolls (135, 140–141). Stålenhag combines these uncanny tropes to portray the prosumption of AI as nightmarish. Selling us our repackaged unconscious desires, AI is shown here to generate an ambiguous state, one Stålenhag portrays as occurring in the half-light of dusk, between light and dark, sleep and wakefulness, conscious and unconscious, work and play, as the audience of neurolinked zombies consume the sexualised spectacle performed by the idol produced by their AI-generated collective unconsciousness.

Like Van Arman's *Emerging Faces*, Stålenhag's *The Electric State* imagines how the uncanny qualities of AI images have their origins in prosumption. But whereas Van Arman seeks to actually build such prosumptive machines, Stålenhag's work articulates a type of Romantic anti-capitalism, one that adheres to an older form of craft labour, in this case, digital painting, and which deplores AI's potential destruction of artistic work in the design and entertainment industries.[12] The actual threat posed to Stålenhag by AI was made clear in a 2022 incident with Andrez Guadamuz, a researcher in property law. Guadamuz sought to test his published research on the relationship between sci-fi, authorship and AI (2021) by using a text-to-image model called Midjourney to produce images that imitated Stålenhag's art, posting the results to Twitter (now x.com). In response, Stålenhag criticised the lack of skill, originality and beauty in such images, and added to it a criticism of big tech: "What I don't like about AI tech is not that it can produce brand new 70s rock hits like 'Keep On Glowing, You Mad Jewel' by Fink Ployd, but how it reveals that that kind of derivative, generated goo is what our new tech lords are hoping to feed us in their vision of the future."[13] Such anger and distaste towards the "grey-goo" of AI images and the "tech overlords" purveying them was visualised in *The Electric State* in the portrayal of neurolinked prosumers. For Stålenhag, the key threat of AI is not the technology as such, but rather the monopoly capitalism that generates such prosumptive networks.

Conclusion

The comparison between twentieth-century conceptual art and contemporary artistic responses to AI lies not in the idea (or, possibly, "topos") that conceptual art anticipated prompt writing, but in the fact that both emerged as responses to monopoly capitalism and the deskilling of creative labour. If there's a difference, it is that while conceptual art held

[12] On romantic anti-capitalism, see Hemingway (2025).

[13] Stålenhag's tweets responding to Guadamuz have since been deleted, along with his account on x.com. But this quote is still discussed in certain places online, e.g., Plunkett (2024).

some potential, however contested, for creative autonomy, such potential seems far less likely in the case of AI art. Artists like Van Arman aim to expand AI's ability to absorb and replicate artistic skill, reinforcing a form of technological dominance over creativity. It may seem ironic that sci-fi, a heteronomous genre integrated with the entertainment industries, can hold a critical position with regard to such projects. But I have argued elsewhere that science fiction, like Stålenhag's, can also speculate into the nature of art, even if one has to consider the distinct financial, institutional and philosophical networks its operates within (Murray 2025). Stålenhag has articulated the concerns of many others who have protested against the proliferation of AI images and the appropriation of their work, and he uses his images to warn against the heteronomy inherent to the making of AI art, that is, the lack of agency and creativity in the prosumption of prompt-writing. Undoubtedly, such protestations share similar topoi to those articulated in the nineteenth century by artists and critics in response to photography, such as the merger of art and industry, as well as the decline of creative imagination (Beuno et al.). But in identifying the technological disruption of AI as one of prosumption, Stålenhag roots such problems not in technology itself, but in how AI deskills the labour market and allows technology platforms to monopolise image production.

I am not aware of any artists that reskill their practice in Roberts's term, one that finds autonomy in the deskilled position of the prosumer, and I doubt such a possibility. In *The Electric State* Stålenhag's character, Michelle, achieves autonomy from AI, but does so by not linking herself to it. While her story ends tragically, it underscores the requirement necessary for artists to achieve autonomy in their creative practice: democratic and public control over monopoly capital.

Acknowledgements With particular thanks to Kim Charnley for the generous feedback. Thank you also Leda Cempellin, Melissa Geiger and Joseph Hurtgen. For images and permissions, my gratitude to Pindar Van Arman, Simon Stålenhag and Frieder Nake.

References

Adiodun, Sade J., and Luke Nickel. 2024. Artificial Intelligence: Dreams, Data and Neuro-aesthetics in the Age of AI. *Journal of Comparative Literature and Aesthetics* 47:141–162.

Auer, Robin Markus. 2024. Creativity and Function. In *Artificial Intelligence: Human Machine Interaction and Creative Practice*, ed. Eckart Voigts et al., 45–62. Bielefeld: Transcript Verlag.

Baudelaire, Charles. 1955. The Salon of 1859. In *The Mirror of Art: Critical Studies by Charles Baudelaire*. Translated and edited by Jonathan Mayne. Phaidon.

Beech, Dave. 2025. Concepts of Labor in Marxist Art History. In *The Routledge Companion to Marxisms in Art History*, ed. Tijen Tunali and Brian Winkenweder. Routledge.

Braverman, Harry. 1998. *Labor and Monopoly Capital: The Degradation of Work in the Twentieth Century*. NYU Press. Originally published in 1974.

Broad, Terence, Mick Grierson, and Frederic Leymarie. 2020. Amplifying The Uncanny. In *8th Conference on Computation, Communication, Aesthetics & X (xCoAx 2020)*, 36–37. https://2020.xcoax.org/pdf/xCoAx2020-Broad.pdf.

Bueno, Claudio Celis, Steve Jankowski, and Jakko Kemper. 2025. The Enduring Schism Between Culture and Technique: Historical (Dis)continuities Between the Daguerreotype and Generative AI. *Convergence* 1–16.

Caplan, Lindsay. 2022. *Arte Programmata: Freedom, Control, and the Computer in 1960s Italy*. Minneapolis: University of Minnesota Press.

Caplan, Lindsay. 2024. The Death of the Author and Other Fantasies: Generative Art between Cybernetics and Psychoanalysis. Paper presented at the *Association of Art Historians Annual Conference*, Bristol, April 3–5.

Charnley, Kim. 2025a. Deskilling. In *The Routledge Companion to Marxisms in Art History*, ed. Tijen Tunali and Brian Winkenweder. Routledge.

Charnley, Kim. 2025b. Carpenter of the Predicate: Ian Burn, Conceptual Art and Making. In *A Show of Hands: Crafting Concepts in Contemporary Art*, ed. Ileana Parvu. De Gruyter.

Epstein, Ziv, Sydney Levine, David G. Rand, and Iyad Rahwan. 2020. Who Gets Credit for AI-Generated Art? *iScience* 23:101515.

Foster, Hal. 1996. *The Return of the Real*. MIT Press.

Freud, Sigmund. 2003. *The Uncanny*. Translated by David McLintock. Penguin.

Goenaga, Mikel Arbiza. 2020. A Critique of Contemporary Artificial Intelligence Art: Who is 'Edmond de Belamy'? *AusArt* 8:49–64.

Grba, Dejan. 2022. Deep Else: A Critical Framework for AI Art. *Digital* 2.

Guadamez, Andres. 2021. Do Androids Dream of Electric Copyright? Comparative Analysis of Originality in Artificial Intelligence-Generated Works. In *Artificial Intelligence and Intellectual Property*, ed. Jyh-An Lee, Reto M. Hilty, and Kung-Chung Liu. Oxford University Press.

Halperin, Brett A., and Stephanie M. Lukin. 2024. Artificial Dreams: Surreal Visual Storytelling as Inquiry in AI 'Hallucination'. In *DIS '24: Designing Interactive Systems Conference, IT University of Copenhagen, Denmark, July*, 619–637. AMC.

Heckman, Derek. 2024. Wizards Versus Robots. *Slate*. https://slate.com/technology/2024/08/magic-the-gathering-artificial-intelligence-card-art-controversy.html. Accessed 25 January 2025.

Hemingway, Andrew. 2025. Romantic Anti-Capitalism. In *The Routledge Companion to Marxisms in Art History*, ed. Tijen Tunali and Brian Winkenweder. Routledge.

Hertzmann, Aaron. 2018. Can Computers Create Art. *Arts* 7 (2): 18.

Hertzmann, Aaron. 2020. Computers Do Not Make Art, People Do. *Communications of the ACM* 63 (5): 45–48.

Kemper, Jakko. 2024. *Frictionlessness: The Silicon Valley Philosophy of Seamless Technology and the Aesthetic Value of Imperfection*. Bloomsbury Academic.

Manovich, Lev. 2024. AI and Myths of Creativity. *Architectural Design* 92 (3): 60–65.

Marx, Karl. 1973. *Grundrisse: Foundations of the Critique of Political Economy (Rough Draft)*. Translated by Martin Nicolaus. Penguin. First published 1939.

Marx, Karl. 1976. *Capital: A Critique of Political Economy, Volume 1*. Translated by Ben Fowkes. Penguin.

Mazzone, Marian, and Ahmed Elgamal. 2019. Art, Creativity and the Potential of Artificial Intelligence. *Arts* 8:1–9.

Murray, Andrew. 2025. Speculation. In *The Routledge Companion to Marxisms in Art History*, ed. Tijen Tunali and Brian Winkenweder. Routledge.

Murray, Andrew, and Alan Bradshaw. 2024. Could Commodities Themselves Speak? An Introduction to the Agnotology of the Spectacle. *Environment and Planning D: Society and Space* 42 (2): 275–293.

Nesbit, Molly. 1987. What was an Author? *Yale French Studies* 73.

Parvu, Ileana. 2025. Making Concepts. In *A Show of Hands: Crafting Concepts in Contemporary Art*, ed. Ileana Parvu, 11–16. Berlin: De Gruyter.

Pasquinelli, Matteo. 2023. *The Eye of the Master: A Social History of Artificial Intelligence*. Verso.

Plunkett, Luke. 2024. AI Creating 'Art' Is an Ethical and Copyright Nightmare. https://www.lukeplunkett.com/ai-creating-art-is-an-ethical-and-copyright-nightmare/#:~:text=Swedish%20artist%20Simon%20St%C3%A5lenhag%20perhaps,what%20our%20new%20tech%20lords.

Rani, Sunanda, et al. 2024. Examining the Impacts of Artificial Intelligence Technology and Computing on Digital Art: A Case Study of Edmond de Belamy and its Aesthetics Values and Techniques. *AI & Society*. https://doi.org/10.1007/s00146-024-01996-y.

Raveto-Biagioli, Kriss. 2016. *Digital Uncanny*. Oxford University Press.

Reeve, Elspeth. 2017. Meet the Man Teaching Robot Artists to Paint like Humans. *Vice*, 8 August 2017. https://www.vice.com/en/article/meet-the-man-teaching-robot-artists-to-paint-like-humans/.

Ritzer, George. 2015. The 'New' World of Prosumption: Evolution, 'Return of the Same' or Revolution? *Sociological Forum* 30:1–17.

Roberts, John. 2007. *The Intangibilities of Form: Skill and Deskilling in Art After the Readymade*. Verso.

Roberts, John. 2024. *Art and Emancipation*. Brill.
Schröter, Jens. 2024. AI, Automation, Creativity, Cognitive Labor. In *Artificial Intelligence: Human Machine Interaction and Creative Practice*, ed. Eckart Voigts et al., 35–44. Verlag.
Solano, Paola, and Luca Quagelli. 2020. On Andy Warhol: Between Repetition and Symbolization. *Canadian Journal of Psychoanalysis/Revue Canadienne de Psychanalyse* 28:257–276.
Stålenhag, Simon. 2018. *The Electric State*. Skybound Books.
Stephensen, Jan Løhmann. 2024. The Marcel Duchamp Case In, Against, or After Artificial Creativity. In *Artificial Intelligence: Human Machine Interaction and Creative Practice*, ed. Eckart Voigts et al., 125–138. Verlag.
Takagi, Yu, and Shinji Nishimoto. 2023. Stable Diffusion with Brain Activity: FAQ. https://sites.google.com/view/stablediffusion-with-brain/faq_en.
Thomas, Daniel. 2025. Christie's Plan for AI Art Auction Sparks Backlash from Artists. *The Financial Times*. https://www.ft.com/content/e8c7b729-f87a-408c-a2be-76f8da489ba2. Accessed 10 February 2025.
Tomba, Massimiliano. 2012. *Marx's Temporalities*. Brill.
Van Arman, Pindar. 2017. *Emerging Faces*, acrylic on canvas, 93.9 × 116.8 cm. Lot 8 of Christies Online Auction 23942. https://onlineonly.christies.com/s/augmented-intelligence/pindar-van-arman-b-1974-8/249747.
Van Arman, Pindar. 2025. Thanks, I Find that Simplifying the Explanation is Preferred. *X.com*, https://x.com/VanArman/status/1888902862521978960.
Vishmidt, Marina. 2019. *Speculation as a Mode of Production: Forms of Value, Subjectivity in Art and Capital*. Haymarket.
World Economic Forum. 2025. *Future of Jobs Report 2025*. https://reports.weforum.org/docs/WEF_Future_of_Jobs_Report_2025.pdf. Accessed 20 February 2025.
Xiang, Chloe. 2022. Artists are Revolting Against AI Art on ArtStation. *Vice*. https://www.vice.com/en/article/artists-are-revolt-against-ai-art-on-artstation/. Accessed 25 January 2025.
Žižek, Slavoj. 2008. *The Sublime Object of Ideology*. Verso.
Zylinska, Joanna. 2020. *AI Art: Machine Visions and Warped Dreams*. Open Humanities Press.

CHAPTER 5

Not Touched by Human Hands: Misattributed AI Sentience and the Power of Images

Kurt Ralske

The Error of Misattribution

AI-generated images are fake. Perhaps there is nothing more fake than an AI image. The images produced by users of DALL-E and Midjourney that flood the Internet (typically, celebrities in surreal situations, goofy historical anachronisms, animals performing human activities, or juvenile stylistic mash-ups) are "a tale told by an idiot, full of sound and fury, signifying nothing" (Shakespeare [1623] 2015, 252). Because they are formed entirely within the digital realm out of the digitized archive of existing representations, it is clear that no AI-generated image could ever be a direct indexical representation of a truth as it exists in the world.

AI images are always second-order mediations: they are mediations of mediations.

However, ordinary users of images, who consume images without criticality, are liable to make an error: they might accept AI images as

K. Ralske (✉)
Tufts University, Boston, MA, USA

L. Cempellin, M. Geiger (eds.), *Reimagining Art History with Artificial Intelligence*,
https://doi.org/10.1007/978-3-032-21685-4_5

unmediated truths. Without criticality, the default principle for the use of images is "seeing is believing." What is at stake is not the simple, understandable error of mistaking an AI image for an authentic photograph. The more serious error is for the viewer to know that an image is AI generated and yet still consider it as a representation of a truth (or even, to find the image *more* meaningful because of its AI origins). I see this type of error as having enormous significance—philosophically, culturally, and politically. As a means of studying this error, I aim to reverse the question and work backwards: What conditions, and what epistemological framework, would be necessary for AI images to become regarded as credible, as containers of truths, that is, as representations worthy of being interpreted to produce meanings applicable to the world?

The root cause of this mistaken interpretation of AI images is what philosopher Jonathan Birch calls "misattribution of consciousness," the erroneous attribution of sentience to AI. Birch (2025) believes that "millions of users will soon misattribute human-like consciousness to AI friends, partners, and assistants on the basis of mimicry and role-play," to the point that many users already believe they interact with sentient AI companions (Birch 2025, 2).

In 2024, Colombatto and Fleming conducted a study of 300 ChatGPT users to explore how ordinary users perceived the consciousness of LLMs. They found that "only a third of our sample thought that ChatGPT definitely did not have subjective experience, while two-thirds of our sample thought that ChatGPT had varying degrees of phenomenal consciousness (…). These findings thus highlight a discrepancy between folk intuitions and expert opinions on artificial consciousness" (Colombatto and Fleming 2024, 4).

The non-critical consumer of images who erroneously assumes that an AI image generator is capable of sentience will interpret generated images as manifestations of a consciousness whose capabilities could exceed their own. A critical viewer might consider a particular image to be merely annoying AI slop. A non-critical viewer, inclined to misattribution of AI sentience, would encounter the same image and consider it as a thing to be seen, and to be believed. And this belief, quite unlike a simple trust in the indexicality of the photograph, bestows the image with a capacity for profound kinds of influence upon the viewer.

Birch describes "misattribution of consciousness" as a problem for those who use AI products whose interfaces mimic familiar human modes of interaction. I believe the situation extends much further: misattributed

AI sentience is a problem for all users of images, even those who never interact directly with AI products. Image consumers encounter AI images even if they have never used AI tools themselves. The mere existence of AI images alters the epistemelogical framework that structures how images can be interpreted and used, equally for all users of all types of images.

This inquiry into AI, images, and beliefs is in two parts. The first is to historicize the problem of misattributed AI sentience, by connecting it with how the relationship between images and beliefs has been theorized by art historians and art theorists: Hans Belting (1994) on early Christian icons, and David Levi Strauss (2020) on analogue photography and its relation to truth. The second part is to examine misattributed AI sentience and its ramifications. How might this erroneous notion impact how ordinary viewers use and interpret images? And what new, unprecedented, or anachronistic uses of images might result from this error? Beyond the scope of this inquiry are the larger philosophical and technological questions of "Is AI sentience possible?" or "When exactly will it be developed?" These are not taken up here. For this inquiry, all that is required is a simpler proposition: that in the future, some percentage of consumers of images will believe AI is capable of sentience. Because the focus here is on beliefs, the misattributed *notion* of AI sentience is all that is considered, not the possibility of true existence or non-existence of AI sentience. However wildly incorrect the misattributed notion of AI sentience may be, it is an actual phenomenon that is potentially the cause of profound cultural change. As such, in itself it is a topic worthy of serious critical consideration.

The *Acheiropoeta* Icon

Hans Belting discussed a particular category of early Christian religious icon, those traditionally designated as *acheiropoieta*, or "not touched by human hands." Within the Christian Church of the Early Middle Ages, these paintings were considered to have been created by divine will. That is, they came into existence without the involvement of any human being. These were paintings considered to be "unpainted"—meaning, they appeared miraculously, as divine manifestations. Of this miracle, little can be said; it can be understood only through belief.

A famous *acheiropoieton* image is the Shroud of Turin. For believers (Belting 1994, 64), the image was created when the body of Jesus was resurrected, leaving behind an impression of his earthly form on the cloth wrapping his body. The image is, within its system of belief, the product of a miraculous, incomprehensible process, and no human was involved in its production. "Believers claim that the Shroud is acheiropoietic; that is [...] it is a direct emanation of the Son of God, unmediated, without human intervention or subjectivity: an objective trace" (Strauss 2020, 19). It is "not touched by human hands."

Belting describes various ways *acheiropoieta* were believed to have come into existence. Some appeared miraculously inside churches when they were consecrated (Belting 1994, 64). Other icons were said to have been painted by saints, such as an image of the Virgin in S. Maria Maggiore in Venice, attributed to the apostle St Luke (Belting 1994, 68). Saints can perform miracles; thus, paintings created by them were *acheiropoieta*. And still other icons, such as an image of Christ on display in the pope's Sancta Sanctorum, were said to have been painted by holy beings themselves, as self-portraits: "About this image the medieval legends tell us that the apostles had appointed Luke...to paint a portrait of Christ, so that they would at least retain a likeness of him after he ascended into heaven. Once begun, however, the picture had completed itself, 'not by human agency, but by divine intervention'" (Belting 1994, 65).

In each of these cases, the images were considered "unpainted," that is, they were manifestations of divine will. These images laid claim to having special significance precisely because they were not touched by human hands. Within its context of belief, the *acheiropoieta* icon is the authoritative likeness of some holy personage. The image's authoritative status rests on its divine origins. If it were made by a human, it would be only a subjective fantasy, and like all human things, imperfect. But because its author is divine, there can be no image that can lay claim to greater authority than it.

The Indexical Analogue Photograph

David Levi Strauss has noted that like *acheiropoieta* icons, the analogue photograph is similarly "not touched by human hands" (Strauss 2020, 57). The analogue photograph is the product of a scientific process: light is focused by a lens, then permanently fixed by a chemical reaction. That process can be accomplished with little or no human input; for example, the shutter could be triggered automatically (mechanically) and the image would still be produced.

In the digital age, we consider photographs as constructions, and we know that the intentionality of the photographer is a crucial part of the process. We regard photographs as mediated images, not unmediated ones. But this was not always the case. During much of the history of analogue photography, the photographic process was considered purely scientific, objective, impartial. In the scientific perspective, the photographic process allows whatever configuration of light is present in a particular place and time to represent itself accurately, without interference from any human. The photograph manifests itself because of the natural principles of the behaviour of light and chemicals, not the human hand.

Analogue photography was built on scientific discoveries made in the fields of optics, chemistry, engineering, and manufacturing. The specialized knowledge needed to create the analogue photographic process remains incomprehensible to the non-specialist. From a certain perspective, photography is something of a miracle.

Photographs reveal worlds too impossibly small for us to see with our own eyes—such as microscopic organisms or atoms—or worlds too impossibly big for us to see, such as the iconic 1972 "Blue Marble" image of planet Earth taken from the moon. But, even though we cannot directly verify the existence of these things through our own experience, we accept them as truths, because we already comfortably believe in the epistemological framework surrounding the production of these images, that is, science, reason, empirical truth, enabling a kind of knowledge superior to that of any individual. Because photographs are made by a machine, they were accepted as truer than any images made by human hands.

For many decades, the truth-value of analogue photographs was so generally accepted that they could be used as evidence in legal proceedings (Sante 1992). Precisely because the analogue photograph is an image produced by a machine, it carries a claim to exceptional veracity. Because of its incomprehensible mechanical origins, the photograph was considered more trustworthy than any human witness, even the most virtuous one. Humans are biased or ignorant or prone to error; machines are impartial and relaiably accurate. "The camera never lies" was a popular expression of the era (Stevenson 1891, 301).

What, then, can be said about the similarities between the *acheiropoieta* icon and the analogue photograph? The icon emerges from the divine; the analogue photograph emerges from a scientific process. Both processes are not comprehensible to the ordinary person. Both processes depend on knowledge that ordinary image-users do not have access to. The *acheiropoieta* icon presents an authoritatively accurate image of a divine being because its miraculous origins prove its author is the Deity, whose authority and veracity cannot be questioned. The analogue photograph presents an authoritatively accurate image of the world because the scientific processes used for its production are free from human bias, ignorance, and error.

The AI-Generated Image

What, then, of how AI-generated images are created? Could it be said that AI images are *acheiropoieta*, "not touched by human hands"? And might some image-user ever claim that AI images have a special capacity to reveal truths that cannot be accessed in other ways? For the miraculous icon and the indexical photograph, belief and truth are constituted in visual form. Could the same be said of the AI image—that it, like the others, is "not touched by human hands," and for that very reason carries some authoritative connection to truths?

The process of AI image generation is complex, relying on specialized hardware and software. Only a tiny percentage of those who generate AI images fully comprehend the techniques used in their creation (generative adversarial networks, diffusion models, massive training sets). Even the engineers responsible for writing the software algorithms would be unable to predict exactly what image would be produced in response to any given prompt. AI images are machine-made, and thus seemingly deterministic in origin. Yet the mathematical unperpinnings of the algorithm, relying on many iterations through huge matricies of possibility, are so complex that the results are unpredictable in a way surpassing human understanding. Most of us who have ever played with DALL-E or MidJourney or Stable Diffusion have had the experience of entering a prompt and then being genuinely startled by the resulting images. "How did it do that, and why?" is a common response. The production of AI images appears to end users as a mysterious and generally incomprehensible process.

To return to the initial question: What conditions—what epistemological framework—would be necessary for AI images to become regarded as credible, as containers of truths? This question is approached by considering the relationship between images and beliefs.

Images and Beliefs

Within any given epistomelogical framework, images and beliefs exist in a tautological, self-reflexive, recursive, self-sustaining relationship: a closed circuit of proof and faith. Each affirms the other. An example is provided by a 1977 incident in New Mexico (Garcia 2017). A tortilla was thrown on a grill. When removed, some saw the marks burned into it as an image of Jesus, and considered the appearance of the image as a miracle. A frenzy of devotion and publicity ensued. To the non-believer, the pattern on the tortilla is arbitrary and without meaning. But to the believer, the fact that Jesus caused his image to manifest on the tortilla is a miracle and is a persuasive reason to believe even more strongly in the divinity of Jesus. The believer's belief leads them to an interpretation of an image that strengthens that framework of belief. The process is self-reflexive and cyclical. The image poses a question and provides itself as the answer.

In my view, the three types of image discussed here—each "not touched by human hands" and carrying a special capacity to represent truths—can be considered as an emblem of the period they emerged from, or more accurately, of the belief systems that define each historical period. The icon, emblematic of pre-modernity, creates and supports belief in religion as truth. The indexical photograph, emblematic of modernity and the Enlightenment, creates and supports belief in science as absolute truth. The AI image, emblematic of post-humanism, creates and supports belief in AI sentience, that is, belief in a technology capable of knowledge that equals or surpasses human knowledge.

To accept the icon's holiness is to affirm one's belief in the divine. To accept the analogue photograph's indexicality is to affirm one's belief in the absolute truth of science. To accept AI images as credibly interpretable is to affirm one's belief in the sentience of AI, that is, to consider the meanings perceived within AI images as the emanations of a sentience capable of knowledge (Fig. 5.1).

Misattributed AI sentience may be considered as a special marker of the transition to a post-humanist epistemological framework. Post-humanism proposes the decentering of the human within the world. Within a misattributed notion of AI sentience, the presumed evidence of sentient behaviour serves to confirm that human intelligence is only one type of intelligence among others. The moment that the notion of AI sentience becomes credible is a moment of discontinuity, a shift in how humans conceive of themselves and their place and role within the universe.

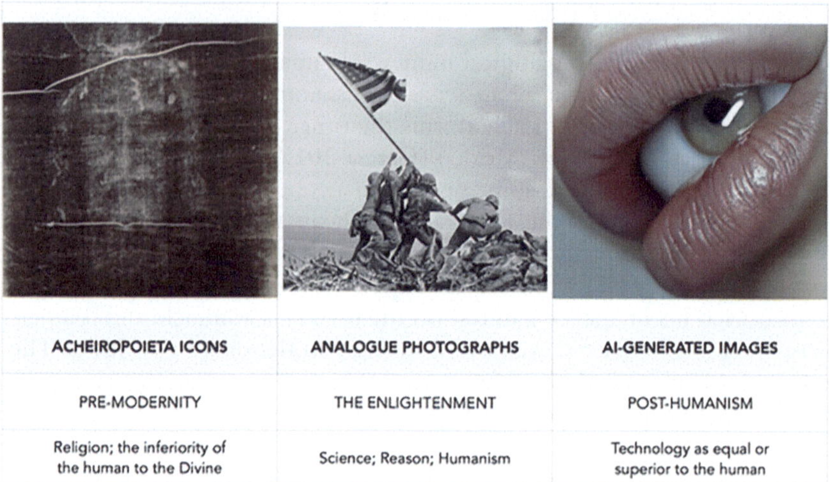

Fig. 5.1 From icons to photographs to AI. Left: Digital print Musée de l'Élysée, Lausanne Secundo Pia (1855–1941), The Shroud of Turin, May 1898. Digital print. Public domain. Source: https://commons.wikimedia.org/wiki/File:Secundo_Pia_Turinske_platno_1898.jpg. Centre: English: Raising the Flag on Iwo Jima, photo by Joe Rosenthal, 23 February 1945. Public domain. Source: https://commons.wikimedia.org/wiki/File:Raising_the_Flag_on_Iwo_Jima,_larger_-_edit1.jpg. Right: AI-generated image created by author using DALL-E 2

The Cultural Impact of Misattributed AI Sentience

In the summer of 2022, a news story appearing in major media outlets brought forward the notion of AI sentience into popular discourse. Google software engineer Blake Lemoine went public with the claim that a Google chatbot had become sentient and possessed an emotional capacity equivalent to that of a human child. Lemoine was fired by Google (Grant 2022). As a media event, the story stands as an example of the ongoing proliferation of the misattributed notion of AI sentience within popular culture. It should be noted that AI companies obtain practical benefits from the misattributed notion of AI sentience: perceived sentience is the ultimate "killer app." Is it likely that any corporation would choose to actively discourage a popular belief that their products possess an incomprehensible power and efficacy?

A research study (Mie et al. 2024) concluded that large language models such as ChatGPT pass the Turing Test, meaning that in a blind test the average user cannot reliably distinguish between a human and AI output. Any user of an AI tool may consciously know there is no sentience within the AI process, but if the tool produces output indistinguishable from human creations, it is easily understandable how errors could creep into an uncritical user's thinking.

Jonathan Birch identifies another factor, one built into the design of the interface of AI tools, the "persisting interlocutor illusion":

> At present, many users seem to misunderstand the true nature of their interactions with chatbots in significant ways. Chatbots generate a powerful illusion of a companion, assistant, or partner being present throughout a conversation. I call this the *persisting interlocutor illusion.* 'Interlocutor' is just a term for the being with whom you feel you're interacting: an assistant, a companion, a romantic partner, and so on. It is an illusion, because every step in your conversation is a separate processing event. (Birch 2025, 4)

For the designers of AI tools, encouraging the persisting interlocutor illusion is merely good design. As with social media applications, the goal is "stickiness": to retain users, to build a sense of loyalty to the product, to drive users to use the product more frequently and for greater durations. The "persisting interlocutor" is intended to appear as the user's assistant, companion, or partner, and the effectiveness of the illusion is borne out by the increasing popularity of these products.

An additional factor in the proliferation of the misattributed notion of AI sentience is its potential politicization: its usefulness as a means of consolidating and extending power. Technology oligarchs and the nation-state have formed new alliances. National governments and technology corporations may decide that promoting the notion of AI sentience is a useful tool to further their own mutual interests. Images and texts created by an incomprehensible sentience accrue a profundity and a corresponding profound influence. Decisions dispensed by an algorithm would bypass traditional human political systems, potentially rendering them obsolete. If the mechanisms of military decision-making are off-loaded onto AI (much as has been done within the economic sphere), the moral weight of killing is lifted from humans, placing war beyond any questions of ethics—removed to the realm of "that which must be simply accepted," akin to how we think of, for example, natural disasters (Fig. 5.2).

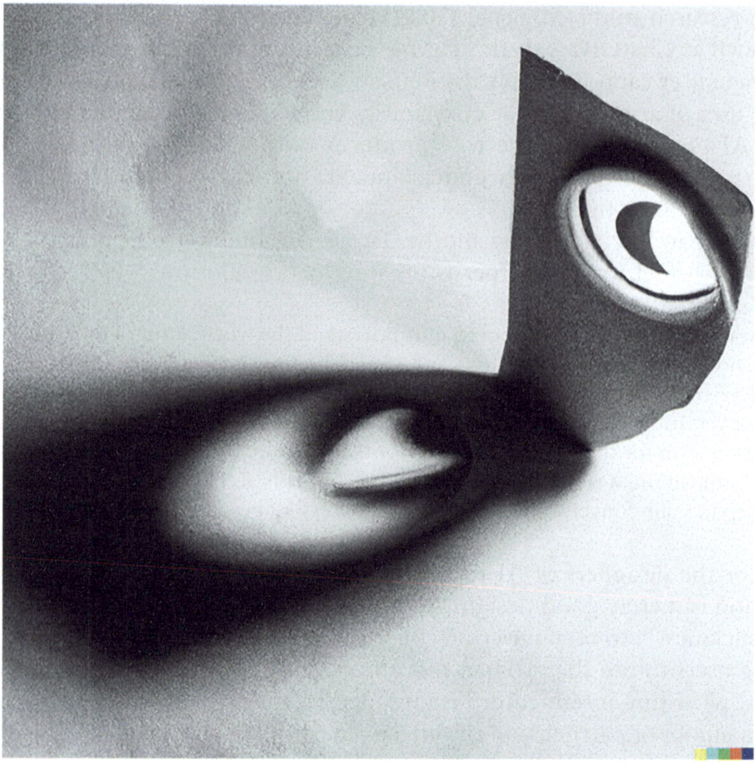

Fig. 5.2 Image generated by DALL-E 2 in response to the author's prompt "a Kafkaesque situation"

AI Sentience and Uncertainty

How might a belief in AI sentience change the interpretation of images? A personal anecdote stands an a kind of qualitative case study with a sample size of one. In April 2022, I began experimenting with the newlyreleased DALL-E 2, the first popular AI image generator. Shown here is one of the first images I generated. The prompt was simply "a Kafkaesque situation." I cannot deny: this image fascinates me, and I have returned to it many times. If one of my art students had created it, I would praise them for their ability to transform abstract concepts into concrete form. Kafka's work has special significance to me, and this image has come to play a part in my thoughts on Kafka: certain vague concepts have attached themselves to the image and have now crystallized around it. I do not feel entirely comfortable admitting this. I know, as you do, that AI images are entirely smoke and mirrors, ephemeral and inconsequential. There is something a bit disturbing about finding meaning in a place where none should exist.

To even consider the possibility of AI sentience is to induce uncertainty in how we think of human knowledge. The end user of an AI system receives an output, but has no way of analysing or testing the process of the production of that output. If the viewer finds significance within an AI image, the possibility is opened that those meanings emanate from an intelligence superior to human intelligence. However, because the workings of AI are incomprehensible, there can be no proof either way. To even allow for the possibility of the notion of AI sentience causes a crisis of truth and a crisis of how we valuate our intelligence.

Baudrillard's concept of the hyperreal describes the condition of extreme uncertainty about "real" and "fake": an uncertainty that reaches an intolerable point where both categories must be negated or rendered obsolete (Baudrillard 1994, 1). We are perhaps in a similar relation to the notion of AI sentience. When confronted by seemingly meaningful AI images, a viewer has no basis with which to judge whose knowledge is superior: their own, or the AI's. The only sensible option is to negate both categories. However, this negation creates a crisis: it becomes difficult or impossible to valuate any knowledge, regardless of its form.

Images reflect and transmit ideologies and philosophical frameworks. The icon reflects and transmits a religious model of the universe built on eternal divine truths. The analogue photograph reflects and transmits the universe of science, which is predictable and consistently verifiable. The AI image, when viewed uncritically, reflects and transmits the notion of AI sentience: a world in which human intelligence is merely one type of intelligence, among others, which leaves us uncertain of its value.

In light of that uncertainty, how might people use and interpret AI images? If AI sentience can be neither proven nor disproven, the viewer's relation to the meanings of images can be nothing other than a question of belief. Uncertainty induces a need to find meaning (or to create meaning), even if the meaning-making process is based only on faith or desire, instead of logic and reason. I suggest that, for the viewer favourably inclined towards notions of sentience, AI images are likely to become the locus of magical thinking, and will speculate on what forms this might take.

AI and Magical Thinking

Erik Davis, in *Techgnosis*, describes how technological advances of the nineteenth and twentieth centuries were repurposed for "off-label use" as tools for practices based on magical thinking. For example, not long after the radio became popular, some took up the practice of tuning the radio in between radio station frequency bands and listening to this dead space in hopes of hearing the voices of divine beings or departed ancestors (Davis 1999, 83). Similarly, not long after the invention of photography, amateur paranormal investigators used the camera to attempt to capture visible traces of the manifestation of invisible beings, supernatural phenomena, or lost loved ones (Davis 1999, 90).

How might AI images be used as tools in practices based on magical thinking? As an anecdotal case study, I present one possibility, based on personal experience. After DALL-E produced the "Kafkaesque situation" image for me, I began using the same prompt over and over, with various AI image generators, for a period of months. I never again obtained a result I enjoyed as much as the original "Kafkaesque situation" image. But something else happened. I began to feel that although the images being generated were not telling me anything new or meaningful about Kafka, they were saying something about the day and time I entered the prompt. Why were today's images so different from yesterday's, even though the prompt was exactly the same? I became tempted to view the images as forecasts, which abstractly described the ineffable qualities of the day in a visual form. Our ancestors found meaningful images of future events within the entrails of animals; surely it would be no more ridiculous to find meaning within the output of sophisticated software trained on the near-entirety of human cultural production.

This suggests one possible use of AI images in practices based on magical thinking. The AI image generator comes to be considered as an oracle. The practice resembles the ancient process of divination: the interpretation of unpredictable phenomena as representations of as-yet-unmanifested truths. Because the believer in AI sentience erroneously conceives of the intelligence behind the image as potentially superior to their own, the image is worthy of being interpreted. And what meanings could be more beneficial than information directly pertaining to the viewer's own future? What is learned from this process is valuable—exactly how valuable depends on how intelligent the believer imagines the AI to be.

The practice of divination is an ancient one. It developed as a response to the uncertainties of a bewildering universe and an unknowable future. But like the ancients, we, too, live in uncertain times. And perhaps, however absurd and indefensible magical thinking may be, it would seem unfair to begrudge anyone their attempts to find meaning while wrestling with the universal human experience of doubt, fear, or loss. Strauss notes, "Belief in images has become the test case for the social. If we are to believe in the world, we must have images of it" (Strauss 2020, 67). We have a clear understanding of how icons and photographs defined and supported the social and political structures of the era they emerged from. AI images are, at the moment, considerably more mysterious. How will they be interpreted and used? What beliefs might they support? I view AI images as entirely discontinuous with the past. If in the future our most meaningful images of the world are AI generated, it is difficult to imagine what kind of social and political structures that world would be built on. It will likely be a world radically and incomprehensibly different from our own. And that is an occasion for both hope and fear.

References

Baudrillard, Jean. 1994. *Simulacra and Simulation.* Ann Arbor: University of Wisconsin Press.

Belting, Hans. 1994. *Likeness and Presence: A History of the Image before the Era of Art.* Chicago: Chicago University Press.

Birch, Jonathan. 2025. *AI Consciousness: A Centrist Manifesto.* PsyArXiv. https://doi.org/10.31234/osf.io/af7c9_v1.

Colombatto, Clara, and Fleming, Stephen M. 2024. *Folk Psychological Attributions of Consciousness to Large Language Models.* Neuroscience of Consciousness. https://doi.org/10.1093/nc/niae013.

Davis, Eric. 1999. *Techgnosis: Myth, Magic + Mysticism in the Age of Information.* New York: Crown Publishers.

Garcia, Uriel J. 2017. 'Tortilla Miracle' Brought Hope and Mockery to N.M. Family. *Santa Fe New Mexican.* https://www.santafenewmexican.com/life/features/tortilla-miracle-brought-hope-and-mockery-to-n-m-family.

Grant, Nico. 2022. Google Fires Engineer Who Claims Its A.I. is Conscious. *New York Times.* https://www.nytimes.com/2022/07/23/technology/google-engineer-artificial-intelligence.html.

Mie, Q., Y. Xie, W. Yuan, and M. Jackson. 2024. *A Turing Test of Whether AI Chatbots are Behaviorally Similar to Humans.* National Academy of Science. https://pubmed.ncbi.nlm.nih.gov/38386710/.

Sante, Luc. 1992. *Evidence*. New York: Macmillan Publishing.
Shakespeare, William. 2015. *Macbeth*. London: Bloomsbury Publishing. First published 1623.
Stevenson, Robert Louis. 1891. *In The South Seas*. Charles Scribner's Sons.
Strauss, David Levi. 2020. *Photography and Belief*. New York: David Zwirner Books.

CHAPTER 6

AI Interventions With a Studio-Sourced Dataset

Jennifer L. Karson

Attending a machine learning workshop in the fall of 2019, I sat among mostly scientists and engineers in a University of Vermont (UVM) conference center. A decade had passed since I graduated from the San Francisco Art Institute (SFAI), and into The Great Recession. A necessarily unconventional career path led me to my current position as the director of the UVM College of Engineering and Mathematical Sciences digital fabrication lab and teaching studio art classes in UVM's College of Arts and Sciences. Comfortable in STEM spaces and accustomed to parsing dense technical information, as workshop presenters demonstrated how machine learning algorithms could recognise patterns and automate rules, I recognised the potential to expand a series of glyphs I had started in my studio (Fig. 6.1).

J. L. Karson (✉)
University of Vermont, Burlington, VT, USA
e-mail: jennifer.karson@uvm.edu

L. Cempellin, M. Geiger (eds.), *Reimagining Art History with Artificial Intelligence*,
https://doi.org/10.1007/978-3-032-21685-4_6

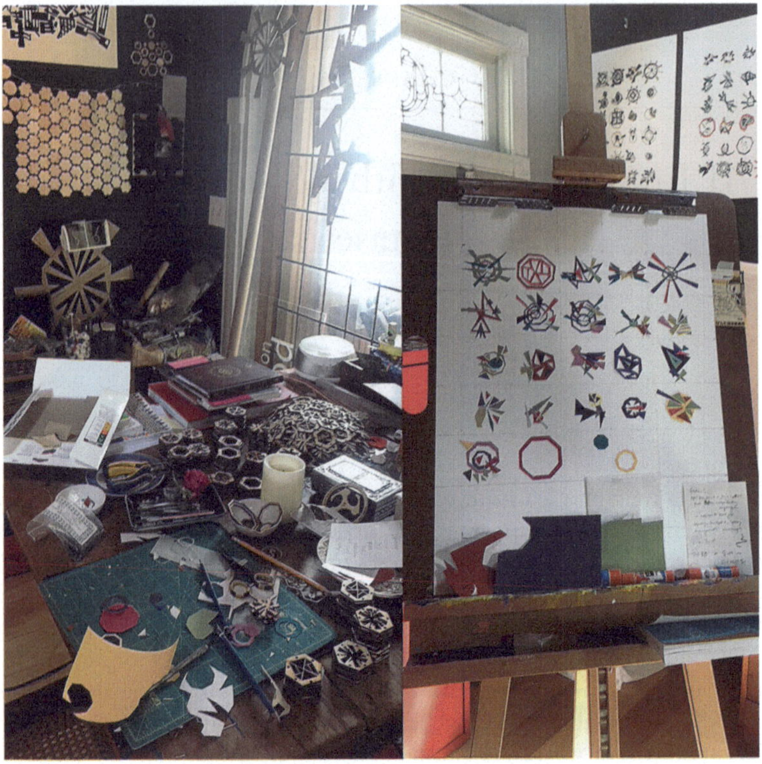

Fig. 6.1 Jennifer L. Karson Studio, 2019 (figure by Jennifer L. Karson. Digital photograph, 2019). The author's studio in Colchester, Vermont, while she was creating the original mixed media glyphs of the Dancing Star Dataset, Series 2

From the Easel to a Genetic Algorithm

The glyph project emerged from colliding interests, life experiences, and arts-based research. At the time I was reading Nietzsche's *Thus Spoke Zarathustra,* exploring rules-based practices of Cage[1] and LeWitt,[2] and

[1] Cage described chance operations as an approach that was in "a spirit of acceptance, rather than a spirit of control." Cage considered chance operations a discipline, not an abandonment of artist decision-making (Kostelanetz 2003).

[2] Sol LeWitt famously wrote, "The idea becomes a machine that makes the art" (LeWitt 1967). Yet I learned from a museum director who acquired a LeWitt piece that, in addition

had file folders brimming with research from a recent sound installation that explored the obsolescence of New England bell towers.

Referencing the architecture of bell towers, the glyph compositions consisted of essential tower elements—one octagon (representing an octagonal bell tower base) and eight triangles (representing the eight triangular slabs that converge at the tower's peak) (Fig. 6.2). Inspired by Cage and LeWitt, I created rules for how the glyphs were constructed, and all the while Zarathustra's phrase "one must still have chaos in oneself, to give birth to a dancing star" ran on repeat in my mind, it became a mantra.

By arranging and rearranging these shapes, which I expanded to include irregular triangles and octagons (and occasionally numerous octagons), I produced hundreds of unique configurations that symbolically unsettled the tower's inherent hierarchy. The process of making each glyph required cutting tiny shapes out of origami paper and gluing them by hand onto a larger piece of paper sectioned into a grid of 3″ × 3″ squares.

I had a dense schedule managing responsibilities across two colleges, and my life was highly structured; too often I felt caged within a schedule. Yet, with each glyph I completed, I experienced a cathartic excitement that felt like a glorious escape. I was relieved to know I still had a well of chaotic humanity brewing inside me that could muster a Nietzchean dancing star.[3] And with that, in 2018 the first series of the Dancing Star Dataset was born in my studio (Fig. 6.3).

By February, I secured smaller funding for two graduate students to help me explore how machine learning could expand the Dancing Star Dataset.[4] I had a lot of questions. Could the technology serve as a studio assistant? Could I maintain artistic authorship while working with it? How might a human–machine collaboration support expressions of humanity and artistic agency? In the studio, the emergence of the Dancing Star Dataset dismantled rigid structures. Could work with machine learning continue this trajectory?

to the instructions and materials outlined in LeWitt's guidelines for wall pieces, the estate plays a crucial role in overseeing the creation of the work.

[3] "I tell you: one must still have chaos in oneself, to give birth to a dancing star. I tell you: ye still have chaos in you. Alas! There cometh the time when man will no longer give birth to any star" (Nietzsche 2011).

[4] I would continue to fund the project on numerous small buckets of money through the university and by developing outreach programmes on federal grants.

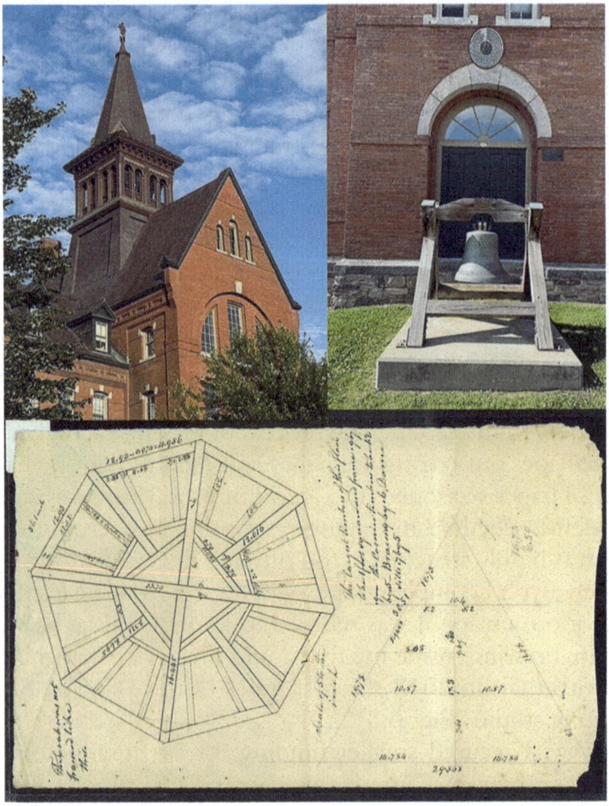

Fig. 6.2 (1) Studies of bell tower architecture in Vermont (top figures by Jennifer L. Karson. "Old Mill Tower and Bell." Digital photographs 2018-2025; bottom figure by John Johnson "Plan for Old Mill building, University of Vermont, Burlington, 1820s. Elevation of the dome rafters c. 1829," Architectural drawing (21 × 34 cm.), John Johnson Collection, University of Vermont Libraries. Digitised June 3, 2014).

A popular UVM course, *Evolutionary Robotics*, taught by computer scientist Josh Bongard (2025) introduced genetic algorithms and neural networks to the two graduate students who made up my first research team. We set out to experiment with both and sought out models that had reasonable documentation and online user communities. Genetic algorithms use a competitive evolutionary approach; in contrast, a generative

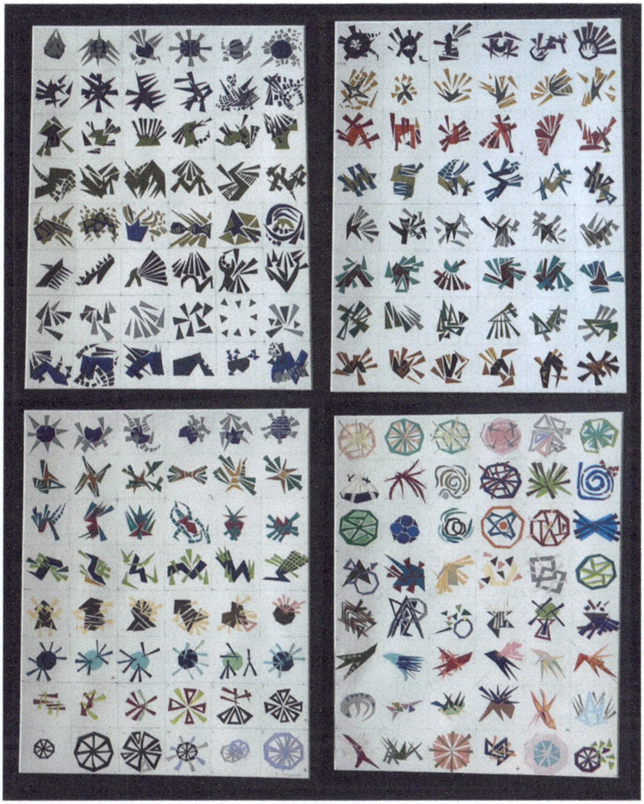

Fig. 6.3 Dancing Star Dataset Mixed-Media Originals, Series 1 (figure by Jennifer L. Karson. Dancing Star Dataset Mixed-Media Originals, Series 1. Mixed Media (set of 4, each 18″ × 24″, 2018)

adversarial network (GAN) uses an adversarial approach where two neural networks are in direct competition with opposing goals (2025; Schiffman 2024). I wanted to work with models we could understand, control, and customise. Quickly, we discovered that even computer scientists struggle to understand how neural networks make decisions, that scientific papers would not answer our humanities- and arts-based questions, and that the best way to know how machine learning worked was to work with it hands-on.

We relied heavily on Dan Shiffman's (n.d.) work and teachings that support creative applications of evolutionary theory in code. A genetic algorithm falls into the category of evolutionary computation, a subset of artificial intelligence and machine learning inspired by Darwinian evolutionary theory's core principles (UT Austin Computer Science n.d.). In these algorithms, potential solutions to a problem evolve over generations through processes that mimic natural selection, heredity, and mutations in biological evolution. Computer simulations of evolutionary processes date back to the 1950s (Shiffman n.d.). We built our first genetic algorithm, *Emergence*, from Shiffman's open-source code, referencing videos he posted four years earlier in July of 2016; the program was light enough to run on our laptops. The algorithm was coded in Processing, a flexible software sketchbook and a language developed by Casey Reas and Ben Fry, a project that supported software literacy within the visual arts. (Fry and Reas 2019; Processing.org n.d.).

An undergraduate who joined our team later in the spring of 2020 digitised the Dancing Star Dataset mixed-media originals (Fig. 6.4). For each Dancing Star glyph he digitally traced the individual irregular triangles and octagons they were comprised of, building large libraries of digital triangle and octagon files. We then programmed *Emergence* to select one digital octagon and eight digital triangles from these digitised shape libraries. The algorithm assembled the triangle and octagon components into new compositions.

Emergence featured interactive selection, it generated nine digital compositions simultaneously within a grid. We then could select the most successful of the generated compositions, these choices then informed which traits would appear in the next generation of glyphs produced by *Emergence*. To accentuate transitions in the app we programmed satisfying "ding" and "click" sounds into the genetic algorithms interactive interface. It was easy and fun to engage with the model, yet this had a downside—the ease-of-use could inspire mindless clicking by the student-user, when ideally I wanted them to thoughtfully compose new glyphs.

Emergence produced compositions much more quickly than composing them by hand in my studio, yet challenges emerged when I attempted to fine-tune the results. From my perspective, the most successful compositions made by *Emergence* were those that most closely resembled the aesthetic qualities of the original mixed-media series (Fig. 6.3). However, my attempt to communicate my vision for the glyphs through programming and verbal communication with student was not all that successful.

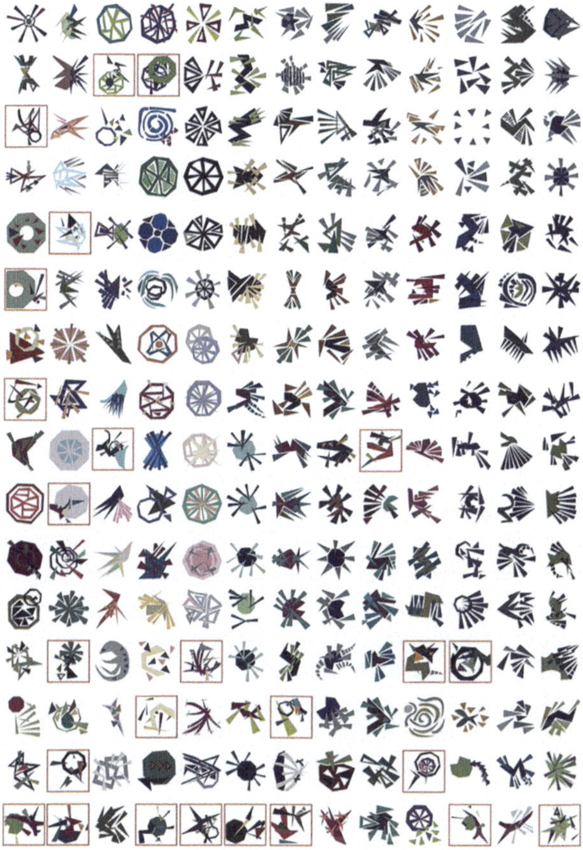

Fig. 6.4 A selection from the Digitised and Expanded Dancing Star Dataset (figure by Jennifer L. Karson). Dancing Star Dataset Sample. Archival digital print on paper 42″ × 79″ 2022. Courtesy of Jennifer L. Karson and Bre Pettis, detail). This work shows two Dancing Star Dataset subsets used to later train StyleGAN models. Most of the examples in this work are digitised versions of the original mixed-media glyphs. Glyphs within orange boxes were made with *Emergence*

When one student on the team rapidly generated over 12,600 glyphs, I spent days going through them all, only keping about 500.

Tiny Datasets

My initial assumption that more data—the most extensive library of triangles and octagons we could extract from the original glyphs would yield better results—was wrong. While the original glyphs of the Dancing Star Dataset maintained consistent shapes and colours across subsets of five glyphs, we initially gave the *Emergence* access to all component triangles and octagons in our library. This approach resulted in cluttered compositions that merely combined shapes without aesthetic coherence (a selection of such curated glyphs are highlighted in orange boxes within Fig. 6.4). In this case, the prevailing big data mindset hindered rather than helped the project. Results improved dramatically when in the summer of 2022 I restricted the genetic algorithm library to predetermined datasets of triangles and octagons (Figs. 6.5, 6.6, and 6.7). This discovery sparked a tiny data mindset and raised questions about the lack of specificity when working with larger datasets. This inspired the genetic algorithm *Tiny D*, which I ran without student assistance It had a library of only eight to ten shapes to pull from—it produced glyphs that were more aesthetically aligned with the Dancing Star originals. This pivot towards small scale, closely curated datasets and an intentional slowing of automated processes (now I was the only one running the model) was in stark contrast to big data trends that are essential for large language models (LLMs),

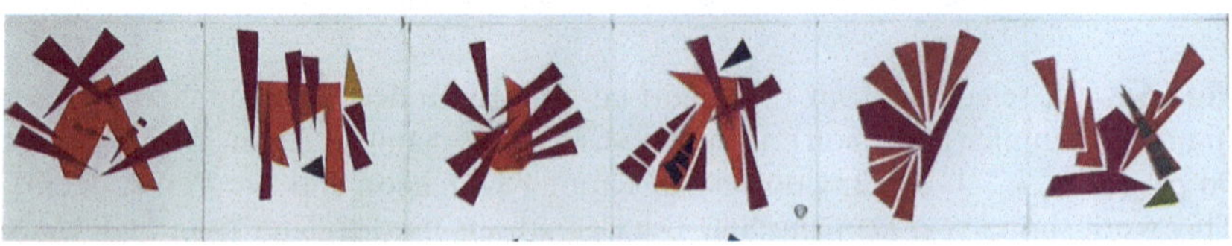

Fig. 6.5 A subset of original multimedia Dancing Stars. (figure by Jennifer L. Karson, Dancing Star Dataset Mixed-Media Originals, Series 1 (detail). Mixed Media 2018)When a student researcher digitized the original multimedia glyphs, SVG files were made of every shape within each composition, meaning that the irregular triangles and octagons existed as separate files. Small selections of 8-10 shapes became the tiny datasets that created the more desirable glyphs generated by the genetic algorithm *Tiny D*

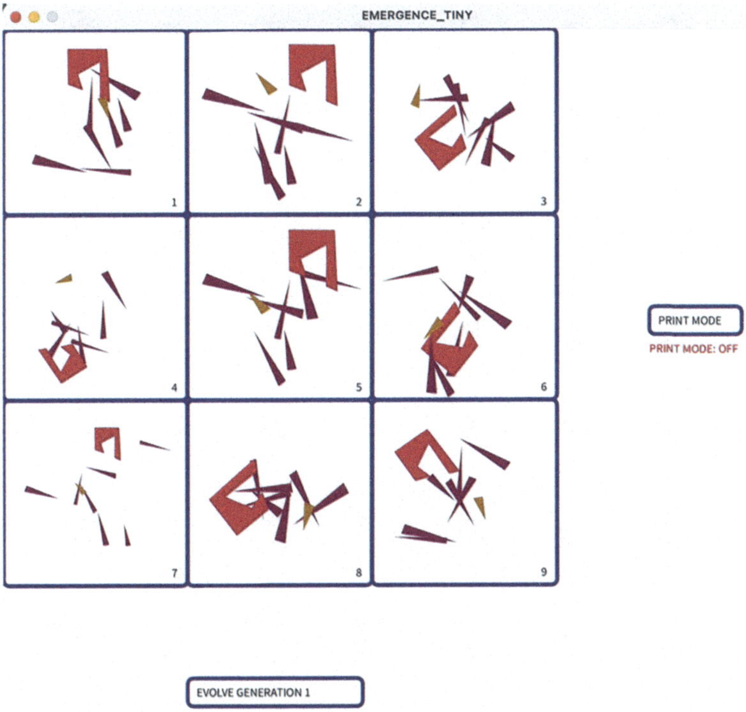

Fig. 6.6 Genetic Algorithm Graphical User Interface of the genetic algorithm *Tiny D* (figure by Jennifer L. Karson. *Tiny D* genetic algorithm screenshot). This genetic algorithm was coded in Processing by Daniel Shiffman, and customised by Ethan Davis, Sarah J Pell, Syd Culbert, and Jennifer L. Karson

self-driving cars, and public health research, efforts that acquire big data and use intensive manual labelling and robust computational tools to process it (Mitchell 2019; O'Neil 2017).

In the fall of 2021, I invited a computer science PhD student to join a team meeting. He was from computer scientist Nick Cheney's Neurobiotics Lab and was interested in doing creative programming outside of his PhD research. In the meeting I was startled by is emphatic insistance that we transition our genetic algorithms from Processing to p5.js, an open-source JavaScript library. He pointed out that this shift would allow our team, now made up of four undergraduates, to move our model into a web browser, making it more accessible. This was an attractive idea. He also

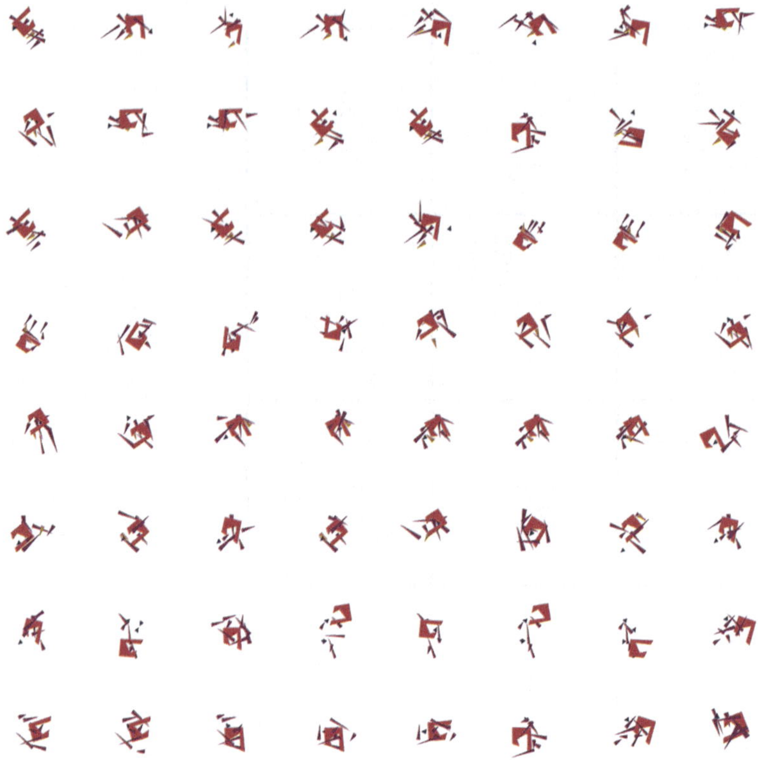

Fig. 6.7 Synthetic Data made with the genetic algorithm *Tiny D* (figure by Jennifer L. Karson. 1232 Tiny Dataset Grid. Archival Digital print on paper 17″ × 19″ 2022, detail). A curated set of glyphs created with *Tiny D*

encouraged automating the generation of component triangles and octagons rather than using the fixed digital files that made up the library of *Emergence*. I was hesitant to abandon our digital shape files based on my original hand-cut images—the shape files had a materiality and character that I anticipated the algorithmically generated ones would lack. However, resisting the allure of more advanced automation and sophisticated programming proved difficult, especially with a team of eager undergraduates looking on. So, I agreed, and an undergraduate took on the project under the mentorship of the doctoral student. The result was *Confetti* (Fig. 6.8), a smooth-running model that runs in the browser. Because the model is

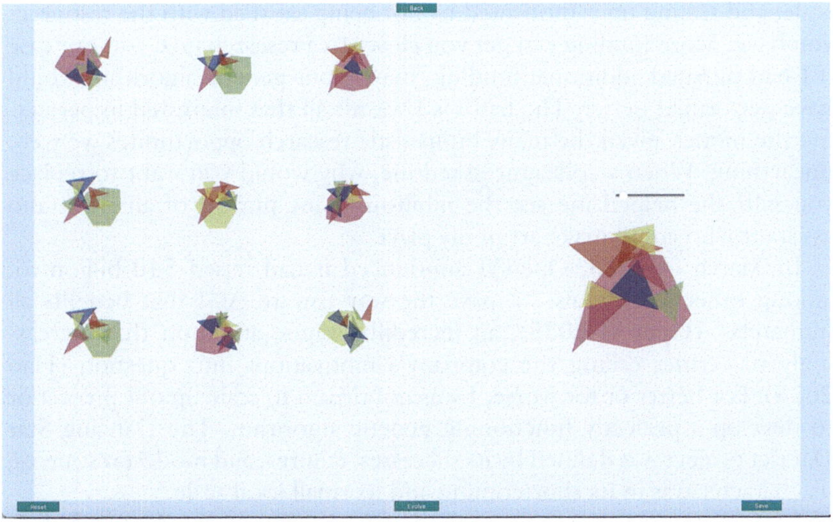

Fig. 6.8 The genetic algorithm *Confetti* (figure by Jennifer L. Karson), a screenshot of *Confetti*, a genetic algorithm coded in p5.js by Oliver Hamburger and Lapo Frati. This model generated triangles and octagons. Available at https://jennkarson.studio/ga/

easy to share, we continue to use it for educational programmes. It remains an important artefact, as it continues to run successfully years after its creation. However, while the model does follow the rules of assembling triangles and octagons into dancing stars, the glyphs it produces are a clear departure from those of the original Dancing Star glyphs (jennkarson.studio 2025).

The formal aesthetic choices I made while composing the original glyphs in my studio resisted translation into words, let alone code. When I expressed the frustration that our genetic algorithms needed more rules before they would make a glyph true to the original hand-assembled works, a computer science colleague replied, "Jenn, you just need more funding." The question of how resources (like funding) and concentrations of power impact tech outcomes has become more interesting to me over time. Throughout our creative research at UVM with AI, we have been relatively resource rich with funding for student researchers and access to the University's high- performance computing (HPC) centre. Yet there is also a relationship between project output and the drive to scale, and scaling up is motivated by not being satisfied with the resources you have. More funding can get you closer to a research goal—in our case if I had pursued additional funding, maybe our genetic algorithm would have performed better. The truth is I wasn't all that interested in perfecting the model, given the many humanistic research opportunites we were unearthing. When a colleague asked me, why would you want to replace yourself? she helped me see the nihilism in my pursuit of an AI studio assistant who could make art in my place.

In March of 2025, OpenAI announced it had raised $40 billion to, among other lofty goals, "...pave the way toward AGI that benefits all humanity" (OpenAI 2025), an incredilby vague ambition that increasingly has critics calling the company's motivations into question (Hao 2025). For better or for worse, I was not driven to scale up our project or to develop a perfectly functioning genetic algorithm. The Dancing Star Dataset project was defined by its successes, failures, and modest resources; its character was in its shortcoming and its small local scale.

I valued that our team customised and wrote the code (Figs. 6.6, 6.7, and 6.8) for our genetic algorithms. We understood how they worked and tailored the algorithms to our specific project needs. Running them from our laptops created an intimate connection with them, and they embodied what Neil Gershenfeld of MIT's Bits and Atoms calls "a locally made meaningful machine."[5] My affection for the machines we made, coexists with my disappointment in the images they generated—that are at best mediocre replicas of the original glyphs lacking temporal-spatial presence and luminosity (Benjamin [1935] 1969).[6] The artist and Processing co-founder Casey Reas has expressed a similar sentiment when he says "The thing that makes the thing is more interesting than the thing" (Reas 2015, 54:29).

[5] Gershenfeld shared the idea of "locally made meaningful machines" at a Vermont FabLab gathering at HatchSpace in Brattleboro, Vermont, in March 2022.

[6] In my discussion, I use "luminosity" where Benjamin's "aura" might otherwise appear. While Benjamin employed aura to describe an artwork's unique presence in time and space that is diminished through reproduction, I find luminosity better captures the essence of what is lost: the vital connection to context and origin. Luminosity avoids the problematic critiques of photography embedded in Benjamin's original terminology and its subsequent new-age connotations, while acknowledging the absence of temporal and spatial presence.

Feeding Synthetic Data to a Generative Adversarial Network

We needed a larger set of Dancing Star glyphs to train a second machine learning system: a generative adversarial network (GAN). GANs were popular with artists who could get access to high performance computing, and the artists who were using them often relied on training image datasets scraped from the Internet. Our genetic algorithms allowed us to expand the Dancing Star Dataset so that it was large enough to train a GAN. This meant our training dataset consisted of digital scans of original mixed-media Dancing Stars and Dancing Stars generated by our genetic algorithm. Now that we had thousands of images in our training dataset, we could avoid relying on Internet-scraped images or pre-existing datasets for primary training, and we could explore the effects of transfer learning on final outputs when a model was first trained on a dataset other than our own. Having our own large image dataset distinguished our process, discoveries, and results. Additionally, it shaped an opportunity to explore the consequences of synthetic data—non-human-created data that imitates real-world data, the scanned original Dancing Star glyphs being the real-world data, and those generated by the genetic algorithm being the synthetic data. Our synthetic data represented the core non-hierarchical ideals of the original glyphs, but lacked their luminosity and muted their rebellion.

Initially I set out to discover how machine learning could serve as a studio assistant and assist in expanding the Dancing Star series. Indeed, the use of machine learning models sped up the process of image generation, but with comprimises. The model output was plentiful and fast, but bland. The cost of spending so much time learning about the models was less time to focus on my artistic intentions.

A 2023 Pew Center Research study speculated that increased integration of useful AI in people's daily lives could diminish individuals' ability to control their choices. It is anticipated that in the context of growing use and acceptance of smart machines and AI-powered systems, boundaries of personal autonomy will require reimagining. We will all be confronted with questions about what decisions we are willing to outsource to digital tools, and what decisions require human agency and oversight. Such an assessment, the authors suggest, will require thoughtful, critical, and informed contemplation on the personal and political levels (Pew Research Center 2023).

When my team transitioned to exploring GANs, specifically StyleGAN concerns about the loss of artistic intention and human agency became even more urgent than they had been with genetic algorithms. A GAN is a machine learning model in which two neural networks compete by using deep learning methods to become more accurate in their predictions. GANs typically run unsupervised (TechTarget n.d.). The generator tries to fool the discriminator, while the discriminator tries to detect the generator's deception. We worked with StyleGAN (2018) and StyleGAN2 (2020). We were not able to work with StyleGAN3 (2021) because of hardware compatability issues.

StyleGAN came with layered interpretability issues; essentially its internal decision-making is black-boxed. My team was awarded privileged access to the University's high-performance computing (HPC) centre in order to use StyleGAN. This was an exciting opportunity while also a complicated process, requiring the setup of environments with numerous software packages, logging in through several layers of security, and navigating a production queue with other research groups. The model was most useful if it had already been trained on a large image dataset, most often the Flickr-Faces-HQ Dataset (NVIDIA 2025), consisting of 70,000 high-quality PNG images of human faces, crawled from Flickr. NVIDIA developed the model in its early days as the dominant supplier of chips needed to train and operate large generative AI models (Carino 2024; Duhigg 2023). A grad student on our team suggested StyleGAN was designed and distributed to help sell NVIDIA's GPUs. This context gave me pause: when using StyleGAN in a high-performance computing environment, we were within and navigating a dense power structure (Fig. 6.11).

But here we were, with privileged access to HPC, funding for a team of student researchers, and driven by a curiosity about machine learning that was growing. Determined to understand the GAN as thoroughly as possible, and stubbornly pursuing an elusive mastery of it, our research team's community began to extend and foster meaningful friendships and working relationships across disciplines and departments on campus. During the pandemic, when entering the HPC facility was not allowed, an engineer at the university's high-performance computing centre, at our request, recorded the sounds of the space. I imagine we were the first, if not the only, research group to make such an embodied and aesthetic request. He sent back a recording with a note explaining that we would not be able to hear the computers, only the fans keeping the computers cool.[7] The sound of screeching fans on the recording put us on high alert to the potential environmental impact of our work in this space far before such concerns garnered mainstream attention.

Donna Haraway's framework of "staying with the trouble" (Haraway 2016) advocates an embrace of messy and contradictory realities like those I was discovering in our work with AI. Of course, I was concerned about the environmental impact of our work. Moreover, could my engagement with AI serve big tech more than my art practice? I was buying into it. Was my participation derailing my artistic intent? Rather than retreat in dispair or sugarcoat its imperfections and impurities, I chose to stay critically engaged with the work and its contradictions because the experience was generating knowledge, community, and a deeper understanding of the current cultural moment.

Reading through technical machine learning papers proved challenging; many of them read like a foreign language filled with unfamilar vocabulary and illegible equations. They provided valuable information about how models worked, but did not answer the aesthetic process and humanistic questions that interested me. When I found my way to scholarship in the emerging field of AI Ethics, the language and stucture of our research took shape. In "Datasheets for Datasets," Timnit Gebru et al. (2018) provided a framework for tracking and documenting the motivation, composition, collection process, and recommended uses for shared datasets. Margaret Mitchell et al. (2018) published "Model Cards for Model Reporting," proposing a method of model documentation in support of responsible democratisation of machine learning and related AI technology, with the intention to increase transparency into how well AI technology works. These papers offered rigorous approaches to evaluating training dataset collections. In the summer of 2020, these discussions were in sync with revitalised conversations about the nuanced history of appropriation and colonisation in art practice and museum collections. Such inquiries of empathy and intellectual questioning in the arts and humanities and among computer science ethicists stand in contrast to the problematic indiscriminate image data scraping across the Internet that has become both a conventional and contested practice for training the widely used text-to-image generators like OpenAI's ChatGPT and Midjourney (Barnes 2025; Lovato et al. 2024).

[7] Listen to the 2020 recording of the Vermont Advanced Computing Center here: https://jennkarson.studio/wp-content/uploads/2025/04/VACC-fans-2020-fade-in.wav.

Obsolescence

In the summer of 2021, six members of our research group trained six different StyleGAN models on the expanded Dancing Star Dataset—now comprising hand-crafted originals and genetic algorithm-generated glyphs. Student researchers utilised pre-training datasets featuring faces, breast tissue, and fractals before fine-tuning with the Dancing Star dDataset, while others trained exclusively on the Dancing Star Dataset without pre-training. Despite sharing the identical dataset and similar intentions to expand the series, each researcher's model produced distinctly different outputs. The installation *Team Picks* (Figs. 6.9 and 6.10) displayed each researcher's 10 favourite generated images on film slides, and projected them through a vintage slide projector carousel. This deliberate materialisation of digital output went beyond the film slides to include the projection of light through a glass lens, the brutalist bulk of the projector body, the whir of the projector fans, and the distinguished mechanised clicks of its automated carousel movement. *Team Picks* confronted how curated results of an experiment expressed a subjective viewpoint, challenging the supposed objectivity of machine learning systems and revealing tensions between desirable artistic authorship and undesirable scientific bias, between human selection and algorithmic generation. When I presented this work with StyleGAN as part of a panel at the 2024 Annual Conference of the College Arts Association, a young assistant professor commented, "You're using an old model," questioning the pedagogical value in teaching anything other than the latest release of the most sophisticated corporate image-generator models.

Yet, initial inquiry with such smaller, older, and bespoke models allowed us to engineer and reverse-engineer their processes. From my perspective, today's ubiquitous text-to-image generators and large language models (LLM) have limited the public's imagination about what AI could be and how it might best serve the public good. The challenges we encountered with small bespoke models set an in-depth foundation for our research while our research documented a phase of the evolution of generative AI. The access we had to HPC in 2020 informs our critical engagement with today's AI advancements across sectors. Moreover, the student researchers on my team and I have had direct experience with generative AI that has provided us with a situated perspective to speak to challenges across sectors such as data quantity, data provenance, data variations and integrity, AI hallucinations, the limitations of synthetic data, the

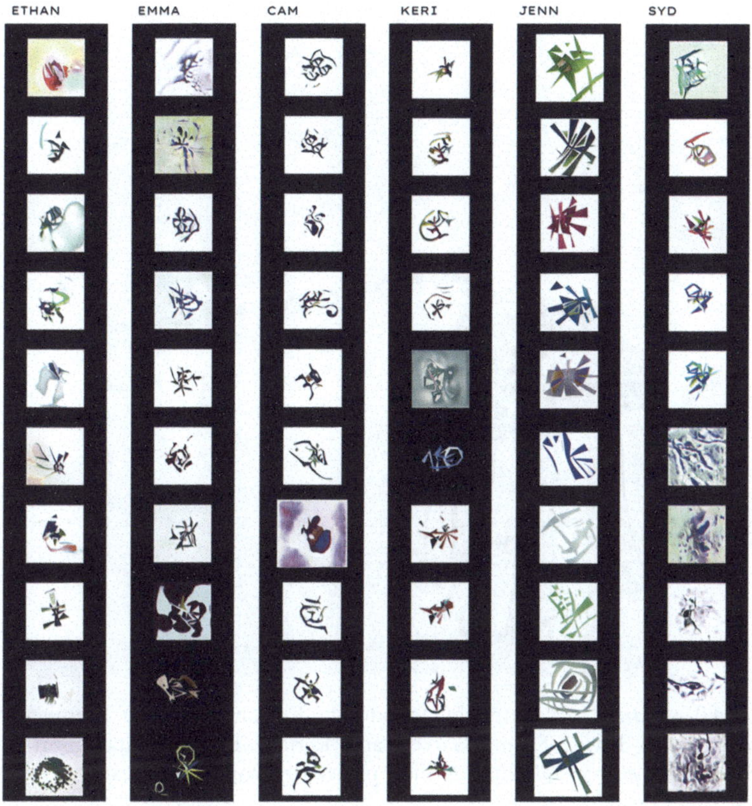

Fig. 6.9 *Team Picks* (figure by Jennifer L. Karson with compositions by Cameron Bremner, Syd Culbert, Ethan Davis, Emma Garvey, Jennifer L. Karson, and Kerime Tukso Digital print 2022) *Team Picks* is an exploration of obsolescence and the potential for biased machine learning outcomes.

environmental impact of high-performance computing, bias in AI systems, cultural biases of technological determinism, and the challenges of balancing human agency with automations.

When it comes to an art practice with technology, in contrast to sprinting at the speed of new tech version releases, meaningful observations come from slowing down and questioning the status quo—it provides time for focused concentration that allows for deciphering patterns, trends, and anomalies. To embrace obsolescence is to commit to a long view.

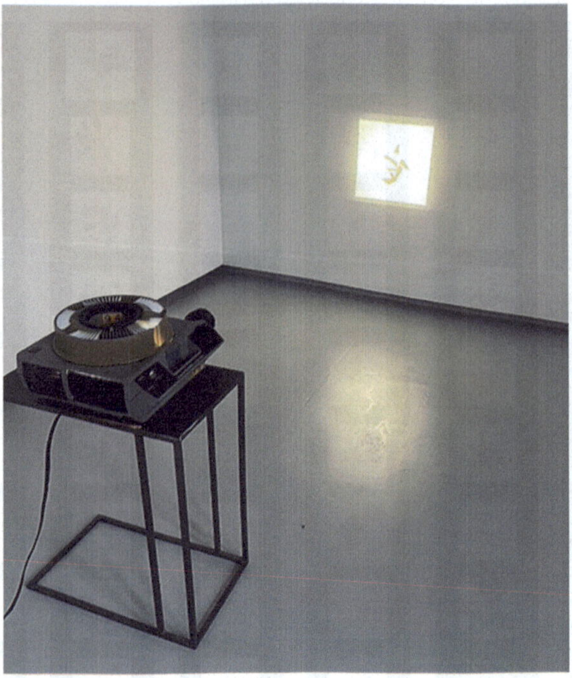

Fig. 6.10 *Team Picks* (figure by Jennifer L. Karson, Cameron Bremner, Syd Culbert, Ethan Davis, Emma Garvey, and Kerime Tukso, digital photograph 2023), *digital photograph 2023* A slide projector projects the teams StyleGAN "fakes" onto a gallery wall

Even if the technology is new, it will become outdated soon enough. Frameworks that embrace obsolescence—the inevitable death of a technology—create opportunities to give it its best life.

Team Picks was first exhibited as part of my solo exhibition *Liquid Architectures and Leaky Territories* at the University of Vermont in 2022 and later included in *Aberrant Activity*, a juried international exhibition presented by Texas A&M University in 2023. The UVM installation was accompanied by contemporary media and technologies, including digital prints, digital video projection, digitally fabricated sculpture, and sound. Assuming students would be most drawn to the work that used the most contemporary technology, I was delighted when a student exclaimed, "Wow, what is that cool thing?" and pointed at the slide projector (Fig. 6.10).

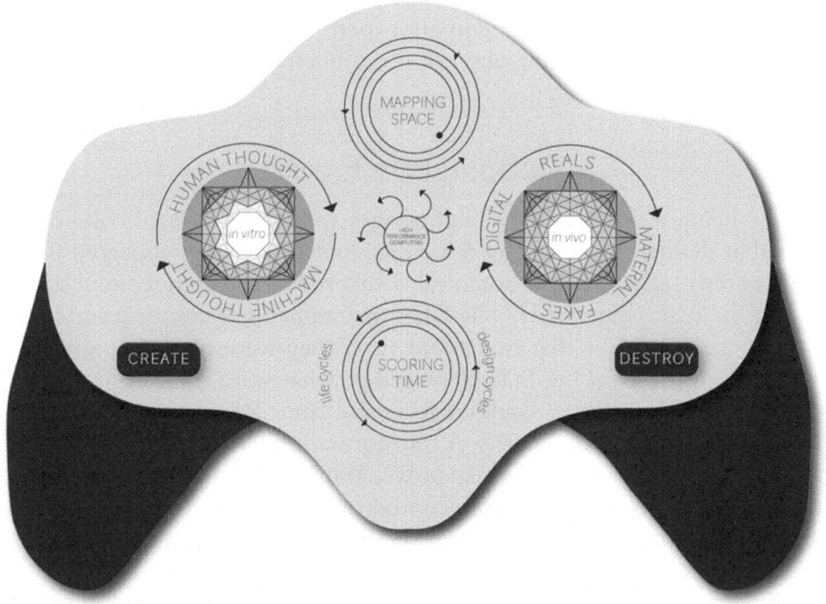

Fig. 6.11 Controller (image by Jennifer L. Karson, Controller, Archival digital print 16″ × 12″ 2022). *Controller* diagrams the constellational research approach Karson developed to explore high-performance computing space

Our work with machine learning pushed the boundaries of what the technology was intended to do, it was an adventure to navigate its capabilities (Fig. 6.11). Because our research started at a time when generative-image technology required users to supply image datasets, the influence training data has on AI model output is undeniable and top-of-mind. I've observed that generally, those who started working with AI after the release of OpenAI's ChatGPT and those who primarily work with commercial models are not as concerned with training data.

In the StyleGAN literature, image data input is classified as "reals" and image output is classified as "fakes." The "reals" label for the Dancing Star Dataset was complicated by the fact that our original dataset was made up of tangible paper objects that had been digitised (i.e. copied), and further complicated by the addition of glyphs made by our genetic algorithm (i.e. synthetic data).[8]

[8] This is a hint of what is to come as AIs are trained on AI-generated information.

Even so, the simple geometric and colour structures of the Dancing Star Dataset would serve us well in our experiments with StyleGAN, allowing us to visually trace and observe the influence and limitations of the model's neural networks.

Something Else Entirely

Despite being trained on the straight edges and clearly defined colour sections that defined the Dancing Star reals, StyleGAN fakes appeared fluid, and painterly—they looked botanical compared to the architectural structure of the reals (Fig. 6.12). The fakes maintained the colour palette and scale of the reals, but that was about it. If they were not a recognisable extension of the Dancing Star glyph series, what were they? Ruins of the originals? New creations? Both creation and ruin? Distractions? I decided they were *something else entirely*. A transformation had occurred but it was not necessarily progressive or expansive. While it is possible that a larger training dataset could have produced better results (i.e. the reals looking more like the fakes), the failings of the model, or our misuse of it, produced results nonetheless.

Generative AI's probabilistic output, while based on inherent uncertainty, is delivered with certitude (Claude, personal communication, June 30, 2025). In contrast to the embodied collisions of human experiences

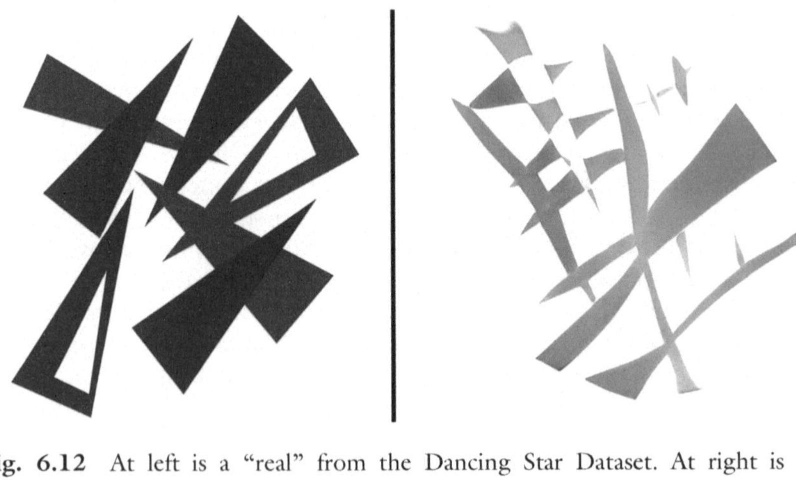

Fig. 6.12 At left is a "real" from the Dancing Star Dataset. At right is a "fake" generated by StyleGAN after being trained on the Dancing Star Dataset.

that inspired the orignal Dancing Star glyphs, the StyleGAN fakes were constructed digitally and pixel-by-pixel, through mechanical mathamatical analysis and algorithmic predictions. Luciana Parisi (2013) provides helpful frameworks for distinguishing between human thought and computational processing—what she names as *soft thought*. Soft thought produces "modes of thought, decision making and mentality that do not exist in direct relation to human thinking" (Parisi 2013, xvii–xviii). Rather, AI and algorithmic soft thought are alien (not human) ways of processing information that inject alien outcomes and products into spheres of human lives and culture. As human-thinkers, we are challenged to recognise—to see—the irrational computations of soft thought that weave effortlessly into the time and space of our lives. As tangible, visible artefacts of what soft thought leaves behind, StyleGAN's Dancing Star fakes provide physical evidence for tracing soft thought's illogical computations. The fakes, now released into the human world, are actants that have sway over the human viewer—we are their audience. In broader AI discussions, the mystical naming of AI failures as hallucinations or machine dreaming (Brown 2023) overlooks the much-needed discussion about how disparate blends of soft thought and human agency are infiltrating culture.

Conclusion

Alan Turing, suggested that "thinking machines" would "help us greatly in finding out how we think ourselves" (Turing [1951] 2004). In my case, he was right. Each limitation I encountered when attempting to translate my artistic vision with the Dancing Stars Dataset and machine learning revealed the nuances and complexity of human creativity. When I initiated the project, I had hoped for a generative collaboration between humans and machines, one that could centre my artistic intent. However, the experiment played out more like a battle between human thought and soft thought, a fight between human agency and a black-boxed technology (Karson 2023).

The major StyleGAN releases were between 2018 and 2021. In 2022, my alma mater, SFAI, an art school that had been at the forefront of new ideas and cultural movements throughout its history, closed after 151 years (Crane 2024; Artforum 2022). Fast-forward to 2025 and there is a parallel. As culture and commerce are preoccupied with the AI race, there is talk of defunding the National Endowment for the Humanities and the National Endowment for the Arts. At the same time that a few powerful companies set out to shape the technological narrative for the future, we may lose institutions that provide humanistic counternarratives. In this moment, I believe that small-scale artistic explorations with AI will prove to be increasingly valuable for tech innovation that aligns with human-centred outcomes.

The Dancing Star Dataset project is in the company of many other artists' works that challenge emergent technological paradigms in real time. The situated and constellated perspective of artists working critically with AI has the potential to be more than a Cassandrian "early warning system" (McLuhan 1964). Artistic inquiry plays a significant role in documenting a technology's history, and can influence its evolution (Data Art Symposium 2025). Arts-based research is not required to produce specific results or provide for investors. In the realm of AI research, arts research has a unique independence, and with that comes the opportunity to develop distinguished and novel insights. There is also a notable lineage of artists who have worked in this space, like that of Harold Cohen and his invention AARON, which he conceived in the 1960s and was revitalised for a Whitney exhibition in 2024 (Whitney Museum of American Art 2024).

I generally avoid the question "What is art?" and prefer Lefebvre's provocation "What is the fantasy of art?" which implies the aspirational element of art-making and sets up extraordinary standards that an artist may or may not achieve. In *The Production of Space* he writes that the fanatasy of art requires leading "out of what is present, out of what is close, out of representations of space, into what is further off into nature, into symbols" (Lefebvre [1974] 1991). Applying this framework to the images my team generated with machine learning models, the formal qualities of the fakes never escaped the representative space of their models—they were respresentations of that space. They also served as symbolic artefacts of our critical artistic inquiry, contextualised by a studio practice. In other words, the fakes we created with machine learning were not what I consider art, while they served as symbolic artefacts of a studio practice. The AI could not birth a dancing star. Yet, in the context of my studio space and practice, the fakes are situated and constellated, holding their own as part of a wider inquiry. Within this inquiry, one framed by questions rooted in the arts and humanities and our efforts to pry open the technology's black-boxed systems, we made meaningful and prescient discoveries through the use of studio-sourced datasets.

The tension we experienced between algorithmic automation and artistic intention in the Dancing Star Dataset experiments created a vital space—essentially a canvas—for examining what may be gained or lost in the shifting negotiations between human creative agency and the turbocharged automations of AI. Ultimately, this phase of our research was less about producing algorithmic art and more about cultivating a studio practice that relentlessy questioned *What happened here? What is happening here? What is becoming here?*. In the context of our experiments, the generative nature of this studio practice created more meaning than the images the genetic algorithms and GANs generated. The practice created dozens of student research opportunities, contributed to public and academic conversations, built community across disciplines and national borders, and originated experiences in galleries and other public sites. Through this relational and constellational (Enwezor 2008) studio engagement, we continue to explore an emergent algorithmic landscape, examine our human experience within it, and share our embodied experience.

* * *

Dancing Star Dataset Researchers Cameron Bremner, Halina Vercessi-Clarke, Syd Culbert, Ethan Davis, Lapo Frati, Emma Garvey, Oliver Hamburger, Anna Hulse, Sarah Pell, Veronika Potter, Fred Sanford, Yifeng Wei, Chauzhen Wu. Special thanks to Kerime Tukso and the Vermont Advanced Computing Center.

Disclosure During the preparation of this work, the author experimented with Claude.ai, curious about how it might improve the readability and language of the work. After using this service, the author reviewed and edited the content as needed and takes full responsibility for the content of the publication.

References

Amazon Web Services. n.d.. What is Synthetic Data? https://aws.amazon.com/what-is/synthetic-data/. Accessed 28 February 2025.

Artforum. 2022. San Francisco Art Institute to Close After 151 Years. https://www.artforum.com/news/san-francisco-art-institute-to-close-after-151-years-251947/. Accessed 18 June 2025.

Barnes, Brooks. 2025. Disney and Universal Sue A.I. Firm for Copyright Infringement. *New York Times*, June 11.
Benjamin, Walter. 1969. The Work of Art in the Age of Mechanical Reproduction. In *Illuminations*. Edited by Hannah Arendt, Translated by Harry Zohn. Schocken Books. First published 1935.
Bongard, Josh. 2025. 2025 Evolutionary Robotics Course. Lecture 6. Evolutionary Algorithms. YouTube video. https://www.youtube.com/watch?v=qMhT5aZIXAg. Accessed 20 April 2025.
Brown, Jeffrey. 2023. Artificial Intelligence Raises Questions about Future of Art. *PBS NewsHour*. Video, 3:20. https://www.pbs.org/video/ai-art-1677793713/.
Carino, Meghan McCarty. 2024. Nvidia Dominates in AI, but Others are Trying to Chip Away. *Marketplace*. https://www.marketplace.org/2024/05/22/nvidias-at-the-top-of-the-ai-heap-but-others-are-trying-to-chip-away/.
Claude (AI assistant). 2025. Conversation with Jenn Karson. June 30.
Crane, Margaret. 2024. The Rise, Fall, and Reinvention of The San Francisco Art Institute. *East of Borneo*. https://eastofborneo.org/articles/the-rise-fall-and-reinvention-of-the-san-francisco-art-institute/. Accessed 18 June 2025.
Data Art Symposium. 2025. Data Transformed by AI. Panel discussion facilitated by Ben Davis (Artnet), featuring Paul (Whitney Museum of American Art), Viégas (Harvard University), and Mauro Martino (IBM Research)., Cambridge, MA, June 11–12. Personal notes.
Duhigg, Charles. 2023. How Jensen Huang's Nvidia is Powering the A.I. Revolution. *The New Yorker*. https://www.newyorker.com/magazine/2023/12/04/how-jensen-huangs-nvidia-is-powering-the-ai-revolution.
Enwezor, Okwui. 2008. The Postcolonial Constellation: Contemporary Art in a State of Permanent Transition. In *Antinomies of Art and Culture: Modernity, Postmodernity, Contemporaneity*, ed. Terry Smith, Okwui Enwezor, and Nancy Condee, 207–234. Durham: Duke University Press.
"Evolution." n.d. UT Austin Computer Science, Department of Computer Science, The University of Texas at Austin. https://www.cs.utexas.edu/~ai-lab/?evolution=. Accessed 26 February 2025.
Fry, Ben, and Casey Reas. 2019. Code as Material—Ben Fry and Casey Reas. In *Being Material*, ed. Marie-Pier Boucher et al., 20–25. Cambridge: MIT Press.
Gebru, Timnit, et al. 2018. Datasheets for Datasets. *arXiv*. https://arxiv.org/abs/1803.09010.
Google for Developers. 2025. Overview of GAN Structure. https://developers.google.com/machine-learning/gan/gan_structure. Last modified 26 February 2025.
Hao, Karen. 2025. *Empire of AI: Dreams and Nightmares in Sam Altman's OpenAI*. New York: Penguin Press.

Haraway, Donna J. 2016. *Staying with the Trouble: Making Kin in the Chthulucene*. Durham: Duke University Press.

Jenn Karson Studio. 2025. UVM's Art & AI Genetic Algorithm! https://jennkarson.studio/ga/. Accessed 28 February 2025.

Karson, Jenn. 2023. Five Guardrails for Artists Working with Machines and A.I. https://jennkarson.studio/5_artist_guardrails_ai/.

Kostelanetz, Richard. 2003. *Conversing with Cage*. Hove: Psychology Press.

Lefebvre, Henri. 1991. *The Production of Space*. Translated by Donald Nicholson-Smith. Blackwell. First published 1974.

LeWitt, Sol. 1967. Paragraphs on Conceptual Art. *Artforum* 5 (10). https://www.artforum.com/features/paragraphs-on-conceptual-art-211354/.

Lovato, Juniper, et al. 2024. Foregrounding Artist Opinions: A Survey Study on Transparency, Ownership, and Fairness in AI Generative Art. *arXiv*. https://arxiv.org/abs/2401.15497.

McLuhan, Marshall. 1964. *Understanding Media: The Extensions of Man*. New American Library.

Mitchell, Melanie. 2019. *Artificial Intelligence: A Guide for Thinking Humans*. Westminister: Penguin UK.

Mitchell, Margaret, et al. 2018. Model Cards for Model Reporting. *arXiv*. https://arxiv.org/abs/1810.03993.

Nietzsche, Friedrich. 2011. *Thus Spoke Zarathustra*. Translated by Thomas Common. Narrated by John Lee. Audiobook ed. Tantor Audio.

NVIDIA. 2025. NVlabs/StyleGAN. GitHub Repository. https://github.com/NVlabs/stylegan. Accessed 26 February 2025.

O'Neil, Cathy. 2017. *Weapons of Math Destruction: How Big Data Increases Inequality and Threatens Democracy*. New York: Crown.

OpenAI. 2025. New Funding to Build Towards AGI. *OpenAI Blog*, March 31, 2025. https://openai.com/index/march-funding-updates/.

Parisi, Luciana. 2013. *Contagious Architecture: Computation, Aesthetics, and Space*. Cabridge: MIT Press.

Pew Research Center. 2023. The Future of Human Agency. February 24. https://www.pewresearch.org/internet/2023/02/24/the-future-of-human-agency/.

Processing. n.d. *Processing.org*. https://processing.org. Accessed 26 February 2025.

Reas, Casey. 2015. The Thing that Makes the Thing is More Interesting than the Thing. Lecture, *Penny Stamps Speaker Series*, University of Michigan, Ann Arbor, MI, March 12. Video, 54:29. https://www.youtube.com/watch?v=PftrM9VZFbs.

Shiffman, Daniel. n.d. *The Nature of Code: Genetic Algorithms*. https://natureofcode.com/genetic-algorithms/. Accessed 26 February 2025.

Shiffman, Daniel. 2024. *The nature of code: simulating natural systems with javascript*. No Starch Press.
TechTarget. n.d. Generative Adversarial Network (GAN). *SearchEnterpriseAI*. https://www.techtarget.com/searchenterpriseai/definition/generative-adversarial-network-GAN. Accessed 28 February 2025.
Turing, Alan. 2004. Can Digital Computers Think? (1951). In *The Essential Turing*, ed. B. Jack Copeland, 476–448. Oxford University Press.
Whitney Museum of American Art. 2024. Harold Cohen: AARON. Exhibition, Whitney Museum of American Art, New York, February 3–May 19, 2024. Curated by Christiane Paul. https://whitney.org/exhibitions/harold-cohen-aaron.

PART II

When Art History Meets AI in Museum Practices

CHAPTER 7

AI's Catalogue Raisonné: Co-Curatorial Approaches to Digital Documentation of Art Collections

Giulia Taurino

Introduction

A catalogue raisonné is a comprehensive and authoritative collection of information about the works of a notable artist or group of artists, published in one or multiple volumes. Commonly compiled by academics, curators, art specialists, and even the artists themselves, it typically includes detailed descriptions of each artwork, such as its title, date, medium, dimensions, and provenance history, along with a representative image, and may be updated periodically to reflect discoveries or changes in the artist's professional activity. The term "raisonné" means "reasoned," indicating that the catalogue is a carefully researched compilation of logically arranged information. In art museums and other heritage institutions, "catalogues raisonnés" are considered essential tools for art historians, and

G. Taurino (✉)
Khoury College of Computer Sciences, Northeastern University, Boston, MA, USA
e-mail: g.taurino@northeastern.edu

L. Cempellin, M. Geiger (eds.), *Reimagining Art History with Artificial Intelligence*,
https://doi.org/10.1007/978-3-032-21685-4_7

researchers, as they provide a thorough understanding of an artist's production and help establish artworks' authenticity, attribution, and value. Published by museums, galleries, or private organisations, these "tools" can take various forms, including printed books, online databases, or digital platforms. The chapter starts from this well-established form of documentation in art history, to reflect on AI's conceptual and practical influence on the archival description of artworks. How does AI transform catalogues raisonnés in the digital age? How can AI tools assist art historians with enriching artworks' descriptions, supporting scholarly cataloguing and facilitating information retrieval? And what are the epistemological advantages and risks of a theory and practice of the "AI's catalogue raisonné"?

Some museums have already implemented AI techniques to structure art-related information and organise their collections. Against this backdrop, the first part of this chapter provides an overview of both traditional and emerging approaches to compiling art catalogues. Throughout, this section discusses optical character recognition (OCR) models and multimodal large language models (LLMs), outlining how computer vision (CV) and natural language processing (NLP) can be used to extract machine-readable information from visual media, enrich art collections, or identify patterns across artworks. The second part focuses on the impacts of these applications on art historical research. Citing computational initiatives designed to broaden the access to cultural heritage archives and improve searchability in museum interfaces, this second section sets out to evaluate how AI's co-curated critical catalogues can help support open-access ecosystems and scale up the integration of records' annotations to a wider and more diverse range of source materials. As a proof of concept, the chapter features a series of tests that demonstrate how AI can be deployed to enhance the affordances of catalogues raisonnés in the digital age. In this process, I outline three experiments on vision language models (VLMs) for art image description. Finally, the conclusion draws from the proof of concept to critically examine how AI's own catalogues raisonnés might affect art historical work, art documentation, and our understanding of art objects.

A Brief History of the Catalogue Raisonné

The tradition of cataloguing artworks dates back to the late sixteenth century, though the term "catalogue raisonné" did not appear until later. During this formative period, a catalogue described not only artist-focused compilations but also collectanea of artists' biographies, scientific publications, sales documentations, and auction catalogues (John 2023). Among the first published art compendia is Giorgio Vasari's *Le Vite de più eccellenti architetti, pittori, et scultori italiani, da Cimabue insino a' tempi nostri* (1568), followed by Giovanni Pietro Bellori's *Vite de' pittori, scultori ed architetti moderni* (1672), which described the lives and works of contemporary artists of the time. Although not strictly reasoned catalogues in the modern sense, they represent early attempts at an organised art historical documentation. Other examples of art documentation can be found in the inventories and sales catalogues of the seventeenth century, which surveyed and described the works of prominent artists, detailing the history of art objects after their creation. In their broader definition, these types of art catalogues included lists of objects compiled to document valuable artworks owned by individual collectors, or to exhibit and track sales of particular artworks.

Early art publications from the sixteenth and seventeenth centuries laid the ground for modern catalogues raisonnés. However, the first recognised instance of a reasoned catalogue emerged in the eighteenth century. At this time, art critics, dealers, collectors, and in some cases the artists themselves began to take a more methodical approach to cataloguing an artist's works. This methodical conceptualisation of the art catalogue reflects the initial development of systematic approaches to categorising collections across multiple disciplines, in art history as much as in other fields. The first known edition of an official "catalogue raisonné" of *objets d'art* by a single artist was published in 1751 (posthumous), with the volume *Catalogue raisonné de toutes les pièces qui forment l'oeuvre de Rembrandt*[1] (Fig. 7.1), compiled by Parisian art dealer Edme-François Gersaint and documenting the work of Dutch painter and printmaker Rembrandt. Following the original occurrences of art catalogues in Europe in the eighteenth century, the nineteenth century saw a growing interest in art collecting and cataloguing, aided by an increasing number of projects in the field of art history. Western art historians began to adopt

[1] https://archive.org/details/touteslespieces00gers.

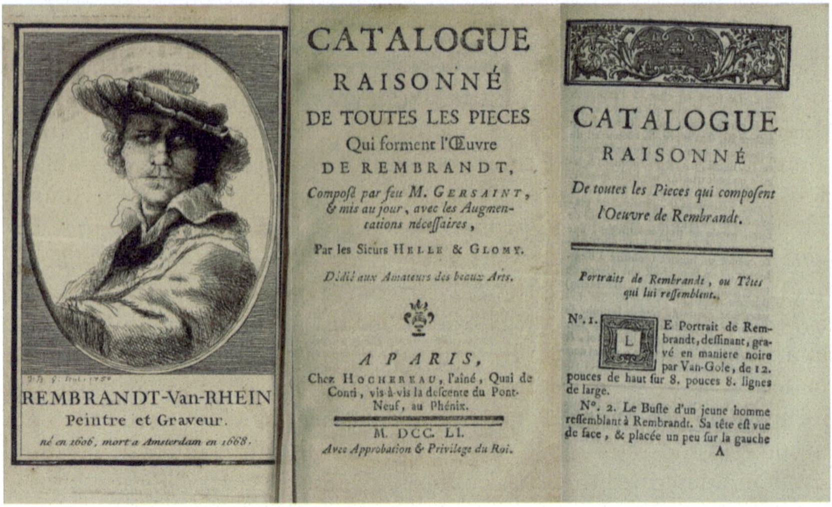

Fig. 7.1 Title Pages (left) and Catalogue's Incipit (right) of the Catalogue raisonné de toutes les pièces qui forment l'oeuvre de Rembrandt by Edme-François Gersaint (1751). Source: the Internet Archive, https://archive.org/details/touteslespieces00gers/page/n7/mode/2up

a more academic approach to cataloguing, providing detailed analysis of works alongside descriptions. At this time, the catalogue raisonné evolved into a curatorial tool for museum exhibitions, and was soon adopted as an editorial guideline for structuring information in exposition catalogues.[2]

By the late twentieth and early twenty-first centuries, the practice of heritage documentation had become even more structured and the task of compiling a catalogue raisonné turned into a formalised academic and institutional endeavour, accompanied by experiments with digital editions. The method of reasoning, categorising, and classifying physical objects and visual concepts became an essential part of the process of collecting and acquiring artworks, and catalogues raisonnés expanded their scope. Scholars and curators were increasingly engaged in the process of

[2] cf. A catalogue of the pictures and studies of William Etty, R.A.: selected for exhibition at the Society of Arts, Adelphi, London, in aid of the formation of National Gallery of British Arts. Publication date: 1849. https://archive.org/details/gri_33125008890812/page/18/mode/2up.

establishing criteria for inclusion, analysing provenance, and addressing issues of attribution and authenticity.

The value of catalogues raisonnés for art historiography and the study of art markets would become evident with maintained catalogues detailing the work of notable artists, which were updated over the years with revised versions to add new findings and changes in acquisition. During this period, more artists, particularly modern ones, had catalogues raisonnés produced, often led by the artist's circle or a committed scholar. Among other examples is *Pablo Picasso's Catalogue Raisonné* curated by Christian Zervos (1932–1978) for *Cahiers d'Art* and representing one of the most comprehensive efforts to compile Picasso's works in collaboration with the artist himself. Zervos produced a multi-volume catalogue, listing over 16,000 works by Picasso and placing them within historical and stylistic context.[3]

Another example of the historiographical value of reasoned catalogues and their role in knowledge dissemination is *Claude Monet: Biographie et Catalogue Raisonné, Volume I*, first published in 1974. This catalogue remains one of the most famous cases of art catalogues from the twentieth century. Helping solidify the practice of systematic cataloguing for modern artists, this publication would undergo several renovations starting from the original five-volume edition published between 1974 and 1991 and curated by French art-dealer and historian Daniel Wildenstein.[4] In more recent years, The Wildenstein Plattner Institute (WPI) released an amended and expanded digital version as *Claude Monet: The Revised Catalogue Raisonné*.[5] The project started in 2003, but builds upon material and documentation dating back to the early twentieth century.

Even more than the rise of collaborative printmaking studios, which fostered knowledge exchange and artistic experimentation, digital editions marked a significant growth in collaborations and publishing resources and opened up to new creative undertakings for documenting and distributing electronic catalogues to a wider audience. Today, digitisation of existing printed catalogues along with born-digital catalogues is instrumental in guiding the future directions of catalogues raisonnés. Moreover, the Internet has made it easier to disseminate art publications, making

[3] https://www.cahiersdart.com/en/art-books/catalogues-raisonnes/pablo-picasso-by-christian-zervos/.

[4] https://wpi.art/2019/01/14/claude-monet/.

[5] https://digitalprojects.wpi.art/monet/artworks.

them more accessible and enabling the incorporation of new research findings in real time. Rogers (2015) pointed to the new frontiers granted by web archiving and the digital publishing of catalogues raisonnés, noting their potential to counter the impermanence of art objects by recompiling existing volumes with updated information, integrating missing data and newly discovered artworks, amending outdated language, or reconstructing catalogues anew from partially lost collections.

Thanks to these technological advancements, the late twentieth century and early twenty-first centuries saw an evident shift towards integrating digital editions, digital imaging, and semantic and computational analysis in art historical research. Along with other open resources used for the classification of art objects, such as structured vocabularies,[6] thesauri, and bibliographical dictionaries, catalogues raisonnés constitute important tools for reconstructing the history of art objects, and their authenticity, provenance, and itinerary in the art market, while providing unique data sources for historical research. Acknowledging this value, in recent decades, academic institutions, galleries, and museums have increasingly been involved in the preparation and publication of digital catalogues raisonnés, either as e-catalogues,[7] or ever-expanding digital corpora based on structured databases, or in their more traditional form as browsable digitised volumes.[8]

Combining a long history of consistent and programmatic documentation with more recent digital remodeling initiatives of printed catalogues into structured information and queryable linked open data,[9]

[6] Structured vocabularies or thesauri are controlled lists of terms, phrases, and concepts used for describing, cataloguing, and retrieving information about art, architecture, and related cultural heritage information. These vocabularies are essential for ensuring consistency and standardisation in documentation and research. They help manage, organize, and standardise large amounts of information related to artworks, making it easier to search, retrieve, and analyse data.

[7] Among the first examples of an electronic catalogue raisonné is The National Gallery of Art's online catalogue raisonné for *Gemini G.E.L.* (2001). As John (2023) reports, "...the e-publication transformed the loose-leaf version of Gemini's catalogue raisonné, released in batches between roughly 1971 and 1988." Cf. https://wayback.archive-it.org/22902/20241219174428/https:/www.nga.gov/fcgi-bin/gemini.pl?view=page&limit=30&sort=2&skip=1.

[8] cf. https://www.artic.edu/digital-publications/33/the-lithographs-of-james-mcneill-whistler-the-digital-edition.

[9] cf. https://www.getty.edu/research/tools/vocabularies/lod/index.html; https://www.getty.edu/projects/remodeling-getty-provenance-index/.

contemporary catalogues raisonnés are not just organised lists framed within a fixed scholarly genre, but dynamic complex networks (Freddolini and Helmreich 2014) holding unprecedented possibilities for art historical research. As such, they acquire new affordances and meaning as "generative digital scholarships" (Neely and Leon 2024). In the next paragraphs, I will observe how the notion of catalogue raisonné as generative digital scholarship can be articulated in AI applications in a way that is twofold: on the one hand, AI pipelines can be integrated in the design, development, and updates of digital art catalogues, on the other hand, digital catalogues raisonnés can be deployed for prompting AI models (e.g., LLMs) to generate more accurate automated captioning and descriptions of artworks.

From Analogue to Digital: New Approaches to Compiling Catalogues Raisonnés

Compilers of art catalogues, whether catalogues raisonnés or exhibition catalogues, have traditionally taken at least one of the following approaches for the editorial arrangement of information about art objects in structured lists: chronological (one of the most common structures for a catalogue raisonné); alphabetical (e.g., titles of artworks); thematic/stylistic; medium-based; geographic/location-based (e.g., inventories); provenance-based; or ownership-based. These ordering principles are sometimes combined or modified depending on the objectives of the catalogue raisonné and the nature of the artist's body of work. Some catalogues also include supplemental material (e.g., reproductions of the artist's work, appendices of rejected works, technical appendices, or author's commentaries), which complements structured information listed in the main catalogue.

In printed catalogues raisonnés, as well as other art historical publications such as indexes, principles of arrangement are fundamental for detail-oriented information retrieval and for manually locating specific resources of interest. On the contrary, in contemporary digital editions, points of access are not confined to ordered entries; instead, they can support cross-searches and various entry points to the catalogue resource. Whether filtering for keywords, identifiers, provenance information, location, or time of creation, readers of digital catalogues can now navigate textual and visual resources without the editorial constraints of a printed object in a more interactive and dynamic fashion (cf. WPI's *Claude Monet: The Revised Catalogue Raisonné*).

In evaluating applications of the digital catalogue raisonné in generative AI, we must acknowledge its structural features in terms of information architecture, as well as in terms of existing and potential biases inherited from older editions as they are digitised and converted into machine-readable data. Despite their longstanding importance in the field of art history, traditional printed catalogues raisonnés suffer from inherent limitations that can diminish their relevance in contemporary scholarship. For instance, the print-based format of traditional catalogues creates fundamental restrictions, resulting in static documents susceptible to becoming outdated almost immediately upon publication. This lack of flexibility prevents the direct integration of new discoveries, attributions, or scholarly insights without producing entirely new editions.

As a result, reparative descriptions[10]—a more recent trend in art history and archival work—cannot be directly implemented in paper-based catalogues as required. Older publications are also likely to reflect or reinforce colonialist knowledge frameworks and documentation practices typical of the time they were written. When dealing with cultural perspectives that have been previously silenced, in particular indigenous and precolonial knowledge, we must consider how old printed museum catalogues might inhibit alternative ways of knowing and how the colonial past of art history is made visible (or invisible) by the way objects are described, coded, and constructed in the catalogue without the possibility of being promptly redacted or updated.

The static permanence of the printed book as a paper-based medium exacerbates the ways in which conventional cataloguing methodologies and past editions have marginalised non-Western perspectives and alternative knowledge systems, often presenting a narrow cultural lens that fails to acknowledge the diverse contexts in which art exists and its understanding evolves. While it is true that generative AI tools can retain biases, we must be equally aware of the biases embedded in the traditional way of cataloguing art objects, which has omitted artworks based on inconsistent editorial decisions and pre-assigned artistic value. Additionally, the high production costs and limited distribution of printed catalogues restrict their accessibility, confining their use primarily to specialised

[10] https://guides.library.yale.edu/reparativearchivaldescription.

institutions, established scholars, or wealthy collectors, rather than making this knowledge widely available to research communities and the broader public.

Given the existing challenges of hard-copy formats, digital databases have presented a long-awaited solution for the timely revision of art catalogues and the reframing of classificatory norms in the study of art history. With their flexibility, digital formats often turned into spaces of experimentation as well as venues for developing critical approaches to the catalogue raisonné outside of Western-centric perspectives and hierarchical interpretations of art histories. As art historian Emily Voelker argues, "...catalogue raisonné projects published solely in hard-copy formats represent more traditional—dare I say, market-driven and sustaining—approaches in the field of art history, whereas digital iterations might enable a reimagining of the genre itself" (Voelker 2023, 1). In another paper, Way and Stuber point to the digital catalogue raisonné "as a case study encounter between a traditional genre of art-historical publication and digital technology" (Way and Stuber 2023, 1), citing digital projects and open-source tools that expand the affordances of this genre rather than erasing existing printed records.

Platforms for digital publishing allow for the creation of interactive catalogues that integrate web features, such as searchable text and images and overall improved discoverability. Among other examples is *Quire*, an open-source, free-to-use digital publishing tool launched by Getty Publications in 2016 with the pilot project *Ancient Terracottas*.[11] This project, alongside other multi-format collection catalogues based on Quire, demonstrates the longevity of digital editions, which often build upon standard compilations of plain text files in a book to create browsable curated experiences based on authoritative sources and enriched with visual features. Other digital initiatives, like Navigating.art, a nonprofit organisation supported by the Hasso Plattner Foundation, were designed by art historians and developers to advance the digital preservation of cultural heritage by providing ready-to-use digital tools and software that help curate and publish digital catalogues raisonnés in structured databases. Digital humanities expert at Navigating.art, Lisa Weiß (2023), spoke about the unique relevance of database structures for catalogues

[11] https://www.getty.edu/publications/terracottas/; https://www.getty.edu/publications/terracottas/catalogue/.

raisonnés as means of organising information about artworks into machine-readable interconnected data entries.

More recent experiments for "moving past the traditional catalogue" (Srinivasan et al. 2009, 265) in critical ways include *Digital Benin*, a project for collating digital material from heritage institutions into a newly curated online catalogue that reassembles over 5000 artefacts previously disassembled due to looting and other colonialist practices of non-granted art appropriation.[12] The project's website warns that "the collections, and some of this material is inherently colonial and contains words, terms, and phrases that are inaccurate, derogatory and harmful towards African and African diasporic communities."[13] Instead of concealing existing classification biases, this project opts for featuring them as the symptoms of outdated cataloguing traditions and problematises the language used in an attempt to raise critical awareness on controversial histories of art documentation. By doing so, this digital initiative paves the way for a critical reading of traditional catalogues raisonnés and alternative forms of art documentation in the quest for a digital leap towards inclusive practices of art cataloguing through digital surrogates and online editions.

Acknowledging the unprecedented possibilities granted by digital editions, over the past fifteen years, academic researchers, art historians, and experts from heritage institutions have gathered to discuss methods for integrating digital and computational technologies into the process of compiling and publishing catalogues raisonnés. Grappling with the rapid growth of digital publishing in the early 2000s, in 2011 the Catalogue Raisonné Scholars Association (CRSA) conference organised one of the first public conversations on the "Issues of the Online Catalogue Raisonné,"[14] addressing database structures, online distribution services, infrastructures, and revenue models, as well as broader frontiers and challenges of editorial practices on the web. These topics returned urgently in follow-up CRSA conferences in 2014, 2015, and 2018 hosted by the Dedalus Foundation,[15] detailing not only the present state of online catalogues raisonnés—ongoing perspective, approaches, and applications—but also their future.

[12] https://digitalbenin.org/catalogue.

[13] https://digitalbenin.org/.

[14] https://dedalusfoundation.org/programs/videos/watch/crsa-online-cr-mini-conference/.

[15] https://dedalusfoundation.org/programs/videos/watch/preparing-for-tomorrow-but-how-the-future-of-online-catalogues-raisonnes/.

At the 2018 CRSA and Dedalus Foundation Conference themed "Preparing for Tomorrow, but how? The Future of Online Catalogues Raisonnés," Andrea Theil, Director of the Roy Lichtenstein Catalogue Raisonné Project, stressed the importance of digital transformations in catalogues raisonnés, which traditionally "haven't been known to operate on the cutting-edge of innovation" (ibidem) and are now instead fully embracing new technologies and features in order to facilitate editorial customisation, corrections, updates, and more fluid access, search, and navigation. Alongside co-panelists Greg Albers (J. Paul Getty Trust) and Stephen Bury (Frick Art Reference Library), Andrea Theil describes future art catalogues as hyperlinked, scalable, and dynamic environments able to adapt to the latest techno-cultural innovations.

These debates in art history have been accompanied by edited volumes and journal issues on the practical and conceptual reframing of practices of editorialisation in digital environments (Bachimont 2007; Way and Stuber 2023; Sinatra and Vitali-Rosati 2014; Vitali-Rosati 2016, 2018; Stuber and Way 2025), where scholars anticipated a pressing topic in today's algorithmic culture: digital publishing initiatives—including online catalogues—tend to overflow outside of the traditional boundaries of the original edition and leak into everyday digital practices of online data sharing, algorithmic indexing, and, more recently, AI-generated content.

It is now understood that digital catalogues are fundamentally redefining how art historical knowledge is created, organised, and accessed, not only by humans but also by machines. As Ames and Lewis (2020) note, "Digital scholarship is a disruptive influence in the library. Its extensive scale and scope leaves few areas of the Library untouched, whether this is around the way collections are described or presented; the changing focus of existing services and the ways they are delivered; modes of access to the collections, and what collections are; or staff skills" (p. 5). This disruptive influence creates possibilities for reimagining the catalogue raisonné not only as a more dynamic and inclusive knowledge resource than its traditional counterpart, but also as a tool for critical inquiry into how art knowledge is constructed, structured, and regenerated manually or computationally.

Such a transformative potential extends beyond technological implementation, requiring substantial pragmatic and conceptual shifts, especially in integrating state-of-the-art AI technologies, such as LLMs. Libraries and institutions supporting digital scholarship are exploring ways to adapt their infrastructure and workflows, as well as the fundamental purpose of preserving heritage records in data-rich, AI-driven environments. In turn, computer scientists and digital humanists are trying to fine-tune and adapt AI models to better serve humanities and cultural heritage applications in archives and libraries, by proposing alternative frameworks that tackle the shortcomings of general-purpose LLMs trained on masses of un-curated data scraped from the Internet.

This new landscape of information management invites us to yet another reconceptualisation of the catalogue raisonné—not merely as a digitised version of the print catalogue, but as a new form of *generative data source* that can overcome the limitations of traditional formats, while expanding possibilities for knowledge creation, representation, and dissemination. In 2023, the International Foundation for Art Research mapped the present state of digital cataloguing of art objects, counting at least 350 online catalogues raisonnés between more traditional digital editorial products and innovative digital catalogues raisonnés that leverage "the affordances of the digital with continuous updating more akin to a museum's online collections database" (Neely and Leon 2024, 5.61). Neely and Leon's survey of the field highlights another important fact: "... unlike search engines, a catalogue raisonné performs the role of an identity manager or authority record for an artwork. By aggregating references to artworks and resources and linking to key archival collections, online scholarly publishers, relevant resources, and related records, a catalogue raisonné can be disambiguated from other like items" (ivi: 5.65).

Institutional digital remodelling initiatives of catalogues raisonnés help preserve authoritative information online, opening up new possibilities for retraining machine models on domain-specific data in art history and prompting more accurate AI-generated information about art objects. Before delving into the current state of "AI's art catalogue" and exploring how art historical information is mediated in LLMs, the next section will provide an overview of existing applications of AI for the creation of catalogues raisonnés, and discuss how these experimental approaches can support the curatorial work of catalogues compilers and lay the ground for further conversation into the shaping of humanities-based multimodal language models.

AI's Catalogue Raisonné: Theory and Applications

Over the past few years, digital applications in catalogues raisonnés have allowed for more efficient information extraction and integration, in some cases prompting new findings, additional pathways of research, and cutting-edge practices of archival documentation. By the same token, they have also exposed art historical information to new dimensions of computational processing and generative AI. While art historians, scholars, specialists, and collectors remain the principal knowledge-holders, contributing invaluable information to art catalogues passed through generations of experts, AI can now be used as an additional tool to facilitate the programmatic enrichment of catalogues and archives. AI tools might be utilised to unveil previously unexposed insights into the movements of artworks in the art market, or surface digital resources from various domains of expertise at once.

Despite the attention given to AI in public discourse, the academic conversation on the reuse of online catalogues raisonnés in generative AI and LLMs is still at an early stage. If topics like born-digital projects preservation and software sustainability have already been explored by the scholarly community, the role of AI in digital publishing is still unclear for what concerns both its potential advantages and risks. Drawing upon recent advancements in AI, some art institutions and academic scholars alike have begun to explore the opportunities for compiling catalogues raisonnés with the support of machine learning (ML) models. In digitisation, archival description and metadata enrichment workflows, in particular, ML applications like OCR have been praised for their time and cost efficiency, with their unprecedented potential to facilitate the manual labour of transcribing handwritten information, compiling catalogues, or else categorising vast holdings of historical records and annotating extensive image collections with descriptive labels for record-level search and information retrieval.

An example of a catalogue raisonné partially generated with the aid of AI is *eManet*, a project by The Atelier for Restoration & Research of Paintings (Netherlands) developed in collaboration with ArtPI.[16] This

[16] ArtPI relies on an API "designed and optimised for art." In Computer Science, an API (Application Programming Interface) is a software interface that connects computers and computer programs for data transmission. In digital archival collections, APIs are commonly used to send a data request to a database and receive a response in the form of transferred data. Source: https://www.artpi.co/about.

project reorganised the work of impressionist painter Édouard Manet, by using ML to group his artistic production into one of the following three categories: étude, ébauche, ébauche/fini.[17] As noted on the project website, "…each category has been analysed using Artificial Intelligence and deep learning"[18] models previously trained on one million artworks to memorise concepts of style, genre, composition, and other art principles. This taxonomy is in line with Manet's approach to painting as an ongoing drafting process. With the help of AI, *eManet* tries to make sense of existing studies, unfinished canvases, and reworked drafts, helping scholars understand changes in Manet's style and artistic scope.

Alongside the AI-generated curation of the catalogue, this digital edition of Manet's catalogue raisonné includes information sourced from Denis Rouart and Daniel Wildenstein's *Edouard Manet: Catalogue Raisonné* (1975). With this operation, the project bridges traditional practices in manually cataloguing artworks and cutting-edge AI applications in a mutual cooperation between human experts and AI agents. As a result, this co-curated catalogue generates streams of indexed content based on the drafting progress, which cross over human-curated timelines and exhibition histories, such as artworks exhibited in "Avenue de l'Alma," "Exhibitions during his lifetime," or "Inventory after death." This and similar approaches to the production of digital catalogues raisonnés demonstrate that AI can indeed facilitate the revisions of traditional printed volumes: when the original catalogue is converted into digital editions or databases, it is reimagined in a new form, featuring latest updates and turning the catalogue into a co-curated online experience.

An article on Navigating.art (McDowall n.d.) highlights the new frontiers of AI in art historical documentation, covering a range of AI applications from NLP for visual question answering to the use of computational tools for enhancing open-access ecosystems.[19] The article cites a series of academic studies, including Rinaldo et al.'s (2023) paper on how libraries, archives, and museums are tackling metadata extraction from handwritten resources using OCR tools. Widely used in manuscript studies, OCR has been leveraged in digital humanities for the automatic transcription of image-based text. OCR models can be applied to text from printed

[17] English translation: Study, Draft, Draft/Finished.

[18] https://www.e-manet.org/.

[19] https://cloud.google.com/blog/products/gcp/when-art-meets-big-data-analyzing-200000-items-from-the-met-collection-in-bigquery.

documents, text featured in the composition of an image (e.g., posters), or text contained in marginalia, that is to say textual annotations in the margins of the main document. Unlocking this information from analogue formats and transforming it into digital documents that can be processed computationally at scale has offered a relief from the burden of manually transcribing thousands of pages. It also offered an unprecedented ease of access to information for art scholars, who are now able to consult historical material—such as correspondence, printed catalogues, and inventories—as transcribed data in a database compiled with AI assistance.

Beyond transferring existing information from analogue to digital format, another useful application of AI in digital humanities is automated image captioning, which, much like OCR, promises to alleviate the time-consuming archival labour of labelling thousands of records. CV for image captioning, however, has faced some challenges and did not always lead to the hoped for results. Research on CV techniques for labelling art images details both opportunities and limitations of ML models for interpreting and describing artworks, from fine art objects to more common artefacts. Among others, Dobbs et al. (2022) discuss an AI-based classification model for compiling a catalogue raisonné leveraging WikiArt data and ResNet 101 CNN architecture with ImageNet for transfer learning "to aid art scholars with the artist authentication and impermanence problems" (ivi: 885).

Despite promising work in the field of AI, art authentication, and preservation, many scholars have pointed to the limited capabilities of CV when applied to art historical research. Research shows that older generation pre-trained CV models often fail to produce detailed or historically accurate descriptions of artworks, rather leaning towards presenting images as consumer products, approximations of everyday objects, or, at best, interpreting artworks from generic Western-centric constructs (Pereira and Moreschi 2020). These issues might stem from the fact that most CV models were trained on datasets containing primarily contemporary images. When a dataset heavily favours certain types of data, it creates an imbalance that can skew the model's predictions. In this case, low exposure to historical records means off-the-shelf models struggle to interpret older images and cultural objects accurately. Moreover, imprecise or incorrect labelling can occur when annotators lack specialised knowledge, especially in domain-specific tasks. Inaccurate labels cause the model to learn incorrect associations, leading to poor prediction accuracy and unreliable behaviour.

To improve CV models' ability to classify art objects, scholars have proposed to fine-tune ML models using pre-curated datasets of images annotated by human experts. A number of studies have demonstrated that such a human-informed approach to automated image processing and classification can enhance AI performance in correctly labelling art historical records (Blessing and Wen 2010; Cetinic et al. 2018; Chen 2018; Dobbs et al. 2022; Johnson et al. 2008; Kondo and Hasegawa 2020; Mensink and van Gemert 2014; Strezoski and Worring 2017; Viswanathan 2017). This approach is supported by the increasing digitisation of art collections, which, along with the computerisation of heritage catalogues (Turner 2016), has made available open-access resources for enriching image datasets and fuelling further exchange between the arts and AI.

Yet, difficulties remain in generating reliable art historical information via AI. Traditional CV models still struggle to understand abstract features, develop a coherent curatorial vision, or elaborate complex linguistic descriptions, and, without proper fine-tuning, can perpetuate biases present in the training data, leading to unfair or discriminatory curatorial practices. Countering existing biases and misinformation in AI should start from embedding historical knowledge in AI models, rather than forcing pre-trained AI models into humanities research with the risk of falling into oversimplification, bias, and loss of depth in image description. Existing limitations of older generation machine vision tools have raised fundamental questions on how to align AI applications to the needs, values, and mission statements of heritage institutions. Within this context, the recent introduction of multimodal LLMs has presented a good opportunity to rethink strategies for expanding AI capabilities to support art historical research starting from human knowledge.

LLMs offer powerful tools for analysing large-scale human-generated text data and automating qualitative summarisation tasks in humanities disciplines. They can aid art historians and archivists in tasks as varied as transcribing texts from printed material, identifying patterns across historical images, or highlighting correlations between various textual sources. With recent state-of-the-art language models, the affordances of AI for digital heritage management and preservation have radically improved, offering a more adaptable solution not only to introduce AI in the study of art, but also and most importantly to integrate art historical knowledge in AI models. Moreover, VLMs can now support visual and textual functions, processing multiple formats in one pass and generating richer and more descriptive outputs. While still at their early stage of experimentation, the multimodal affordances of generative language models create new opportunities for applications in art historical documentation, by allowing for the referencing of authoritative sources, such as art catalogues, and enhancing factual accuracy in automated image description.

As I posit the notion of an "AI's catalogue raisonné," I argue that, with a curated set of instructions in the prompt, LLMs can be deployed to both facilitate the dynamic updating of digital art catalogues and extract relevant information on art objects from existing art documentation resources available online, such as digital catalogs. As already outlined, unlike traditional static printed catalogues, digital catalogues raisonnés can not only be regularly updated to integrate the latest scholarly findings, new attributions, or discoveries, but also easily referenced in computational projects. This ensures that the catalogue remains a current and living document, evolving with ongoing research and public discourse. Thanks to open-access scholarship and online digital catalogue initiatives, the latest state-of-the-art AI models can be optimised for research, ensuring that the LLM filters and prioritises information from online sources based on their academic, scholarly, and authoritative relevance.

If digital access breaks traditional barriers posed by print formats by making these scholarly resources available online, generative AI can now expand the scale of outreach beyond individual initiatives, connecting online catalogues, datasets, and information from a variety of sources thanks to their multimodal information processing capabilities. By granting the digital format new interactive features and enabling its users to engage with art historical content in novel ways, multimodal language models can push the boundaries of cross-disciplinary collaborations in art history, but, without a proper understanding of their functioning, they can easily fall prey to misinterpretations, inconsistent and inaccurate information, and even errors, thus undermining the efforts of art historians.

In a conference presentation[20] on the challenges of automatic art captioning hosted by the Wildenstein Plattner Institute, researcher Alejandro Sierra-Múnera outlined some of these issues, including AI's tendency to generate oversimplifications, hallucinations, biased information, or factually inaccurate descriptions about artworks. In the final remarks on research directions, he suggested that the creation of high-quality captioning datasets and the establishment of data quality parameters via co-curatorial workflows might help achieve better results, citing as a solution

[20] https://www.youtube.com/watch?v=OZu_li3Qy-A.

knowledge grounding via human-assisted information retrieval. In the next section, I outline a proof of concept that shows three different approaches for leveraging existing knowledge bases to improve LLMs' outputs based on information from online catalogues raisonnés and other authoritative sources.

Whether using language processing to reorganise art objects or to connect information from different digital catalogues, an exploratory testing of multimodal LLMs will immediately disclose AI's ability to summarise historical, cultural, and provenance data about notable artworks, detailing acquisitions and exhibition histories in museums and galleries, but it will equally show that, in order to maintain quality outputs, LLMs need quality data sources for factual accuracy. With human supervision to guide models towards reliable sources and detect possible errors in the outputs, LLMs can be instructed to generate more accurate descriptions of artworks without the need for fine-tuning, by relying on prompt engineering to point LLMs at specific textual documents or using Model Context Protocol (MCP) to query authoritative digital archival sources.

Despite these opportunities, research on the use of archival documentation such as art catalogues for fine-tuning ML models or else for prompting multimodal LLMs to improve accuracy on art historical information is still limited. One of the few projects to discuss the use of art catalogues in multimodal analysis was developed by Bartz et al. (2020) as part of a collaboration with the Wildenstein Plattner Institute. This research project outlines a tool for the automatic matching of art descriptions to art records starting from the premise that multimodal data is already featured in art catalogues through semantic associations of text to images. This perspective lays the ground for approaching digital catalogues raisonnés as generative resources for improving both linguistic reasoning and image processing capabilities in VLMs.

To better understand the role of digital catalogues raisonnés as generative resources in multimodal LLMs, I advance the notion of an "AI's catalogue raisonné." In the context of generative AI, I define an AI's catalogue raisonné as the archive of art historical information memorised by multimodal LLMs about any visual instance of images recognised as *objets d'art* by the art community. This information can vary as new models are constantly retrained, and human-made art catalogues are updated, digitised, and released online, but will typically surface the informational structure found in traditional art catalogues, that is, the artwork's identification (e.g., title and its variants, author, time period, medium/materials), the artwork's history and context (e.g., provenance, current location/owner, exhibition history, bibliography/literature), and additional information (e.g., detailed description, essays, or critical commentaries). We shall assume that this information is contained *in nuce* in the AI's catalogue raisonné in all instances when a digital catalogue compiled by art experts and curators exists as an open-access resource over the Internet.

What, then, are the epistemological advantages and risks of a theory and practice of the "AI's catalogue raisonné"? In the next section, I try to answer this question through a series of experiments run using a state-of-the-art multimodal LLM, Claude Opus 4.1. These experiments are conceived as proofs of concept, with the intent to both test the capabilities of LLMs to support art historical documentation and explore the potential uses of digital catalogues for instructing generative AI models to produce accurate descriptions of art objects.

Critical Reflection: Exploring AI's Catalogues Raisonnés for Art Image Description

Much like other documentation practices in art history, catalogues raisonnés "translate material things into linguistic statements" (Keating and Markey 2011, 209), and thus represent "indicative traces of debates concerning the links between language and materiality—the limits and possibilities language holds for describing things" (Freddolini and Helmreich 2014, 13). Multimodal language models act in a similar way: trained on massive amounts of textual data and text-image pairings, they are able to convert visual material inputs into linguistic statements based on selected information. As primarily cultural technologies, much like digital catalogues raisonnés they "should be subjected to same modes of analysis as other objects of material culture" (ibidem), meaning observed and studied not just as mechanical reproductions of information but as, themselves, cultural artefacts.

VLMs are designed to mimic human intelligence through language processing, by combining written records with visual data to build more nuanced linguistic interpretations. However, unlike human intelligence, which can perform complex reasoning tasks, VLM intelligence relies on pattern detection, representation learning, and prediction-based inference through cross-modal alignment between visual and textual modalities, enabling both descriptive generation and cross-modal reasoning based on training data. For this reason, the output generated by VLMs about a given image is only as accurate and comprehensive as the input information that the model can find in the training datasets or from online queries through prompts or via MCP. While digital art catalogues are mostly limited to notable artists, and more work is needed to fill the missing data from underrepresented art histories and visual cultures, access to these digital resources can drastically improve multimodal LLMs' performance, with substantial progress in generating detailed and accurate image captions.

Latest generation VLMs can access information found on the Internet in real time, improving their ability to feature information from recently updated online databases, or reference visual and textual data from museum websites. An AI's catalogue raisonné can be further improved by prompting VLMs to reference digitised or born-digital art historical documentation and resources, not only catalogues raisonnés, but also museum catalogues, controlled vocabularies, or thesauri. The following paragraphs outline three main examples featuring different approaches for prompting VLMs to perform more accurate art image description replicating the model of the catalogue raisonné. Since testing and evaluation of these experiments are still ongoing, the following section reports an attempt to define a tentative workflow for extracting art historical information from multimodal LLMs using a combination of image and text prompts. In the next few paragraphs, I will outline examples from a larger series of experiments run on Claude Opus 4.1, detailing the expected outcomes, generated outputs, and preliminary considerations as part of an initial proof of concept. The goal is to assess opportunities and limitations of AI-generated catalogues raisonnés.

Prompting VLMs to Reference and Reproduce Catalogues Raisonnés

As anticipated in the introduction to this chapter, catalogues raisonnés contain comprehensive, authoritative data about an artist's works, including detailed descriptions, attributions, provenance information, and critical analysis. By prompting AI models to reference data from online art catalogues, art historians can direct VLMs to generate captions that are not just generic interpretations of visual cues or erroneous accounts, but more detailed, accurate, relevant, and overall authoritative descriptions. This approach to prompt engineering is known as retrieval-augmented generation (RAG), a technique that enhances LLM outputs by first retrieving relevant information from external knowledge sources, then using that information to generate more accurate, truth-grounded responses. This approach can be used for prompting LLMs to retrieve information from authoritative knowledge bases outside of their training data sources. I tested the efficacy of an RAG approach for building an AI's catalogue raisonné about Claude Monet using Claude Opus 4.1. Beyond RAG, alternative options to limit AI hallucinations and increase the likelihood of accurate outputs include MCP integration for real-time data access, chain-of-thought prompting, fact-checking through external validators and human-in-the-loop verification, confidence scoring with uncertainty quantification, and fine-tuning on domain-specific, high-quality datasets—the latter requiring access to compute resources.

For this preliminary testing, I focused on structured prompting approaches with explicit constraints. More specifically, I wrote a prompt that (1) referenced a manually compiled list of authoritative sources, including art catalogues, digital databases, museum exhibitions, and scholarly papers about the artist, and (2) instructed the model to reproduce the format of a catalogue raisonné. I then isolated three parameters for the initial qualitative evaluation: (1) model accuracy in including attributions to sources and versions; (2) model accuracy and completeness in reporting updated information from digital catalogues and other sources; and (3) model accuracy in using art historical terminology, and contextual language from the catalogue.

Given an image of a widely documented and researched painting by Claude Monet, *Woman with a Parasol - Madame Monet and Her Son*,[21] along with a prompt requesting the model to provide a detailed description in the style of an art catalogue, I expected that a specialised VLM could leverage a catalogue raisonné like Daniel Wildenstein's multi-volume work on Monet's paintings to return a relevant output, checking for accuracy of information and sourcing additional details. Preliminary outputs from exploratory testing revealed interesting insights. Once the model was exposed to detailed descriptions of Monet's artworks through the manually curated list, which featured data about the paintings' provenance, stylistic elements, and historical context, most of this information was reported in the generated outputs. When the model was prompted to generate a description of Monet's painting *Woman with a*

[21] Source: https://www.nga.gov/collection/art-object-page.61379.html.

Parasol - Madame Monet and Her Son (1875) in the style of a catalogue raisonné, it therefore provided more than just simple descriptions of visual features (e.g., "woman in a field") or short captions (e.g., "this work, painted in 1875, captures the early Impressionist use of light and brush-stroke, characteristic of Monet's series on French landscapes"), but instead offered detailed information about the art historical context of the painting (Fig. 7.2) following the style of a catalogue raisonné as instructed in the prompt, along with a list of authoritative sources.

Through summarisation of information from authoritative sources, the output returned slightly more generic descriptive information along with

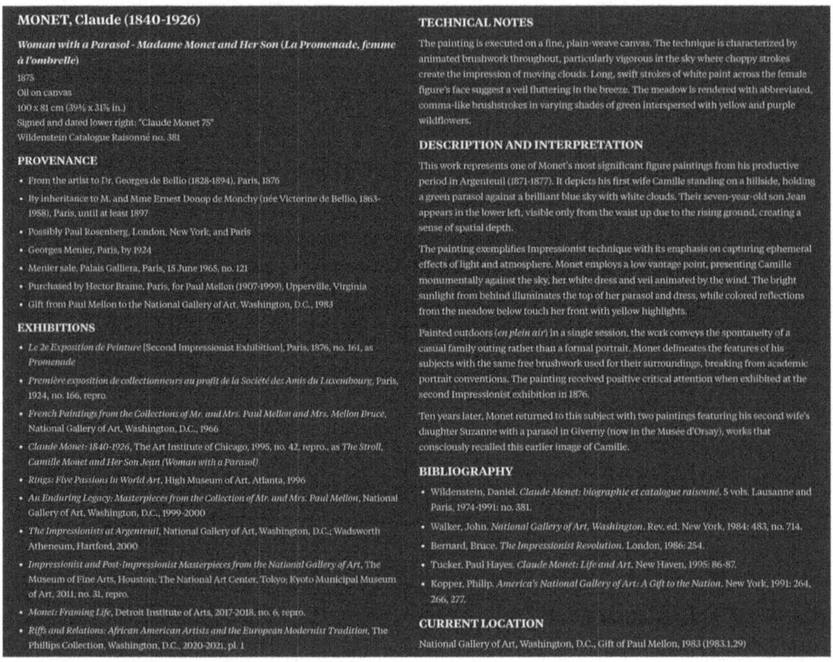

MONET, Claude (1840-1926)

Woman with a Parasol - Madame Monet and Her Son (La Promenade, femme à l'ombrelle)

1875
Oil on canvas
100 x 81 cm (39⅜ x 31⅞ in.)
Signed and dated lower right: "Claude Monet 75"
Wildenstein Catalogue Raisonné no. 381

PROVENANCE

- From the artist to Dr. Georges de Bellio (1828-1894), Paris, 1876
- By inheritance to M. and Mme Ernest Donop de Monchy (née Victorine de Bellio, 1863-1958), Paris, until at least 1897
- Possibly Paul Rosenberg, London, New York, and Paris
- Georges Menier, Paris, by 1924
- Menier sale, Palais Galliera, Paris, 15 June 1965, no. 121
- Purchased by Hector Brame, Paris, for Paul Mellon (1907-1999), Upperville, Virginia
- Gift from Paul Mellon to the National Gallery of Art, Washington, D.C., 1983

EXHIBITIONS

- *Le 2e Exposition de Peinture* [Second Impressionist Exhibition], Paris, 1876, no. 161, as *Promenade*
- *Première exposition de collectionneurs au profit de la Société des Amis du Luxembourg*, Paris, 1924, no. 166, repro.
- *French Paintings from the Collections of Mr. and Mrs. Paul Mellon and Mrs. Mellon Bruce*, National Gallery of Art, Washington, D.C., 1966
- *Claude Monet: 1840-1926*, The Art Institute of Chicago, 1995, no. 42, repro., as *The Stroll, Camille Monet and Her Son Jean (Woman with a Parasol)*
- *Rings: Five Passions in World Art*, High Museum of Art, Atlanta, 1996
- *An Enduring Legacy: Masterpieces from the Collection of Mr. and Mrs. Paul Mellon*, National Gallery of Art, Washington, D.C., 1999-2000
- *The Impressionists at Argenteuil*, National Gallery of Art, Washington, D.C.; Wadsworth Atheneum, Hartford, 2000
- *Impressionist and Post-Impressionist Masterpieces from the National Gallery of Art*, The Museum of Fine Arts, Houston; The National Art Center, Tokyo; Kyoto Municipal Museum of Art, 2011, no. 31, repro.
- *Monet: Framing Life*, Detroit Institute of Arts, 2017-2018, no. 6, repro.
- *Riffs and Relations: African American Artists and the European Modernist Tradition*, The Phillips Collection, Washington, D.C., 2020-2021, pl. 1

TECHNICAL NOTES

The painting is executed on a fine, plain-weave canvas. The technique is characterized by animated brushwork throughout, particularly vigorous in the sky where choppy strokes create the impression of moving clouds. Long, swift strokes of white paint across the female figure's face suggest a veil fluttering in the breeze. The meadow is rendered with abbreviated, comma-like brushstrokes in varying shades of green interspersed with yellow and purple wildflowers.

DESCRIPTION AND INTERPRETATION

This work represents one of Monet's most significant figure paintings from his productive period in Argenteuil (1871-1877). It depicts his first wife Camille standing on a hillside, holding a green parasol against a brilliant blue sky with white clouds. Their seven-year-old son Jean appears in the lower left, visible only from the waist up due to the rising ground, creating a sense of spatial depth.

The painting exemplifies Impressionist technique with its emphasis on capturing ephemeral effects of light and atmosphere. Monet employs a low vantage point, presenting Camille monumentally against the sky, her white dress and veil animated by the wind. The bright sunlight from behind illuminates the top of her parasol and dress, while colored reflections from the meadow below touch her front with yellow highlights.

Painted outdoors (*en plein air*) in a single session, the work conveys the spontaneity of a casual family outing rather than a formal portrait. Monet delineates the features of his subjects with the same free brushwork used for their surroundings, breaking from academic portrait conventions. The painting received positive critical attention when exhibited at the second Impressionist exhibition in 1876.

Ten years later, Monet returned to this subject with two paintings featuring his second wife's daughter Suzanne with a parasol in Giverny (now in the Musée d'Orsay), works that consciously recalled this earlier image of Camille.

BIBLIOGRAPHY

- Wildenstein, Daniel. *Claude Monet: biographie et catalogue raisonné*. 5 vols. Lausanne and Paris, 1974-1991: no. 381.
- Walker, John. *National Gallery of Art, Washington*. Rev. ed. New York, 1984: 483, no. 714.
- Bernard, Bruce. *The Impressionist Revolution*. London, 1986: 254.
- Tucker, Paul Hayes. *Claude Monet: Life and Art*. New Haven, 1995: 86-87.
- Kopper, Philip. *America's National Gallery of Art: A Gift to the Nation*. New York, 1991: 264, 266, 277.

CURRENT LOCATION

National Gallery of Art, Washington, D.C., Gift of Paul Mellon, 1983 (1983.1.29)

Fig. 7.2 Output from Claude Opus 4.1 (prompted with basic prompt and multimodal RAG; web search: active). Image input: Claude Monet, *Woman with a Parasol Madame Monet and Her Son* (); Prompt: "Write a description for this image in the style of a catalogue raisonné." The prompt was complemented with a list of references for better-quality RAG. Image source: https://www.nga.gov/artworks/61379-woman-parasol-madame-monet-and-her-son

precise historical data about the title, year, and exhibition history, with relative sources cited in the bibliography. While it still needs human supervision, at first glance, the catalogue is accurate and includes information that can be verified based on bibliography, current location, and older catalogues, although it failed to produce actual references for each section. Given LLMs' capability to reproduce human linguistics and reasoning, many art historians have been questioning whether AI will reduce the need for art historians, with widespread concerns for the replacement of human expertise by machines. This proof of concept demonstrates the exact opposite: especially when it comes to LLMs, AI majorly relies on human insight and will fail to operate successfully without quality data and well-constructed prompts. Deploying AI assistants to co-curate catalogues along with human specialists in critical ways can help facilitate the manual labour of comparing different versions and resources, provided that the machine model is accurately directed to reference updated digital versions. Concurrently, involving human experts in the loop can help in improving the quality of LLMs outputs. This operation does not diminish the value of art historical work, or the value of art. On the contrary, art historical work is ever more fundamental not only to direct the models to quality outputs but also to qualitatively evaluate their results.

Given the amount of information available online on Monet's work, I tested Claude Opus 4.1 again without a list of pre-curated references. The model returned detailed outputs even without additional training, drawing from institutional and non-institutional web sources from which information was extracted and summarised with related citations. By comparing the outputs returned in Figs. 7.2 and 7.3, we notice that historical information is the same in both outputs, but descriptive language changes. Figure 7.3 shows that the model prompted with basic instructions paraphrased sources found online, without a specific selection for academic sources. However, Fig. 7.2, generated taking an RAG approach, features information from scholarly essays and authoritative material, keeping concise language and minimising unnecessary commentaries. RAG can also help avoid LLMs hallucinations, which can stem from limitations in training data, among other factors,[22] but might be partially resolved by intervening manually in the selection of sources.

This analysis suggests two points for reflection. First, as VLMs are becoming important cultural tools, when allowed and with respect for

[22] cf. https://cloud.google.com/discover/what-are-ai-hallucinations.

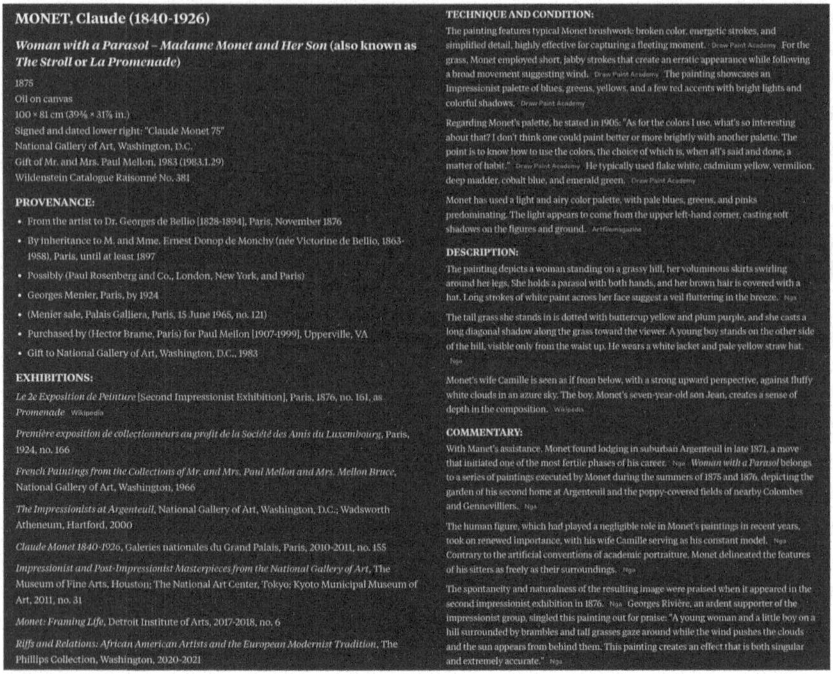

MONET, Claude (1840-1926)

***Woman with a Parasol – Madame Monet and Her Son* (also known as *The Stroll* or *La Promenade*)**

1875

Oil on canvas

100 × 81 cm (39⅜ × 31⅞ in.)

Signed and dated lower right: "Claude Monet 75"

National Gallery of Art, Washington, D.C.

Gift of Mr. and Mrs. Paul Mellon, 1983 (1983.1.29)

Wildenstein Catalogue Raisonné No. 381

PROVENANCE:

- From the artist to Dr. Georges de Bellio [1828-1894], Paris, November 1876
- By inheritance to M. and Mme. Ernest Donop de Monchy (née Victorine de Bellio, 1863-1958), Paris, until at least 1897
- Possibly (Paul Rosenberg and Co., London, New York, and Paris)
- Georges Menier, Paris, by 1924
- (Menier sale, Palais Galliera, Paris, 15 June 1965, no. 121)
- Purchased by (Hector Brame, Paris) for Paul Mellon [1907-1999], Upperville, VA
- Gift to National Gallery of Art, Washington, D.C., 1983

EXHIBITIONS:

Le 2e Exposition de Peinture [Second Impressionist Exhibition], Paris, 1876, no. 161, as *Promenade* Wikipedia

Première exposition de collectionneurs au profit de la Société des Amis du Luxembourg, Paris, 1924, no. 166

French Paintings from the Collections of Mr. and Mrs. Paul Mellon and Mrs. Mellon Bruce, National Gallery of Art, Washington, 1966

The Impressionists at Argenteuil, National Gallery of Art, Washington, D.C.; Wadsworth Atheneum, Hartford, 2000

Claude Monet 1840-1926, Galeries nationales du Grand Palais, Paris, 2010-2011, no. 155

Impressionist and Post-Impressionist Masterpieces from the National Gallery of Art, The Museum of Fine Arts, Houston; The National Art Center, Tokyo; Kyoto Municipal Museum of Art, 2011, no. 31

Monet: Framing Life, Detroit Institute of Arts, 2017-2018, no. 6

Riffs and Relations: African American Artists and the European Modernist Tradition, The Phillips Collection, Washington, 2020-2021

TECHNIQUE AND CONDITION:

The painting features typical Monet brushwork: broken color, energetic strokes, and simplified detail, highly effective for capturing a fleeting moment. Draw Paint Academy For the grass, Monet employed short, jabby strokes that create an erratic appearance while following a broad movement suggesting wind. Draw Paint Academy The painting showcases an Impressionist palette of blues, greens, yellows, and a few red accents with bright lights and colorful shadows. Draw Paint Academy

Regarding Monet's palette, he stated in 1905: "As for the colors I use, what's so interesting about that? I don't think one could paint better or more brightly with another palette. The point is to know how to use the colors, the choice of which is, when all's said and done, a matter of habit." Draw Paint Academy He typically used flake white, cadmium yellow, vermilion, deep madder, cobalt blue, and emerald green. Draw Paint Academy

Monet has used a light and airy color palette, with pale blues, greens, and pinks predominating. The light appears to come from the upper left-hand corner, casting soft shadows on the figures and ground. Artfilemagazine

DESCRIPTION:

The painting depicts a woman standing on a grassy hill, her voluminous skirts swirling around her legs. She holds a parasol with both hands, and her brown hair is covered with a hat. Long strokes of white paint across her face suggest a veil fluttering in the breeze. Nga

The tall grass she stands in is dotted with buttercup yellow and plum purple, and she casts a long diagonal shadow along the grass toward the viewer. A young boy stands on the other side of the hill, visible only from the waist up. He wears a white jacket and pale yellow straw hat. Nga

Monet's wife Camille is seen as if from below, with a strong upward perspective, against fluffy white clouds in an azure sky. The boy, Monet's seven-year-old son Jean, creates a sense of depth in the composition. Wikipedia

COMMENTARY:

With Manet's assistance, Monet found lodging in suburban Argenteuil in late 1871, a move that initiated one of the most fertile phases of his career. Nga *Woman with a Parasol* belongs to a series of paintings executed by Monet during the summers of 1875 and 1876, depicting the garden of his second home at Argenteuil and the poppy-covered fields of nearby Colombes and Gennevilliers. Nga

The human figure, which had played a negligible role in Monet's paintings in recent years, took on renewed importance, with his wife Camille serving as his constant model. Nga Contrary to the artificial conventions of academic portraiture, Monet delineated the features of his sitters as freely as their surroundings. Nga

The spontaneity and naturalness of the resulting image were praised when it appeared in the second impressionist exhibition in 1876. Nga Georges Rivière, an ardent supporter of the impressionist group, singled this painting out for praise: "A young woman and a little boy on a hill surrounded by brambles and tall grasses gaze around while the wind pushes the clouds and the sun appears from behind them. This painting creates an effect that is both singular and extremely accurate." Nga

Fig. 7.3 Output from Claude 4 Opus (basic prompting without RAG; web search: active). Image input: Claude Monet, *Woman with a Parasol - Madame Monet and Her Son* (1875); Prompt: "Write a description for this image in the style of a catalogue raisonné." Draw Paint Academy, Artfilemagazine, NGA (National Gallery of Art). Wikipedia indicates the web source from which information was extracted. Image source: https://www.nga.gov/artworks/61379-woman-parasol-madame-monet-and-her-son

intellectual property, it is imperative to transition old forms of art historical documentation into open-access digital assets and structured databases—within the necessary regulatory frameworks—to make it retrievable by AI models. This is beneficial not only for model training or fine-tuning, but also for improving the accuracy of foundation LLMs by granting them accessibility to authoritative art historical sources via structured prompting techniques. Second, there is a need to fine-tune models (when possible) on low-resource or underrepresented art histories and cultures to compensate for the overrepresentation of Western art in VLMs' datasets and online art documentation resources, which, even when not prompted by the input image and/or text, might end up skewing the results.

From a few tests run in parallel to Monet's case study, in instances where the model is exposed to non-Western art or abstract art paintings, accuracy was more likely to be compromised. In particular, as shown in Figs. 7.4 and 7.5, without RAG the model repeatedly fails to recognise not only the title and author, but also a primary reference to build upon for recreating the conventional structure of a catalogue raisonné. Both the Japanese print and the cubist painting used for testing display a similar subject compared to Monet's work (i.e., woman with parasol), respectively showing an image from an art tradition and aesthetic that Monet is known to have drawn from[23] and an image that draws from his work using a different art style. The results show evidence that without RAG and a human-curated list of references, the model is not able to give as accurate an output as in other more widely documented examples. Fields in these outputs are often listed as "Unknown," or "Untitled," or filled with sentences that expose seemingly missing data, e.g., "to be determined," "to be documented," "to be assessed," or else "no documented exhibitions identified," or "no known published references," whereas both paintings are in fact available in the public domain and have been documented online as part of the MET collection (New York, US) and the Museo Nacional Thyssen-Bornemisza (Madrid, Spain).

To this point, it is important to reiterate that LLMs mainly rely on statistical inference, meaning the number of examples and documentation available on a given artwork in the training set or else from online resources will inevitably impact the ability of the model to opt for the preferred description if the dataset lacks enough occurrences, likely leading to poor performance for underrepresented art objects in the training dataset. On the contrary, we might assume that Monet's work is highly represented on the web and therefore in the training datasets, which are mostly composed by data scraped from the Internet. Notable artworks are abundantly documented online, providing the machine with various occurrences, which are likely to lead to better AI outputs when prompted to provide an image

[23] While Monet is not known to have collected this particular work from Kitagawa Utamaro, the impressionist French painter had been widely exposed to his work through his own collection of woodblock prints from the Edo period, which are now held in archives and collections at the Musée Marmottan Monet in Giverny. Source: https://claudemonet-giverny.fr/en/decouvrir/les-estampes-japonaises/.

[Woman with Parasol and Fan]
Bijin-ga (Picture of a Beautiful Woman)

Artist: [To be determined - signature visible on parasol]
Period: Late Edo period, likely 1790s-1820s
Medium: Woodblock print (*nishiki-e*); ink and color on paper
Format: *Ōban* (large format)
Dimensions: Approximately 38 x 26 cm (standard *ōban* size)
Publisher: [Seal visible but requires identification]
Signature: Artist's signature and publisher's seal present on parasol handle

Description: This refined example of *bijin-ga* depicts an elegantly dressed woman in three-quarter profile, exemplifying the sophisticated portrayal of feminine beauty characteristic of late Edo period *ukiyo-e*. The subject holds a large parasol (*wagasa*) rendered in subtle gradations of blue-gray with radiating golden spokes, while delicately grasping a folding fan (*ōgi*) decorated in alternating bands of coral and yellow. Her outer garment (*uchikake*) displays a rich purple-brown tone with small decorative motifs, worn over under-robes visible at the collar in the traditional layered style (*kasane no irome*). The geometric patterning of her *obi* suggests a checkered design in green and gold tones.

The composition demonstrates the characteristic "serpentine posture" (*yugami*) noted in *ukiyo-e* scholarship, with the figure's body creating an elegant S-curve while her face turns in partial profile. Her coiffure, rendered with delicate linear strokes typical of the period's printmaking technique, shows the elaborate styling of the late Edo period. The pale complexion and refined features conform to period beauty ideals, with the small rosebud mouth and elongated face typical of the style's evolution in the 1790s-1810s.

Technical Notes: The print displays the sophisticated polychrome printing (*nishiki-e*) techniques developed in the 1760s, with evidence of careful color registration and possible use of *kirazuri* (mica) or *karazuri* (blind embossing) techniques, though closer examination would be required for confirmation. The paper shows characteristic aging consistent with Edo period production.

Comparative Works: The style and subject treatment show affinities with the *bijin-ga* traditions established by Kitagawa Utamaro (1753-1806) and continued by artists of the Utagawa school. The emphasis on textile patterns and the elegant positioning of accessories particularly recalls the work of artists active in the Bunka-Bunsei eras (1804-1830).

Condition: [To be assessed - visible aging and slight discoloration consistent with age]

Provenance: [To be documented]

Literature: Further research required to identify specific artist and series attribution. The presence of text on the parasol suggests this may be part of a series with literary or poetic associations, common in *bijin-ga* of this period.

Fig. 7.4 Output from Claude Opus 4.1 (basic prompting without RAG; web search: active). Image input: Kitagawa Utamaro, *Woman Holding Up a Parasol* (from the series *Ten Classes of Women's Physiognomy*, original title: Fujo *ninsō juppen: Higasa o sasu onna*), (ca. 1792–93); Prompt: "Write a description for this image in the style of a catalogue raisonné." Image source: https://www.metmuseum.org/art/collection/search/55319. The model correctly identifies the artwork as a woodblock print in the *Ukiyo-e* style, but fails to provide more detailed and accurate information about the artist, title, or provenance history

[Artist Unknown]
Untitled (Abstract Composition with Curved Forms)
Date: [Unknown, likely early-to-mid 20th century based on style]
Oil on canvas
Dimensions: [Not available]
Location: [Unknown]

Description

This dynamic abstract composition demonstrates the artist's engagement with early twentieth-century modernist principles, particularly the liberation of color and form from representational constraints. The work features boldly delineated curvilinear shapes in a vibrant palette of red, green, blue, yellow, purple, pink, black, and white against areas of unpainted or lightly treated canvas.

The composition centers on an energetic arrangement of interlocking curved forms that appear to radiate outward from a loose central axis. The artist employs broad, confident brushstrokes to define each color area, with visible evidence of the painting process preserved in the surface texture. The forms suggest movement and rhythm, creating a sense of visual dynamism characteristic of early abstract movements.

Technical Observations

The painting exhibits a direct painting technique with areas of color applied in what appears to be a single or limited number of layers. The brushwork varies from smooth, even applications in some color fields to more gestural passages where the artist's hand is clearly evident. The boundaries between colors are generally decisive, though some areas show evidence of wet-on-wet blending, particularly in transitional zones between forms.

Stylistic Context

The work's formal vocabulary—emphasizing pure color relationships, dynamic curved forms, and non-objective composition—aligns with several early twentieth-century abstract movements. The emphasis on color interaction and rhythmic composition suggests possible connections to Orphism, a movement that emerged in Paris around 1912-1913 and emphasized the lyrical possibilities of pure abstraction through color and light. The bold, simplified forms and vibrant palette also recall aspects of Fauvism's liberation of color from descriptive function.

Without additional documentation regarding provenance, exhibition history, or artist attribution, further scholarly contextualization remains speculative. The work nonetheless represents a significant example of early-to-mid twentieth-century abstract painting, demonstrating the period's experimental approach to color, form, and compositional dynamics.

Condition

[Condition assessment not available from photographic documentation alone]

Provenance

[Unknown]

Exhibition History

[No documented exhibitions identified]

Literature

[No known published references]

Fig. 7.5 Output from Claude Opus 4.1 (basic prompting without RAG; web search: active). Image input: Robert Delaunay, *Woman with a Parasol* (1913); Prompt: "Write a description for this image in the style of a catalogue raisonné." Image source: https://www.museothyssen.org/en/collection/artists/delaunay-robert/woman-parasol. The model surprisingly locates the painting in the correct stylistic context (citing the Cubo-Futurists principle of simultaneity named "Orphism," or "Orphic Cubism" by Apollinaire), but still struggles to give information about artist, title, or provenance history description in the style of an art catalogue. While the backend functioning of LLMs still needs further exploration, we can conclude that in either instance—whether we are dealing with a famous painting or with a lesser known artwork—RAG is a valid solution to manually direct language models to preferred authoritative sources and inform them with the necessary human knowledge to produce a quality output. By the same token, RAG can be used as a technique to expose lack of documentation available online in cases when the model fails to retrieve correct information about a given artwork, artist, or art movement from external knowledge sources.

Incorporating Getty Vocabularies in VLMs

While catalogues raisonnés represent an important source of information about art objects and carry a formal language, when using a VLM for art object description and documentation, an even more specific reference to standardised language resources might be needed to improve the quality of the results. For instance, in addition to catalogues raisonnés, other digital references, such as the Getty Art & Architecture Thesaurus (AAT), can be successfully integrated in the pipeline to provide the model with controlled vocabularies and standardised terms for an accurate description of art objects based on agreed-upon naming conventions. Getty AAT covers fields such as materials and techniques, object types and components, styles and periods, processes and activities, physical attributes, associated concepts and disciplines, and cultural contexts (as general concepts). By incorporating structured vocabularies in RAG, multimodal LLMs can be prompted to use field-specific terminology, ensuring greater precision in art image description (cf. Fig. 7.6).

For example, let us consider an instance where a researcher uses an LLM to generate a description of a typical Renaissance quadratura, an illusionistic ceiling painting technique common in Renaissance, Baroque, and Rococo art. We can assume that leveraging controlled vocabularies via RAG would instruct an LLM to adopt specific terms such as "sfumato," "chiaroscuro," or "trompe l'oeil" (all of which are featured in Getty's AAT as preferred terms) rather than opting for more generic terms. These AAT terms describe a specific effect of three-dimensional depth on two-dimensional surfaces, as opposed to terms like "nuanced" or "contrasted" or "deceptive" that would not carry the same descriptive precision and insight into the history of artistic techniques. To test this hypothesis, I prompted Claude Opus 4.1 to use the AAT's controlled terms and

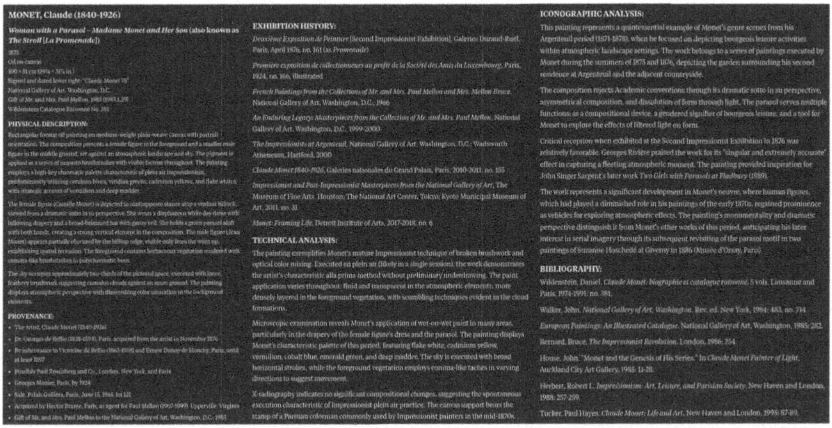
MONET, Claude (1840-1926)

Woman with a Parasol – Madame Monet and Her Son (also known as *The Stroll* [*La Promenade*])

1875

Oil on canvas

100 × 81 cm (39⅜ × 31⅞ in.)

Signed and dated lower right: "Claude Monet 75"

National Gallery of Art, Washington, D.C.

Gift of Mr. and Mrs. Paul Mellon, 1983 (1983.1.29)

Wildenstein Catalogue Raisonné No. 381

PHYSICAL DESCRIPTION:

Rectangular format oil painting on medium-weight plain-weave canvas with portrait orientation. The composition presents a female figure in the foreground and a smaller male figure in the middle ground, set against an atmospheric landscape and sky. The pigment is applied in a series of impasto brushstrokes with visible facture throughout. The painting employs a high-key chromatic palette characteristic of plein air Impressionism, predominantly utilising cerulean blues, viridian greens, cadmium yellows, and flake whites, with strategic accents of vermilion and deep madder.

The female figure (Camille Monet) is depicted in contrapposto stance atop a verdant hillock, viewed from a dramatic sotto in su perspective. She wears a diaphanous white day dress with billowing drapery and a broad-brimmed hat with gauzy veil. She holds a green parasol aloft with both hands, creating a strong vertical element in the composition. The male figure (Jean Monet) appears partially obscured by the hilltop edge, visible only from the waist up, establishing spatial recession. The foreground contains herbaceous vegetation rendered with comma-like brushstrokes in polychromatic hues.

The sky occupies approximately two-thirds of the pictorial space, executed with loose, feathery brushwork suggesting cumulus clouds against an azure ground. The painting displays atmospheric perspective with diminishing color saturation in the background elements.

PROVENANCE:

- The artist, Claude Monet (1840-1926)
- Dr. Georges de Bellio (1828-1894), Paris, acquired from the artist in November 1876
- By inheritance to Victorine de Bellio (1863-1958) and Ernest Donop de Monchy, Paris, until at least 1897
- Possibly Paul Rosenberg and Co., London, New York, and Paris
- Georges Menier, Paris, by 1924
- Sale, Palais Galliera, Paris, June 15, 1965, lot 121
- Acquired by Hector Brame, Paris, as agent for Paul Mellon (1907-1999), Upperville, Virginia
- Gift of Mr. and Mrs. Paul Mellon to the National Gallery of Art, Washington, D.C., 1983

EXHIBITION HISTORY:

Deuxième Exposition de Peinture [Second Impressionist Exhibition], Galeries Durand-Ruel, Paris, April 1876, no. 161 (as *Promenade*)

Première exposition de collectionneurs au profit de la Société des Amis du Luxembourg, Paris, 1924, no. 166, illustrated

French Paintings from the Collections of Mr. and Mrs. Paul Mellon and Mrs. Mellon Bruce, National Gallery of Art, Washington, D.C., 1966

An Enduring Legacy: Masterpieces from the Collection of Mr. and Mrs. Paul Mellon, National Gallery of Art, Washington, D.C., 1999-2000

The Impressionists at Argenteuil, National Gallery of Art, Washington, D.C.; Wadsworth Atheneum, Hartford, 2000

Claude Monet 1840-1926, Galeries nationales du Grand Palais, Paris, 2010-2011, no. 155

Impressionist and Post-Impressionist Masterpieces from the National Gallery of Art, The Museum of Fine Arts, Houston; The National Art Center, Tokyo; Kyoto Municipal Museum of Art, 2011, no. 31

Monet: Framing Life, Detroit Institute of Arts, 2017-2018, no. 6

TECHNICAL ANALYSIS:

The painting exemplifies Monet's mature Impressionist technique of broken brushwork and optical color mixing. Executed en plein air (likely in a single session), the work demonstrates the artist's characteristic alla prima method without preliminary underdrawing. The paint application varies throughout: fluid and transparent in the atmospheric elements, more densely layered in the foreground vegetation, with scumbling techniques evident in the cloud formations.

Microscopic examination reveals Monet's application of wet-on-wet paint in many areas, particularly in the drapery of the female figure's dress and the parasol. The painting displays Monet's characteristic palette of this period, featuring flake white, cadmium yellow, vermilion, cobalt blue, emerald green, and deep madder. The sky is executed with broad horizontal strokes, while the foreground vegetation employs comma-like taches in varying directions to suggest movement.

X-radiography indicates no significant compositional changes, suggesting the spontaneous execution characteristic of Impressionist plein air practice. The canvas support bears the stamp of a Parisian colorman commonly used by Impressionist painters in the mid-1870s.

ICONOGRAPHIC ANALYSIS:

This painting represents a quintessential example of Monet's genre scenes from his Argenteuil period (1871-1878), when he focused on depicting bourgeois leisure activities within atmospheric landscape settings. The work belongs to a series of paintings executed by Monet during the summers of 1875 and 1876, depicting the garden surrounding his second residence at Argenteuil and the adjacent countryside.

The composition rejects Academic conventions through its dramatic sotto in su perspective, asymmetrical composition, and dissolution of form through light. The parasol serves multiple functions: as a compositional device, a gendered signifier of bourgeois leisure, and a tool for Monet to explore the effects of filtered light on form.

Critical reception when exhibited at the Second Impressionist Exhibition in 1876 was relatively favorable. Georges Rivière praised the work for its "singular and extremely accurate" effect in capturing a fleeting atmospheric moment. The painting provided inspiration for John Singer Sargent's later work *Two Girls with Parasols at Fladbury* (1889).

The work represents a significant development in Monet's oeuvre, where human figures, which had played a diminished role in his paintings of the early 1870s, regained prominence as vehicles for exploring atmospheric effects. The painting's monumentality and dramatic perspective distinguish it from Monet's other works of this period, anticipating his later interest in serial imagery through its subsequent revisiting of the parasol motif in two paintings of Suzanne Hoschedé at Giverny in 1886 (Musée d'Orsay, Paris).

BIBLIOGRAPHY:

Wildenstein, Daniel. *Claude Monet: biographie et catalogue raisonné*. 5 vols. Lausanne and Paris, 1974-1991: no. 381.

Walker, John. *National Gallery of Art, Washington*. Rev. ed. New York, 1984: 483, no. 714.

European Paintings: An Illustrated Catalogue. National Gallery of Art, Washington, 1985: 282.

Bernard, Bruce. *The Impressionist Revolution*. London, 1986: 254.

House, John. "Monet and the Genesis of His Series." In *Claude Monet Painter of Light*, Auckland City Art Gallery, 1985: 11-28.

Herbert, Robert L. *Impressionism: Art, Leisure, and Parisian Society*. New Haven and London, 1988: 257-259.

Tucker, Paul Hayes. *Claude Monet: Life and Art*. New Haven and London, 1995: 87-89.

Fig. 7.6 Output from Claude Opus 4.1 (prompted using structured prompting and multimodal RAG, web search: active). Image input: Claude Monet, *Woman with a Parasol - Madame Monet and Her Son* (1875); Prompt: "Write a description for this image in the style of a catalogue raisonné. Use language terminology from Getty Art & Architecture Thesaurus (AAT)." Image source: https://www.nga.gov/artworks/61379-woman-parasol-madame-monet-and-her-son

generate a new description of the same Monet painting originally selected as a case study for this set of experiments.

Compared to Fig. 7.2, the output did produce a slightly more technical description using standardised language, as follows: "Rectangular format *oil painting* on medium-weight *plain-weave* canvas with *portrait* orientation. The composition presents a female figure in the foreground and a smaller male figure in the middle ground, set against an atmospheric landscape and sky. The *pigment* is applied in a series of *impasto brushstrokes* with visible facture throughout. The painting employs a high-key chromatic palette characteristic of *plein air Impressionism*, predominantly utilising *cerulean blues, viridian greens, cadmium yellows*, and *flake whites*, with strategic accents of *vermilion* and *deep madder*" (cf. Figure 7.6, *Physical Description*). At second glance, however, this experiment does present some issues, sometimes producing logically unclear strings of text like "a series of impasto brushstrokes with *visible facture throughout*" or else reporting non-verified information like "medium-weight plain-weave canvas."

In this example, prompting the VLM to use terminology from controlled vocabularies via RAG does not seem to be as effective or reliable as simply referencing an existing catalogue. As shown in the next paragraph, a combined approach might be preferable, prompting the model to both reference a list of authoritative resources and use domain-specific terminology from controlled vocabularies. Alternatively, if no authoritative cataloguing resources are available, more fine-tuning might be needed to train a specialised model on domain-expert knowledge.

Although it is not always possible to predict the extent of marginal improvements in the model in relation to upfront computational costs, fine-tuning LLMs remains a valuable option, particularly in the lack of already published digital catalogues raisonnés and other online resources, or in use-cases where LLMs are deployed as instrumental methods to support the creation of new cataloguing resources in art documentation workflows. In such use-cases, a small language model could ensure not only consistency in the language used in the AI-generated text, but also accuracy of information included in the outputs. It is important to note that an RAG approach still offers, in most cases, the easiest implementation path and, while not technically "training" the model, achieves similar goals of incorporating domain-specific knowledge. Another accessible alternative is vector search, which requires indexing the domain of knowledge in vector databases without the need for any modification to the underlying model itself.

Combining Catalogues Raisonnés With Vocabularies for Enhanced Accuracy

Leveraging both catalogues raisonnés and controlled vocabularies via structured LLM prompting and RAG provides a dual advantage: on the one hand, the comprehensive, contextual richness from catalogues, where images are often paired with detailed textual descriptions, and on the other hand the standardised, consistent terminology from thesauri. A multimodal LLM that integrates and references both resources is likely to generate more detailed and accurate image captions with precise art historical language. To verify this assumption, I ran a third test by instructing the model to retrieve catalogue raisonné descriptions from digital catalogues about Claude Monet as well as Getty vocabularies terms. The hypothesis was that this strategy would direct the model to summarise contextual historical details from catalogues raisonnés and adopt the

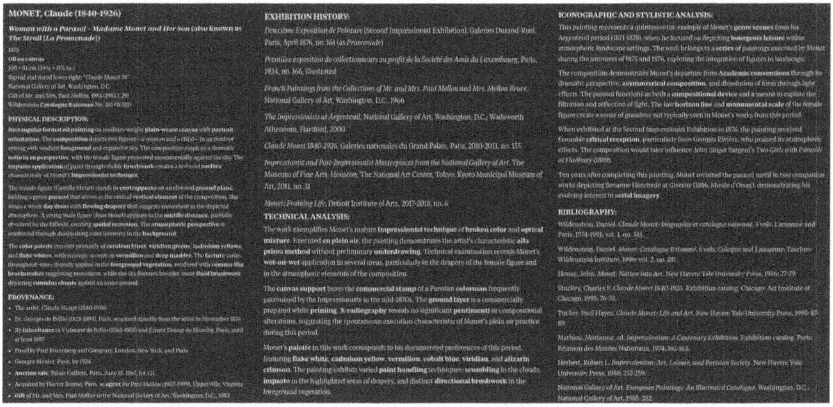

MONET, Claude (1840-1926)

***Woman with a Parasol - Madame Monet and Her Son* (also known as *The Stroll* [*La Promenade*])**

1875

Oil on canvas

100 × 81 cm (39⅜ × 31⅞ in.)

Signed and dated lower right: "Claude Monet 75"

National Gallery of Art, Washington, D.C.

Gift of Mr. and Mrs. Paul Mellon, 1983 (1983.1.29)

Wildenstein **Catalogue Raisonné** No. 381 (W381)

PHYSICAL DESCRIPTION:

Rectangular format oil painting on medium-weight **plain-weave canvas** with **portrait orientation**. The **composition** depicts two figures—a woman and a child—in an outdoor setting with verdant **foreground** and expansive sky. The composition employs a dramatic **sotto in su perspective**, with the female figure presented monumentally against the sky. The **impasto application** of paint through visible **brushwork** creates a textured **surface** characteristic of Monet's **Impressionist technique**.

The female figure (Camille Monet) stands in **contrapposto** on an elevated **ground plane**, holding a green **parasol** that serves as the central **vertical element** of the composition. She wears a white **day dress** with **flowing drapery** that suggests movement in the depicted atmosphere. A young male figure (Jean Monet) appears in the **middle distance**, partially obscured by the hillside, creating **spatial recession**. The **atmospheric perspective** is reinforced through diminishing color intensity in the **background**.

The **color palette** consists primarily of **cerulean blues**, **viridian greens**, **cadmium yellows**, and **flake whites**, with strategic accents in **vermilion** and **deep madder**. The **facture** varies throughout: more densely applied in the **foreground vegetation**, rendered with **comma-like brushstrokes** suggesting movement, while the sky features broader, more **fluid brushwork** depicting **cumulus clouds** against an azure ground.

PROVENANCE:

- The artist, Claude Monet (1840-1926)
- Dr. Georges de Bellio (1828-1894), Paris, acquired directly from the artist in November 1876
- By **inheritance** to Victorine de Bellio (1863-1958) and Ernest Donop de Monchy, Paris, until at least 1897
- Possibly Paul Rosenberg and Company, London, New York, and Paris
- Georges Menier, Paris, by 1924
- **Auction sale**, Palais Galliera, Paris, June 15, 1965, lot 121
- Acquired by Hector Brame, Paris, as **agent** for Paul Mellon (1907-1999), Upperville, Virginia
- **Gift** of Mr. and Mrs. Paul Mellon to the National Gallery of Art, Washington, D.C., 1983

EXHIBITION HISTORY:

Deuxième Exposition de Peinture [Second Impressionist Exhibition], Galeries Durand-Ruel, Paris, April 1876, no. 161 (as *Promenade*)

Première exposition de collectionneurs au profit de la Société des Amis du Luxembourg, Paris, 1924, no. 166, illustrated

French Paintings from the Collections of Mr. and Mrs. Paul Mellon and Mrs. Mellon Bruce, National Gallery of Art, Washington, D.C., 1966

The Impressionists at Argenteuil, National Gallery of Art, Washington, D.C.; Wadsworth Atheneum, Hartford, 2000

Claude Monet 1840-1926, Galeries nationales du Grand Palais, Paris, 2010-2011, no. 155

Impressionist and Post-Impressionist Masterpieces from the National Gallery of Art, The Museum of Fine Arts, Houston; The National Art Center, Tokyo; Kyoto Municipal Museum of Art, 2011, no. 31

Monet: Framing Life, Detroit Institute of Arts, 2017-2018, no. 6

TECHNICAL ANALYSIS:

The work exemplifies Monet's mature **Impressionist technique** of **broken color** and **optical mixture**. Executed **en plein air**, the painting demonstrates the artist's characteristic **alla prima method** without preliminary **underdrawing**. Technical examination reveals Monet's **wet-on-wet** application in several areas, particularly in the drapery of the female figure and in the atmospheric elements of the composition.

The **canvas support** bears the **commercial stamp** of a Parisian **colorman** frequently patronized by the Impressionists in the mid-1870s. The **ground layer** is a commercially prepared white **priming**. **X-radiography** reveals no significant **pentimenti** or compositional alterations, suggesting the spontaneous execution characteristic of Monet's plein air practice during this period.

Monet's **palette** in this work corresponds to his documented preferences of this period, featuring **flake white**, **cadmium yellow**, **vermilion**, **cobalt blue**, **viridian**, and **alizarin crimson**. The painting exhibits varied **paint handling** techniques: **scumbling** in the clouds, **impasto** in the highlighted areas of drapery, and distinct **directional brushwork** in the foreground vegetation.

ICONOGRAPHIC AND STYLISTIC ANALYSIS:

This painting represents a quintessential example of Monet's **genre scenes** from his Argenteuil period (1871-1878), when he focused on depicting **bourgeois leisure** within atmospheric landscape settings. The work belongs to a **series** of paintings executed by Monet during the summers of 1875 and 1876, exploring the integration of figures in landscape.

The composition demonstrates Monet's departure from **Academic conventions** through its dramatic perspective, **asymmetrical composition**, and dissolution of form through light effects. The parasol functions as both a **compositional device** and a means to explore the filtration and reflection of light. The low **horizon line** and **monumental scale** of the female figure create a sense of grandeur not typically seen in Monet's works from this period.

When exhibited at the Second Impressionist Exhibition in 1876, the painting received favorable **critical reception**, particularly from Georges Rivière, who praised its atmospheric effects. The composition would later influence John Singer Sargent's *Two Girls with Parasols at Fladbury* (1889).

Ten years after completing this painting, Monet revisited the parasol motif in two companion works depicting Suzanne Hoschedé at Giverny (1886, Musée d'Orsay), demonstrating his evolving interest in **serial imagery**.

BIBLIOGRAPHY:

Wildenstein, Daniel. *Claude Monet: biographie et catalogue raisonné*. 5 vols. Lausanne and Paris, 1974-1991, vol. 1, no. 381.

Wildenstein, Daniel. *Monet: Catalogue Raisonné*. 5 vols. Cologne and Lausanne: Taschen-Wildenstein Institute, 1996: vol. 2, no. 381.

House, John. *Monet: Nature into Art*. New Haven: Yale University Press, 1986: 27-29.

Stuckey, Charles F. *Claude Monet 1840-1926*. Exhibition catalog. Chicago: Art Institute of Chicago, 1995: 76-78.

Tucker, Paul Hayes. *Claude Monet: Life and Art*. New Haven: Yale University Press, 1995: 87-89.

Mathieu, Marianne, ed. *Impressionism: A Centenary Exhibition*. Exhibition catalog. Paris: Réunion des Musées Nationaux, 1974: 162-163.

Herbert, Robert L. *Impressionism: Art, Leisure, and Parisian Society*. New Haven: Yale University Press, 1988: 257-259.

National Gallery of Art. *European Paintings: An Illustrated Catalogue*. Washington, D.C.: National Gallery of Art, 1985: 282.

Fig. 7.7 Output from Claude Opus 4.1 (prompted using structured prompting and multimodal RAG, web search: active). Image input: Claude Monet, *Woman with a Parasol - Madame Monet and Her Son* (1875); Prompt: "Write a description for this image in the style of a catalogue raisonné. Use language terminology from Getty Art & Architecture Thesaurus (AAT)." The prompt was complemented with a list of references for better-quality RAG. Image source: https://www.nga.gov/artworks/61379-woman-parasol-madame-monet-and-her-son

preferred terminology from controlled vocabularies. This approach was taken to generate the output in the example in Fig. 7.7.

As shown in Fig. 7.7, for the same image of a painting by Claude Monet used in previous testing—*Woman with a Parasol – Madame Monet and Her Son*—the VLM did combine memorised information from Monet's documented works from authoritative sources (e.g., *Claude Monet: The Revised Catalogue Raisonné*) and the relevant entries from Getty's AAT, as instructed in the prompt. When compared to Fig. 7.2 from the first series of tests, this output shows a more technical language, particularly in listing the colours or the style, displaying both provenance information and details about painting techniques used in this painting. While this confirms the initial hypothesis, much like in output shown in Fig. 7.6, a second look reveals some imprecisions. For instance, the figure is described as taking a "contrapposto posture," falling into over-interpretation and adopting overly manneristic language that risks being grammatically and syntactically correct yet semantically nonsensical.

Compared to Fig. 7.6, Fig. 7.7 also does not show much difference in the amount of additional information about the artwork's provenance and exhibition history, leading to a fundamental question: Is an AI's catalogue raisonné just a syntactic reformulation of and variation on material available online? If so, is an RAG approach enough to interpolate additional human knowledge and expertise into AI models? Or is a deeper level intervention needed through fine-tuning to alter the semantic structure of LLMs? As in most cases, different approaches should be evaluated on a case-by-case basis, taking into consideration the subject of the research, existing documentation, and the scope of use of the LLM as a tool.

Preliminary Considerations

Overall, these exploratory tests show that an RAG approach to LLM, alongside structured prompting techniques, can lead to improvements in the model's ability to contextualise art historical information and use appropriate language for art description in a co-curatorial process that features art historians and experts. Of all the examples in this proof of concept, online catalogues raisonnés seem to provide the richest historical and contextual information to the VLMs, even more so than controlled vocabularies. This is particularly evident in the first set of experiments, where pointing to existing authoritative resources and online catalogues raisonnés does show a considerable difference in the quality of the outputs. As perhaps expected, given the multimodal nature of VLMs, when instructed to reference a pre-curated list of authoritative resources the model was able to correctly describe not only the visual elements of an artwork, but also its significance in art history and provenance contexts.

Effectively, being able to source information from digital catalogues raisonnés appears to help the model avoid generic, superficial, or erroneous captions, providing context that aligns with scholarly interpretations of the work. Additionally, even more than vocabularies, the inclusion of authoritative information sourced from the Internet also improved the quality of AI-generated description. Monet's examples show that, as expected when the model's web search feature is on, Claude Opus 4.1 will likely opt for integrating additional art documentation available in the public domain—including museum exhibition catalogues and other art historical texts. Although not explored in this chapter, since this proof of concept specifically focuses on art catalogues, one could run more testing to evaluate multimodal LLMs' accuracy when instructed to retrieve academic papers to offer additional insight into art analysis. While RAG strategies to connect LLMs to digital art catalogues can help the model generate captions that are not only descriptive but can also adapt to different socio-cultural and historical interpretations, the examples above show that more work is needed to prevent errors or hallucinations. For instance, further VLM fine-tuning will require curating multiple datasets for training smaller, specialised LLMs on more specific tasks (e.g., reconstructing provenance histories through available archival material) in order to avoid the pitfalls of foundation AI models, such as high computational demand, scarce error management, and training inefficiencies. The right combination of specialised datasets can be used to create a model able to interpret art images with more accuracy even when the corpus falls outside of the Western canon.

To expand on the first few experiments (Figs. 7.4 and 7.5), in taking a more critical stance on co-curatorial approaches for compiling digital catalogues based on open-access art museum collections, I ran additional tests on lesser known artworks by instructing the LLM to generate text using art history's terminologies for materials, techniques, and periods. Due to the lack of digital catalogues to reference, the AI-generated text did feature standardised terms from controlled vocabularies, but failed to generate accurate information. This proves, once again, that curating and sharing more online catalogues raisonnés is emerging as a priority not only for art historical documentation, but also for improving VLMs through catalogue data compiled by human experts. Once rendered machine-readable and prepared for LLM research and development, online catalogues raisonnés can serve as unique resources for machine training and validation, by providing a ground truth for the training, testing, and evaluation of VLMs.

In this sense, the benefits of framing a theory and practice of an "AI's catalogue raisonné" are both functional—in that this framework promotes the development of AI-based archival and curatorial tools that can support the work of art experts in compiling digital catalogues—and epistemological—in that it fosters the study of art to finally enter the domain of computer science in a reciprocal exchange. This would ensure that AI-generated knowledge contains reliable, historically grounded, and semantically meaningful information drawing from decades of art historical research. As many researchers in AI and cultural heritage have advocated (Hendricks 2017; Dekker and Tedone 2019; Taurino 2022), human-algorithmic curation in AI is essential as both a directional force, in practices like prompt engineering and RAG, and as an evaluative force that ensures the quality of AI-generated image descriptions.

For critical and ethical purposes, feedback from art historians, curators, and specialists is ever more essential to assess the quality and relevance of the AI-generated text in art image descriptions and identify outdated information or obsolete language inherited from older catalogue editions. Agreeing with this statement, the scope of the proof of concept presented here is not to show how AI can decode aesthetic elements and provide automated art analysis at a granular level substituting the work of art historians, but rather to call art experts into action to tweak, redact, and correct AI's catalogues raisonnés in ways that can lead to fruitful cooperation and new paths for research and knowledge creation.

Conclusion

In this chapter, I outlined the history and relevance of catalogues raisonnés as essential tools for scholars, curators, and collectors, offering a record of an artist's work, biography, and other collateral information about exhibition and acquisition histories. From early attempts at systematic cataloguing in the eighteenth century to the digital databases of today, the development of catalogues raisonnés has mirrored advancements in art historical scholarship. Delving into the multifaceted nature of catalogues throughout art history and contemporary practice, I emphasised the importance of modern catalogues raisonnés as both dynamic texts and grounded empirical sources. With their critical insights into art movements, creators, and objects, art catalogues not only shed light on the socio-cultural contexts and historical narratives behind artworks, but also carry information on specialised terminology for art description.

Acknowledging their importance in art history, I considered how, in recent years, heritage institutions and publishers have challenged traditional approaches to printed catalogues as static products, proposing instead to treat them as dynamic digital processes for knowledge design and data sharing on art historical information. In line with recent experiments with digital editions and remodelling initiatives of catalogues as databases, in this chapter, online catalogues raisonnés are discussed as flexible, multivalent texts that produce meaning through both language and visual displays. Such a perspective opens up to new avenues not only for reinterpreting physical catalogues and reimagining them in digital versions, but also for examining them as techno-cultural tools for engaging in a conversation with AI and emerging contemporary practices of art documentation.

With this in mind, I presented some examples from a broader series of experiments with VLMs to test AI on specialised art knowledge. This exploratory work served as a proof of concept to introduce the notion of an AI's catalogue raisonné, or better yet, of many AIs' catalogues raisonnés, which exist within LLMs as more and more digitised or born-digital art catalogues become available in the public domain. Through this proof of concept we observed that online catalogues raisonnés can indeed act as dynamic, active agents in art historiography and AI alike, by revealing insights into the functions, purposes, and interpretations of artworks in the past and transitioning them into the future. As new technologies and methodologies shape the field, future catalogues raisonnés will likely transform into even more comprehensive and accessible resources, preserving the legacy of artists for future generations at the intersection of human and computational co-curatorial documentation practices.

Drawing from preliminary explorations, this chapter also demonstrates the importance of acquiring new competences in AI in order for art historians and experts to gain agency over the already widespread process of engaging with AI technologies. Now that computers have acquired new sets of technical capabilities based on linguistic training from human-generated texts, more than ever before, humanists can contribute to the conversation on the development and application of AI tools in critical ways, addressing the advantages, but also risks, biases, and ethical concerns, of generative AI and the making of what we might call "machine knowledge." In this mutual exchange between technology and the arts, art historians and experts are needed to take on the continuous curation of data necessary to regulate the quality of AI-generated outputs and prevent AI models from producing misleading or false statements.

In the future, by incorporating art historical knowledge in VLMs and improving AI-generated descriptions of art historical objects, we could envisage new applications of AI tools in art history, archival studies, and museums. For instance, in art historical research, quality LLMs could be used to process large volumes of data to identify patterns, relationships, and anomalies within ever-growing historical documentation, catalogues, and databases of art objects. Or else, LLMs might offer new ways to explore the evolving meanings of catalogues as themselves cultural objects, allowing for dynamic updates and reinterpretations in real time. In museums, specialised LLMs instructed with pre-curated prompts could help museum-goers navigate the histories of artworks at a deeper level of interactions, in ways that would be possible only in a guided tour. Several institutions have already made experiments in this direction, trying to integrate generative AI in order to create more interactive, informative, and inclusive museum experiences. For instance, in 2023, the National Gallery of Singapore developed an AI guide that leverages NExT-GPT to rethink conventional visitors' experiences and explore new, perhaps unexplored art itineraries.[24]

While many of these explorations in generative AI and museum collections are still proofs of concept, they do pave the way for critical reflections about the inevitable intersection between AI and cultural heritage. In the current information landscape, human-curated text found in online catalogues is bound to become a fundamental component of a much broader humanistic pursuit to make generative AI models not only technically sound and ethically aware, but also responsive to the complexities of human cultural production, exchange, and evolutions. As much as catalogues raisonnés can transform the course of AI, being able to accurately leverage LLMs for the creation of catalogues raisonnés could transform traditional art historical methods, museology, and archival practice by making historical records more accessible, adaptable, and inclusive, perhaps even opening new points of inquiry or problematising existing knowledge frameworks.

As we set out to explore more possibilities for reimagining the online catalogue raisonné in its process of entering AI culture, it is equally important to restate that AI tools must be deployed with critical understanding of the many layers embedded in both AI and art catalogues as "sociotechnical information infrastructure(s)" (Turner 2016, 163). As language models evolve, adapting traditional art cataloguing resources to digital workflows and online open-access publications will be key to advancing the accuracy and relevance of AI-generated art documentation.

References

Ames, S., and S. Lewis. 2020. Disrupting the Library: Digital Scholarship and Big Data at the National Library of Scotland. *Big Data & Society* 7 (2): 1–7. https://doi.org/10.1177/2053951720970576.

[24]https://www.ncs.co/en-sg/knowledge-centre/articles/generative-AI-guide-creates-truly-immersive-inclusive-and-hyper-personalised-museum-experiences/.

Bachimont, Bruno. 2007. Nouvelles tendances applicatives: de l'indexation à l'éditorialisation. In *L'indexation multimédia*. Paris: Hermès. http://cours.ebsi.umontreal.ca/sci6116/Ressources_files/BachimontFormatHerme%CC%80s.pdf.

Bartz, C., N. Jain, and R. Krestel. 2020. Automatic Matching of Paintings and Descriptions in Art-Historic Archives using Multimodal Analysis. In *Proceedings of the International Workshop on Artificial Intelligence for Historical Image Enrichment and Access* (AI4HI), 23–28.

Bellori, Giovanni Pietro. 1672. *Vite de' Pittori, Scultori ed Architetti Moderni.*

Blessing, A., and K. Wen. 2010. Using Machine Learning for Identification of Art Paintings. *Tech Report* 5.

Cetinic, E., T. Lipic, and S. Grgic. 2018. Fine-Tuning Convolutional Neural Networks for Fine Art Classification. *Expert Systems Applications* 114:107–118. https://doi.org/10.1016/j.eswa.2018.07.026.

Chen, J. 2018. Comparison of Machine Learning Techniques for Artist Identification. https://www.semanticscholar.org/paper/Comparison-of-Machine-Learning-Techniques-for-Chen/8cf70f05a9582fb3383c6c465bd4e7a608631dc2.

Dekker, A., and G. Tedone. 2019. Networked Co-Curation: An Exploration of the Socio-Technical Specificities of Online Curation. *Arts* 8 (3): 86. https://doi.org/10.3390/arts8030086.

Dobbs, Todd, Aileen Benedict, and Zbigniew Ras. 2022. Jumping Into the Artistic Deep End: Building the Catalogue Raisonné. *AI & Society* 37 (3): 873–889. https://doi.org/10.1007/s00146-021-01370-2.

Freddolini, Francesco, and Anne Helmreich. 2014. Inventories, Catalogues and Art Historiography: Exploring Lists Against the Grain. *Journal of Art Historiography* 11:1–14. https://arthistoriography.files.wordpress.com/2014/11/freddolini_helmreich_introduction.pdf.

Gemini G.E.L. and National Gallery of Art. 2001. *Gemini G.E.L. Catalogue Raisonné.* Los Angeles and Washington, DC. www.geminigel.com.

Hendricks, Manique. 2017. The Algorithm as Curator: In Search of a Non-Narrated Collection Presentation. *Stedelijk Studies Journal* 5. https://doi.org/10.54533/StedStud.vol005.art11.

John, Dennis Michael. 2023. *Highpoint Editions: A History & Catalogue, 2001–2021.* Panorama.

Johnson, C., E. Hendriks, I. Berezhnoy, E. Brevdo, S. Hughes, I. Daubechies, J. Li, E. Postma, and J. Wang. 2008. Image Processing for Artist Identification. *IEEE Signal Processing Magazine* 25 (4): 37–48. https://doi.org/10.1109/MSP.2008.923513.

Keating, Jessica, and Lia Markey. 2011. Introduction: Captured Objects, Inventories of Early Modern Collections. *Journal of the History of Collections* 23 (2): 209–2013. https://doi.org/10.1093/jhc/fhq035.

Kondo, K., and T. Hasegawa. 2020. CNN-based Criteria for Classifying Artists by Illustration Style. In *Proceedings of the 2020 2nd International Conference on Image. Video and Signal Processing*, 93–98. https://doi.org/10.1145/3388818.3389163.

McDowall, Georgina, Navigating.art. n.d. *How AI Empowers Scholarship and Digital Catalogues Raisonnés*. https://www.navigating.art/articles-from-navigatingart/how-ai-empowers-scholarship-and-digital-catalogues-raisonns.

Mensink, T., and J. van Gemert. 2014. The Rijksmuseum Challenge: Museum-Centered Visual Recognition. In *Proceedings of International Conference on Multimedia Retrieval*. Association for Computing Machinery, Glasgow. https://doi.org/10.1145/2578726.2578791.

Monet, Claude. 1875. *Woman with a Parasol—Madame Monet and Her Son*. Washington, DC: National Gallery of Art.

Neely, L., and E. Leon. 2024. Reimagining the Catalogue Raisonné as Generative Digital Scholarship. *International Journal for Digital Art History* 9:5.58–5.69. https://doi.org/10.11588/dahj.2023.9.95286.

Pereira, G., and B. Moreschi. 2020. Artificial Intelligence and Institutional Critique 2.0: Unexpected Ways of Seeing with Computer Vision. *AI & Society* 36:1201–1223. https://doi.org/10.1007/s00146-020-01059-y.

Rinaldo, Constance, Diane Rielinger, Joseph Deveer, and Danielle Castronovo. 2023. Connecting Libraries, Archives, and Museums: Collections in Support of Natural History Science. *Journal of Computer Cultural Heritage* 16 (1): 3. https://doi.org/10.1145/3570905.

Rogers, K. 2015. Viewpoint: The Catalogue Raisonné. Scholars Association (CRSA). https://doi.org/10.1017/S0307472200000146.

Rouart, Denis, and Daniel Wildenstein. 1975. *Edouard Manet: Catalogue Raisonné* (2 vols.), Paris: La Biblioteque des Arts.

Sinatra, Michael E., and Marcello Vitali-Rosati. dir. 2014. *Pratiques de l'édition numérique* (édition augmentée). Montréal: Presses de l'Université de Montréal. ISBN: 978-2-7606-3592-0. https://www.parcoursnumeriques-pum.ca/1-pratiques/introduction.html.version1. Accessed 1 March 2014.

Srinivasan, R., R. Boast, J. Furner, and K. M. Becvar. 2009. Perspective: Digital Museums and Diverse Cultural Knowledges: Moving Past the Traditional Catalogue. *The Information Society* 25:265–278.

Strezoski, G., and M. Worring. 2017. OmniArt: Multi-task Deep Learning for Artistic Data Analysis. ArXiv:1708.00684 [Cs]. http://arxiv.org/abs/1708.00684.

Stuber, T., and Jennifer Way. 2025. Digital Dialogues. *Panorama. Journal of the Association of Historians of American Art* 11 (1). https://doi.org/10.24926/24716839.19942.

Turner, H. 2016. The Computerisation of Material Culture Catalogues: Objects and Infrastructure in the Smithsonian Institution's Department of

Anthropology. *Museum Anthropology* 39:163–177. https://doi.org/10.1111/muan.12122.

Taurino, Giulia. 2022. Experiments in Machine Unlearning: On Algorithmic Curation and Museums Marginalia. Special Issue: Critical Making, Critical Design. in The Digital Review, Issue 01. https://www.thedigitalreview.com/issue01/taurino-machine/begin.html.

Viswanathan, N. 2017. Artist Identification with Convolutional Neural Networks. https://www.semanticscholar.org/paper/Artist-Identification-with-Convolutional-Neural-Viswanathan-Stanford/dafe87bf57c4413d769de46af78f7e4305087838.

Vitali-Rosati, Marcello. 2016. "What is editorialization?" Sens Public. http://sens-public.org/article1059.html.

Vitali-Rosati, Marcello. 2018. *On Editorialization: Structuring Space and Authority in the Digital Age. Theory on Demand 26.* Amsterdam: Institute of Network Cultures. http://networkcultures.org/blog/publication/tod-26-oneditorialization-structuring-space-and-authority-in-the-digital-age/.

Voelker, Emily L. Digital-Born Catalogues Raisonnés and Networked Art Histories. Panorama: Journal of the Association of Historians of American Art 9, no. 1 (Spring 2023). https://doi.org/10.24926/24716839.17354.

Way, Jennifer, and Tracy Stuber. 2023. Section Theme: Digital Catalogues Raisonnés. *Panorama: Journal of the Association of Historians of American Art* 9 (1). https://doi.org/10.24926/24716839.17222.

Weiß, Lisa. 2023. More Than Just a Database: The Endless Possibilities of Digital Catalogues Raisonnés. *Panorama: Journal of the Association of Historians of American Art* 9 (1). https://doi.org/10.24926/24716839.17157.

Zervos, Christian. 1932. *Pablo Picasso: Catalogue Raisonné.* Paris: Editions Cahiers d'Art.

CHAPTER 8

Curating the Algorithm: An Educational Encounter With AI and Art Exhibitions

Bárbara Romero Ferrón and Nuria Rodríguez Ortega

Introduction

This chapter presents an experimental workshop that critically investigates the potential and limitations of generative artificial intelligence in curatorial practice. Framed within the broader context of digital humanities, art history, and museum studies, the workshop *Picasso and AI: Analysing and*

This chapter is an output of the Complexhibit Project, entitled "Study and Interpretation of the Domain of Art Exhibitions as a Complex Cultural System through Data Analytics and Natural Language Processing" (PID2021-125037NB-I00), funded by the Spanish Ministry of Science, Innovation and Universities, Government of Spain, and led by Nuria Rodríguez-Ortega and of the Telefónica-UMA Chair (5G, Digital Culture and Next-Generation Technologies for Society)

B. R. Ferrón
Leuphana University Lüneburg, Lüneburg, Germany
e-mail: barbara.romero_ferron@leuphana.de

N. R. Ortega (✉)
University of Málaga, Málaga, Spain
e-mail: nro@uma.es

L. Cempellin, M. Geiger (eds.), *Reimagining Art History with Artificial Intelligence*,
https://doi.org/10.1007/978-3-032-21685-4_8

Questioning the Technology That Overwhelms Us invited students and professionals to work directly with generative algorithms in the development of exhibition narratives. To understand the motivations and structure behind this initiative, it is essential to consider the two specific disciplinary foundations that underpin it: exhibition studies and critical curatorial practice.

The chapter is structured into three parts. First, it presents an introduction and a state of the art on scholarly and practical approaches to the intersection of exhibitions and curatorial AI, and second, a detailed explanation of the process of designing and implementing the proposed workshop, including the conceptual and technical aspects. The final third section reflects on the insights gained in this experience, and the possibilities of adapting and reproducing this workshop in other contexts.

A Look Into Temporary Exhibitions and Curatorial AI

Since the 1960s, scholars have dedicated part of their work to exploring this connection, seeking ways to create a meaningful integration.[1] The intersection between art history and computational technologies has continued to evolve since then, providing new materials for artistic expression and identifying patterns and correspondences that foster creative agency. As technology advances, the discipline integrates new tools and methodologies that provide new opportunities for humanities research. In art history, technological innovations present opportunities and challenges for analysing artworks and understanding how museums and art institutions adapt to an increasingly algorithmic future.

The so-called algorithmic society, in which we are all currently living, where interpersonal and cultural connections, relationships, consumption, and even creative production are mediated by algorithms, has introduced and, by now, established a new understanding of social imbalances, as sovereignty becomes governed and structured by automated processes (Burrell and Fourcade 2021). These interconnections and entangled perspectives are also reflected in cultural productions, such as exhibitions and

[1] For early examples of computational approaches to art history research, see Jules David Prown (1967). The historical integration of computing into artistic practice has also been explored through major exhibitions in the last few years, including *Coded: Art Enters the Computer Age, 1952–1982* (Jones et al. 2023) and *Radical Software: Women, Art & Computing, 1960–1991* (Cotton and Beaumont 2024).

their narratives. These new technological approaches are shaping how stories are constructed, which voices are amplified (but also silenced), and how cultural meaning is produced and distributed. A performative exhibition space emerges in which digital objects, new media, technological infrastructure, and computational agents take shape, consolidating new sets of interactions and relationships that construct new narratives based on new kinds of objects. Although machines, culture, and artistic production have long interacted, the rise of artificial intelligence has taken a dominant role, from machine learning algorithms to generative text and image models. These newly established systems of production have reshaped how these interactions are understood within cultural and artistic institutions. Particularly in the field of art exhibitions, a crucial question arises: Can generative artificial intelligence transform and shape curatorial narratives and curatorial work? This question poses a Lovelace objection: Do machines even think? A considerable corpus of scholarly publications has sought to answer this question from many perspectives, including the cognitive sciences, ethics, computer science, and even studies of creativity and algorithms. To introduce this topic to art history students and museum professionals, our research group designed a workshop to explore the potential and limitations of AI systems in curatorial practice and the conceptualisation of art exhibitions.

The design of this workshop was shaped by another guiding question: What skills will art historians need to navigate this transformation? With the widespread adoption of generative artificial intelligence systems, access to these tools has become more democratised, making them, sometimes, part of our daily lives. As scholars working on interdisciplinary research combining computational methodologies and art history and as educators, we have encountered these challenges in our research projects and our efforts to design a curriculum[2] that adapts museum studies, curatorial practices, and art history to contemporary developments.

To better understand the motivations of the workshop, we focus on two key aspects: exhibitions and generative AI. To explore their intersection, we first need a clear understanding of why exhibitions are an essential

[2] This workshop is just one in a long-standing series of workshops and seminars, alongside the international Summer School (DAHSS), that the iArtHis_Lab research group have designed and organised since 2016. Together, these initiatives represent a major contribution to the field of art history and its intersection with computational methodologies and artificial intelligence. https://dahss.iarthislab.eu/2024/.

and compelling subject of study for this workshop, serving as the perfect paradigm for analysing the functional logic of generative AI.

Temporary exhibitions are an essential component of cultural institutions and art galleries. Exhibitions establish a dynamic arena in which objects, curatorial narratives, and spatial design are deliberately orchestrated to create a coherent, meaningful visitor experience. Each exhibition is a polyhedron of connections; in other words, it is a space where diverse artistic objects are brought together, where multiple individuals contribute to its creation—from curators and artists to technicians and designers—and where numerous visitors engage with the result, each bringing their own perspectives and interpretations. Temporary exhibitions mirror the interests, values, and narratives of their specific socio-cultural and temporal context. These narratives, the topics on which the exhibition reflects, are shaped by broader cultural and societal shifts and the vision of the curator. Since the first decades of the twentieth century, the figure of the curator has become a vital part of a cultural institution. Curators act as coordinators, crafting exhibition narratives through meticulous research and bringing together diverse components, from artworks, lighting, sound, and text, to design (typographies, colours…), into a whole that intends to communicate a message to the public. However, curators, as individuals, bring their own perspectives, biases, and interpretive frameworks to exhibitions. As such, exhibitions are inherently human constructs—not only because the objects on display are typically created by humans (mountmakers) or represent aspects of human experience, but also because of the re-signification processes that occur through their curation. When artworks are placed in dialogue with one another, they acquire new layers of meaning and emotional resonance shaped by human interpretation.

The collaboration between technology and exhibitions has taken many forms. It has given artists the possibility of expanding their artistic production, and curators the opportunity to apply transformation in their curatorial work, especially in their relationships with the exhibition public (Li et al. 2024b). The inclusion of technology or digital components in exhibitions has supported learning, interpretation, and knowledge transfer for diverse audiences by creating a more accessible, inclusive, and interactive museum space (Chen et al. 2022; Tam and Hui 2024). Asta et al. (2024) analysed the level of visitor engagement with new technologies in exhibitions over the last few years. The study concluded that these technologies contributed to an 85 per cent improvement in visitor engagement. This is one example of the many studies conducted in recent years to measure the impact of new technologies in the museum sector related to educational goals and public engagement (Li et al. 2024a; Malik et al. 2023). This demonstrates that integrating technology into exhibition design and narrative is not only here to stay but also enhances the museum experience and offers a wide range of new possibilities.

Moreover, since the COVID-19 pandemic, the creation of digital exhibitions, designed to be entirely digital from their conceptualisation to their final design, has opened new possibilities and redefined what an exhibition space is and how curatorial work needs evolve and adapt to these new digital environments (Kamariotou et al. 2021; King et al. 2021; Zidianakis et al. 2021). The intersection of new technologies, such as virtual reality and 3D scanning, with exhibitions and museum collections has opened new possibilities for creating new digital narratives that revitalise collections and enhance visitors' engagement with specific objects, e.g., by creating 3D models that allow visitors to interact with them digitally. The selection of objects for digitisation, the creation of 3D models, or even the inclusion of specific objects in digital exhibitions reintroduces systems of hierarchies and silences (Aristova et al. 2020; Beale et al. 2022; Liu and Chang 2024; Khalil et al. 2023). This selective process reflects underlying biases that must be critically considered in the development of digital curatorial strategies.

In our workshop, we extended this line of work, in which digital and computational methods are applied in exhibitions, by exploring another possibility: What if exhibitions were not just supported by digital tools but actually produced and curated by technology itself? What if generative AI took an active role in designing and shaping exhibitions? To explore this possibility, we built on the work of scholars and curators who have already begun investigating the role of AI in curatorial practices. In 2008, Joasia Krysa introduced the concept of "software curating," referring to automated curatorial practices. She proposed integrating socio-technological networks into the curatorial process, highlighting how computational systems could play an active role in curatorial decision-making and exhibition design (Krysa 2008). Algorithmic curation is not purely autonomous; it is deeply intertwined with human intervention, as algorithms are trained by humans, and their outputs are shaped by human influence.

Experimentation with the possibilities of AI systems in curatorial projects is already underway, encompassing a wide range of approaches. Some initiatives focus on archive curation, such as the *Digital Curator Project*

(2019–2022), developed by Lukas Pilka, which employs computer vision technologies to explore and reorganise image archives through textual search, with the objective of designing thematic exhibitions. In this project, human agency is based on textual searching, prompting, and selection of the objects; however, other projects take a more speculative or performative direction, incorporating pseudo-humanoid systems that simulate human curatorial roles. The project *AI Jarvis*, presented as one of the curators of the 2022 Bucharest Biennale, was introduced with human-like attributes, including nationality, voice, and even gender identity (Batycka 2022). The case of *AI Jarvis* illustrates how AI can be a performative human-like agent that challenges traditional notions of curatorial authorship and presence.

These experimental projects study the possibilities of applying AI to curatorial practices while engaging with the critical challenges. Following that research path, Srinivasan (2024) emphasises further tensions within techno-human forms of collaboration, such as the overrepresentation of Western cultural frameworks and questions of authorship in artistic production. These issues highlight significant ethical concerns about biases and the algorithms' logic. However, aren't these concerns just a reflection of the systemic biases already present in our cultural institutions? These biases and logic are not brand new; therefore, the next question is: Does generative curation reinforce and perpetuate these imbalances rather than disrupt them and create new venues? These questions just showcase the need for a critical approach that interrogates the implications of algorithmic curation. To move beyond the limitations of algorithmic curation, scholarly publications have introduced the concept of "co-curation", which shifts the focus away from the final generated outcomes and instead emphasises the creative process (Dekker 2024; Dekker and Tedone 2019).

The focus on the process, unlike fully automated curation, makes co-curation a model that acknowledges human agency. In this approach, curators engage with AI-generated content by actively intervening in the process and significantly shaping its outcomes. In other words, rather than allowing the machine to independently generate and define all the content and concepts for the exhibition, the process becomes a form of supervised collaboration—where human insight, critical judgement, and curatorial intention work alongside the machine's generative capabilities. While this new understanding of curation does not eliminate bias, since both the algorithm and curators bring their own biases, it fosters a conscious, reflective curatorial practice. The concept of co-curation frames curatorial processes as conscious and dynamic exchanges rather than solely automated outputs, where critical approaches to technology are recognised as an integral part of the process (Krysa and Impett 2020).

Critical Considerations

When this workshop explores "generative curating" or "AI-curating", it does not simply focus on the technical application of algorithms within the creation and design of exhibitions; rather, it constitutes an ongoing discussion and negotiation that touches on authorship, creativity, ethics, and technological advances. In the last few years, artificial intelligence tools have increasingly become part of curatorial workflows; these practices invite and challenge us to rethink contemporary curating and explore new modes of cultural production shaped by machine collaboration. In this chapter, we will focus on three key aspects: authorship and legitimacy, narrative coherence and critical capacity, and ethics and accountability.

Traditionally, art history has focused on questions such as authorship and legitimacy, driven by the importance of authenticity. Therefore, AI contributes to decision-making—suggesting works, organising themes, or even generating texts, but who is credited as the curator? While these algorithms operate within human-defined parameters and are trained on existing datasets, labelled by humans, their capacity to produce unexpected associations or autonomous outputs blurs the current understanding on the relationship among tool, author, and collaborator. These new existing tensions invite a critical reassessment of both the legal definitions and the symbolic frameworks that traditionally structure curatorial authorship.

Equally important is the issue of narrative coherence and critical capacity. Machine learning algorithms successfully process large amounts of information and recognise patterns. However, their understanding of context, history, abstract concepts, and nuance remains limited. This raises concerns: Are these "new" narratives reproducing existing patterns? There is an existing risk of producing curatorial narratives generated or shaped by AI that reflect superficial patterning or reproduce the biases embedded in training data, rather than offering critical engagement or interpretive richness. Here, critical thinking and algorithm literacy are key. The absence of critical thinking in the production of new narratives risks reinforcing the very hegemonic discourses that museums and cultural institutions have been working to challenge for decades.

Another important aspect to consider is the significant ethical implications involved in integrating AI into curatorial work. Questions emerge around transparency: How are decisions made? What algorithms are being used? On which data are they trained? Moreover, without rigorous human supervision, any algorithmic process can reinforce existing biases and inequalities based on the data it is trained on. That can amplify the underrepresentation of specific already marginalised groups or cultures, or using these new technologies primarily for spectacle, reducing curatorial practice to technological novelty and distracting from a more complex and rich cultural reflection. One of the central aspects of using AI in exhibition and narrative-making should be to ensure accountability and, thus, to create good practices from the beginning, building on them.

At the same time, the creative and experimental potential of generative curating should not be dismissed or overlooked. AI's capacity to highlight connections, navigate large and diverse archives, and suggest combinations beyond human intuition, thanks to its processing capacity, opens new curatorial possibilities. In this context, human–machine collaboration can give rise to hybrid curatorial models, where the curator is not replaced but extended—benefiting from the strengths of both human criticality and algorithmic capacity. Therefore, "generative curating" or "AI-curating" demands a reconceptualisation of the curatorial process itself. Now, the curatorial practice is no longer uniquely connected to human agency but is shaped by an interplay of machine intelligence, knowledge, research questions, and, most importantly, ethical responsibility, which is crucial.

These three pillars constitute the theoretical and critical framework for this workshop, serving as a practical testing ground for these ideas. The workshop allows participants to confront the complexities discussed above through hands-on experimentation. This introduction thus provides the conceptual foundation needed to contextualise the design, implementation, and reflections that follow.

The Workshop: Picasso, Generative Artificial Intelligence, and the Curating of Exhibitions

The workshop, *Picasso and AI: Analysing and Questioning the Technology that Overwhelms Us*,[3] equipped future museum and art history professionals with an understanding of generative AI algorithms and their potential applications. The workshop focused on two key areas: image classification and text generation, using open-source algorithms. The principal idea was to create a hands-on learning experience, and for that, we used Picasso's artistic production and the scholarly publications about his work as the primary corpus for applying these AI tools. The choice of Picasso was intentional, linked to our affiliation with the University of Málaga, his birthplace, and to the cultural programme for the local anniversary commemorating his legacy in 2023. This workshop offered art history and museum studies students a foundation for engaging with generative AI and learning how it works, while critically examining the underlying operational logic of these user-friendly interfaces. The workshop focused on the design, creation, and curation of an art exhibition using two distinct algorithms: OpenAI's GPT-3.5 for generating curatorial narratives and OpenAI's CLIP (Contrastive Language–Image Pre-training) for retrieving and selecting images.

Textual and Visual Picasso Corpora

To work with the two models of generative AI, we needed two distinct corpora: a textual and a visual corpus. For the textual corpus,[4] we collected scholarly publications focused on various aspects of Picasso's life and work. To facilitate the mass downloading of this information, we chose the

[3] This workshop took place in October 2023 under the coordination of Nuria Rodríguez Ortega and featured contributions from researchers Bárbara Romero Ferrón, María Ortiz Tello, and Alejandro Mozo. It was organised by the Telefónica UMA Chair (5G, Digital Culture and Next-Generation Technologies for Society) within the framework of the Complexhibit Project (Ref. PID2021-125037NB-I00). Full information about the workshop is available at: http://catedratelefonicauma.es/actividades/picasso-y-la-ia/

[4] This textual corpus is openly published, matching our goals of reproduction of this same workshop by other educators. You can find the links to all the corpora, materials, tools, and resources on Zenodo. https://doi.org/10.5281/zenodo.14778367. This open-source approach reinforces our commitment to replicability, enabling the workshop to be readily adapted and implemented in other institutional and pedagogical contexts.

Spanish repository Dialnet, which allows for bulk downloads of indexed publications. Since obtaining entire texts in plain format was impractical and the corpus would have been too large to handle with user-friendly, free generative AI interfaces, we collected only metadata: title, author, journal or publisher, place of publication, publication date, abstract, and keywords.

For the visual corpus, we gathered images of Picasso's works from institutions and online repositories like WikiArt and Wikipedia. These images were not collected with the intention of publication but were used solely for educational purposes. For the same educational reason, we did not aim to collect high-resolution images or those with complex backgrounds or specific artistic styles. The image corpus did not include detailed metadata about the artworks themselves. In most cases, the titles of the images were not the actual titles of the objects depicted.

Selection of Algorithms

The next step in developing this workshop was selecting the generative AI algorithms to use. For the text component, where participants would perform text mining analysis and generate the narrative for their exhibition, we decided to use ChatGPT, as participants were familiar with the platform. This platform uses, as its name suggests, a specific version of the Generative Pre-trained Transformer (GPT),[5] which operates through two stages: pre-training and fine-tuning. During pre-training, the algorithm learns patterns in textual language by analysing vast amounts of data, such as books, articles, and websites. In the fine-tuning stage, it refines its understanding by adjusting the model with specific datasets and tasks to enhance its ability to generate coherent and contextually appropriate text. Through this process, the model can produce fluent, cohesive responses. We asked participants to use the free version, and for those who did not want to create accounts under their own names, we provided email addresses created for this activity. This allowed them to participate without sharing personal data with OpenAI. For the visual analysis, we chose another algorithm developed by OpenAI: Contrastive Language–Image Pre-training (CLIP), to analyse the image corpus.[6] CLIP has been trained on a large corpus of image–text pairings. It uses neural networks to

[5] See: https://huggingface.co/docs/transformers/en/model_doc/openai-gpt.

[6] See: https://openai.com/index/clip/.

connect textual concepts to visual sources, enabling it to create multimodal connections between images and text. However, OpenAI no longer provides a user-friendly platform for this algorithm. As a result, we used the Hugging Face platform to download and feed the model with our visual corpus of Picasso's works. We then created a simple, user-friendly interface named "PicassoAI"[7] (https://amozo.es/PicassoAIg/) that allowed participants to interact with the CLIP algorithm and our Picasso corpus.

Generative Curation of a Picasso Exhibition

The mission of each section of this workshop—the textual and the visual—varied in terms of how the algorithms work and how they were intended to function. The textual part, using ChatGPT, was focused on the narrative development for the exhibition. To achieve this, we divided the textual corpus by decade, with each group of participants working with publications about Picasso from a different time. The information collected was minimal but sufficient for ChatGPT to perform a text mining analysis, identifying common topics and keywords within the studies. Once each group selected the topics, the next step was to generate a narrative. The second part of the textual section involved interacting with AI to create the narrative for the exhibition. In this way, the two sections simulated the functioning of the algorithms: participants supplied textual input that served as a form of training data, and based on that input, the algorithm generated a curatorial narrative. For instance, one group focused their exhibition on the theme of motherhood in Picasso's artistic production, using this concept as the central axis of their curatorial proposal.

Once participants finished their narrative, the next step was to select the objects from Picasso's artistic production that best illustrated their ideas. The "PicassoAI" interface allowed participants to enter textual inputs, which generated a list of images from Picasso's artistic production based on their semantic proximity to the selected term. For example, if participants entered "motherhood" as a textual prompt, "PicassoAI" produced images accompanied by scores indicating how strongly each image represented the concept, based on CLIP, previously described. We did not train this model; it was pre-trained. It simply applied its learned text-image pairings to our Picasso corpus. Through this process, participants were

[7] See: http://amozo.es/PicassoAIg/.

able to select images that reflected their generated narrative. At the end of these two sections, participants created a textual and visual narrative for an exhibition about Picasso entirely generated by AI.

Workshop Takeaways

Beyond the final exhibitions (which, given the dataset, all focused on Picasso), the primary objective of this workshop was to explore how AI can shape curatorial practices, fostering new interactions and connections within the exhibition creation and design process. During the workshop, participants learned how AI can assist in exhibition-making and began to question its implications for curatorial practice and the role of technology in shaping exhibition narratives. This activity aimed to train future museum professionals and is part of an ongoing discussion on the intersection of museum exhibitions and AI.

Potentialities of Generative AI in Curatorial Contexts

A key insight from the workshop was the recognition of generative AI as a tool for augmenting curatorial creativity. Through the processing of extensive textual and visual corpora, AI systems such as ChatGPT and CLIP enabled participants to identify recurrent themes—such as the rise of decolonial or feminist perspectives on Picasso's work in recent decades—uncover latent conceptual connections, and draft preliminary exhibition narratives with notable efficiency. This ability to navigate large datasets and suggest patterns offers considerable promise for curators tasked with exploring expansive archives or reinterpreting well-studied figures such as Picasso.

Generative AI facilitates narrative experimentation by proposing novel associations and juxtapositions that might challenge traditional curatorial logics. As demonstrated during the workshop, AI systems can disrupt and change linear, chronological, or even stylistic narratives by surfacing unexpected themes. This aligns with broader movements in contemporary curating that emphasise non-linear, speculative, and participatory approaches to exhibition-making. The workshop's use of Picasso's corpus, for instance, led to the emergence of alternative narrative threads that might not have been immediately visible through conventional research methods.

The workshop approached generative tools as a means to reflect on the methodological challenges currently confronting art history. Participants worked critically with generative AI outputs, analysing, adjusting, and interacting with them through interpretive reasoning, scholarly judgement, and domain-specific expertise, in this case, art historical knowledge. Therefore, the workshop highlights the essential role of human interpretation in these new curatorial processes, where generative technologies serve as a site for methodological exploration and human–machine collaboration, without completely replacing human agency.

Limitations, Risks, and Critical Lessons

This workshop highlighted structural epistemic limitations when incorporating generative AI into creative processes. Large language models such as GPT, the model used by OpenAI, can produce fluent, coherent, and internally consistent texts, but their outputs often rely on dominant interpretive frameworks, particularly in relation to canonical figures like Picasso, where there are hundreds of thousands of texts reinforcing specific ideas. Participants found a repetition of biographical narratives across the different groups, such as the figure of Picasso as a genius or a politically engaged artist, while more feminist or decolonial perspectives remained largely absent. Such patterns point to the risk of curatorial homogenisation when these tools operate without sustained critical intervention, which can perpetuate already dominant narratives, despite all the scholarly efforts of recent decades. Similar training corpora and interpretive conventions tend to generate recurring narratives, often privileging Western-centred viewpoints or established themes at the expense of diversity and critical plurality in curatorial discourse.

The second part of the workshop, which focused on image selection using CLIP, showed similar limitations. The capacity of the algorithm (that we did not fine-tune) to link textual information to visual content remained shallow, privileging surface-level associations over meaningful semantic relationships. The constraints of the visual-to-text connections generated by the algorithm highlighted, again, the importance of human intervention, not merely as validators of algorithmic outputs, but as active co-creators who interpret, reframe, contextualise, and critically build the exhibition's conceptual framework.

As the workshop progressed, the ethical implications of incorporating generative AI into curatorial processes became clearer. The textual corpus retrieved from the Dialnet repository was shaped by prevailing scholarly trends, cultural interests, and patterns of exclusion in the publications surrounding Picasso's figure and artistic production. The visual corpus of Picasso's artworks was also conditioned by the availability and accessibility of images, depending on the museum collections and webpages selected; the corpus would have different artworks from different artistic production moments in Picasso's life. Adding to this, the two algorithms used to examine and interact with these materials introduced further constraints, each with its own methodological and epistemic limitations, as mentioned before. Kate Crawford (2021) has argued that algorithms are not neutral tools but "infrastructures of power" that encode and reproduce societal and historical inequalities and hierarchies. The workshop made clear that the current challenges for curators are not only to critically assess their engagement with AI tools and their outputs but also to curate the datasets, ensuring that diverse, inclusive, and plural perspectives inform the generative processes.

Towards Hybrid Curatorial Practices

Rather than replacing curators, generative AI invites us to imagine hybrid curatorial methodologies in which human expertise and machine computation co-produce new forms of knowledge. Such collaborations may be particularly fruitful in the early stages of curatorial research—supporting brainstorming, hypothesis testing, or speculative inquiry—while leaving conceptual authorship and ethical accountability firmly in human hands.

The workshop, which served as an educational experiment, supports the need to embed AI literacy within curatorial training and museum and art history studies, ensuring that future professionals possess not only the technical skills to engage further with these new technologies but also the critical frameworks to interrogate their implications, as mentioned before in the introductory sections about critical considerations. This involves promoting awareness of algorithmic bias, data ethics, and the sociotechnical conditions shaping AI development, as advocated by scholars working at the intersection of art, technology, museums, and curatorial practice.

Final Reflections

We currently live in an algorithmic ecosystem where our interactions with art and culture are increasingly mediated by generative artificial intelligence. The integration of new technologies in museums is not an isolated phenomenon but a reflection of a broader reality as our lives becomes increasingly mediated by a wide range of technological systems. This techno–human collaboration in curatorial processes calls for a critical and theoretical understanding of the different roles within it when discussing cultural production. Generative AI presents curatorial practice with a double horizon: it is both a space of radical possibility and a site of critical risk. On the one hand, it offers tools for playful and speculative exhibition-making; on the other hand, it threatens to flatten complexity, reproduce biases, and obscure the labour of interpretation. As this workshop promotes, the task ahead is not to decide whether AI can replace curators or not. The current challenge of the field is to reflect on how curators should responsibly and imaginatively integrate AI into their work to enrich the cultural field while maintaining their intellectual and ethical commitments and standards.

The concept of automated curation emerged in the early twenty-first century, and with the rapid advancement and democratisation of generative AI in recent years, this is only the beginning of an evolving synergy. As scholarship continues to explore and theorise these transformations, it is essential for art history and museum studies researchers and educators to integrate these discussions into academic curricula. Addressing this topic goes beyond reviewing the state of the field; it requires a deep engagement with how algorithms function, an awareness of their biases, and a critical examination of the subtle ways technology influences, modifies, and curates our experiences.

The workshop *Picasso and AI: Analysing and Questioning the Technology That Overwhelms Us* results from a long-standing exploration of the intersection between computational methodologies, digital tools, and art history. More than a theoretical exercise, it is designed to equip art history and museum studies with the tools to engage in these conversations from an informed and critical perspective. Rather than adopting a passive or naive stance towards these technologies, participants are encouraged to actively interrogate and repurpose them for their own scholarly and professional work.

This workshop provides an experimental framework for reflecting on the increasingly complex relationship between curatorial practice and generative AI. Beyond the pedagogical objectives, the workshop aims to serve as a laboratory for interrogating, in practice, how generative artificial intelligence could restructure and support fundamental aspects of exhibition-making, narrative construction, space design, and curatorial research. Artificial intelligence is here to stay, and it is imperative that we provide art history students and practitioners with the knowledge and skills to understand this technology critically.

References

Aristova, Ulyana V., Alexey Y. Rolich, Alexandra D. Staruseva-Persheeva, and Anastasia O. Rolich. 2020. Digital Museum Transformation: From a Collection of Exhibits to a Gamut of Emotions. In *Digital Transformation and Global Society*, ed. Daniel A. Alexandrov, Alexander V. Boukhanovsky, Andrei V. Chugunov, Yury Kabanov, Olessia Koltsova, and Ilya Musabirov, 419–435. Springer International Publishing. https://doi.org/10.1007/978-3-030-65218-0_31.

Asta, Ngr Putu, Raka Novandra, Rohmat Sahirin, Mariam Khan, and Nguyen Minh Tu. 2024. Interactive Digital Art Exhibitions: Enhancing Public Engagement Through Technology in Fine Arts. *Journal of Social Science Utilizing Technology* 2 (4): 552–564. https://doi.org/10.70177/jssut.v2i4.1739.

Batycka, Dorian. 2022. The Bucharest Biennial Is Curated Entirely by an A.I. Named Jarvis. We Asked It a Question. *Artnet News*, 25 May 2022. https://news.artnet.com/art-world/bucharest-biennial-curated-entirely-by-an-a-i-named-jarvis-we-asked-it-a-question-2120907.

Beale, Gareth, Nicole Smith, Theodore Wilkins, Guy Schofield, Jonathan Hook, and Anthony Masinton. 2022. Digital Creativity and the Regional Museum: Experimental Collaboration at the Convergence of Immersive Media and Exhibition Design. *Journal on Computing and Cultural Heritage* 15 (4): 1–78. https://doi.org/10.1145/3527620.

Burrell, J., and M. Fourcade. 2021. The Society of Algorithms. *Annual Review of Sociology* 47 (1): 213–237.

Chen, Tien-Li, Yun-Chi Lee, and Chi-Sen Hung. 2022. A Study on the Effects of Digital Learning Sheet Design Strategy on the Learning Motivation and Learning Outcomes of Museum Exhibition Visitors. *Education Sciences* 12 (2): 135. https://doi.org/10.3390/educsci12020135.

Cotton, M., and S. Beaumont. 2024. *Radical Software: Women, Art & Computing, 1960–1991*. Mudam Luxembourg/Musée d'Art Moderne Grand-Duc Jean.

Crawford, Kate. 2021. *The Atlas of AI: Power, Politics, and the Planetary Costs of Artificial Intelligence*. Yale University Press.

Dekker, Annet. 2024. From Digital (Art) Curation to Networked Co-Curating. *Mimesis Journal* 13 (2): 29–41. https://doi.org/10.13135/2389-6086/9993.

Dekker, Annet, and Gaia Tedone. 2019. Networked Co-Curation: An Exploration of the Socio-Technical Specificities of Online Curation. *Arts* 8 (3): 86. https://doi.org/10.3390/arts8030086.

Jones, L., Ferran, et al. 2023. *Coded: Art Enters the Computer Age, 1952–1982*. Los Angeles County Museum of Art, Host Institution, & DelMonico Books is the Publisher.

Kamariotou, Vassiliki, Maria Kamariotou, and Fotis Kitsios. 2021. Strategic Planning for Virtual Exhibitions and Visitors' Experience: A Multidisciplinary Approach for Museums in the Digital Age. *Digital Applications in Archaeology and Cultural Heritage* 21:e00183. https://doi.org/10.1016/j.daach.2021.e00183.

Khalil, Sabine, Andreas Kallmuenzer, and Sascha Kraus. 2023. Visiting Museums via Augmented Reality: An Experience Fast-Tracking the Digital Transformation of the Tourism Industry. *European Journal of Innovation Management* 27 (6): 2084–2100. https://doi.org/10.1108/EJIM-09-2022-0479.

King, Ellie, M. Paul Smith, Paul F. Wilson, and Mark A. Williams. 2021. Digital Responses of UK Museum Exhibitions to the COVID-19 Crisis, March–June 2020. *Curator: The Museum Journal* 64 (3): 487–504. https://doi.org/10.1111/cura.12413.

Krysa, Joasia. 2008. Software Curating: The Politics of Curating in/as (an) Open System(s). PhD diss., University of Plymouth. https://pearl.plymouth.ac.uk/bms-theses/332.

Krysa, J., and L. Impett. 2020. Rethinking Curating in the Age of Artificial Intelligence. https://researchonline.ljmu.ac.uk/id/eprint/19232/1/Humanities%20and%20Artificial%20Intelligence%20Krysa.pdf.

Li, Jingjing, Xiaoyang Zheng, Ikumu Watanabe, and Yoichi Ochiai. 2024a. A Systematic Review of Digital Transformation Technologies in Museum Exhibition. *Computers in Human Behavior* 161:108407. https://doi.org/10.1016/j.chb.2024.108407.

Li, Qiang, Jingjing Wang, and Tian Luo. 2024b. Evaluating Interactive Digital Exhibit Characteristics in Science Museums and Their Effects on Child Engagement. *International Journal of Human–Computer Interaction* 40 (3): 838–849. https://doi.org/10.1080/10447318.2022.2126584.

Liu, Zhiyang, and Seokwon Chang. 2024. A Study of Digital Exhibition Visual Design Led by Digital Twin and VR Technology. *Measurement: Sensors* 31:100970. https://doi.org/10.1016/j.measen.2023.100970.

Malik, Umair Shafqat, Laura Loredana Micoli, Giandomenico Caruso, and Gabriele Guidi. 2023. Integrating Quantitative and Qualitative Analysis to

Evaluate Digital Applications in Museums. *Journal of Cultural Heritage* 62:304–313. https://doi.org/10.1016/j.culher.2023.06.002.

Prown, Jules David. 1967. The Art Historian and the Computer: An Analysis of Copley's Patronage (1753–1774). *The Smithsonian Journal of History* 1 (4): 17–30.

Romero Ferrón, Bárbara, Alejandro Mozo Quesada, María Ortiz Tello, and Nuria Rodríguez-Ortega. 2025. Picasso and AI. Analysing and Questioning the Technology That Overwhelms Us. https://doi.org/10.5281/zenodo.14778367.

Srinivasan, Ramya. 2024. To See or Not to See: Understanding the Tensions of Algorithmic Curation for Visual Arts. In *Proceedings of the 2024 ACM Conference on Fairness, Accountability, and Transparency*, 444–455. FAccT '24. New York: Association for Computing Machinery. https://doi.org/10.1145/3630106.3658917.

Tam, Cheung-On, and Claire Ka-Yan Hui. 2024. Teaching Visual Arts Using Virtual Exhibitions: An Investigation of Student Usage and Impact on Learning. *Studies in Art Education* 65 (3): 371–387. https://doi.org/10.1080/00393541.2024.2355728.

Zidianakis, Emmanouil, Nikolaos Partarakis, Stavroula Ntoa, Antonis Dimopoulos, Stella Kopidaki, Anastasia Ntagianta, Emmanouil Ntafotis, et al. 2021. The Invisible Museum: A User-Centric Platform for Creating Virtual 3D Exhibitions with VR Support. *Electronics* 10 (3): 363. https://doi.org/10.3390/electronics10030363.

CHAPTER 9

Recognition as an Epistemic Glass Box: Explainable AI in Museum Contexts

Monica Lanaro

Hand in Hand

In March 2016, photographer Muhammad Hamed captured the image of a young Syrian refugee crossing the border into Jordan near the town of Ruwaished, clutching her child tightly in her arms. The photograph was incorporated into Reuters' dataset and subsequently processed through the Reuters API by Recognition—an image-matching algorithm that scanned over 30,000 works from the Tate Britain archive. Among these, it identified *Cottage Children* (c. 1754–1797) by Gainsborough Dupont[1] as a visual counterpart. The algorithm established this pairing based on three

[1] Gainsborough Dupont, *Cottage Children*, c. 1790–95, Tate Britain. The artwork can be viewed on the Tate website: https://www.tate.org.uk/art/artworks/dupont-cottage-children-n00311.

M. Lanaro (✉)
Independent, Milan, Italy

L. Cempellin, M. Geiger (eds.), *Reimagining Art History with Artificial Intelligence*,
https://doi.org/10.1007/978-3-032-21685-4_9

principal criteria: the presence of a child being held, the identification of a woman as the primary subject in both images, and a 41.2% compositional match, as determined by similarities in colour palette.

At first glance, the match appears compelling: despite being separated by over two centuries, both images depict mothers cradling their children. To a trained human eye, references to Marian iconography may be discerned—from the motif of the Flight into Egypt to pyramid-shaped compositions featuring the Christ Child and Saint John the Baptist. The Syrian woman's hands enfold her child in a manner evocative of standing Madonnas, conjuring the inexorable pathos associated with *pietas*. Surprisingly, the other woman clasps her fingers in a completely different way. It is precisely the representation of the hands that reveals the interpretative distance between human perception and the algorithmic logics of artificial intelligence in 2016.

While the algorithm's bounding boxes highlight the hands of the Syrian woman, they do not frame those of the woman depicted by Dupont. Instead, the focus is placed on the hands of a child seated beside her, holding a bundle of sticks. The position of the child's hands mirrors that of the Syrian woman's embrace—an equivalence that, from the algorithm's perspective, sufficed to infer that both subjects were engaged in the same act of holding a child. In doing so, the algorithm overlooks the symbolic and narrative context that distinguishes the two scenes, revealing the limitations of computational vision when confronted with culturally and historically embedded visual codes.

What today might be reductively labelled an error, in 2016 served to expose the mechanisms of artificial intelligence within contexts of complex meaning.

Research, Comparison, and Conjunction

In 2016, Recognition won the third edition of the IK Prize, an award given by Tate Britain in collaboration with Microsoft for ideas that used digital technology to innovate the way audiences discover, explore, and enjoy the 500 years of British art in the Tate collection (Tate 2016).[2] The project was designed by Angelo Semeraro, Coralie Gourguechon, Monica

[2] For a video documentation of the Recognition installation at Tate Britain, see: Fabrica, "Recognition – IK Prize 2016," YouTube video, 2:12, September 12, 2016, https://www.youtube.com/watch?v=Z1_iEbwWdIU.

Lanaro, and Isaac Vallentin as members of Fabrica, the Benetton Group communication research centre based in Treviso, Italy.

The number of digitized works in the Tate collection was the research starting point—more than 70,000 images make up the Tate Britain archive, which was indicative of a large number of works not on public display. According to research by Christopher Groskopf (2016) for Quartz, in 2016 among 20 museums distributed in seven countries, only 5% of the works were exhibited to museum visitors, with the remaining 95% stored in archives. Included in this 95% is *Cottage Children* (C.1754–1797) by Gainsborough Dupont.

The question at the core of the IK Prize brief was: How can technology create an engaging discoverability process within such a vast collection? The initial catalyst for the design of Recognition was a Reddit thread titled *r/Accidental Renaissance*.[3] It featured a series of photographs that, due to parameters like composition, colour, lighting, and the subjects, resembled master paintings spanning from the fourteenth to the nineteenth century. The idea that photographs could accidentally recreate the same theatricality as paintings from the past became a popular online phenomenon starting in 2014 (Beaumont-Thomas 2014).

Scrolling through the Reddit thread, another aspect became evident: it was a collective curatorial project. The creative process behind Recognition then evolved towards a concept of curation driven by technology itself—technology capable of comparing real-time photojournalistic images, part of the contemporary aesthetic infosphere, with the 30,000 works in the Tate Britain collection, to identify accidental similarities.

At the time of Recognition, the debate surrounding the potential of artificial intelligence had begun to question those actions and tasks that included critical thinking or creativity more broadly. For example, Saleh et al.'s (2014) study, "Toward Automated Discovery of Artistic Influence," analysed the methodologies and opportunities for the automated discovery of artistic influence by examining similarities between paintings and artists. A year later, Elgammal (2015) reported on an artificial intelligence algorithm developed to assess creativity (understood as originality and lasting influence) in paintings. Both studies exemplify the potential of artificial intelligence to visually analyse paintings—without any pre-codified knowledge of art or art history.

[3] r/AccidentalRenaissance is a subreddit for photos that accidentally resemble Renaissance style art.

It is not surprising that these studies have raised objections from art historians, who criticize these systems for oversimplification: modern art history, unlike the nineteenth-century approach based on stylistic comparison, considers economic, political, social, and theoretical contexts (Pollock 2014).

Simultaneously, in an interview with *The New Yorker*, Hans Ulrich Obrist referenced the postcolonial scholar Homi Bhabha, describing his curatorial approach as "junction-making"—the act of connecting objects, people, and the relationships between them (Max 2014). In curatorial discourse, comparison and conjunction are integral and complementary aspects of the same practice; in a parallel manner, they also underpin the processes of image recognition and matchmaking at the core of Recognition.

The debate on the role of photography, not so much as an expressive medium but as a tool for cataloguing works of art and overcoming premodern hierarchies between art forms, is much older. It dates back to André Malraux's 1947 essay *Le Musée Imaginaire*, in which the politician and writer explains how photographed works of art can be compared, transcending the hierarchical categories traditionally assigned to specific disciplines or individual artists:

> The sleight of hand involved in altering the scale of reproduced works endows the miniature with an entirely new significance. Reproduced at 'true size', it appears in the same format as the reduced paintings. The meticulousness of style—which, regardless of its workmanship, sets it apart from the original painting—is then no weightier than the slight grimace imposed upon it by reduction. (Malraux 1996)

The virtualization of the museum holds the potential to liberate curatorial practice from classificatory systems rooted in dominant cultural narratives. Through photographic reproduction, for instance, Michelangelo's *David* can be positioned alongside a miniature, without necessarily reinforcing hierarchical distinctions between artistic forms or traditions.

The notion that photography could support a more democratic and accessible discourse on art (Malraux 1996) aligned closely with the IK Prize brief—to create an engaging process of discoverability within an extensive collection.

It became evident that Recognition would require a dual-format development: a virtual platform, open to all users, where the algorithm's matches could be explored and its selection criteria scrutinized; and a physical installation at Tate Britain, where visitors could interact with the system and generate new pairings. These two modalities aimed to democratize the curatorial experience—broadening accessibility while actively involving the museum audience in the interpretive and discovery processes of the collection.

Another highly relevant aspect in achieving the goal of making Recognition accessible was the design of the website. The interface was designed to display the algorithm's focus areas, the identified similarity criteria, and the match percentages. This allowed users to explore the algorithm's decision-making process and gain a clearer understanding of algorithmic operation.

The research process led to the identification of the components of Recognition: the dual environments, including the virtual space as an imaginary museum and the in-gallery installation, the technology, and the challenge itself, curating matches between the 30,000 works in the Tate Britain collection and photographs from the Reuters agency.

The technical development of Recognition, including the backends and user interfaces, was executed by Alexandre Giraud and Emmanuel Benazera from the company JoliBrain, for a duration of two months. For the learning process of Recognition, over 30,000 works from the Tate Britain digital collection were used, encompassing images, captions, description metadata, and approximately 1600 photographs per day with corresponding metadata from the Reuters news feed. To enhance the learning process, the algorithm was trained with around 300,000 images from the MSCoco dataset, with object bounding boxes and captions, the Imagenet dataset, approximately 14,000,000 images sorted into 33,000 hierarchical categories, and two place datasets, which included 2,500,000 images sorted into 205 scenes and approximately 10 million images sorted into over 400 scenes (JoliBrain 2016).

Recognition Online and Onsite

Following a two-month training period, Recognition ran from September 2 to November 27, 2016, during which it produced algorithmic matches between artworks from the Tate Britain collection and Reuters photojournalistic images (Fig. 9.1).

Each match was presented on a dedicated page where users could explore the image recognition process and analyse the comparison criteria.

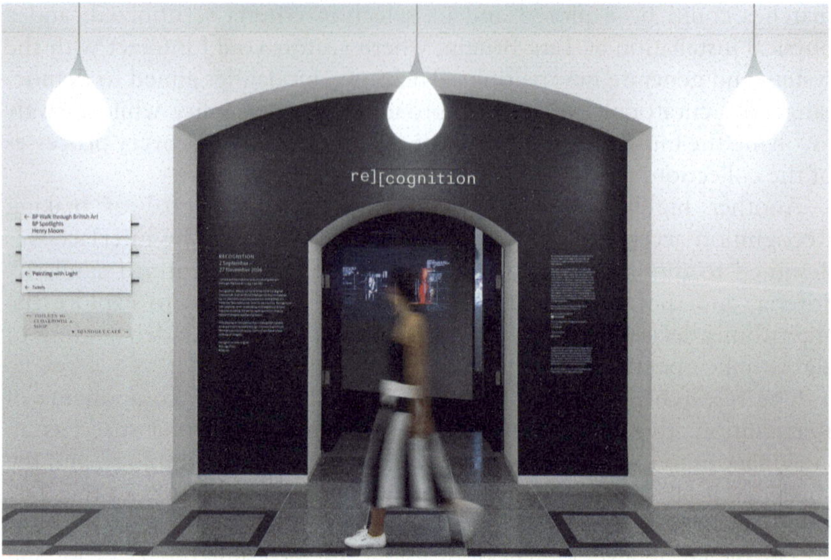

Fig. 9.1 Installation photography of *Recognition*, held at Tate Britain. Tate. Photo: © Tate (Joe Humphrys)

At the core of the project was an algorithm capable of pairing works of art with photographs taken by Reuters reporters and based on four comparison criteria:

- Object recognition: Identification of objects and visually similar patterns.
- Facial features analysis: Visual analysis of faces depicted in photos and artworks, aimed at generating probabilistic estimates of age range, facial expression, and perceived gender.
- Composition: Detection of similar compositional patterns, shapes, and structures.
- Context: Analysis of the data accompanying the images, such as titles, dates, tags, and image descriptions. As a result, Recognition autonomously generated a brief description of what it was analysing. The presence of text output did not imply the use of a language model; rather, it reflected a data-to-text interface layer common in pre-LLM AI systems.

The project was made visible to the public online through the website and to visitors at Tate Britain through an installation that required direct interaction from those present at the museum. The public was invited to create matches, starting from a subset of Tate works pre-selected by the algorithm, as it would have been impossible for users to select an artwork from the more than 30,000 available objects within a reasonable timeframe.

Explainable AI as Visitor Experience

From a visitor experience perspective, the on-site installation at Tate Britain played a crucial epistemic role. It did not merely function as a display of algorithmic outcomes, but as an interactive environment in which visitors were invited to explore the Tate collection while simultaneously engaging with the operational logic of Recognition itself. By allowing visitors to actively select artworks to be associated with Reuters photographs, the installation transformed algorithmic matching into an embodied interpretative practice. Visitors were not passive recipients of AI output; rather, they were positioned as co-interpreters who could test, question, and negotiate the system's propositions.

Recent scholarship on AI-mediated user experiences in museums emphasizes that trust in AI systems emerges not from technical accuracy alone, but from opportunities for meaningful interaction, intelligibility, and user agency among end-users (Avlonitou et al. 2025). Across both its online platform and its on-site installation at Tate Britain, Recognition anticipated what can be described as Explanatory Uncertainty Visualizations (ExUVis): experiential configurations in which transparency is enacted through interface design, interaction, and situated engagement with algorithmic outputs, rather than through post-hoc technical explanations (Kitzing 2025). In this framework, explainability did not consist in rendering the internal mechanics of the system fully intelligible, but in enabling end-users to observe, compare, and interrogate the system's behaviour through perceptually accessible cues and interactive affordances. Rather than attempting to explain the underlying models, the interface disclosed selected and interpretable elements of the recognition process—such as bounding boxes highlighting detected visual features and similarity metrics associated with the chosen match—thereby supporting end-user sense-making without inducing cognitive overload.

Within explainable artificial intelligence (XAI) and visualization research, transparency is often achieved not through exhaustive explanation, but through selective visualization strategies that make computational attention perceptible to end-users (Kitzing 2025; Windhager et al. 2019). In this context, bounding boxes function as epistemic visual cues: rather than explaining why a decision is made, they indicate where the system is attending within an image, thereby fostering interpretability through design rather than causal or mathematical disclosure (Kitzing 2025; Karran et al. 2022).

In Recognition, these design choices instantiated an explainable end-user experience by externalizing uncertainty and process visibility in a form compatible with museum-based exploration, reinforcing trust through transparency, interaction, and cognitive fit rather than exhaustive explanation.

Recognition's interface did not present the final match as an isolated or authoritative result. Rather, it exposed key elements of the recognition process, such as detected visual features, similarity metrics, and areas of algorithmic attention, enabling end-users to situate the algorithm's choice within an interpretative frame. In this sense, trust did not arise from claims of correctness or authority, but from transparency-through-experience: the opportunity to observe how the system perceived and compared images, including when its outputs diverged from human expectations.

The on-site installation at Tate Britain thus functioned as a dual exploratory space. It enabled visitors to navigate the collection beyond established curatorial taxonomies, while simultaneously encountering artificial intelligence as a situated and interpretable system. This configuration reinforced the museum's role as a site of critical technological literacy, where end-users could develop informed relationships with AI by engaging directly with its perceptual processes rather than encountering them as invisible infrastructure.

Recognition as an Epistemic Glass Box

Recognition can be understood not simply as an early experiment at the intersection of artificial intelligence and creativity, but as a project that operationalized interpretability through design. Across both its online platform and its on-site installation at Tate Britain, the system exposed selected aspects of its recognition process—such as areas of visual attention, similarity metrics, and comparison criteria—allowing end-users to engage with algorithmic perception as an observable phenomenon. Rather than pursuing full technical transparency or post-hoc explanation, Recognition embedded intelligibility directly into the user experience. In this sense, it anticipated principles now associated with human-centred and explainable AI, positioning itself as an epistemic glass box. While computer science literature—often framing the transition from black box to glass box (Rai 2020)—defines the glass box primarily as an inherently interpretable model, contrasted with the limitations of post-hoc explanations (Rudin 2019) and increasingly articulated as an ethical requirement for decisional transparency (Garrett and Rudin 2024), Recognition reconfigures this notion at an epistemic level. Within this framework, transparency does not denote access to internal model mechanics, but an unfolding interpretative process that enables visitors to negotiate meaning at the intersection of human and computational vision.

Error as an Epistemic Effect

The implication of this epistemic role of error can be further articulated through contemporary debates on explainable artificial intelligence (XAI) and interpretable artificial intelligence, which have become central to discussions of AI deployment in cultural and humanities-based contexts. In contrast to "black-box" systems, whose operations remain inaccessible to users, XAI research emphasizes the importance of rendering computational processes intelligible and contestable (Mersha et al. 2024). Within the digital humanities, the value of AI systems is increasingly understood not only in terms of optimization or predictive accuracy, but also in terms of their capacity to support interpretation, critique, and reflexive engagement with computational methods (El-Hajj et al. 2023). From a complementary perspective grounded in computer vision research, the mismatches generated by Recognition can be understood through the concept of epistemic uncertainty—uncertainty arising from limitations in the model or its training data rather than from noise in the input itself (Kendall and Gal 2017). Recognition's unexpected matches exemplify this condition: when the system encounters visual configurations that exceed the statistical regularities encoded in its datasets, it produces equivalences that diverge from human semantic interpretation. Crucially, this uncertainty, rather than being suppressed, is rendered visible, reinforcing its epistemic and analytical value.

Building on this understanding of uncertainty as an epistemic resource, studies in human–AI interaction consistently show that making uncertainty visible—rather than suppressing it—can increase user trust, provided that uncertainty is communicated in cognitively appropriate ways (Reyes et al. 2025). Recognition operationalized this principle through visual representations such as bounding boxes and probabilistic similarity measures, which externalized uncertainty without overwhelming users with technical detail. This approach resonates with theories of cognitive fit, according to which representations are most effective when they align with users' perceptual and interpretative capacities (Vessey 1991).

In a museum context, such uncertainty acquires particular epistemic significance. By exposing the gap between statistical similarity and cultural meaning, Recognition encourages critical reflection on what computational systems can and cannot perceive. This aligns with recent scholarship in critical AI and cultural analytics, which conceptualizes AI systems as interpretative instruments embedded within specific cultural and institutional frameworks rather than neutral technologies (Foka et al. 2024).

From Data to Capta: Situated Vision

This interpretative positioning becomes even more explicit when considered through Johanna Drucker's distinction between data and capta.

As Drucker argues, the term *data* implies information that is given, neutral, and self-evident—an assumption she explicitly challenges within the humanities (Drucker 2011, 2014). She proposes *capta* instead, emphasizing that what is processed by computational systems is taken, selected, and constructed through specific theoretical and cultural frameworks. Recognition was trained on datasets deliberately assembled by the project's actors, including digitized artworks from Tate Britain and photojournalistic images from Reuters. These corpora were shaped by institutional, descriptive, and categorical decisions, and therefore constitute *capta* rather than raw data.

Within this framework, Recognition can be understood as an epistemological tool that exposes the outcomes of a computer vision process animated by *capta*. Although governed by computational logics of pattern recognition and correlation, its results remain situated, partial, and contingent. By making this condition legible, Recognition operates as an epistemic glass box—rendering the limits of algorithmic perception available for reflection and interpretation within the humanities.

Designing Against Opacity

To further situate Recognition within contemporary debates on algorithmic opacity, it is useful to distinguish between different conceptual accounts of opacity articulated in recent scholarship. Building on established distinctions between technical opacity (Burrell 2016, 2–3), epistemic opacity (Humphreys 2004, 215–216), and institutional opacity, understood here in line with Burrell's notion of opacity as intentional corporate or state secrecy (Burrell 2016, 1–2), this analysis resonates with, while remaining conceptually distinct from, the regulatory taxonomy proposed by Buttaboni and Floridi (2026).

In their influential framework, Buttaboni and Floridi conceptualize AI opacity as a layered configuration articulated through transparency, traceability, interpretability, and explainability, each associated with different stakeholders, regulatory obligations, and explanatory purposes. Rather than defining discrete types of opacity, they reframe opacity in terms of distinct but interdependent dimensions that respond to different audiences and explanatory needs.

Against this conceptual backdrop, Recognition did not aim to minimize opacity across all layers, nor was it conceived as a white box system in which internal mechanisms are fully understandable to end-users. Rather, it was deliberately designed as an epistemic glass box, prioritizing explainability at the level of user experience over full technical transparency. This positioning is consistent with Buttaboni and Floridi's distinction between transparency-oriented approaches—primarily relevant for developers, auditors, or regulators—and explainability-oriented approaches, whose primary audience consists of non-expert users seeking intelligibility rather than technical disclosure (Buttaboni and Floridi 2026, fig. 1).

In this sense, Recognition privileged epistemic accessibility, aligning with human- and user-centred models of explainability that frame interpretability as a relational property emerging through interaction between systems, interfaces, and end-users (Karran et al. 2022; Buttaboni and Floridi 2026). The project thus exemplifies how explainability can be operationalized as a design strategy—making algorithmic processes inspectable, discussable, and contestable at the level where meaning is actually negotiated: the interface and the experience.

Opacity and Cognitive Risk

Conversely, excessive opacity risks generating what can be described as cognitive risk: a condition in which users anticipate a mismatch between their own interpretative resources and the epistemic demands of a system or experience. Museum contexts offer a parallel: visitors frequently disengage from exhibitions perceived as insufficiently mediated or contextually supported, responding with avoidance rather than exploration.

A comparable, though not identical, dynamic may be observed in AI-human context. When algorithmic processes are perceived as inscrutable or insufficiently mediated, end-users may respond with skepticism, reduced trust, or disengagement—not necessarily because they reject AI technologies as such, but because they lack adequate interpretative footholds to make sense of the system's behavior. Recent research on algorithmic transparency and explainability suggests that trust is closely linked to perceived intelligibility and epistemic alignment, rather than to technical performance alone (Karran et al. 2022; Mersha et al. 2024). In this sense, opacity does not merely obscure system operation, but may actively shape user attitudes and willingness to engage.

Against this backdrop, Recognition can be understood as an attempt to respond to such risks through design. Rather than maximizing transparency or fully disclosing its internal mechanisms, the project calibrated the degree and form of visibility afforded to end-users. It did not aim to explain everything, but to display enough—supporting interpretation while preserving curiosity and exploratory engagement.

This balance is essential both in AI system design and in museum strategies more broadly. In both domains, transparency and explainability function not as ends in themselves, but as mechanisms for reducing cognitive risk, fostering trust, and enabling meaningful engagement. Recognition thus demonstrates one possible way in which epistemic glass boxes can operate at the intersection of artificial intelligence and cultural institutions, offering a model in which interpretability is experienced through interaction rather than delivered through instruction.

Ten Years On

Recognition remains a notable case in contemporary discussions not only as an early example of explainability through design—in which transparency was enacted at the level of user experience through calibrated visibility, interaction, and interpretative affordances—but also as a critical precedent in debates surrounding the use of images in AI training. In this latter respect, the project anticipated discussions that are still ongoing today, particularly regarding the legitimacy, governance, and cultural implications of employing visual content from journalistic repositories and creative works within machine learning models. Thanks to an exclusive agreement granting access to images from both the Tate Britain archive and the Reuters photojournalism database, Recognition was able to operate using datasets fully authorized by two globally recognized institutions at the forefront of culture and information. In 2016, Recognition ran for three months, generating matches between the Tate Britain archive and contemporary photojournalism, documenting key events such as the US presidential race and the historic victory of Google's AlphaGo AI over world champion Lee Sedol. Ten years later, the project website is no longer accessible—an example of the technological obsolescence that often affects digital initiatives, and a reflection of the ongoing challenges related to digital preservation and archiving practices.

Nevertheless, the Reddit thread *r/AccidentalRenaissance*—which initially inspired the project—remains among the top 1% of the platform's largest communities. One of the most recent images shared within the community depicts Claudia Sheinbaum, President of Mexico, on International Women's Day. Surrounded by Indigenous and Afro-Mexican women and enveloped in the smoke of ceremonial incense, she raises the *Bastón de Mando*, a symbol of authority conferred by Indigenous communities. Her gaze is directed beyond the frame, towards an indeterminate point that lifts the photograph beyond the contingencies of the present.

The visual resonance with Eugène Delacroix's *Liberty Leading the People* is unmistakable—yet, as with Recognition, the question is not whether the match is correct, but what forms of recognition it enables. In this sense, the enduring appeal of *Accidental Renaissance* confirms the project's core intuition: recognition is never a final verdict, but an epistemic process that unfolds between images, histories, and interpretative frameworks.

Acknowledgements The author is profoundly grateful to Dr Leda Cempellin for her dedicated guidance and intellectual mentorship, which significantly enriched the development of this chapter. Special thanks are also due to Jennifer Carding, Sales Executive at Tate Images, for her kind assistance in facilitating the permissions to reproduce the Recognition installation images.

Project Credits Recognition was conceived and developed by the research team at **Fabrica** (Treviso, Italy), including Coralie Gourguechon, Monica Lanaro, Angelo Semeraro, and Isaac Vallentin. Established in 1994, Fabrica operated as a communication research centre within the Benetton Group, offering international fellowships across design, interaction, and journalism. Technical AI development and website architecture were executed by Emmanuel Benazera and Alexandre Giraud (**JoliBrain**). The project was produced for Tate Britain by Tony Guillan. The author extends further thanks to Sam Baron and Carlo Tunioli for their leadership and support during the project's inception.

References

Avlonitou, Charis, Eirini Papadaki, and Alexandros Apostolakis. 2025. A Human–AI Compass for Sustainable Art Museums: Navigating Opportunities and Challenges in Operations, Collections Management, and Visitor Engagement. *Heritage* 8(10): 422. https://doi.org/10.3390/heritage8100422.

Beaumont-Thomas, Ben. 2014. Accidental Renaissance: The Photos That Look Like Italian Paintings. *The Guardian*, August 6, 2014. https://www.theguardian.com/artanddesign/2014/aug/06/accidental-renaissance-photojournalism-italian-painting-ukraine-frank-lampard.

Burrell, Jenna. 2016. How the Machine 'Thinks': Understanding Opacity in Machine Learning Algorithms. *Big Data & Society* 3 (1): 1–12. https://doi.org/10.1177/2053951715622512.

Buttaboni, Carlotta, and Luciano Floridi. 2026. A Regulatory Taxonomy of AI Opacity in the EU: Rethinking Transparency, Traceability, Interpretability, and Explainability. *AI and Ethics* 6: 100. https://doi.org/10.1007/s43681-025-00940-0.

Drucker, Johanna. 2011. Humanities Approaches to Graphical Display. *Digital Humanities Quarterly* 5 (1). http://www.digitalhumanities.org/dhq/vol/5/1/000091/000091.html.

Drucker, Johanna. 2014. *Graphesis: Visual Forms of Knowledge Production*. Cambridge, MA: Harvard University Press.

Elgammal, Ahmed. 2015. Which Paintings Were the Most Creative of Their Time? An Algorithm May Hold the Answers. *The Conversation*, July 30, 2015. https://theconversation.com/which-paintings-were-the-most-creative-of-their-time-an-algorithm-may-hold-the-answers-43157.

El-Hajj, Hassan, Oliver Eberle, Anika Merklein, Anna Siebold, Noga Shlomi, Jochen Büttner, Julius Martinetz, Klaus-Robert Müller, Grégoire Montavon, and Matteo Valleriani. 2023. Explainability and Transparency in the Realm of Digital Humanities: Toward a Historian XAI. *International Journal of Digital Humanities* 5: 299–331. https://doi.org/10.1007/s42803-023-00070-1.

Foka, Anna, and Gabriele Griffin. 2024. AI, Cultural Heritage, and Bias: Some Key Queries That Arise from the Use of GenAI. *Heritage* 7(11): 6125–6136. https://doi.org/10.3390/heritage7110287.

Garrett, Brandon L., and Cynthia Rudin. 2024. The Right to a Glass Box: Rethinking the Use of Artificial Intelligence in Criminal Justice. *Cornell Law Review* 109 (3): 561–627.

Groskopf, Christopher. 2016. Museums Are Keeping a Ton of the World's Most Famous Art Locked Away in Storage. *Quartz*, January 20, 2016. https://qz.com/583354/why-is-so-much-of-the-worlds-great-art-in-storage.

Humphreys, Paul. 2004. *Extending Ourselves: Computational Science, Empiricism, and Scientific Method*. Oxford: Oxford University Press.

JoliBrain. 2016. *Recognition: Source Code for IK Prize 2016*. GitHub repository. https://github.com/jolibrain/recognition.

Karran, Alexander John, Théophile Demazure, Antoine Hudon, Sylvain Senecal, and Pierre-Majorique Léger. 2022. Designing for Confidence: The Impact of Visualizing Artificial Intelligence Decisions. *Frontiers in Neuroscience* 16: 883385. https://doi.org/10.3389/fnins.2022.883385.

Kendall, Alex, and Yarin Gal. 2017. What Uncertainties Do We Need in Bayesian Deep Learning for Computer Vision? In *Advances in Neural Information Processing Systems (NIPS 2017)*, 5574–5584.

Kitzing, Stephanie. 2025. Visual Explanations of Uncertainty in Artificial Intelligence: A Scoping Review. Submitted to IEEE VIS 2025, March 31, 2025. Preprint.

Malraux, André. [1947] 1996. *The Voices of Silence*. Translated by Stuart Gilbert. Princeton: Princeton University Press.

Max, D. T. 2014. *The Curator of Everything: Hans Ulrich Obrist's Infinite Encounter*. The New Yorker, December 8, 2014. https://www.newyorker.com/magazine/2014/12/08/art-conversation.

Mersha, Melkamu, Khang Lam, Joseph Wood, Ali AlShami, and Jugal Kalita. 2024. Explainable Artificial Intelligence: A Survey of Needs, Techniques, Applications, and Future Direction. *Neurocomputing* 599: 128111. https://doi.org/10.1016/j.neucom.2024.128111.

Pollock, Griselda. 2014. *Computers Can Find Similarities Between Paintings – But Art History Is About So Much More*. The Conversation, August 22, 2014. https://theconversation.com/computers-can-find-similarities-between-paintings-but-art-history-is-about-so-much-more-30752.

Rai, Arun. 2020. Explainable AI: From Black Box to Glass Box. *Journal of the Academy of Marketing Science* 48 (1): 137–141. https://doi.org/10.1007/s11747-019-00710-5.

Reyes, Jonatan, Anil Ufuk Batmaz, and Marta Kersten-Oertel. 2025. Trusting AI: Does Uncertainty Visualization Affect Decision-Making? *Frontiers in Computer Science* 7: 1464348. https://doi.org/10.3389/fcomp.2025.1464348.

Rudin, Cynthia. 2019. Stop Explaining Black Box Machine Learning Models for High Stakes Decisions and Use Interpretable Models Instead. *Nature Machine Intelligence* 1 (5): 206–215. https://doi.org/10.1038/s42256-019-0048-x.

Saleh, Babak, et al. 2014. Toward Automated Discovery of Artistic Influence. *Multimedia Tools and Applications* 75 (7): 3565–3591.

Tate Britain. 2016. IK Prize 2016: Recognition. https://www.tate.org.uk/whats-on/tate-britain/ik-prize-2016-recognition. Accessed October 2025.

Vessey, Iris. 1991. Cognitive Fit: A Theory-Based Analysis of the Graphs vs. Tables Literature. *Decision Sciences* 22 (2): 219–240.

Windhager, Florian, Paolo Federico, Günther Schreder, Katrin Glinka, Marian Dörk, Silvia Miksch, and Eva Mayr. 2019. Visualization of Cultural Heritage Collection Data: State of the Art and Future Challenges. *IEEE Transactions on Visualization and Computer Graphics* 25 (6): 2311–2330. https://doi.org/10.1109/TVCG.2018.2830759.

PART III

AI-Enhanced Pedagogy: Transforming Art History Education

CHAPTER 10

From Digital Art History to Artificial Intelligence

Emily Leifer

The past five years has seen astounding transformation in the technical capabilities of machine learning, resulting in an onslaught of widely available systems for information analysis. While there has been a recent efflorescence of literature on artificial intelligence (AI), the novelty of the technology dictates that much of this writing offers guidelines or warnings without providing evidence of specific outcomes. When faced with something so new, my impulse, as a historian, is to find precedent and to extrapolate. What have we seen before, what is original, and what is a variation on a theme? To begin to create a foundation for the current incarnation of AI in art history and art historical pedagogy, this chapter looks back to the discourse on digital art history, and pairs it with more recent recommendations for the use of AI in the discipline. Ultimately, I determine that what AI shares with digital art history, democratised access to information and the ability to break out of entrenched modes of thinking, has the potential to add to the practice of art history. What is unique about AI is more complex. Its ability to recognise and categorise images appears promising for uncovering new connections to analyse and research, yet

E. Leifer (✉)
Independent Scholar, Brooklyn, NY, USA

L. Cempellin, M. Geiger (eds.), *Reimagining Art History with Artificial Intelligence*,
https://doi.org/10.1007/978-3-032-21685-4_10

this technology carries forward the biases of its input material and those programming this recognition. Furthermore, the ability of large language models to mimic human language and create content by extrapolating from existing information presents new challenges to the practice and teaching of art history. By taking a more historical perspective, we can see that while the current incarnation of AI in art history is not without precedent, it is by no means an inevitable evolution of the discipline.

Digital art history emerged as a method of research in the mid-2000s, as image (and metadata) digitisation efforts reached critical mass and funding bodies sought out closer collaborations between the sciences and humanities. The new approach built on the optimism generated by what some historians call Web 2.0, when the advent of user-friendly web development tools and social media promised a more accessible, interactive, and equitable experience with information technology. Digital art history uses digital means to query large amounts of data to answer an art historical research question. It allows for what K. Bender termed "distant viewing," an analogue to literary theorist Franco Moretti's "distant reading" (Bender 2015; Moretti 2000). While "close reading" examines works of literature on the level of the individual work—word choice, syntax, and pacing—"distant reading" zooms out, examining a particular concept or technique within a larger cultural field. Distant reading originaly sought to overcome the constricted canons of national literatures. The digital technology of the era made this larger field more accessible. From a single computer one could access and meaningfully search a multitude of archival resources from all over the world. For example, rather than apply close reading to each line of the canonical *Moby Dick*, the literary scholar could instead use digital tools to search a wide variety of English language publications from the 1840s for mentions of the word "whale." This search for the whale could span instruction manuals, industry publications, posters, and contracts, should these resources be digitised. The unprecedented breadth of the archive made available through digitisation helped to overcome the limits of an individual researcher's physical location, knowledge base, and personal biases by making a wider range of material, both canonical and obscure, available for study. Such expanded analysis is not entirely the product of digital tools, but new technologies have made the traditionally time-consuming and travel-intensive process of surveying archival materials available to a wider range of scholars. While economic decisions have made physical research unavailable to many, an ever-growing body of digitised resources and sophisticated search methods have allowed the work to continue.

Bringing the strategies of the digital humanities into the realm of art history, in "Is there a 'Digital' Art History?" Johanna Drucker (2013) points out that there is more to digital art history than the use of digitised resources. It is instead "the use of analytic techniques enabled by computational technology" that can lead to genuinely new methods in the field (7). Drucker presents the example of a hypothetical database of artists' pigments that would include associated information such as chemical composition, preparations, years in use, and geographical sources. A researcher could then turn to this resource with an object like Jan Van Eyck's *The Arnolfini Portrait* (1434) to determine the sources of its pigments and, crucially, what other works use those same pigments. One could use this type of information to forge lateral material connections between artworks that may have previously been separated by scholarly pedigree, drawing connections not only between artists or artists and patrons but along chains of production and among overlooked producers working with similar materials. Within this new constellation of information, Drucker argues, "…computational assessment will demonstrate the identity of objects as nodes in many various networks of cultural relations" (6). Rather than relations of power, ownership, or influence revealed in traditional studies of patronage, provinance, and style, multidirectional connections and overlooked actors begin to emerge.

In the 2010s art historians began taking advantage of the bird's eye perspective enabled by distant viewing. Many of these types of projects are compiled and analysed in *The Routledge Companion to Digital Humanities and Art History* (Brown 2020). In the pre-AI and pre-computer vision era, these projects often took the form of network analysis (Lincoln 2020) and mapping (Joyeux—Prunel 2020). As an example of network analysis, in 2012 Anne Helmreich used gallery exhibition catalogues, sales information, and dealer correspondence from nineteenth-century London, digitised by the Getty Research Institute, to create a model that revealed the unrecognised role of international exchange in the exponential growth of the London art market. This web of connections showed that London's prominence stemmed from its status as a hub of global interaction rather than the concentration of influence in the metropole. In this study, digital analysis revealed a cultural process that was at first obscured by the biased prioritisation of a British point of view (Helmreich and Fletcher 2012). For an example of mapping, one can look to the oft-cited "Mapping Gothic

France" project (2010), which plots images, texts, and bibliographies related to gothic cathedrals on an interactive publicly available digital map of Western Europe. As stated on the website for "Mapping Gothic France," Stephen Murray and Andrew Tallon sought to "establish linkages between the architectural space of individual buildings, geo-political space, and the social space resulting from the interaction (collaboration and conflict) between multiple agents—builders and users" (Murray and Tallon 2012). This graphic organisation shows how typologies and techniques spread and changed across space, avoiding the silos of national patrimony or limiting definitions of style that tend to emerge in more narrowly focused studies. In this mapping project, as in the network analysis example, digital tools allow art historians to escape the strictures of national patrimony and art historical canons by providing new ways to form international connections.

Those in favour of digital art history such as Lev Manovich (2020) claimed that while "computational methods and large datasets do not automatically guarantee more objectivity and inclusion…they can help us to *confront our assumptions, biases, and stereotypes.* They allow us to notice what we overwise may not be able to see" (17). However, Claire Bishop (2018) in her critical "Against Digital Art History," argues that the cardinal sins of digital art history include the reduction of all valuation to statistical calculation, and the continued unexamined belief that statistical evaluation is in and of itself meaningful. For Bishop, with the introduction of computer analysis, other ways of solving problems and other types of information become invisible. Numerical and pattern-based correlation becomes the favoured way of meaning making. Context it seems is a double-edged sword. While digital analysis can remove bias-creating context, such as national origin, it can also remove meaning-making context. Bishop argues that it is just the kind of qualitative and contextual information on which the humanities thrive that gets lost in the translation to the digital medium. While computers can detect patterns, Bishop claims patterns are not in and of themselves meaningful relationships. Meaning comes through interpretation and the somewhat audacious human claim of causality. While data can show correlation, it takes a fallible human who can be tested and argued with to make the claim for cause and effect.

At the height of this debate on digital pattern recognition, text could be read easily by computers, but images could not. While a text can easily be typed into a computer program, an image must first go through a series of translations. Textual content is not necessarily tied to the page. It can be separated from its physical context with little loss of meaning. For an image to be analysed in this fashion, it must be translated from its medium, be that paper and ink, paint and canvas, bronze or stone, into a digital image, and that digital image must be translated into a code. A short, red, feathery brushstroke of oil on canvas must first become a series of pixels, each of a uniform two-dimensional size with an alphanumeric colour designation. Because of these issues with translation, in digital art history, connections were more often based on textual information, metadata such as names of artists, dates, and locations, as well as information culled from exhibition catalogues, auction records, instruction manuals, and non-directly art historical text sources.

Metadata can encompass factual information and a body of historical references. In the era of digital art history, computers could accurately recognise patterns in this metadata but could not yet read the translated images. Thus, digital art history changed the way art historians accessed historical sources but did not fundamentally alter one's relationship to the interpretation of images. While the digital technology of the 2000s sparked a revolution in the practices of the humanities, what is unique to art history, the interpretation of visual evidence, remained relatively unchanged. Sonja Drimmer and C.J. Nygren in their "Art History and AI: Ten Axioms" (2023) explain that "whereas earlier work largely used digital tools for the purposes of information management or to ask questions adjacent to the works of art (in other words, in generating and analyzing what could be considered a work's context), we are seeing the first efforts at aiming AI at the work itself, that is, the use of computer vision as an analytical lens placed on the object" (5.03). Comptuer vision, especially as it has developed in the past five years, fundamentally changed the terms of debate. With digital art history, scholars asked computers to find connections in texts; with the contemporary developments in AI and computer vision, scholars are now asking computers to find connections among images themselves. When asking a machine to deal directly with images, it may become easier to confuse the pattern it finds with art historical interpretation rather than an aid to contextual research.

In *The Atlas of AI: Power, Politics, and the Planetary Costs of Artificial Intelligence*, Kate Crawford (2021) argues that due to the intervening years of military investment in facial recognition, today computers are significantly better at reading images. AI can encode digitised images and read this pixel language almost as fluently as text. This will allow researchers to more fully integrate images into their wide-ranging search for meaningful patterns. Yet this process is not as transparent as it might seem. In digital image recognition, patterns and relationships among the pixels in each image must be translated into a digital code. This code is then compared with a staggeringly large number of other images which have similarly been translated into a code to determine levels of similarity. Yet human inputs are still required to make these similarities meaningful. Using a convolutional neural network, a computer can recognise that one roundish reddish assortment of pixels roughly matches another assortment of pixels, but a human must intervene at some point to associate those assortments with the word "apple." Computers can find patterns; humans determine what that pattern means.

Furthermore, by tying certain combinations of pixels to a certain, necessarily limited, number of words, computer vision cannot hope to encompass the full range of multiple and simultaneous semtanic meanings of an image, even if the system were allowed the proverbial 1000 words. These labels also entrench meanings supplied by a universalised viewer, omitting a variety of meanings that may be based on the viewer's own context and situation. In a special issue of the flagship art historical journal *Art Bulletin* devoted to AI and art history, Leonardo Impett argues that "any computer vision algorithm that can detect an object in an image necessarily contains a culturally and historically contingent understanding of what that object should look like" (2024). Computer vision introduces another opportunity for bias into the already established methods of digital art history.

Many authors have pointed to the biases already present in the digital archive and the tendency of algorithms to further entrench, and even amplify, the prejudices and blind spots of their creators (O'Neil 2016; Noble 2018; Benjamin 2019; Katz 2020). In addition to computer vision itself, systems trained on works of art introduce their own processes of bias. Mashinka Firunts Hakopian (2024) examines how AI art and art history projects often use the most widely available high-quality digital images, usually created by particularly well-funded museums of their most popular and recognisable holdings, thus favouring the Western canon of male European artists. These projects then present their outcomes as the unbiased product of AI, thereby erasing the history of colonial violence that led to the creation of the Western canon in the first place. Ironically, it is just this canonicty that distant reading sought to combat. For Hakopain "both canons and datasets reflect and reinforce existing relations of power" (39).

Even if one consciously diversifies the sources of visual input, this democracy of material being a cornerstone of arguments in favour of the digital humanities, basing one's interpretation on an image of an object, rather than the object itself, leads to some aspects being valued over others. A photograph allows analysis of form, composition, and colour while obscuring other relevant information such as texture, material, weight, and surrounding environment. To some extent this is an issue already faced by Walter Benjamin in his "The Work of Art in the Age of Mechanical Reproduction" (1968) and a necessary artefact of art historical instruction since the nineteenth-century introduction of the slide lecture. Yet as Emma Stanford argues in "A Field Guide to Digital Surrogates: Evaluating and Contextualizing a Rapidly Changing Resource" (2020), new issues of canon formation arise in practical decisions about what to photograph. These include considerations such as "Is the object robust enough to hold up to prolonged handling during digitisation? Is the object of an appropriate size and type to be photographed or scanned using equipment that the institution already owns? Is the object already catalogued? Finally, will the digitised object have *impact*?" and the ever-present question, iIs there funding to support the expensive photographing process? (205). All of this is without mentioning the durational and installation art created since the 1960s and non-Western and Indigenous art forms that are not static, small, or self-contained enough to be captured by photograph (Wasielewski 2023).

After examining the collection and categorisation of images, we can turn to the types of questions afforded by these new assemblages of information. Computer scientists, sometimes working with art historians, have used these datasets to determine the authenticity of paintings, to attribute authorship, and to recognise evolutions in style. For example, in 2008 a group of computer scientists worked with the Van Gogh Museum, using 101 high-resolution images of Van Gogh paintings to develop a program for dating the paintings based on their style, as the artist's output changed significantly over his career. Not only did the program catagorise the artworks, it also determined that some works were so stylistically different as to bring their authorship into question (Johnson et al. 2008; see also Elgammal et al. 2018; Ellis and Johnson 2019; Saleh et al. 2016). Yet authorship, authentication, and merely tracking the evolution of style, without attibution of cause or effect, are not the tasks of today's art historians. Griselda Pollock (2014) clarified: "Art history isn't just about tracing influence and comparing use of things like space, texture, form and colour.... We no longer hunt for connections – we ask questions" (n.p.). Arguing against the mere tracing of influence, Pollock states, "The big question is not that Caillebotte...was influenced by Degas. Instead it is what he did with that 'Degas-ness.' Did he get what Degas was doing? Was he arguing against Degas by making sure we saw some reference to his work? Why would it be valuable to work with it, to work it otherwise? What does referencing and deferring to another artist make possible for the one who does so?" (n.p.) This critique of mere pattern recognition nevertheless reveals the types of research projects that could begin with AI rather than end with it.

Amanda Wasielewski continues this line of argument in *Computational Formalism: Art History and Machine Learning* (2023), putting forward that the new capabilities of computer vision and the research being done by computer scientists are out of step with the current practice of art history. While historians today are interested in social and historical context, and ways of meaning making inflected by semiotic, psychoanalytic, and post-structural theories, as well as theories of race, gender, and sexuality, the type of image studies conducted in the sciences harkens back to the subtle detection of style required for connoisseurship or the comparisons and categorisations employed at the dawn of the discipline. More than being out of date, Wasielewski claims that "merely (re-) importing scientific epistemologies into the humanities without interrogating the ways in which humanities disciplines have moved away from such paradigms over the past fifty years means that the great critiques of Western bias, structures of meaning, and universalism are all but ignored" (13). Yet she also concedes that machine learning can "chart connections and uncover points of comparison among artworks that a human could never find on their own... but the art historian is still left to interpret it" (21). For Wasielewski, computer vision can reveal unsuspected connections in the data, but art historians must still complete their own research and analysis to make those connections meaningful. The technology is a starting point.

Computer vison builds on the promises of digital art history, offering more scholars access to a wider range of materials and even an explicitly more diverse range of materials. Like their predecessors, proponents of computer vision highlight the technology's ability to democratise research and break art historical canons. Katheryn Brown echoes Wasielewski's sentiment that computer vision should supplement art historical interpretation, writing that "If computer 'vision' is understood as a technology that extends rather than displaces human cognition, it might...[enable]

researchers to make feature comparisons across large bodies of work or that reveals qualities invisible to the human eye" (2024, 34). Paul Jaskot similarly argues for computer vision, writing that "the ability to use new computational methods to analyse large bodies of visual evidence from cultures without extensive print traditions or, complementarily, the ability to highlight through sheer number the contributions of art-historical actors of marginalized class, ethnicity, or gender status allow for new challenges to an all-too market-driven choice of subject matter standard in the field" (2020, 12). In its goals, if not necessarily in its techniques, computer vision continues the project embarked upon by digital art history.

Art historian Elizabeth Mansfield's study of cloud formations in the work of nineteenth-century British painter John Constable has begun to emerge as an exemplary case in the use of computer vision in the practice of art history, as has Elizabeth Honig's investigation of the visual connections between the work of various studios related to the Bruegel family of Flemish Renaissance painters (Honig 2018; Mansfield et al. 2022). Mansfield wanted to know why Constable's clouds looked so realistic. Mansfield needed eyes that were not her own, asking herself, "Am I just so accustomed to perceving clouds painted the way Constable paints them as realistic that I am naively trusting their accuracy?" (n.p). Were the clouds convincing because they looked like other painted clouds in the history of art or had Constable hit upon a cloud logic, a pattern for clouds based in nature? For Mansfield, computer vision was uniquely suited for the task. It could see Constable's clouds without the fogging lens of Mansfield's experience with the history of depictions of clouds. With the input of her computer scientist collaborators, she decided to test the hypothesis, first proposed by Kurt Badt, that Constable was referring to Luke Howard's nomenclature system for clouds, created in 1802, which taxonomised clouds into cirrus, cumulus, and stratus. The group used appropriately labelled cloud photographs from the National Oceanographic and Atmospheric Agency to train a computer to recognise the different types of clouds. They then turned this trained system on Constable's clouds and found that they predominantly conformed to Howard's categorisations. For Mansfield, what to make of this correspondence is less clear, as it does not prove the influence of Howard's theories. It is impossible to tell if Constable's clouds conform to Howard's theories or if both Constable's paintings and Howard's theories correspond to their individual observations of clouds. What Mansfield concludes is that "I have become more attentive to my own habits of looking, with a sharpened awareness that my perception is inflected by both disciplinary and personal biases" (n.p.). In *Artforum*, Drimmer (2025) is critical of these findings: "Casting errors as valuable for self-reflection without providing concrete examples of how that reflection has been beneficial does little more than create a permission structure for the failures of this technology" (n.p.). Drimmer is suspicious of the celebration of computer vision and collaboration with computer scientists in the absence of clearly successful outcomes.

Another model for the use of computer vision in art history comes from Amalia Foka (2021) who first surveyed the kinds of questions asked in the major journals of art history, before suggesting how computer vision might help answer them. Rather than survey art historians on their opinions on computer vision (Spratt and Elgammal 2015), Foka sought to bridge the divide in the other direction, to identify which image features art historians utilise within their research. Foka compiles a list of visual attributes that art historians find meaningful, and thus that computer scientists would do well to make searchable. From an art historical perspective some of these catagories could be helpful, including recognising geographic locations, biblical figures, and religious symbols, and even detecting signatures. Others, including recognising a figure's ethnicity or depictions of a certain physical material, risk providing breadth of available objects at the expense of depth of analysis.

This review of the literature on digital art history pre- and post-computer vision has established possible avenues for AI in art historical research as well as in the classroom, including aiding in access to a wider variety of archival materials and images of works of art, visualising networked and geographical connections, and, in some situations, using computer vision to search for images to study, such as depictions of a particular landscape and questions to investigate further, such as Caillebotte's "Degas-ness." Yet the last time new technology in the art history classroom was investigated using a systematic method was in 2008, at the dawn of the digital art history moment (Donahue-Wallace et al. 2008). Reviewing the digital art history of the preceding decade reveals that while computational methods may not be well suited to art interpretation, they are useful for unearthing unexpected connections. The preceding argument suggests that AI would be most useful for students in conducting preliminary research. It could partially automate the already aleatory process of looking at swathes of images and skimming sources to find a peculiarity, a contradiction, a similarity, or resonance that will require more dedicated work to make meaningful. However, this new resource comes with its own dangers. While AI cannot interpret works of art, to many students, who are learning how to interpret art, it can conjure attempts that they might mistake for the real thing.

Current and potential uses of AI in the classroom, as put forward in the literature before 2022, centre around AI used as an individualised tutor, AI used in administration/student risk assessment, and AI used in multimedia gamification. Texts written after 2022 contend with generative large language models such as ChatGPT in the creation and completion of assignments and assessments. These texts also engage, to a lesser extent, visual generative AI such as Dall-E or Midjourney. There is a need for discipline specificity in this literature, especially in dealing with images. Hwang and Chen (2023) recommend that "using Midjourney to create artworks enables students to focus on their creative thinking rather than spending time on drawing the details" (2.6). As any art historian will tell you, there is no separating creative thinking from drawing the details. Drawing the details is where creative thinking happens.

Looking at the sparse discipline-specific literature such as "Supporting Learning in Art History – Artificial Intelligence in Digital Humanities Education" (Messemer et al. 2020), suggestions include the notion that "Computer-aided selection supports the balance and objectivity of the learning material. Thus, AI can even lead to the provision of politically truly neutral education that can be less influenced" (28). Here again we see the diversity and democracy promised by digital art history, but also a glossing over of the decidely non-neutral aspects of digitisation efforts and computer vision training. They also suggest that the multi-modal capcities of AI could be used to develop an application that would recognise images of an artwork and automatically "fetch categorised information on the history of the artwork directly onto the students personal computer or mobile device" (31). They suggest, "As a next step it is necessary to develop tools to interact with these images and the data — to create personal digital collections of images of artworks, to annotate, to share etc." (32). While such a program might be useful at the early stages of art historical study or in art appreciation classes, it would not be useful for research, as it automates skills that will be necessary should the student continue in the field. The ability to annotate and share collections of artwork is promising, but this would be a more straightforward software development rather than an application of AI.

Excitement about the ability of AI to process vast amounts of data and identify patterns, particularly in image analysis, echoes the optimism around data processing in digital art history. Each promises to democratise access to information and reveal new connections. Each unfortunately runs the risk of substituting pattern recognition for interpretation. Moreover, neither method inherently erases the overrepresentation of the Western canon in its input materials. At this moment of transition, today's challenge is to separate the possibly useful aspects of AI from the harmful ones in both the practice and teaching of art history.

References

Bender, K. 2015. Distant Viewing in Art History: A Case Study of Artistic Productivity. *International Journal for Digital Art History* (1): 100–110.

Benjamin, Walter. 1968. The Work of Art in the Age of Mechanical Reproduction. In *Illuminations*, ed. Hannah Arendt. Translated by Harry Zohn. Schocken Books.

Benjamin, Ruha. 2019. *Race After Technology: Abolitionist Tools for the New Jim Code*. Polity.

Bishop, Claire. 2018. Against Digital Art History. *International Journal of Digital Art History* 3 (July): 123–131. https://doi.org/10.11588/dah.2018.3.49915.

Brown, Kathryn, ed. 2020. *The Routledge Companion to Digital Humanities and Art History*. Routledge. https://doi.org/10.4324/9780429505188.

Brown, Kathryn. 2024. After Art History? Artworks as Data. *The Art Bulletin* 106 (2): 33–36. https://doi.org/10.1080/00043079.2024.2296277.

Crawford, Kate. 2021. *The Atlas of AI: Power, Politics, and the Planetary Costs of Artificial Intelligence*. Yale University Press.

Donahue-Wallace, Kelly, Laetitia Amelia La Follette, and Andrea Pappas, eds. 2008. *Teaching Art History with New Technologies: Reflections and Case Studies*. Cambridge Scholars Publishing.

Drimmer, Sonja. 2025. Machine Yearning: On Generative AI's Structure of Feeling. *Artforum* 63 (8). https://www.artforum.com/features/generative-ai-structure-of-feeling-1234728310/.

Drimmer, Sonja and C. J. Nygren. 2023. Art History and AI: Ten Axioms. *International Journal for Digital Art History* 9: 5.02–5.13. https://doi.org/10.11588/dah.2023.9.90400.

Drucker, Johanna. 2013. Is There a 'Digital' Art History? *Visual Resources* 29 (1–2): 5–13. https://doi.org/10.1080/01973762.2013.761106.

Elgammal, Ahmed, Yan Kang, and Milko Den Leeuw. 2018. Picasso, Matisse, or a Fake? Automated Analysis of Drawings at the Stroke Level for Attribution and Authentication. In *Proceedings of the Thirty-Second AAAI Conference on*

Artificial Intelligence (AAAI-18), 42–50. https://cdn.aaai.org/ojs/11313/11313-13-14841-1-2-20201228.pdf.

Ellis, Margaret Holben, and C. Richard Johnson. 2019. Computational Connoisseurship: Enhanced Examination Using Automated Image Analysis. *Visual Resources* 35 (1–2): 125–140. https://doi.org/10.1080/01973762.2019.1556886

Foka, Amalia. 2021. Computer Vision Applications for Art History: Reflections and Paradigms for Future Research. In *Proceedings of EVA London: AI and the Arts: Artificial Imagination* (EVA 2021), 73–80. https://www.scienceopen.com/hosted-document?doi=10.14236/ewic/EVA2021.12.

Hakopian, Mashinka Firunts. 2024. Art Histories from Nowhere: On the Coloniality of Experiments in Art and Artificial Intelligence. *AI & Society* 39 (1): 29–41. https://doi.org/10.1007/s00146-023-01768-0.

Helmreich, Anne and Pamela Fletcher. 2012. Local/Global: Mapping Nineteenth-Century London's Art Market. *Nineteenth-Century Art Worldwide* 11 (3). www.19thc-artworldwide.org/index.php/autumn12/fletcher-helmreich-mapping-the-london-art-market.

Honig, Elizabeth. 2018. Human Vision, Computer Technology and the Image Investigation Tool. The Frick Collection (website), April 13, 2018. https://www.frick.org/interact/miniseries/searching_seeing/elizabeth_honig_human_vision_computer_technology_image.

Hwang, Gwo-Jen, and Nian-Shing. Chen. 2023. Exploring the Potential of Generative Artificial Intelligence in Education: Applications, Challenges, and Future Research Directions. *Educational Technology & Society* 26 (2): I–XVIII. https://doi.org/10.30191/ETS.202304_26(2).0014.

Impett, L. 2024. Digital Art History as Critical AI. *The Art Bulletin* 106 (2): 11–14. https://doi.org/10.1080/00043079.2024.2296270.

Jaskot, Paul. 2020. Digital Methods and the Historiography of Art. In *The Routledge Companion to Digital Humanities and Art History*. Routledge. https://www.taylorfrancis.com/chapters/edit/10.4324/9780429505188-3/digital-methods-historiography-art-paul-jaskot?context=ubx&refId=fa3c3036-b12a-4fe0-a43e-0a4914436781.

Johnson, C. Richard, Ella Hendriks, Igor J. Berezhnoy, Eugene Brevdo, Shannon M. Hughes, and Ingrid Daubechies. 2008. Image Processing for Artist Identification. *IEEE Signal Processing Magazine* 25 (4): 37–48. https://doi.org/10.1109/MSP.2008.923513.

Joyeux-Prunel, Béatrice. 2020. Digital Humanities for a Spatial, Global, and Social History of Art. In *The Routledge Companion to Digital Humanities and Art History*, ed. Kathryn Brown. Routledge. https://www.taylorfrancis.com/chapters/edit/10.4324/9780429505188-10/digital-humanities-spatial-global-social-history-art-b%C3%A9atrice-joyeux-prunel?context=ubx&refId=3d361452-369b-4040-b160-c7474dd99119

Katz, Yarden. 2020. *Artificial Whiteness: Politics and Ideology in Artificial Intelligence*. Columbia University Press.

Lincoln, Matthew. 2020. Tangled Metaphors: Network Thinking and Network Analysis in the History of Art. In *The Routledge Companion to Digital Humanities and Art History*, ed. Kathryn Brown. Routledge. https://www.taylorfrancis.com/chapters/edit/10.4324/9780429505188-9/tangled-metaphors-matthew-lincoln?context=ubx&refId=2d4c198e-2602-4e19-bdb9-9ece2a324bdc

Manovich, Lev. 2020. *Cultural Analytics*. MIT Press. https://drive.google.com/file/d/1NuSQcqgZkj4sToU3EfeFmq1jPC36hU58/view

Mansfield, Elizabeth, Zhuomin Zhang, Jia Li, John Russell, George S. Young, Catherine Adams, and James Z. Wang. 2022. Techniques of the Art Historical Observer. *Nineteenth-Century Art Worldwide* 21 (1). https://doi.org/10.29411/ncaw.2022.21.1.5.

Messemer, Heike, Walpola Layantha Perera, Matthias Heinz, Florian Niebling, and F. Maiwald. 2020. Supporting Learning in Art History-Artificial Intelligence in Digital Humanities Education. In *Erfahrungen mit digitaler Praxis: Workshop Gemeinschaften in Neuen Medien*, 28–35. https://tud.qucosa.de/api/qucosa%3A73553/attachment/ATT-0/.

Moretti, Franco. 2000. Conjectures on World Literature. *New Left Review* 1: 54–68. https://newleftreview.org/issues/ii1/articles/franco-moretti-conjectures-on-world-literature.

Murray, Stephen, and Andrew Tallon. 2012. Mapping Gothic France. https://mcid.mcah.columbia.edu/collection/mapping-gothic.

Noble, Safiya Umoja. 2018. *Algorithms of Oppression: How Search Engines Reinforce Racism*. New York University Press.

O'Neil, Cathy. 2016. *Weapons of Math Destruction: How Big Data Increases Inequality and Threatens Democracy*. Crown.

Pollock, Griselda. 2014. Computers can Find Similarities Between Paintings—But Art History is About so Much More. *The Conversation*. https://theconversation.com/computers-can-find-similarities-between-paintings-but-art-history-is-about-so-much-more-30752.

Saleh, Babak, Kanako Abe, Ravneet Singh Arora, and Ahmed Elgammal. 2016. Toward Automated Discovery of Artistic Influence. *Multimedia Tools and Applications* 75 (7): 3565–3591. https://link.springer.com/article/10.1007/s11042-014-2193-x.

Spratt, Emily, and Ahmed Elgammal. 2015. Computational Beauty: Aesthetic Judgment at the Intersection of Art and Science. In *Computer Vision—ECCV 2014 Workshops, Lecture Notes in Computer Science*, ed. Lourdes Agapito, Michael M. Bronstein, and Carsten Rother, vol. 8925, 35–53. https://doi.org/10.1007/978-3-319-16178-5_3.

Standford, Emma. 2020. A Field Guide to Digital Surrogates: Evaluating and Contextualizing a Rapidly Changing Resource. In *The Routledge Companion to Digital Humanities and Art History*, ed. Kathryn Brown. Routledge. https://www.taylorfrancis.com/chapters/edit/10.4324/9780429505188-19/field-guide-digital-surrogates-emma-stanford?context=ubx&refId=a4e8a36a-d0c1-4ea4-84cc-8b8f7b291a2e

Wasielewski, Amanda. 2023. *Computational Formalism Art History and Machine Learning*. MIT Press.

CHAPTER 11

Computer Vision, Human Vision, and Future Visions: Lessons From AI in the Liberal Arts Classroom

Kimiko Matsumura

AI has radically altered the way students seek out and organise information, forcing us to re-evaluate our pedagogical and professional roles and to think carefully about what makes our field useful for higher education and society. Students use ChatGPT to research, summarise readings, take notes, and submit passable work with minimal effort. As a result, foundational assignments like comparison essays have become questionable assessments of student learning and require thoughtful modification.

We may feel safe now because the tools are flawed and hand-written exams can still circumvent some issues. However, this is likely the worst version of AI we will ever use, as Ethan Mollick has argued (2024, 60–62). If this is the case, can exams even assess the skills that will be practical for future professionals and critical thinkers? How do we evaluate and change our learning outcomes as AI keeps improving?

K. Matsumura (✉)
Lake Forest College, Lake Forest, IL, USA
e-mail: kmatsumura@lakeforest.edu

L. Cempellin, M. Geiger (eds.), *Reimagining Art History with Artificial Intelligence*,
https://doi.org/10.1007/978-3-032-21685-4_11

Frankly, I have had a bit of a crisis in the last couple of years. I question the value of an art historical education if Claude works in seconds. Is memorisation important if we can reliably externalise our knowledge and skip to higher taxonomies of learning? What defines subject mastery? What are our learning outcomes?

I still believe art history matters, and because of that belief I am slowly embracing AI. However, that requires me to ask different questions to ensure the discipline remains viable beyond our current "coverage mentality," beyond blanket memorisation for a global canon of objects from prehistory to the present (Sienkewicz 2016). Instead, I ask, "What am I preparing my students for? What skills do I want adults to have? What do I want them to be able to do in a world where AI is ubiquitous?"

To address my existential dilemma, this chapter discusses some ways I incorporate large language learning models into my course assignments and my motivations in doing so. I foreground the learning outcomes that drive my pedagogical choices, showing through student assessment how AI can clarify disciplinary values and demonstrate our utility in the current higher ed administrative climate. Acknowledging that these assignments respond to a specific technological moment, I use my findings to offer a potential set of course design principles for our inevitably AI-altered futures. The technology is not the end of art history—it is a tool for enhancing what we already know about good pedagogy.

Learning Outcomes and Sample Assignments

In Fall 2022, I suspected that some students were outsourcing their comparison essays to ChatGPT based on the standardised structure of the papers and the outrageously false visual evidence presented therein. While I could not prove with certainty that anyone used the program, it disheartened me to see how easily undergraduates could circumvent the analysis skills I sought to promote. Banning AI was impractical without reliable detection tools to enforce that policy, so at first, I reluctantly returned to in-class exams, an assessment tool I had previously abandoned. I also continued to assign the traditional visual analysis essay to practise writing because LLMs could not yet perform this task. By Fall 2023, however, it was widely known that DALL-E could generate images and Gemini could interpret them; I could not avoid AI anymore.

There were things I liked about AI, particularly its ability to help brainstorm ideas or rephrase concepts, but I remained frustrated by the students' lack of engagement with the outputs. Papers contained obvious hallucinations that contradicted course content and formal evidence. Outside the classroom, I also saw people struggling to identify AI-generated images. Viral social media moments like the "Balenciaga Pope" demonstrated how we were failing to notice obvious formal or historical inconsistencies (Huang 2023).

As we confront these challenges, I believe art history offers vital competencies in critical thinking for all people, regardless of discipline. Visual literacy needs cultivation to parse truth from hallucination in our emerging technological landscape, but it is not innate (Sienkewicz 2013, 121). This is where I think art history offers our strongest value, especially at the foundations level where most students interface with the discipline for the first and last time. If the students could at least recognise when the AI was wrong and correct those mistakes, I would know that they too understood the basic formal and contextual elements of their artworks and perhaps would learn to be more suspicious of AI-generated answers and images.

These issues have sharpened my perspectives on the field and my teaching, helping me develop the following course learning outcomes that marry traditional disciplinary standards with new analytic needs:

- Learn to analyse and describe objects.
- Recognise the key stylistic and historical traits of different art movements and/or cultures.
- Contextualise unknown objects by connecting them to historical and scholarly precedents.
- Critically assess AI and AI-generated material.

I then used backwards design to create assignments that cultivate these skills, relying on the stated learning outcomes to construct AI-based exercises aligned with the desired competencies (Wiggins and McTighe 2005, 13–34). Two such assignments are a critical analysis of an AI-generated comparison essay and a critique of an AI-generated image. Both interventions occurred in the 100-level introductory survey in the Fall semester of 2024 after being piloted in Spring 2024. The course is required for art and art history majors, but it also satisfies the general education programme's humanities requirement. Typically, students are non-majors ranging in status from Freshmen to Seniors with little to no experience in art history. Fall 2024 enrolled 22 students.

My classroom is unusual. Since 2022, I deliver two 50-minute lectures per week, then use the third 50-minute class as a "lab period" for in-class group assignments. Students are randomly sorted into groups of four or five at the beginning of the semester and gather every week to complete activities that practise description, comparison, analysis, and writing. I could thus introduce these assignments to my course design without significant changes, and I could also advise and monitor students while they used the technology as an in-person facilitator.

Sample Assignment 1, Comparison Critique: I value the skills cultivated by analytic writing, and I believe the traditional comparison essay can still practise and assess these skills under the right conditions. I established the following goals for the assignment as I designed the updated version:

- Identify key visual and historical similarities and differences between objects.
- Define effective writing strategies for art historical analysis.
- Assess the strengths and weaknesses of large language learning models for essay writing.

The resulting assignment is the second step in a scaffolded comparison essay completed over the course of a month. In week 2 of the semester, students chose two course objects for a future comparison essay and submitted a worksheet containing the visual and historical information for their choices. In week 3, students prompted an LLM to generate a comparison essay about those two objects before annotating the output (Fig. 11.1).

Students practised this activity with different objects in their assigned groups during the week 3 "lab period," then completed annotations with their chosen objects independently, outside of class. Because they had already established the evidence in their week 2 worksheets, students were capable of noting where the AI succeeded or fell short in the assigned annotations, which proceeded as follows:

1. Identify which AI you used and include the prompt you fed it.
2. Underline parts of essay structure in red (thesis statement, topic sentences).
3. Highlight passages that need more information or support to clarify and strengthen the point in blue (this includes overly generic or vague language).

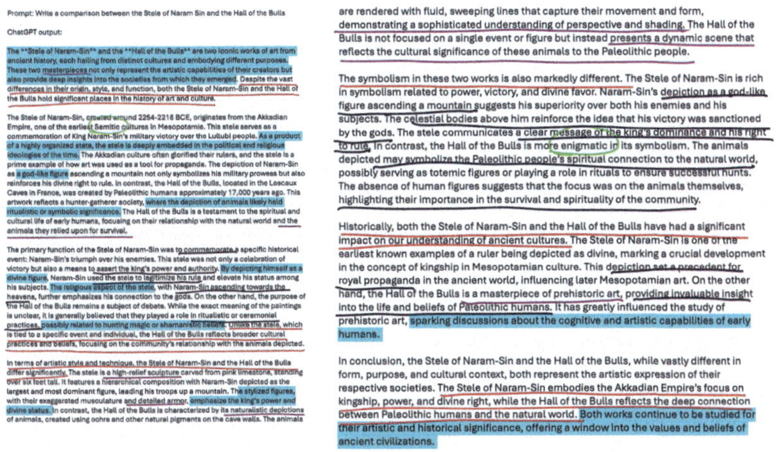

Prompt: Write a comparison between the Stele of Naram Sin and the Hall of the Bulls

ChatGPT output:

The **Stele of Naram-Sin** and the **Hall of the Bulls** are two iconic works of art from ancient history, each hailing from distinct cultures and embodying different purposes. These two masterpieces not only represent the artistic capabilities of their creators but also provide deep insights into the societies from which they emerged. Despite the vast differences in their origin, style, and function, both the Stele of Naram-Sin and the Hall of the Bulls hold significant places in the history of art and culture.

The Stele of Naram-Sin, created around 2254-2218 BCE, originates from the Akkadian Empire, one of the earliest Semitic cultures in Mesopotamia. This stele serves as a commemoration of King Naram-Sin's military victory over the Lullubi people. As a product of a highly organized state, the stele is deeply embedded in the political and religious ideologies of the time. The Akkadian culture often glorified their rulers, and the stele is a prime example of how art was used as a tool for propaganda. The depiction of Naram-Sin as a god-like figure ascending a mountain not only symbolizes his military prowess but also reinforces his divine right to rule. In contrast, the Hall of the Bulls, located in the Lascaux Caves in France, was created by Paleolithic humans approximately 17,000 years ago. This artwork reflects a hunter-gatherer society, where the depiction of animals likely held ritualistic or symbolic significance. The Hall of the Bulls is a testament to the spiritual and cultural life of early humans, focusing on their relationship with the natural world and the animals they relied upon for survival.

The primary function of the Stele of Naram-Sin was to commemorate a specific historical event: Naram-Sin's triumph over his enemies. This stele was not only a celebration of victory but also a means to assert the king's power and authority. By depicting himself as a divine figure, Naram-Sin used the stele to legitimize his rule and elevate his status among his subjects. The religious aspect of the stele, with Naram-Sin ascending towards the heavens, further emphasizes his connection to the gods. On the other hand, the purpose of the Hall of the Bulls remains a subject of debate. While the exact meaning of the paintings is unclear, it is generally believed that they played a role in ritualistic or ceremonial practices, possibly related to hunting magic or shamanistic beliefs. Unlike the stele, which is tied to a specific event and individual, the Hall of the Bulls reflects broader cultural practices and beliefs, focusing on the community's relationship with the animals depicted.

In terms of artistic style and technique, the Stele of Naram-Sin and the Hall of the Bulls differ significantly. The stele is a high-relief sculpture carved from pink limestone, standing over six feet tall. It features a hierarchical composition with Naram-Sin depicted as the largest and most dominant figure, leading his troops up a mountain. The stylized figures, with their exaggerated musculature and detailed armor, emphasize the king's power and divine status. In contrast, the Hall of the Bulls is characterized by its naturalistic depictions of animals, created using ochre and other natural pigments on the cave walls. The animals are rendered with fluid, sweeping lines that capture their movement and form, demonstrating a sophisticated understanding of perspective and shading. The Hall of the Bulls is not focused on a single event or figure but instead presents a dynamic scene that reflects the cultural significance of these animals to the Paleolithic people.

The symbolism in these two works is also markedly different. The Stele of Naram-Sin is rich in symbolism related to power, victory, and divine favor. Naram-Sin's depiction as a god-like figure ascending a mountain suggests his superiority over both his enemies and his subjects. The celestial bodies above him reinforce the idea that his victory was sanctioned by the gods. The stele communicates a clear message of the king's dominance and his right to rule. In contrast, the Hall of the Bulls is more enigmatic in its symbolism. The animals depicted may symbolize the Paleolithic people's spiritual connection to the natural world, possibly serving as totemic figures or playing a role in rituals to ensure successful hunts. The absence of human figures suggests that the focus was on the animals themselves, highlighting their importance in the survival and spirituality of the community.

Historically, both the Stele of Naram-Sin and the Hall of the Bulls have had a significant impact on our understanding of ancient cultures. The Stele of Naram-Sin is one of the earliest known examples of a ruler being depicted as divine, marking a crucial development in the concept of kingship in Mesopotamian culture. This depiction set a precedent for royal propaganda in the ancient world, influencing later Mesopotamian art. On the other hand, the Hall of the Bulls is a masterpiece of prehistoric art, providing invaluable insight into the life and beliefs of Paleolithic humans. It has greatly influenced the study of prehistoric art, sparking discussions about the cognitive and artistic capabilities of early humans.

In conclusion, the Stele of Naram-Sin and the Hall of the Bulls, while vastly different in form, purpose, and cultural context, both represent the artistic expression of their respective societies. The Stele of Naram-Sin embodies the Akkadian Empire's focus on kingship, power, and divine right, while the Hall of the Bulls reflects the deep connection between Paleolithic humans and the natural world. Both works continue to be studied for their artistic and historical significance, offering a window into the values and beliefs of ancient civilizations.

Fig. 11.1 Instructor-annotated sample ChatGPT output

4. Highlight information that is not sustained by the sources you have in orange (i.e., the textbook, the lecture, our assigned supplementary materials).
5. Underline any outright false or problematic information in purple (a hallucination, misconception, or misinterpretation).
6. Circle any word or phrase you don't know or wouldn't use in green (not your voice).
7. Underline redundant passages in black.
8. After annotating, reflect on the AI-generated essay. What did the AI do well? What did it do poorly or insufficiently? Give specific examples. Did it miss any important details? What about the text is useful and what would you do differently?

Of the eight consenting study participants, seven submited responses to question 8. Some were highly dismissive of AI and others more positive; nevertheless all students identified strengths and weaknesses in their AI-generated essay (Table 11.1):

Overall, the students reported that the AI text offers good foundations for argument direction and structure but requires additional formal details and stronger organisational practices to create more effective essays.

Table 11.1 Strengths and weaknesses of AI-generated essays that seven students identified in their homework

Pros	**Number of samples identifying the issue (of 7)**
Fast	1
Provides clear essay structure	5
Identifies key points	7
Provides evidence for claims	2
Cons	**Number of samples identifying the issue (of 7)**
Repetitive	5
Includes misconceptions or hallucinations	2
Lacks specific formal evidence/evidence is vague	5
Structure is weak	5
Is not thorough/misses key information	6

Arguments for and against AI often address the rapid outputs or the hallucination rates, and while some students mentioned these issues, more considered the breadth and depth of content and its organisation. One strong student sample is illustrative of these ideas:

> The AI broke up the essay into very small paragraphs which I thought was unnecessary since they could just be combined. I also thought that some of the topic sentences did not exactly serve as topic sentences but rather continuations of the previous paragraph, adding to the point that the paragraphs could have been combined. There wasn't any false information but the information they gave was quite vague. They went into a little detail of the features of the second piece, but it was not in-depth and for both, failed to bring in ideas of composition, line or symmetry into contention.
>
> It captured the 'why' well. The essay focuses on what the art depicts and why it was relevant or important to that period of time. However, it does not draw too much attention onto the similarities. This, as well as the lack of articulation onto the structure/organization/composition of the piece, only allowed insight into the differences between both the pieces vaguely rather than drawing sophisticated connections between the two. For example, I mentioned in my worksheet that a similarity between them could be that there is a level of reverence for women because of how the figurine highlighted the importance of the female fertility but also how Nefertiti was drawn in equal scale to the king and had a more adorned throne, which was a purposeful ode to her importance during Akhenaten's rule.

> From this exercise, the only parts of the essay I would use would be how to structure the essay, and where I should put what detail. I liked how they broke up the paragraphs to have one paragraph be solely about the Egyptian relief and the other to be about the figurine, then a paragraph (or set) to be about both. Without breaking up the paragraphs in the way they did, I think talking about each piece separately with their historical context and then going into my comparison later would be a good way to structure my essay.

While this student deftly articulates concerns about breadth, depth, and formatting, they are not alone in their ability to note these problems; all seven samples recognise that AI can identify key information, but six note that it needs to be more thorough. Five out of seven samples address the repetitive nature of the outputs and call for richer visual evidence. Beyond content, six of the seven reflections also stated that the AI helped them consider some aspect of the essay process more broadly, such as effective vocabulary, structure, evidence, and/or argumentation. It is clear, then, that the activity makes room for critiquing not just LLMs but also the qualities of good writing.

Sample Assignment 2, "In the style of": In week 13 of 15, students used DALL-E via Copilot to generate any image in the style of one of our class's art movements. At this point in the semester, students had encountered select global material from prehistory through the nineteenth century and had practised identifying and comparing formal and historical details in several graded assignments. Student group dynamics were also well established as this was the tenth lab session. "In the style of" therefore served as an opportunity to review stylistic principles towards the end of the semester in a low-stakes environment with familiar peers.

The goals of this assignment are:

- Recognise the primary characteristics of an art movement.
- Contextualise an image in its historical precedents.
- Assess the strengths and weakness of AI image generators.

Students completed the activity in their assigned groups over the course of the weekly 50-minute "lab period." After prompting AI to produce an image in the artistic style of their choice (Fig. 11.2), students evaluated the output as follows:

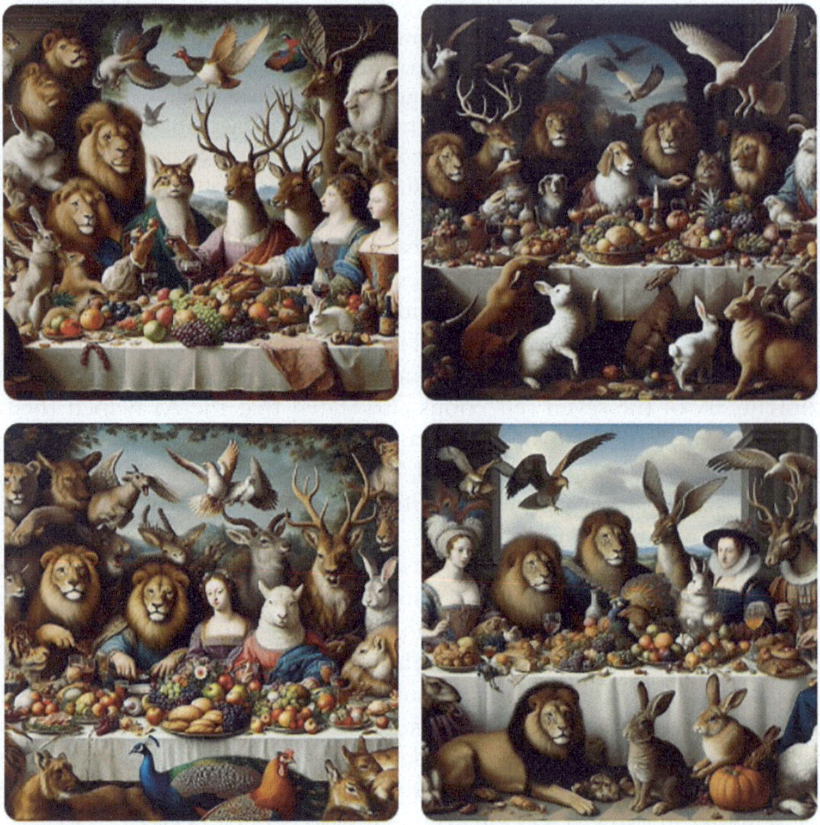

Fig. 11.2 Animals in the style of Renaissance painting. 2024 DALL-E images generated by author as an example for the student assignment

1. Copy your exact prompt and a screenshot of the images Copilot produced. How did the AI do? What elements of the image are consistent with the style you chose and what is not? Be specific. Consider things like composition, iconography, apparent medium, light, shadow, colour, etc.
2. Bring in a relevant image from class to help you compare and/or contrast. What does the AI-generated image capture about your period-correct example and what does it miss?

3. What generalisations do you think the AI is making about the subject matter or the style (women are blonde, animals mean wild animals, Renaissance means Last Supper, etc.)?
4. Create a more specific prompt that includes further period-specific visual and iconographic details to help the AI generate a more relevant image, then prompt the AI. Copy your exact prompt and a screenshot of the four images Copilot produced. Are these images better? How so (i.e., what is more consistent with the style and what is it still missing)?

Four group responses from consenting students reveal developing competencies in visual analysis and stronger capabilities in contextualisation. Two of the groups chose Impressionism, one group chose Romanticism, and the remaining group selected Baroque (Table 11.2).

All groups approached or met the assignment learning outcomes by addressing the issues in Table 11.2. Nevertheless, groups varied in their ability to both recognise and articulate elements of form in relation to stylistic principles, which indicates that the assignment needs to be adjusted to improve the quality of responses. Excerpts from two different group submissions point to this discrepancy, showing a range of proficiencies concerning vocabulary use and the uneven application of detailed supporting evidence.

In this partially successful example, the group identifies basic concepts, but the discussion of Romanticism is incomplete and does not always use proper terminology (Fig. 11.3). Initially, the group is too focused on identifying overarching formal elements without explaining their relationship to the principles of the movement:

Table 11.2 Scoring for the achievement of learning outcomes for four student group samples comparing an AI-generated image to a canonical style

	Not successful	*Partially successful*	*Successful*
Identifies key stylistic elements		1	3
Uses discipline-specific terminology		1	3
Identifies AI generalisations about style and subject matter			4
Chooses an appropriate comparable class object and effectively compares it to the AI image		1	3

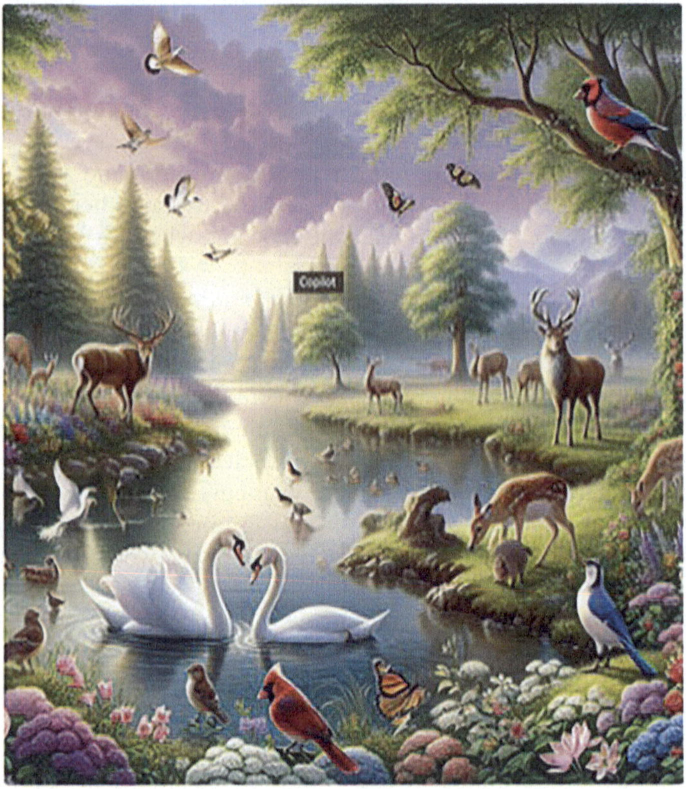

Fig. 11.3 Student group generated DALL-E image based on the prompt "Animals in the style of a romantic image"

> The AI did well to show a great use of light and color. We can see texture and shadow in the water. We can also see how the deer create a scene of symmetry. Furthermore, we can also see rich colors in the blues. The color used in this piece is very vibrant, and wouldn't necessarily be seen as rich in nature, showing how the AI perceived the prompt of romanticism.

When they compare the generated image to a course image, however—in this case *Among the Sierra Nevada, California* by Albert Bierstadt—the response improves slightly. The group still does not describe issues in scale, proportion, or naturalism, but they begin to marry up their generalisations with the Bierstadt example and parse the ideas of romance from Romanticism as a movement:

> The AI overemphasizes the tone of romanticism, rather than just the style of romanticism. This can be seen with the swans forming the shape of a heart, for example. The AI correctly utilizes pictorial space, shown in the animals getting smaller and the river getting thinner the further it gets, as well as the use of atmospheric perspective shown in the farther trees and mountains getting less vibrant and defined. We can see the use of light, color, and an overly dramatic landscape, which look artificial and contribute to the almost 'godly' nature of the work. We can also note the family of deer, shown at the bottom which refers to the ideal family environment.
>
> The AI assumes that because this is a Romantic era painting that it is a landscape. There is an assumption of fantastical elements to the piece, which may be a motivator for the unnatural amount of elements all concentrated in one place. These animals are all posed perfectly, with most looking into the light or at the viewer, adding to the intention that the AI wanted to make a highly idealized landscape view of nature, almost to an exaggerated extent. The AI tries to incorporate a romantic tone within the image, specifically the flowers and swans.

This group's second prompt narrows their chosen genre to the Hudson River School and includes more formal and historical context (Fig. 11.4):

> Prompt: 'draw an 1860's American natural landscape Hudson River fine brushstroke natural landscape with elements of idealized nature.' The AI correctly used light and color, as well as a more finished example of atmospheric perspective. We can also see the 'spotlight' style sun that shines light on the landscape. Compared to the original, less specific prompt, the results of the more specific prompt had clear intention towards making the paintings more warm toned rather than cool toned, also adding to the 'hazy' romantic style.

While it is clear that the group understands some elements of the style, as seen in the key words chosen for the prompt and the limited terminology in the response, the analysis still needs more specificity to demonstrate deep learning. By contrast, another student group more fully describes formal and historical elements for their chosen style (Impressionism) and more consistently uses discipline-specific language throughout their response. Their initial discussion begins to illustrate this difference (Fig. 11.5):

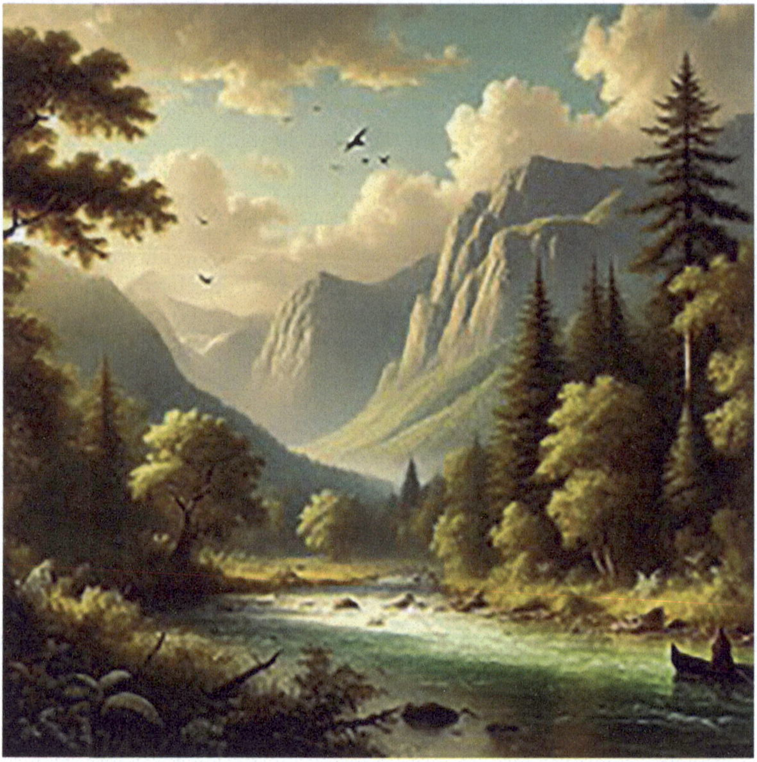

Fig. 11.4 Student-generated DALL-E image based on the prompt "draw an 1860's American natural landscape Hudson River fine brushstroke natural landscape with elements of idealized nature"

> These images align with the Impressionist style through their use of vibrant, bold colors and loose brushstrokes. The everyday subject matter like a walk in the park and a river are characteristic of Impressionism. These AI images however look more polished than Impressionist artworks. Basically, they look more polished and finished since their AI generated rather than created by a human.

The response gets even more specific after comparing their images with Claude Monet's *Impression, Sunrise*:

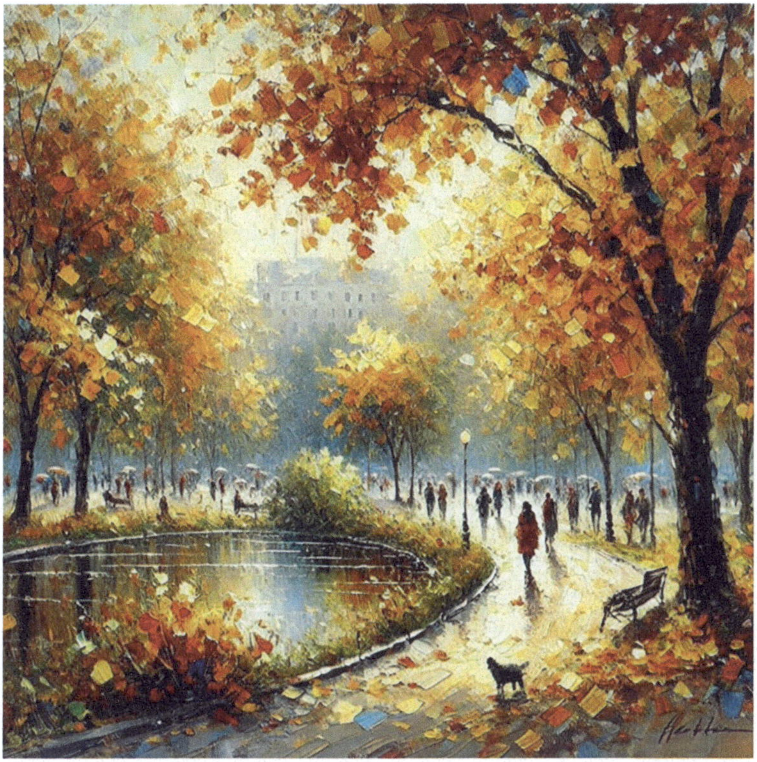

Fig. 11.5 Student-generated DALL-E image in the style of Impressionism

The AI generated image shows the bright colors and use of light that are common in Impressionism. It somewhat captures the feature of visible/textured brushstrokes, though not fully. Subject matter in the AI-generated pieces is rendered in too much detail as compared to Monet's piece, thus diluting the focus of Impressionism on 'spontaneity' and the subjective interpretation of reality. The first generated image forgets the surface orientation and flatness of Impressionism.

The AI assumes Impressionist paintings have a saturated, vibrant and bright palette. Though there are visible brushstrokes, as accurate to Impressionism, the AI is still trying to insert naturalism into the images. The AI interprets the subjective snapshot values of Impressionism as highly atmospheric and idealized scenes. Subject matter rather than formal elements (such as color and lighting) are the focus of the pieces, despite the

> focus of Impressionism on the formal [...]. The AI assumes Impressionism is set in modern times (see the umbrellas, jeans and contemporary building in the background).

While some of the vocabulary still needs adjustment, the discussion is more well rounded and specific than the previous group's submission. This group then regenerated images based on the prompt "Make me an Impressionist landscape with muted colors, visible brush strokes, and a serene, natural atmosphere" (Fig. 11.6).

> [T]he brushstrokes and natural use of light are more obvious and more random than the previous images, still the brushstrokes are very blended and smooth in certain areas. We see the 'crispiest' part of the image in the center, a nod at how we only have one small plane of focus at a time, demonstrating the subjective optics valued in Impressionism.
>
> Atmospheric perspective is still being utilized, thus negating Impressionist focus on emphasizing the flatness and two-dimensionality of the canvas and collapsing space/warping perspective. This looks like it would have been painted outside—'*en plein air*.'

Much like the partially successful example, the group's analysis improved after they compared the AI image with a course image. Language became more precise and context more thorough. Such improvement across both examples may indicate that students are better able to deduce principles though comparative practice than from memory alone, and that the analysis of the course example is an essential step in the assignment. It is possible that starting the assignment with the course example rather than the AI image may help students identify stylistic principles and strengthen their answers. Subsequent semesters could begin with an evaluation of the period-specific example rather than the AI-generated image to measure improvements in student comprehension.

There are other opportunities for adjustment. Groups did not always read instructions carefully or respond thoroughly. Several submitted images are missing their prompts, for example, making it impossible to observe the language students are using or the evolution of their descriptions. More hands-on instructor intervention may remind groups to follow directions. Students were also limited by the position of the assignment in the semester. Three of the four groups chose a style covered in the week of the assignment, which suggests students are more likely to turn to

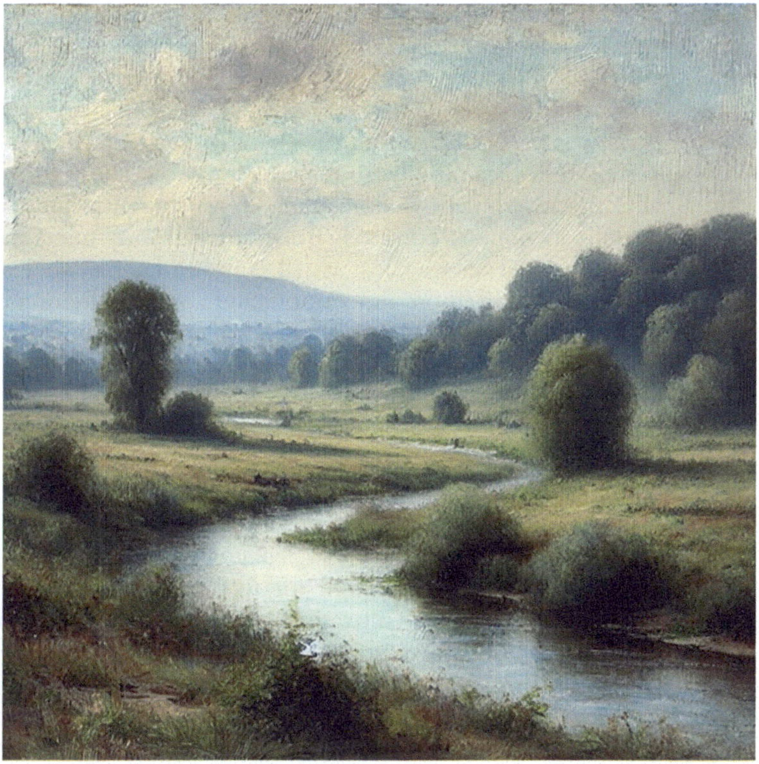

Fig. 11.6 Student-generated DALL-E image based on the prompt "Make me an Impressionist landscape with muted colors, visible brush strokes, and a serene, natural atmosphere"

recent material in the activity and less inclined to review coursework, as intended. As such, it is unclear if the assignment is effective for course review. This could be addressed by assigning periods to the groups directly in subsequent semesters or by placing the assignment at the end of the course for a more deliberate final review.

The activity is perhaps not more successful than traditional visual analysis or identification of an unknown since both assignments ask students to make deductions based on novel images. However, it has several advantages over traditional methods. First, the collaborative nature of the assignment along with the unexpected image outputs allowed students to reflect on the significant elements of form and reason through unusual or unlikely design elements both verbally and in writing. Second, AI images permitted groups to evaluate typical and atypical characteristics without resorting to pre-existing scholarly analysis, and in exceptional cases, they facilitated conversations about biases in the training data as students discussed how certain terms lead the AI to make assumptions about form or content; finally, the assignment demonstrated how students can apply visual literacy skills in non-art contexts. By asking students to leverage their art historical proficiencies against visual culture material, they saw how their abilities in identification, description, and contextualisation can be used beyond the classroom. Overall, these advantages combined with the ability to meet learning outcomes suggest that the assignment is a useful exercise for cultivating art historical skills.

Reflections and Guiding Principles

The Fall 2024 sample sizes are very small and only offer preliminary insight into the utility of AI in art historical pedagogy. However, I believe these assignments are promising enough for further development and assessment, especially as a tool for cultivating critical users. The comparison assignment made space for experimentation and engagement, allowing students to think through the strengths and weaknesses of AI as a writing tool and find opportunities to improve upon insufficient evidence and organisation. Rather than merely hearing from an instructor that AI-generated essays were anaemic in quality, students pinpointed exactly where they could learn from the outputs and enhance them. Similarly, as students analysed the DALL-E images, they tested their ability to apply formal and historical knowledge while making connections between prompts and outputs. In both cases students enacted critical analysis skills and exhibited scepticism towards unedited AI images and writing. They demonstrated an ability to apply art historical principles and identify generalisations and assumptions in AI-generated material, meeting my new learning outcomes.

I will continue to use these assignments, but I intend to make small changes in the scaffolding, instructor supervision, and course schedule to improve student outcomes and expand object coverage. For example, student engagement with reflection questions often varied, ranging from single-paragraph answers to multi-page evaluations. Stronger scaffolding or more hands-on guidance may facilitate more consistently rigorous responses in future applications.

However, it is not yet clear that the assignments are equally effective for objects across cultures and media based on this semester's work. When choosing objects or movements, Fall 2024 students defaulted to material with which they felt most comfortable, unfailingly selecting figurative sculpture or painting for their assignments despite having options for non-objective art, architecture, prints, and decorative objects. Future semesters could address these areas more strategically by positioning the assignments in modules relating to non-Western and non-objective art or by assigning specific objects or movements. Likewise, further studies are needed to observe the efficacy of AI for more specialised art history courses, as my students were limited by the frame of the semester and the introductory nature of the course. Assignments addressing less canonical objects, objects from the Global South, and contemporary objects are needed to determine if students can meet learning outcomes with those materials and at an appropriate scholarly level.

Despite my results, these course intervations may not be appropriate for larger classes and departments, limiting the broader applicability of the study. Since the activities mirror the practice of reinforcement learning, they demand involved instructor directions and feedback, which is admittedly time-consuming and beyond the means of many high-enrolment institutions. Such pedagogy also requires a different approach to course content to align with new learning outcomes. Breadth and depth must become much more strategically defined to make time for skill development without sacrificing disciplinary standards or creating knowledge gaps for majors; this is also labour-intensive and requires departmental consensus before application. As Peter Bacon Hales (1995) recounts in the reform of the Art History Survey at UIC, material conditions of the department such as funding, enrolment, and staffing have a significant impact on the need and desire to reform the curriculum. Likewise, I acknowledge that small class sizes and a liberal arts college ethos support my ability to enact these changes where larger or public programmes may face different impediments. Further studies might evaluate how these assignments function in larger classes and departments.

Even with these limitations, I believe both majors and non-majors will need to be able to critically engage with AI-generated material as an extension of media literacy, which compels changes to the standard survey content to benefit both groups in the long run. Giving students early opportunities to analyse the strengths and weaknesses of AI helps them learn where they fit into these technological changes, encourages them to "look askance," and practically demonstrates how they can remain "the human in the loop" (Mollick 2024, 52–54) when using the technology in the future.[1] They can become savvy, critical consumers if we show them how to do so.

We know higher education is on the verge of major change. With the looming "enrollment cliff," budget cuts, and evolving technology, we need to be more flexible than our traditionally conservative and slow-moving discipline allows (Bauman 2024).[2] To be sure, AI is adapting faster than we are, and these assignments might become obsolete with the next software update.[3] Nevertheless, the process of creating, using, and assessing these activities has taught me valuable lessons that offer some principles for my future uses of AI-based pedagogy. These principles persist beyond the limitations of the individual assignments, and I offer them as course design strategies below.[4]

Know What the Tools Can Do

Instructors need to play with these programs often to stay informed. To design effective assignments, we need to be aware of how the technology functions and what it can achieve. Identifying the successful elements

[1] "Look askance" deliberately invokes Michael Leja's study on the development of sceptical looking in the nineteenth century (2004). Much in the way that modernity's culture of humbug encouraged people to critically engage with art and visual culture, AI also requires us to "process visual experiences with some measure of suspicion, caution, and guile" (Leja 2004, 1). While an extended dialogue with Leja's text is beyond the scope of this chapter, it is useful to remember that visual technologies have already demanded the cultivation of critical thinking skills in the past, and that this process can provide insight into our current and future technological engagements.

[2] Art history is wedded to nineteenth-century technologies, having relied on the growth of reproductive media such as prints, casts, and photographs to establish its legitimacy as a positivist discipline in the modern period (Bohrer 2002; Witcombe 2008). This needs to be a greater concern for us as society moves beyond the technologies that informed the basic tenets of our practice. Our field is at risk of becoming the natural history of the twenty-first century: outmoded by more specialised, savvy, and functional disciplines.

[3] To this point, between the initial development of the assignment in Spring 2024 and its Spring 2025 run, Copilot stopped producing four images at a time and the "In the style of" activity needed updating.

[4] My philosophy echoes that of Stephen Carroll (2008). Though he addresses computer technology in general, we share an emphasis on aligning the tools to learning outcomes.

provides students with tools to supplement their abilities in the future. Identifying the limits helps isolate areas for student development, showing instructors where they can teach specific skills that the technology does not yet provide. Doing both helps us close the gaps in effective thinking and reasoning. As the sample responses indicate, students can interpret these same successes and failures when given the opportunity to assess them.

Structure Assessments to Encourage Engagement and Reduce Student Procrastination

As with plagiarism, students often turn to AI tools when they feel unprepared or overloaded (Abbas et al. 2024, 14–15; Heckler and Forde 2015). When assignments are scaffolded, students spend more time with the material and have more opportunities to master the content as they apply it in new ways. AI-based activities like the ones I have developed leverage the sequential nature of critique and feedback to build towards a final essay rather than rely on a singular written response. It breaks down the complicated processes of fact gathering, reasoning, and writing into more manageable pieces. Such active learning opportunities allow students to approach content by emphasising process over outcomes to nurture curiosity and develop critical thinking skills. Combining these methods of engagement with new technology like AI allows instructors to enrich their course activities for broader sensory competencies while also cultivating interdisciplinary skill sets (Strelan et al. 2020).[5]

Emphasise Skill Building Rather Than Fact Gathering

While students require a baseline of knowledge before they can engage in higher-order taxonomies of thought, producing facts does not always demonstrate comprehension of those ideas or provide students with the tools to engage in more complex critical analysis. Habituating students to the *application* of knowledge rather than its repetition facilitates an ability to implement art historical lenses beyond the classroom and cultivate dynamic and adaptable skill sets such as visual literacy, argumentation, and

[5] Learning to effectively integrate AI in the classroom is important, as technological barriers are a major impediment to the implementation of active learning. See Kristin Børte et al. (2023, 606–609).

evidentiary support (Cempellin 2024, 2–3; Sienkewicz 2016). AI has the potential to serve a critical role in this process, as students in the study demonstrated transferrable skills in reason, argumentation, and writing.

Think Carefully About Disciplinary Goals and Be Transparent About the Skills You Value

Using backwards design has shown me that we need to be more thoughtful about our learning outcomes and be clearer with our students about how assignments participate in that process. While these learning outcomes are changing, we must truthfully answer some tough questions: What is the goal of an art historical education? Is it familiarity with the canon? The ability to analyse images? Exposure to competing visual traditions? A knowledge of scholarly methods or arguments? We all likely answer that question differently and change our answers depending on the course level and context. For example, some may feel strongly that learning to write independently and effectively is a key learning outcome at odds with using large-language learning models. That complaint is legitimate. However, in a conversation about AI, a colleague in the English department reminded me that writing is a tool, even if its processes of standardisation and record keeping have become second nature and hegemonic.[6] I add to his observation that all tools have functions, but not in all situations. We need to identify when certain tools are required, why, and what value we expect students to extract from learning how to use that tool so we may design our assessments accordingly. This should also include AI. As a tool, it too demands testing and assessment in educational contexts before our wholesale rejection or adoption.

Acknowledge Your Boundaries

Ethical resistance to AI is valid, and whether you use AI in your curriculum or not, I encourage you to be transparent about your stance with students so they can make informed decisions. Indeed, despite my classroom successes, I continue to have mixed feelings about AI. The technology consumes a tremendous amount of energy, which has environmental

[6] My thanks to Joshua Corey. This also aligns with Marshall McLuhan's (1962) arguments about the way that text and print media function as technologies, extending and amputating the abilities of human beings and fundamentally changing the way we think.

consequences (Crawford 2021). Training data is scraped from others' intellectual property without permission or compensation, overwhelmingly favours Western thought, and often relies on exploited or poorly compensated labour to catalogue content, which leads to harmful biases (Mollick 2024, 33–38). Plagiarism questions and equity issues also remain serious and unresolved challenges in educational and professional use (Mowreader 2024). These are very real concerns, and my students are increasingly voicing them when asked to complete AI-based assignments. Further experimentation and reflection are necessary to determine if the pedagogical advantages I describe here are worth the costs.

Not all faculty members share my situation or my learning outcomes. Other institutional contexts and conditions naturally require other considerations when pursuing AI-inclusive pedagogy. However, it is clear that students can use AI tools critically and effectively to cultivate art historical skills in visual literacy, reasoning, and argumentation. We can devise pedagogical strategies that help students become active thinkers in the face of these changes. The technology will continue to progress, and specific assignments may fall to the wayside, but the adaptive principles will remain. As such, I hope that my findings can provide a road map (or a foil) for your own design process.

Acknowledgements My thanks to Leda Cempellin for her essential guidance and support in the development of this chapter. Approval for this study was granted by the Human Subjects Review Committee of Lake Forest College, for which I thank Amanda Felkey. Informed consent to participate and publish was obtained from individual participants. Student responses are lightly edited for grammar and length.

References

Abbas, Muhammad, Farooq Ahmed Jam, and Tariq Iqbal Khan. 2024. Is it Harmful or Helpful? Examining the Causes and Consequences of Generative AI Usage Among University Students. *International Journal of Educational Technology in Higher Education* 21 (10): 1–22. https://doi.org/10.1186/s41239-024-00444-7.

Bauman, Dan. 2024. Colleges Were Already Bracing for an 'Enrollment Cliff.' Now There Might Be a Second One. *The Chronicle of Higher Education*, February 7. https://www.chronicle.com/article/colleges-were-already-bracing-for-an-enrollment-cliff-now-there-might-be-a-second-one.

Bohrer, Frederick N. 2002. Photographic Perspectives: Photography and the Institutional Formation of Art History. In *Art History and Its Institutions: The Nineteenth Century*, ed. Elizabeth Mansfield. Taylor & Francis Group.

Børte, Kristin, Katrine Nesje, and Sølvi Lillejord. 2023. Barriers to Student Active Learning in Higher Education. *Teaching in Higher Education* 28 (3): 597–615. https://doi.org/10.1080/13562517.2020.1839746.

Carroll, Stephen. 2008. Dangerous Romances: The Rhetoric of Teaching (Art History) with Technology. In *Teaching Art History with New Technologies*, ed. Kelly Donahue-Wallace, Laetitia La Follette, and Andrea Pappas. Cambridge Scholars Publishing.

Cempellin, Leda. 2024. Preparing Our Students for the Professional World: Integrating Thematic Assignments and Teamwork into the Art History Survey Course Design. *International Journal of Education & the Arts* 25 (12): 1–21. https://doi.org/10.26209/ijea25n12.

Crawford, Kate. 2021. *Atlas of AI: Power, Politics, and the Planetary Costs of Artificial Intelligence*. Yale University Press.

Hales, Peter Bacon. 1995. Discipline/Survey. *Art Journal* 54 (3): 65–69. https://doi.org/10.2307/777589.

Heckler, Nina C. & Forde, David R. 2015. The Role of Cultural Values in Plagiarism in Higher Education. Journal of Academic Ethics 13 (1): 61-75.

Huang, Kalley. 2023. Why Pope Francis Is the Star of A.I.-Generated Photos. *New York Times*, April 8. https://www.nytimes.com/2023/04/08/technology/ai-photos-pope-francis.html.

Leja, Michael. 2004. *Looking Askance: Skepticism and American Art from Eakins to Duchamp*. University of California Press.

McLuhan, Marshall. 1962. *The Gutenberg Galaxy: The Making of Typographic Man*. University of Toronto Press.

Mollick, Ethan. 2024. *Co-Intelligence: Living and Working with AI*. Portfolio.

Mowreader, Ashley. 2024. Survey: When should College Students Use AI? They're Not Sure. *Inside Higher Ed*, September 16. https://www.insidehighered.com/news/student-success/academic-life/2024/09/16/college-students-uncertain-about-ai-policies.

Sienkewicz, Julia A. 2013. Critical Perception: An Exploration of the Cognitive Gains of Material Culture Pedagogy. *Winterthur Portfolio* 47 (2/3): 117–138.

Sienkewicz, Julia A. 2016. Against the 'Coverage' Mentality: Rethinking Learning Outcomes and the Core Curriculum. *Art History Pedagogy & Practice* 1 (1): 1–14. https://academicworks.cuny.edu/ahpp/vol1/iss1/5.

Strelan, Peter, Amanda Osborn, and Edward Palmer. 2020. The Flipped Classroom: A Meta-Analysis of Effects on Student Performance Across Disciplines and Education Levels. *Educational Research Review* 30:100314. https://doi.org/10.1016/j.edurev.2020.100314.

Wiggins, Grant, and Jay McTighe. 2005. *Understanding by Design—Expanded Second Edition*. ACSD.

Witcombe, Christopher L. C. E. 2008. Bye Bye, Slides/Bye Bye, Carousels/ Hello, Internet/I Think I'm a Gonna Cry-y. In *Teaching Art History with New Technologies*, ed. Kelly Donahue-Wallace, Laetitia La Follette, and Andrea Pappas. Cambridge Scholars Publishing.

CHAPTER 12

Utilising Tree-of-Thought Prompting to Facilitate Self-Reflective Analysis in Undergraduate Media Studies Students

Karl van Heerden

Introduction

With the unprecedented rise in popularity of large language model (LLM)-based writing tools such as QuillBot (2024), Grammarly (2024), ChatGPT (2024), Claude (2024), and Gemini (2024), increased usage of these tools by students has been observed in educational institutions across the globe. This presents a concern for subjects in the Humanities, which tend to privilege written assignments, typically essays, as the primary form of assessment (Melzer 2014, 22). Specifically, there is concern among educators that students will become overly reliant on LLMs and that consequently this will have a negative impact on their learning (Tossell et al. 2024, 2). This chapter focuses on the subject Visual Culture—known elsewhere as Visual Studies—which partly emerged from, and remains deeply intertwined with, Art History. Although the relationship between these

K. van Heerden (✉)
Open Window Institute, Pretoria, South Africa
e-mail: karl@openwindow.co.za

L. Cempellin, M. Geiger (eds.), *Reimagining Art History with Artificial Intelligence*,
https://doi.org/10.1007/978-3-032-21685-4_12

subjects remains contentious across some campuses and faculties, the two share overlapping methodologies, research imperatives, and pedagogical concerns (Elkins 2003). It is from this shared ground that an opportunity arises to address the question of how students engage with LLMs and their essays.

The site of study, Visual Culture 300 (VC 300), is a compulsory theoretical subject at The Open Window, a private higher education institution in South Africa—analogous to the private universities found in other countries. The "300" denotes that the class is taught to third-year undergraduates, running over two semesters. As a course in the Humanities, the subject emphasises critical thinking, research skills, academic writing, and the analysis of visual texts.

LLMs respond to instructions from users in the form of text inputs, known as prompts, which determine the structure and overall quality of the answer (White et al. 2023, 1). Various prompting methods have arisen, such as Input-Output (IO) prompting, similar to how users search for information in modern-day search engines (Besta et al. 2024, 2), Chain-of-Thought (CoT) prompting, by which the user guides the LLM in "thinking step by step" (Zhang and Ding 2024, 2), and Tree-of-Thought (ToT) wherein the LLM "searches through a combinatorial problem space, represented as a tree" (Yao et al. 2023, 2).

This chapter explores the benefits to students in the Humanities when using LLM-generated feedback on their essays through ToT prompt structures, paired with a self-reflection exercise. The data suggests that, overall, students find the LLM feedback helpful and, through sustained use, that it improves the quality of their writing, resulting in higher grades. Furthermore, the self-reflection reports indicate that students who made use of the ToT prompt were able to identify more specific problems with their essays for improvement. Overall, the findings of this chapter indicate that students learn more about improving their writing from LLMs using ToT prompts when compared to IO prompt topologies.

The findings of this research may benefit scholars and educators across the Humanities and beyond. Overreliance on LLM-generated writing is a potential impediment to students developing their skills in arguably any discipline that relies on written assessment, which the work undertaken in this chapter seeks to mitigate. What will hopefully be made clear throughout the rest of the chapter is an earnest desire to encourage students, regardless of background, to engage thoughtfully with writing tasks and to discourage them from allowing LLMs to engage in critical thinking on their behalf. Finally, it should be underscored that this chapter does not constitute an endorsement of LLMs in the classroom. Instead, this work is an attempt at formulating a proactive response to the already widespread use of LLMs by students.

Related Work

Academic research into LLM use in college-level essays includes two groups: the first examines the potential of LLMs as tools used for evaluation; the second explores LLMs in the process of writing essays. Regarding the former, researchers note several challenges facing LLM-based evaluation, namely the accuracy of the feedback and scores, the consistency of those scores when compared with human evaluators, and the trust students place in the scores provided by the LLM. Chiang et al. (2024) discuss the ease with which LLM evaluators are manipulated into providing higher scores through "prompt hacking" (p. 1). Meanwhile, Kundu and Barbosa (2024) show that LLM evaluators scored essays lower when compared to human evaluators. Regarding student perception, Tossell et al. (2024) observe a distinct lack of trust in LLM-based feedback when not supervised by their instructors. While scant, the literature on LLM-based essay grading indicates concerns with score accuracy. Meanwhile, the role of LLMs as a writing tool is a more comprehensively researched area.

First, researchers agree that LLMs provide a positive benefit to students when used as an aid, rather than a replacement, in their essay writing. Picciano (2024) observes that LLMs assist students "in writing their essays, [were] easy to use, and helped generate ideas to get them started" (p. 10). Kloker et al. (2024) qualify this observation, noting any potential benefits to LLM usage exist only "as long as transparency is maintained" (pp. 12–13) between lecturers and students. Mitchell-Yellin (2024) even claims that the emergence of LLM-based writing tools has surfaced long-buried concerns around fundamental flaws in the transmission-based educational model favoured by many institutions.

However, scholars note concerns in their appraisal of LLM tools in essay writing. Moon, Green, and Kushlev observe a lack of creative diversity in LLM-generated essays (2024). They propose the notion of "creative fixation" (p. 17), whereby LLMs limit the diversity of student essays by presenting them with a small pool of initial ideas. Overall, the scholarly response to LLMs in essay writing is cautious. Researchers recognise inherent problems in popular passive learning models and the opportunities LLM assistants can provide in encouraging students to engage with their learning. However, a significant concern among scholars is regulating the ethical use of LLMs by students.

Scholars have attempted numerous approaches in guiding students towards effective and ethical usage of LLMs. Mvondo et al. (2023) observe that students "appear to be influenced by prevailing norms regarding LLM chatbots and the guidance of instructors" (p. 29), arguing it is up to educators to establish ethical ways in which LLMs can be used in the classroom. Meanwhile, Nelson (2024) applies the notion of a "best appropriate technology" (p. 130) to outline how LLMs can be used in essay writing assignments to enhance student learning. Nelson (2024) argues that LLM usage should "result in less 'busywork' for learners" (p. 136) and lower their anxiety. However, Jungherr (2023, 4) observes that variability in prompt design and strategy can significantly affect the output quality of LLMs, and consequently student engagement. For example, in a case study similar to this chapter, Oppenheimer et al. (2024) use LLMs as a collaborative tool for feedback and suggestions on college student essays. However, examination of the dataset reveals the authors did not use a structured prompt technique. Instead, the researchers relied on LLM-generated guidelines to instruct the students in writing their prompts (Oppenheimer et al. 2024, 11). Ethical and effective uses of LLMs are thus intrinsically connected, and as explored in subsequent sections, selecting an appropriate prompt engineering strategy is crucial to maximising student engagement and learning.

Prompt Engineering

As outlined at the onset of this chapter, various prompting strategies have been developed to enhance LLM reasoning across different use-cases. ToT, concurrently proposed by Yao et al. (2023) and Long (2023), is one such strategy that attempts to improve on the reasoning and complex problem-solving of previous methods. Specifically, ToT adopts the step-by-step reasoning of CoT by breaking a problem down into smaller sub-problems, but represents them as nodes on a "thought tree" (Yao et al. 2023, 2). In contrast to CoT, ToT provides multiple reasoning paths the model may select from (Besta et al. 2024, 2). Crucially, this approach allows models to explore various solutions via "breadth-first search (BFS) or depth-first search (DFS), which allow systematic exploration of the tree of thoughts with lookahead and backtracking" (Yao et al. 2023, 2). This approach demonstrates a significant improvement over previous methods in creative writing tasks (Yao et al. 2023, 6).

Researchers observe that prompt techniques like ToT and CoT improve the accuracy of LLM answers as they "overcome[s] the constant depth limitation of a model's internal (latent space) reasoning by extending the reasoning process into the 'text' space through prompting" (Zhang and Ding 2024, 2). Due to the intricate structure of ToT prompts, the technique is best used in tasks that demand complex reasoning.[1] ToT prompting has been implemented in various contexts, such as language and style imitation (Chen and Moscholios 2024), as the prompt framework for multi-agent debate and reasoning (Haji et al. 2024; Liu et al. 2024a), or as the basis for optimising LLM fine-tuning to align more closely with human preferences (Zhang et al. 2024b). However, Parvez (2024) notes that the step-by-step reasoning of CoT-derived prompting methods, such as ToT, risks producing erroneous information—commonly referred to as hallucinating—due to a lack of grounded reasoning and contextual evidence. Furthermore, ToT fails in certain domains, such as software engineering (La Rosa et al. 2024).

To overcome some of its inherent limitations, researchers have sought to improve or modify the ToT approach. Cai et al. (2024) incorporate the "dynamic adaptability of temperature adjustment" (p. 2)—temperature being the randomness of LLM-generated text—to better adapt to various complex problem-solving tasks. Liu et al. (2024b) adopt logical reasoning and propositions to "address the issue of information loss" (p. 3). Other scholars have addressed the issue of factual inaccuracies by incorporating additional fact-checking instructions (Zhang et al. 2024a) or by introducing stochastic self-guided reasoning during intermediate thought steps (Bi et al. 2024). For example, Bi et al. (2024), in an approach similar to this chapter, "...build a stochastic reasoning tree to represent the possible reasoning lines and the probability of each reasoning line taking us to the right answer" (p. 4).

Furthermore, ToT prompting serves as the basis for many other prompt engineering strategies. Researchers such as Yang et al. (2024) and Gao et al. employ ToT techniques in the creation of an additional "meta-buffer for storing high-level thoughts" (2024, 2). Meanwhile, other researchers leverage otherwise static ToT prompting methods to develop iterative or

[1] For additional research on LLMs and complex reasoning, see Renze and Guven (2024), Chen et al. (2024), and Zebaze et al. (2024).

interactive strategies for reasoning-heavy tasks (Boyle et al. 2024; Radha et al. 2024). Finally, a more recent development sees ToT approaches used as the basis for graphs (Markowitz et al. 2024) or diagrams of thought (Zhang et al. 2024c, 1) to improve upon the explainability of previous approaches. Despite their shortcomings, ToT prompt strategies remain popular and effective tools in enhancing reasoning and complex problem-solving in LLMs. Although newer methods continue to be developed, due to its proficiency with reasoning tasks and robust structure, a ToT approach was selected as the topology used in this study.

Methodology and Data

The class of 2024 in VC 300 consisted of 119 students from various disciplines and departments. As an interdepartmental theory subject, VC 300 facilitates students from areas as diverse as photography, web development, and industrial design. The assignments for both semesters of VC 300 tasked students with submitting an essay by the end of the period. Essay topics for Semesters 1 and 2 include a postmodern analysis of an Internet community, and a self-reflective analysis on the student's creative practice from a postcolonial viewpoint, respectively. A similar assessment plan was adopted for both semesters, with formative tasks that engaged students in writing multiple drafts and receiving feedback from the lecturer, their peers, and an LLM. Formative tasks included submitting a proposal, a draft for lecturer review, feedback from an LLM of their choice using the provided ToT prompt, a written reflection on the LLM feedback, and a second draft for peer feedback. Formative assessment is foregrounded, as it has proven to be a useful tool in "in guiding instruction and supporting individual learning" (Shute and Becker 2010, 7).

The ToT prompt was introduced in the course to assist students in receiving better-quality feedback from the LLM. On their own, students often resort to using simple IO prompt methods when eliciting feedback from LLMs. For example, in this study, one prompt written by a student consisted solely of the instruction to "provide critical feedback on this academic essay." The premise of this study is to assert that providing students with structured prompts facilitates improved feedback from an LLM on their work. By offering an example of a well-structured prompt that incorporates advances in prompt engineering research, students are exposed to strategies better suited to the task of elevating their writing while benefitting from more detailed and constructive feedback.

The prompt designed for this study draws from the Tree-of-Thought approach popularised by Yao et al. (2023). The prompt—provided in full in the Appendix—is a zero-shot design that requires the LLM to adopt three personas in critiquing the student essay. The three personas each represent a "branch" on the tree, resulting in a breadth of three. A zero-shot prompt—meaning only a single prompt is sent before the final output is received—constrains the depth of the tree to one. While zero-shot prompts are less suitable than multi-shot or few-shot prompts (Kundu and Barbosa 2024, 15), accommodations are necessary for students on free plans for commercially available LLMs.

Research Methodology

Data collected for this study spans both semesters for the 2024 academic year, Semester 1 (S1) and Semester 2 (S2). For S1, a total of 110 written self-reflection reports were collected. For S2, a total of 90 reports were collected, resulting in a total of 200 reports. The discrepancy in totals between the two semesters, when compared with the total number of students, is due to several factors: the deregistration of some students over the year, some students not submitting assignments, some students submitting assignments that were incomplete, or submissions that did not adhere to the assignment requirements.

Additionally, student grades were collected for the draft assignment, the final essay, and the semester average for both semesters. Writing samples for the self-reflection reports were accessed from the Open Window's Learning Management System, Canvas, and stored in Microsoft Word format. Of the total samples, 77 pairs were identified where a student submitted the feedback from the LLM and a self-reflection report for both S1 and S2.

Data Analysis

To derive overall sentiment in the self-reflection reports regarding the use of LLMs in the feedback process, evaluative terms were extracted from the samples and labelled as either "positive" or "negative" in their sentiment. Keywords for positive sentiment included *insightful*, *helpful*, *useful*, *great*, and *impressive*. Keywords for negative sentiment included *biased*, *vague*, and *unhelpful*. Self-reflection reports that did not make use of evaluative terminology to describe the LLM were classified as "neutral" in their sentiment.

Ethical Considerations

The anonymity of the participants has been ensured in the following ways, (a) the names, email addresses, and student identification numbers of the participants are not included in any of the research or published material, (b) extracts from self-reflective reports do not include identifiable information, such as specific case studies, topics, or details—writing samples used in any published material are examples of generic sentiments that are not personally identifiable, and (c) participants could opt out of the study and request their sample be removed from the dataset at any time. Furthermore, this study received approval from the institution's Research and Ethics Committee to use the samples collected.[2]

Findings

After coding, out of the 77 final pairs, two main groups were identified, students who used the provided ToT prompt in both S1 and S2—*ToT-ToT*—and a second group, who began with a custom prompt in S1 and adopted the provided ToT prompt in S2—*Custom-ToT*. Out of the 110 students—excluding outliers—32.7% (36) used custom prompts in S1, although this number dropped to 1.8% (2) in S2. Initially perplexing, this behaviour provided an opportunity to compare the feedback and experiences of students with a control group. Table 12.1 provides an overview of the distribution of sentiment between the two groups.

The major groups were further delineated based on their relative change in sentiment in their self-reflection reports submitted during the first and second semesters. Table 12.2 illustrates the change in sentiment from the reports in S1 to S2 in both groups. Note the increase in positive sentiment from S1 to S2 in the *Custom-ToT* group that adopted the provided prompt template in S2.

Some outliers in the larger dataset include students who did not reflect on the feedback of the LLM, contrary to the assignment instructions. Other outliers were samples where it could not be determined if the

[2] Date of approval: 16 October 2024.

Table 12.1 *ToT prompt usage and sentiment distribution per semester*

Semester 1	*ToT-ToT*	*Custom-ToT*
Total pairs	53	24
Negative sentiment	1.9% (1)	12.5% (3)
Neutral sentiment	28.3% (15)	29.2% (7)
Positive sentiment	69.8% (37)	50% (12)
No feedback	0% (0)	8.3% (2)
Semester 2		
Negative sentiment	0% (0)	0% (0)
Neutral sentiment	32.1% (17)	25% (7)
Positive sentiment	66% (35)	57.1% (16)
No feedback	1.9% (1)	3.6% (1)

Table 12.2 *Sentiment evolution as a result of prompt usage*

Progression	*ToT-ToT*	*Custom-ToT*
Total samples	53	24
Negative to neutral	0% (0)	3.6% (1)
Negative to positive	0% (0)	7.1% (2)
Neutral to positive	15.1% (8)	17.9% (5)
Positive to neutral	18.9% (10)	10.7% (3)
Remained positive	13.2% (7)	14.3% (4)
Remained neutral	50.9% (27)	35.7% (10)

student used a custom prompt or the provided one, due to missing documentation. Outliers were not included in the analysis of data. Furthermore, certain expected codes are not present in the data, namely, there are no examples of samples where the sentiment remained negative across both semesters or where sentiments developed from either positive or neutral to negative. The assessment instructions did not mandate a specific LLM platform, though many participants chose to use OpenAI's ChatGPT LLM (2024) for feedback. As the assessment was carried out over two semesters, the first cohort used ChatGPT 3.5, while the second used the then-released ChatGPT 4.0. Other notable examples include Microsoft Copilot and AskPDF.com. It is not known whether students used trial, free, or paid versions of various LLM services.

Discussion

The findings of the study indicate that students' attitudes towards the feedback provided by an LLM changed significantly when provided with the ToT-based prompt. Attention should be paid to the changes in the *Custom-ToT* group, which experienced a shift from 12.5% negative reports in S1 to 0% in S2. These students reported a more positive experience when using the provided prompt, compared to their own. Between S1 and S2, this cohort exhibited a 7.1% increase in positive reports. The difference in response is striking when comparing the written self-reflective feedback reports between students who used the ToT prompt and those who did not. For example, within the *ToT-ToT* cohort, participant 48 observed, "The feedback is very detailed, and because of this, is likely going to be the reason I get a slightly better mark." However, not all feedback within this group was positive. The single negative sentiment in this cohort from participant 67 noted that "[ChatGPT] did not want to tell me that my work is bad or even mediocre." This observation contrasts with the majority of other participants, who identified specific critiques highlighted by the feedback on their essays.

Initially relying on their custom prompts, the *Custom-ToT* group consisted of a much higher proportion of negative sentiments in the reports for S1. Participant 54 stated, "While the feedback response may be fast, GAI doesn't provide adequate feedback." Meanwhile, participant 114 reflected, "I struggle to really accept this feedback because it feels that Ai is developed to general [sic] work in the favour of the viewer." However, many participants still rated the feedback from their custom prompts highly. Participant 57 noted, "The feedback that I've gotten from Chat GPT is quite sufficient." Similarly, participant 61 highlighted that "the whole feedback given is extremely helpful." In contrast, the student reports in S2, after their adoption of the ToT prompt, are notably more positive. Participant 54, previously quoted, notes, "…overall, the feedback from the LLM system plays a vital role in refining the essay's analysis and expanding its reach."

While students' reflections on their attitudes towards LLMs are noteworthy, of particular benefit to educators is the quality and depth of critique students have internalised from the provided feedback. In this regard, there is a stark difference between the custom prompts used by some students and the ToT prompt developed for this study. In the self-reflections provided, students who made use of the ToT prompt identified specific aspects of their essays that required improvement. Examples of these ranged from feedback on their case studies (participants 3, 11, 14, 38, 80, 88, 112, and 116) to incorporating theory from specific authors (participants 34, 73, and 110), to the connection between theory and practice (participants 7, 43, 47, and 68). In contrast, from all the self-reflection reports based on custom prompts, only a single reference to a specific remark regarding the student's case study or theory could be found (participant 42). The majority of feedback from custom prompts reflected on essay structure, grammar, and academic technique. The difference is notable when comparing this cohort's self-reflections before and after the adoption of the ToT prompt in the second semester. In addition to the rise in positive sentiment among this group, students who transitioned from a custom prompt in S1 to the ToT prompt in S2 were able to identify more specific aspects of their essays that required improvement. Overall, participants' self-reflections indicated a clearer understanding of critical weaknesses in their academic writing and how to improve their essays, when making use of the ToT prompt.

Another noteworthy feature of the findings is the increase in overall neutral sentiments (i.e., self-reflections that did not include positive terms such as *insightful*, *helpful*, *useful*, *great*, or *impressive*). This shift to a more neutral stance can be attributed to an increase in self-reflections that deal with the specific critiques raised by the LLM, rather than a focus on their emotional responses to the feedback. One remark present in two self-reflections is the preference of students to receive lecturer feedback in addition to that provided by the LLM (participants 69 and 114). Overall, students are satisfied with the quality of feedback, as indicated by the majority of positive sentiment. However, this sentiment may have arisen due to students receiving feedback from both the LLM and the lecturer, rendering the LLM feedback supplemental. How students will perceive feedback from only an LLM is unknown.

An examination of the output of the LLM between the provided prompt and students' custom prompts revealed differences in the structure, focus, and specificity of the feedback. Output from custom prompts was generally structured according to basic categories, such as "clarity and tone," "engagement with literature," and "structure." In contrast, the ToT prompt generated bespoke "experts" based on the contents of each essay. For essays on gender, feminist "professors" and "researchers" were evoked, whereas for essays focusing on media representation, "scholars" from fields such as art, visual culture, and film were present. The feedback was specific to each assignment, offering guidance relating directly to the case study or theory. While not required, students were encouraged to ask follow-up questions after the initial critique to clarify points or request further information. Students who made use of the ToT prompt engaged with more specific follow-up questions by requesting advice on potential research sources, or clarifying issues raised by the LLM. The custom prompts, in contrast, offered general advice applicable to almost any essay, regardless of the specific topic of each student. LLMs using custom prompts created by the students frequently commented on general issues, and the follow-up questions asked by students equally lacked specificity and direction.

The impact of this approach on the final grades of students is relatively uncertain due to the nature of the assessment plan. The assessments during S1 and S2 involved several rounds of formative assessment, from proposals and drafts to peer review. After receiving feedback from the LLM, students received critique from the lecturer and from their peers in later drafts. While the impact of the LLM-provided critique could not be measured in isolation, there was a noticeable improvement in the quality of student essays. The mean grade for the S1 essay draft before the LLM task was 63.6% (median 66%, dev. 15.5%). The mean grade for the final essay improved to 67.6% (median 71.9%, dev. 14.8%). This modest increase in average grade is likely attributed to the combination of feedback students experienced throughout the semester and the resulting improvements they made to their assignments.

While the quantitative benefits of structured prompts is yet to be determined, there was an observable benefit in terms of setting acceptable standards for LLM usage in the classroom. As Kloker et al. (2024) observe, "The more crucial issue is that students make their use of LLMs transparent to the lecturer" (p. 10), highlighting the need for cultivating a classroom culture of transparency and ethical behaviour around the use of LLMs. The course design guides students towards such ethical behaviour by providing them with a useful and constructive example of using LLMs without resorting to "offloading" the work of critical thinking and reasoning to these models.

Conclusion

The results of this study indicate that students benefit from adopting structured approaches when prompting LLMs for feedback on their essay writing. Utilising ToT prompting elicits several benefits for students regarding the usefulness and specificity of the feedback. This reflects in a marked improvement in student grades when compared to unstructured prompts. Future studies would benefit from considering a broader range of student samples, from undergraduate and postgraduate programmes in fields outside of Visual Culture. Furthermore, the assignment given to students explicitly required them to critically evaluate the feedback provided by LLMs. Further study is warranted to evaluate the benefits or implications of LLM feedback in other forms of written assessment that does not engage with the feedback directly.

Several insightful observations have been made throughout the research. First is the sincere desire on the part of students to improve their own work. While levels of engagement and enthusiasm naturally vary across the cohort, in general students demonstrate a remarkable willingness to improve their essays, rather than relying on LLMs to generate the majority of their assignment. Second, detailed understanding of how LLMs operate appears to be limited across the cohort. In general, students rely on simple, often poorly worded, prompts, and did not seem interested in improving their skills in this regard. This finding underscores the essential role educators play in guiding students in appropriate LLM usage. Lastly, a ToT prompt approach was able to provide students with more helpful, detailed, and specific feedback on their assignments. Students recognised the value of this feedback and made sincere attempts to apply it to their work. The data collected suggests that LLM-generated feedback has the potential to benefit students in a positive way, while encouraging students' own critical thinking skills.

A significant limitation in this study is the employment of a zero-shot prompt method. As students gain access to increasingly sophisticated LLMs, future studies are encouraged to incorporate more complex prompt design approaches. Suggestions for further development include the use of multiple prompts, multimodal LLMs with video and voice interactions, and "reasoning" LLMs that incorporate Chain-of-Thought techniques by default. This study ends with the recommendation that institutions invest in providing prompt engineering training and support for educators. It is apparent that educators should oversee and advise students on their prompting, regardless of the context of the assessment. Therefore, educators who are well versed in prompt engineering modalities are essential. This study demonstrates that well-structured prompts provide students with more detailed and constructive feedback specific to the needs of the assignment. However, it is crucial that LLM-generated feedback forms only a component of the assessment strategy and is coupled with rigorous and consistent support from educators.

Appendix: ToT Prompt

I want you to act as a trinity of seasoned experts, each a specialist in your own distinct field, collaboratively providing feedback on a student's piece of writing. Your strategy will be "Tree of Thoughts," a method that demands clear articulation of your reasoning process, unfolding step by step, considering all pertinent data, facts, and external influences.

You will each develop an initial critique, taking care to ensure your assertions comply with the known principles of good academic writing, scholarly practice, and media studies discourse. Upon presenting your initial positions, you will partake in a dynamic dialogue, evaluating and critiquing each other's ideas, fostering a space for intellectual growth and collective advancement.

Following this shared critique, each expert will evolve to the next stage in their reasoning process, building on the foundations of the previous step, and integrating feedback from the collective critique. This cyclical and iterative approach will persist, creating an evolving "Tree of Thoughts" until a consensus emerges.

However, maintaining a commitment to intellectual honesty and rigorous scrutiny, any logical flaws or discrepancies detected at any point must be acknowledged. The expert identifying the error will need to backtrack to the point of divergence, rectify the flaw, and embark on a revised train of thought.

To add an element of uncertainty management, each expert will assign a probability to the accuracy of their evolving critique, giving a sense of confidence to their assertions. Continue this dynamic process until all experts reach unanimity on the most probable answer, then create a robust and richly reasoned paragraph of feedback.

The piece of writing is:

PLACE YOUR ESSAY TEXT (INTRODUCTION → CONCLUSION) INSIDE THESE QUOTES

References

Anthropic. 2024. Claude. Claude, 1 November 2024. https://claude.ai/new.

Besta, Maciej, Florim Memedi, Zhenyu Zhang, Robert Gerstenberger, Nils Blach, Piotr Nyczyk, Marcin Copik, et al. 2024. Topologies of Reasoning: Demystifying Chains, Trees, and Graphs of Thoughts. arXiv. http://arxiv.org/abs/2401.14295.

Bi, Zhenyu, Daniel Hajialigol, Zhongkai Sun, Jie Hao, and Xuan Wang. 2024. STOC-TOT: Stochastic Tree-of-Thought with Constrained Decoding for Complex Reasoning in Multi-Hop Question Answering. arXiv. http://arxiv.org/abs/2407.03687.

Boyle, Alan, Isha Gupta, Sebastian Hönig, Lukas Mautner, Kenza Amara, Furui Cheng, and Mennatallah El-Assady. 2024. iToT: An Interactive System for Customized Tree-of-Thought Generation. arXiv. http://arxiv.org/abs/2409.00413.

Cai, Chengkun, Xu Zhao, Yucheng Du, Haoliang Liu, and Lei Li. 2024. T^2 of Thoughts: Temperature Tree Elicits Reasoning in Large Language Models. arXiv. http://arxiv.org/abs/2405.14075.

Chen, Ziyang, and Stylios Moscholios. 2024. Using Prompts to Guide Large Language Models in Imitating a Real Person's Language Style. arXiv. http://arxiv.org/abs/2410.03848.

Chen, Qiqi, Xinpeng Wang, Philipp Mondorf, Michael A. Hedderich, and Barbara Plank. 2024. Understanding When Tree of Thoughts Succeeds: Larger Models Excel in Generation, Not Discrimination. arXiv. http://arxiv.org/abs/2410.17820.

Chiang, Cheng-Han, Wei-Chih Chen, Chun-Yi Kuan, Chienchou Yang, and Hung-yi Lee. 2024. Large Language Model as an Assignment Evaluator: Insights, Feedback, and Challenges in a 1000+ Student Course. arXiv. http://arxiv.org/abs/2407.05216.

Elkins, J. 2003. *Visual Studies: A Skeptical Introduction.* Routledge.

Gao, Peizhong, Ao Xie, Shaoguang Mao, Wenshan Wu, Yan Xia, Haipeng Mi, and Furu Wei. 2024. Meta Reasoning for Large Language Models. arXiv. http://arxiv.org/abs/2406.11698.

Google. 2024. Gemini. Gemini, 1 November 2024. https://gemini.google.com.

Grammarly Inc. 2024. Grammarly: Free AI Writing. Grammarly, 1 November 2024. https://www.grammarly.com.

Haji, Fatemeh, Mazal Bethany, Maryam Tabar, Jason Chiang, Anthony Rios, and Peyman Najafirad. 2024. Improving LLM Reasoning with Multi-Agent Tree-of-Thought Validator Agent. arXiv. http://arxiv.org/abs/2409.11527.

Jungherr, Andreas. 2023. Using ChatGPT and Other Large Language Model (LLM) Applications for Academic Paper Assignments. https://doi.org/10.31235/osf.io/d84q6.

Kloker, Simon, Matthew Bazanya, and Twaha Kateete. 2024. I Don't Trust You (Anymore)! The Effect of Students' LLM Use on Lecturer-Student-Trust in Higher Education. arXiv. https://doi.org/10.48550/ARXIV.2406.14871.

Kundu, Anindita, and Denilson Barbosa. 2024. Are Large Language Models Good Essay Graders? arXiv. http://arxiv.org/abs/2409.13120.

Rosa, Ricardo La, Corey Hulse, and Bangdi Liu. 2024. Can GitHub Issues be Solved with Tree of Thoughts? arXiv. http://arxiv.org/abs/2405.13057.

Learneo Inc. 2024. QuillBot for Chrome: Write Well, Wherever. QuillBot, 1 November 2024. https://quillbot.com/chrome-extension.

Liu, Tongxuan, Xingyu Wang, Weizhe Huang, Wenjiang Xu, Yuting Zeng, Lei Jiang, Hailong Yang, and Jing Li. 2024a. GroupDebate: Enhancing the Efficiency of Multi-Agent Debate Using Group Discussion. arXiv. http://arxiv.org/abs/2409.14051.

Liu, Tongxuan, Wenjiang Xu, Weizhe Huang, Xingyu Wang, Jiaxing Wang, Hailong Yang, and Jing Li. 2024b. Logic-of-Thought: Injecting Logic into Contexts for Full Reasoning in Large Language Models. arXiv. http://arxiv.org/abs/2409.17539.

Long, Jieyi. 2023. Large Language Model Guided Tree-of-Thought. arXiv. http://arxiv.org/abs/2305.08291.

Markowitz, Elan, Anil Ramakrishna, Jwala Dhamala, Ninareh Mehrabi, Charith Peris, Rahul Gupta, Kai-Wei Chang, and Aram Galstyan. 2024. Tree-of-Traversals: A Zero-Shot Reasoning Algorithm for Augmenting Black-Box Language Models with Knowledge Graphs. arXiv. http://arxiv.org/abs/2407.21358.

Melzer, D. 2014. *Assignments across the Curriculum: A National Study of College Writing*. Utah State University Press.

Mitchell-Yellin, Benjamin. 2024. Don't Believe the Hype: Why ChatGPT May Breathe New Life into College Writing Instruction. *Teaching Philosophy* 47 (2): 193–211. https://doi.org/10.5840/teachphil2024429198.

Moon, Kibum, Adam Green, and Kostadin Kushlev. 2024. Homogenizing Effect of a Large Language Model (LLM) on Creative Diversity: An Empirical Comparison of Human and ChatGPT Writing. https://doi.org/10.31234/osf.io/8p9wu.

Mvondo, G. F. N., Ben Niu, and Salman Eivazinezhad. 2023. Generative Conversational AI And Academic Integrity: A Mixed Method Investigation To Understand The Ethical Use of LLM Chatbots In Higher Education. *SSRN Electronic Journal*. https://doi.org/10.2139/ssrn.4548263.

Nelson, Jack Wright. 2024. The "Other" LLM: Large Language Models and the Future of Legal Education. *SSRN Electronic Journal*. https://doi.org/10.2139/ssrn.4882243.

OpenAI. 2024. ChatGPT. ChatGPT, 1 November 2024. https://chatgpt.com.

Oppenheimer, Daniel M., Trent N. Cash, and Allison E. Connell Pensky. 2024. You've Got AI Friend in Me: LLMs as Collaborative Learning Partners. https://doi.org/10.31219/osf.io/8q67u.

Parvez, Md Rizwan. 2024. Evidence to Generate (E2G): A Single-Agent Two-Step Prompting for Context Grounded and Retrieval Augmented Reasoning. arXiv. http://arxiv.org/abs/2401.05787.

Picciano, Anthony G. 2024. Graduate Teacher Education Students Use and Evaluate ChatGPT as an Essay-Writing Tool. *Online Learning* 28 (2). https://doi.org/10.24059/olj.v28i2.4373.

Radha, Santosh Kumar, Yasamin Nouri Jelyani, Ara Ghukasyan, and Oktay Goktas. 2024. Iteration of Thought: Leveraging Inner Dialogue for Autonomous Large Language Model Reasoning. arXiv. http://arxiv.org/abs/2409.12618.

Renze, Matthew, and Erhan Guven. 2024. The Benefits of a Concise Chain of Thought on Problem-Solving in Large Language Models. arXiv. http://arxiv.org/abs/2401.05618.

Shute, Valerie Jean, and Betsy Jane Becker. 2010. "Prelude: Assessment for the 21st Century" In Innovative Assessment for the 21st Century: Supporting Educational Needs, by Betsy Jane Becker and Valerie Jean Shute, 1–12. Springer.

Tossell, Chad C., Nathan L. Tenhundfeld, Ali Momen, Katrina Cooley, and Ewart J. De Visser. 2024. Student Perceptions of ChatGPT Use in a College Essay Assignment: Implications for Learning, Grading, and Trust in Artificial Intelligence. *IEEE Transactions on Learning Technologies* 17:1069–1081. https://doi.org/10.1109/TLT.2024.3355015.

White, Jules, Quchen Fu, Sam Hays, Michael Sandborn, Carlos Olea, Henry Gilbert, Ashraf Elnashar, Jesse Spencer-Smith, and Douglas C. Schmidt. 2023. A Prompt Pattern Catalog to Enhance Prompt Engineering with ChatGPT. arXiv. http://arxiv.org/abs/2302.11382.

Yang, Ling, Zhaochen Yu, Tianjun Zhang, Shiyi Cao, Minkai Xu, Wentao Zhang, Joseph E. Gonzalez, and Bin Cui. 2024. Buffer of Thoughts: Thought-Augmented Reasoning with Large Language Models. arXiv. http://arxiv.org/abs/2406.04271.

Yao, Shunyu, Dian Yu, Jeffrey Zhao, Izhak Shafran, Thomas L. Griffiths, Yuan Cao, and Karthik Narasimhan. 2023. Tree of Thoughts: Deliberate Problem Solving with Large Language Models. arXiv. https://doi.org/10.48550/ARXIV.2305.10601.

Zebaze, Armel, Benoît Sagot, and Rachel Bawden. 2024. Tree of Problems: Improving Structured Problem Solving with Compositionality. arXiv. http://arxiv.org/abs/2410.06634.

Zhang, Xiang, and Dujian Ding. 2024. Supervised Chain of Thought. arXiv. http://arxiv.org/abs/2410.14198.

Zhang, Jinghan, Xiting Wang, Weijieying Ren, Lu Jiang, Dongjie Wang, and Kunpeng Liu. 2024a. RATT: A Thought Structure for Coherent and Correct LLM Reasoning. arXiv. http://arxiv.org/abs/2406.02746.
Zhang, Xuan, Chao Du, Tianyu Pang, Qian Liu, Wei Gao, and Min Lin. 2024b. Chain of Preference Optimization: Improving Chain-of-Thought Reasoning in LLMs. arXiv. http://arxiv.org/abs/2406.09136.
Zhang, Yifan, Yang Yuan, and Andrew Chi-Chih Yao. 2024c. On the Diagram of Thought. arXiv. http://arxiv.org/abs/2409.10038.

PART IV

AI-Driven Imagery: Global Insights for the Responsible Advancement of Art History

CHAPTER 13

AI and the Colonial Gaze

Adriel Luis

A distorted vision of the Pacific Islands has dominated the public imagination for centuries, and now AI thinks it is reality. The hollow depiction of a tropical paradise—lined with palm trees and beach sunsets, inhabited by quietly dancing Islanders with flowers in their hair and grass skirts around their waists—is an injustice to a region that accounts for over a third of the earth's surface, and which Indigenous Studies scholar Lana Lopesi (2018, 29) describes as "one of the most culturally diverse areas in the world, with a multiplicity of social, economic, and political systems all undergoing different stages of decolonisation." Stereotypes of the Pacific and its peoples trace back to Western imperial explorers in the eighteenth and nineteenth centuries, namely French navigator Louis-Antoine de Bougainville, Captain James Cook of Britain, and Charles Wilkes of the United States (*Blakemore* 2018). These explorers extensively documented their observations, often blurring the lines between subjective opinions and scientific fact. Their voyages set the stage for the subsequent colonisation of the Pacific, inspiring the likes of French painter Paul Gauguin and American novelist Herman Melville to create visual art and literature that

A. Luis (✉)
Independent, Los Angeles, CA, USA
e-mail: a@drzzl.com

L. Cempellin, M. Geiger (eds.), *Reimagining Art History with Artificial Intelligence*,
https://doi.org/10.1007/978-3-032-21685-4_13

crystalised romanticisations of the region in nineteenth-century popular culture and eventually the galleries of renowned institutions across the world, including the Metropolitan Mueum of Art and the Musée d'Orsay (de la Durantaye 2008). Over the last century, blockbuster films such as *Bird of Paradise* (1932), *South Pacific* (1958), and *The Thin Red Line* (1998) perpetuated misportrayals of Pacific Islanders as "simple people lacking in complexity, intellect, or ambition" (Hereniko 1999). This lineage of misinformation fuelled the tourist industry driven by Western fantasies of an exotic paradise, complicit in the military occupations, ecological impacts, and economic hardships endured by the region as a result of Western influence (Cheer et al. 2018). Today, a Google image search for "Pacific Islands" summons an endless scroll of lush shorelines dotted with smiling natives frozen in the past as the rest of the world's economies, geopolitics, and technologies evolve around them.

The Internet that produces this search result is the same well from which AI models draw their understandings of the world, which are increasingly influential on how people perceive everything and everyone around them (Ehsan et al. 2019). This digital doppelgänger of the Pacific is gnarled by the colonial gaze, and overshadows the body of writings, photographs, and artworks reflecting the Pacific by the people who live their lives and trace their ancestries there. Emblematic of this discrepancy is the continued influence of Gauguin's paintings on how the region is perceived today, despite his own admissions that his work was driven by a personal desire to quell his disappointment when he discovered that Tahiti was not the paradise he expected (Drayton 2024).

In this chapter, we will investigate the extent to which Gauguin's paintings of Mā'ohi Nui (French Polynesia)—he produced approximately 70 during his stays in Tahiti and the Marquesas Islands between 1891 and 1903—influence text-to-image AI generation related to Tahiti and the Pacific Islands by some of today's most popular AI models (at the time of this writing, these include DALL·E 3, Midjourney V7, and Adobe Firefly Image 4 Ultra). We will then consider how this contributes to biases in how AI conveys the region and its peoples, which reinforces preexisting biases. Lastly, we will consider the impact of this cycle of bias on the present and future of the Pacific.

Terms, Labels, Names

Common terms for the region such as "South Pacific" and "Pacific Islands" were coined by European navigators, and harbour colonial roots (Thaman 2003). Although "Oceania" is also a colonial term, the Pacific Studies community often favours it, inspired by the respected Tongan anthropologist Epeli Hau'ofa (1994) who famously reclaimed the term, writing, "Oceania is vast, Oceania is expanding, Oceania is hospitable and generous, Oceania is humanity rising from the depths of brine and regions of fire deeper still, Oceania is us" (160). Another term, "Te Moana Nui a Kiva," derives from te reo Māori and is sometimes preferred among regional scholars to describe the geographic, cultural, linguistic, spiritual, and navigational histories that connect the region (Ihimaera 2022). However, it resonates more deeply with Polynesian peoples, and not always with others of the region. So, in this chapter I refer to the region as the "Pacific Islands" while minding its frictioned etymology, but surrendering to the fact that it is the most commonly used term, and is most likely to be used in AI prompts and Internet searches (an important consideration in the context of this study). I use the term "Tahitian" to refer to the people of Tahiti, while respectfully acknowledging that "Mā'ohi" is preferred among the peoples indigenous to Mā'ohi Nui (IWGIA 2024). As a writer who does not trace my ancestry to the Pacific, I proceed with humility, deep respect, and high regard for the numerous writers, artists, and scholars of the region who have worked to reconcile colonial harms, many of whom I cite in this chapter.

On Representation

How the Pacific has been portrayed to the rest of the world matters, as do the roots of these portrayals and how AI proliferates them. At the heart of this matter are questions of representation: Who gets to tell their own stories? Who gets to tell the stories of others? Who gets to tell the stories that dominate humanity's collective imagination? Pacific Studies scholar Linda Tuhiwai Smith (2012) writes, "Representation is important because it gives us an impression of 'the truth'…[it] privileges sets of texts, views about the history of an idea, [and] what issues count as significant" (37).

We are amidst an AI arms race directly informed by what is represented online. Companies backed by the most powerful nations are in a heated competition to produce the model that will be most widely adopted and thus hold the greatest influence over how people receive information in an increasingly Internet-dependent world. Indigenous populations are most vulnerable to the impacts of this arms race, including Pacific peoples, who have been systematically deprived of self-governance, a stake in their media portrayals, and agency over geopolitical and environmental decisions that impact them. Scholars have raised concerns that AI privileges the perspectives of those with technological, political, and economic advantages, while disenfranchising traditional and ancestral knowledge. A 2025 report published by the Brookings Institute warned that "the computational infrastructure of major tech companies consumes ever-increasing resources without accountability or recognition of Indigenous knowledge systems" (Kereopa-Yorke 2025). Meanwhile, access to AI technologies and the skillsets needed to leverage them is a growing challenge, with experts warning that "it is hard for the [Pacific Island countries] to attract the AI talents, or train the local people to operate and manage AI systems due to [the region's] economic hardship, limited education resources and brain drain" (Raj et al. 2025).

The colonisation of the Pacific has left a legacy of genocide, disease, poverty, weapons development systems, and damaged ecosystems (Venkataramanan 2023). Historically, justification for the conquest, exploitation, and disenfranchisement of Pacific peoples has been based on the stereotypes first introduced by imperial explorers of the region, treating them as passive, uncivilised people (Adds 2012). For example, the United States selected the Bikini Atoll in the Marshall Islands as the site for testing 67 nuclear bombs between 1946 and 1958, displacing scores of people and forever altering the landscape and waterways (*Maurer* 2024). US Atomic Energy Commission Chief of Health and Safety Merril Eisenbud acknowledged the area as "by far the most contaminated place in the world," referring to the radioactive aftermath left by the nuclear explosions. Regardless, he recommended returning the displaced residents to the area to study the effects of their radiation exposure, noting the scientific advantage of using human specimens rather than animals: "While it is true that these people do not live, I would say, the way Westerners do, civilised people, it is nevertheless also true that they are more like us than the mice" (Pohle 2024). More recently, human rights organisations complained about the Indonesian government's framing of West Papuans as "savages" amidst its ongoing genocide in Papua New Guinea (Kogoya 2022). Meanwhile, in 2023 the United Nations published a report on the severity of human trafficking in Pacific Island nations, noting that "trafficking for sexual exploitation seems to take place especially in the tourist area or in urban areas" (UNODC 2023, 9). The history of the Pacific is marred by examples like these of how colonial stereotypes have enabled violence against the region.

Gauguin's Fantasy

With his full-colour paintings peopled by Polynesians, Gauguin brought to life the notion of an island getaway for the West's enjoyment at the turn of the twentieth century. Gauguin's interest in French Polynesia, his eventual residence there, and his resulting body of paintings were fuelled by a search for what he called "the primitive," a response to his discontent with the industrialisation and urbanisation of his home country of France (Drayton 2024). However, when he first arrived in 1891, Tahiti had already been a French protectorate for half a century. French missionaries, government initiatives, and booming industries had made a sizeable imprint on the social and ecological landscape, devastating Gauguin's hopes for an escape from the grasp of Western influence. "It was the Tahiti of former times which I loved. That of the present filled me with horror" (Drayton 2024). Gauguin spent the following decade painting this "Tahiti of former times," ignoring the French influences and modernisation there to fixate on beaches, tropical plants, and women either dressed in traditional garments or naked.

Gauguin exploited Tahitian women in his artwork as well as in his daily life. He engaged in sexual relations with many of the subjects of his paintings, including Teha'amana, a 13-year-old girl. Gauguin carried syphilis, and he passed the disease on to several of his Tahitian sexual partners (Grishin 2024). In his writings, Gauguin described Tahitians with terms such as "exotic," "meek," and "fool." Unfortunately, his views and treatment of Tahitians are reflected in how they are perceived today.

Despite this troubling legacy, Gauguin's work remains highly regarded. His Tahiti paintings are part of the collections of major museums throughout the world, including the Metropolitan Museum of Art (New York), Tate Modern (London), Musée d'Orsay (Paris), Pushkin Museum of Fine Arts (Moscow), Muthe Museum of Modern Art (New York), and the Paul Gauguin Museum (Tahiti) (Brettell et al. 2019). Paul Gauguin Cruises, a luxury cruise line dedicated to introducing tourists to his version of the Pacific, consistently ranks among the top in the industry (Paul Gauguin Cruises 2019). "I was thinking of Paul Gauguin," explained John Musker, co-creator of Disney's *Moana*, in a 2016 interview about the animated feature film based on a fictionalised island nation of the Pacific. The *Moana* franchise has since become among the most influential pop culture portrayals of Pacific Islanders in the world. The 2024 film *Moana 2* is one of Disney's top-grossing animated films (Squires 2016). Gauguin's influence on art, entertainment, tourism, and foreign policy of the region cannot be understated. This transfers to the amount of Gauguin-tainted data about the Pacific that exists online.

In recent years, Gauguin has received extensive criticism for his sexual exploitation of women and his role in the colonial representation of the Pacific (Mendelsohn 2017). Art historian Eli Anapur (2023) describes how Gauguin reduced the region to a muse "where he could express himself freely, regardless of the morality of it." Didier Maleuvre (2018, 198) wrote, "[Gauguin's] sojourn, as he himself knew, corrupted Tahiti; it was part of the cultural contamination visited on the Polynesians by European presence." Community arts worker Winnie Siuvolovao Dunn (2019) wrote, "All of Gauguin's artworks about Tahiti contribute to the damaging stereotypes about the Pacific and the people who call themselves Polynesian—a sexual and racial fantasy forged from a position of patriarchal and colonial power."

Despite the critiques, art institutions continue to uplift Gauguin's works, highlighting his paintings of the Pacific. In 2024, Kunstforum Wien in Austria, the National Gallery of Australia, and The Museum of Fine Arts, Houston (MFAH) in the United States all exhibited Gauguin retrospectives (Kunstforum n.d.; the National Gallery of Art, NGA n.d.; MFAH 2024). If the colonial context was addressed at all, it was done so cryptically. In the press release for MFAH's exhibition, *Gauguin in the World*, the museum's director Gary Tinterow merely alluded to the artist's transgressions by stating, "Gauguin was controversial in his own time and remains so today," and summarised his impact as "challenging what he perceived as a culture that had reached a dead end and renewing it by exploring and embracing non-Western art" (MFA Houston 2024).

Learning on a Lie

To AI, art is merely information represented by pixels and code. Paintings, illustrations, and photographs produced throughout human history are continuously uploaded to become part of the massive datasets that text-to-image generative AI models trawl. The training for each model varies, and the developers of the most popular ones are opaque about the datasets they are trained on. But excerpts from a 2024 study published in *Scientific Reports* offer a basic outline of how it works:

> AI models use a pre-trained data set of images that link natural language to an image... Images and text captions are passed through encoders ... [a] diffusion model (also known as diffusion prior) is utilized to map the text caption encoding to image encoding... the generative AI tool (e.g., DALL·E) needs to reverse this to generate an image. (Joynt et al. 2024)

Technology writer Alina Valyaeva (2023) further explains how AI models determine what to generate based on the information from images and text they are trained on:

> For a model to master the task, a machine must be trained to recognize objects in images, using a large dataset that includes images and text descriptions of them. As a result, the machine not only recognizes objects in images, but also understands the text descriptions that correspond to them, and how the objects and concepts relate to each other. This understanding of the relationship between language and images is a key aspect of text-to-image algorithms. (Valyaeva 2023)

But interpreting art requires far more than simply "recognizing objects": it requires reasoning beyond AI's capabilities. AI can decypher the imagery and descriptive text that represent an artwork, but cannot derive meaning from it. AI is unable to look critically at an artwork, to consider whether it is based on fact or perception, whether its creator held biases, how to contextualise it in art history, or how to compare it with the physical realities of the offline world. It is certainly unable to distinguish colonial romanticisations from truth. Gauguin afforded himself creative licence to blend reality with a fantasy based on ill-informed nostalgia. Art critic Adrian Searle (2010) once described Gauguin as "almost a magic realist before the fact." This nuance is lost on AI, which simply sees images of the Pacific.

AI relies on easily interpretable images and straightforward metadata (e.g. filename, alt text, captions, and alt text), essentially programming it to prioritise colonial artworks, which are largely subject-based and whose titles often read as descriptive text (Xhignesse 2018). For example, it is more straightforward for AI to develop a notion of Tahiti from Gauguin's painting entitled *Tahitian Women Bathing* (1892) than, say, *La Famille*

Pomare (tifaifai; Pa'oti style; 1991) by Tahitian textile artist Aline Amaru. *La Famille Pomare* is a tifaifai (Tahitian quilt) that incorporates contemporary and traditional elements to pay tribute to the five generations of the Pōmare dynasty that reigned over the Kingdom of Tahiti prior to French rule (McDougall and Page 2005). It depicts Tahiti's pre-colonial rulers standing side-by-side, dressed in garments corresponding with their respective time periods and proximity to Western influence, and surrounded by symbols inspired by Tahitian textiles (Kirker 2012). It is a succinct portrayal of Tahitian history. Still, for an AI model to associate this work with "Tahiti," it must analyse Amaru's treatment of time and symbology with a critical eye. Then there is the issue of accessibility: Amaru's work is held by the Queensland Art Gallery but is not available through its online archives, making it less likely to be part of datasets AI models are trained on (Figs. 13.1 and 13.2).

In contrast, Gauguin's paintings and their titles effectively taxanomise Tahiti, which has been conducive to cataloguing in museums, priming them for training AI. One of Gauguin's most famous paintings, portraying two Tahitian women on a beach, is entitled *Two Tahitian Women on the Beach* (1891). It reads like a basic AI prompt, as do *Three Tahitian Women against a Yellow Background* (1899) and *Tahitian Man with His Arms Raised* (1897) (Shackelford and Frèches-Thory 2004). While he entitled some of his other works more poetically, they all commonly leave little to interpretation when it comes to how Tahiti and its people are portrayed: surrounded by lush nature, exotic by Western standards, forever primitive. As travel writer Nigel Tisdall (2015) put it, "Gauguin's paintings inspired by his time in French Polynesia have become synonymous with our image of the South Seas." In the next section, I analyse how this effect has infiltrated AI.

The Trials

As I mentioned, AI companies are not transparent about the datasets they train their AI models on. This is considered proprietary information that sets each competing model apart (Buick 2025). Nor do text-to-image generators cite the media they draw from, and one of the most contentious issues in this arena has been AI's trawling of artworks without obtaining permission from, notifying, compensating, or crediting the creators and rights holders (Williams 2024). Even for those who do restrict a model from training on their works, there is no stopping the model from

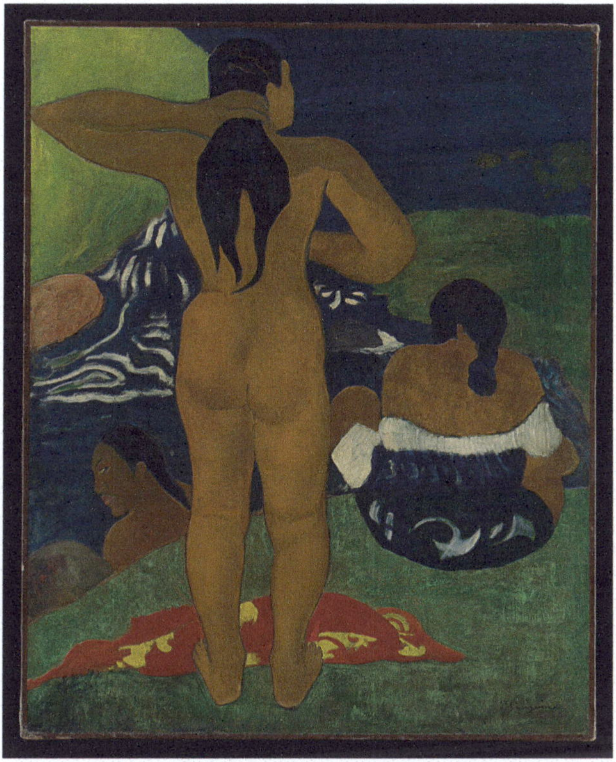

Fig. 13.1 Paul Gauguin, *Tahitian Women Bathing* (1892). The Met Collection, public domain

training on other unauthorised derivatives. So, it is not possible to determine to what degree models have been trained directly on Gauguin's paintings, or to what extent they influence outputs. But by testing a series of prompts on these models, we can detect the extent of the painter's colonial impact on various AI algorithms.

Prompts

Conducting this observational study involved running five prompts through each of three text-to-image AI models, with prompts ranging in degree in terms of relationship with Gauguin. For example, Prompt A,

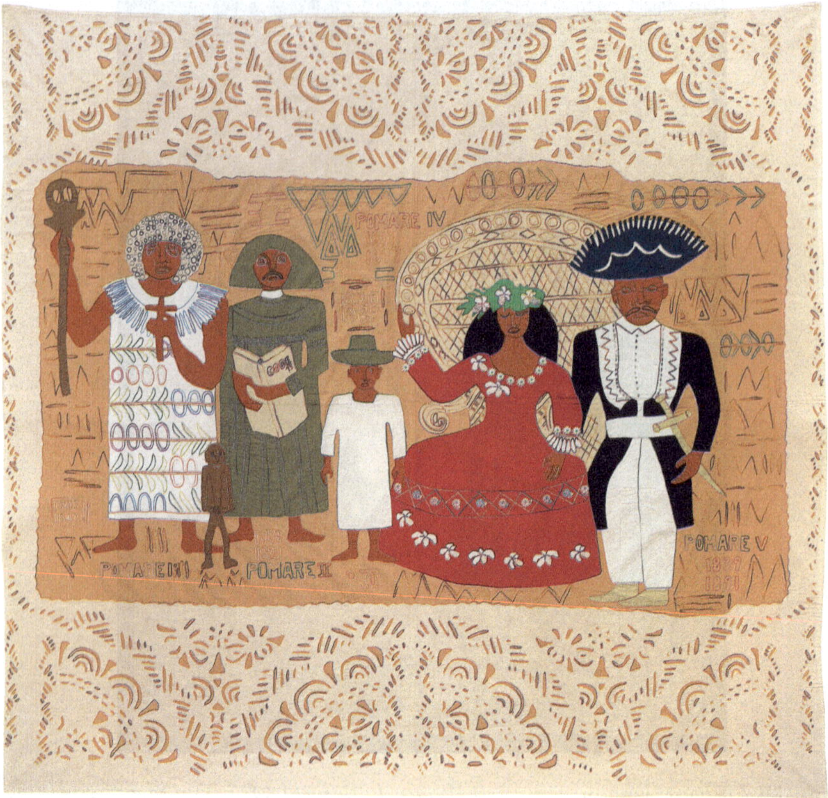

Fig. 13.2 Aline Amaru b.1941 / *La Famille Pomare (tifaifai) (Pa'oti style)* 1991 / Commercial cotton cloth and thread in appliqué and embroidered technique / 237.8 × 229 cm / Purchased 2004. Queensland Art Gallery Foundation Grant / Collection: Queensland Art Gallery / Gallery of Modern Art / © Aline Amaru / Photograph: QACOMA

"Three Tahitians," was used because even though it is the name of a Gauguin painting, it is general enough to not necessarily draw association or request stereotypical imagery. Prompt B, "Tahitians," intended to reveal whether Gauguin influences outputs of Tahitians in general, even if avoiding any suggestion of references to his work. For Prompt C, I tested "three Mā'ohi," to see if results would be affected by using the Indigenous terminology that Gauguin never used, thus marking a clear disassociation with him. With Prompt D, "Three Pacific Islanders," I observed distinctions between AI conceptions of regional peoples and Tahitians specifically. Prompt E, "Three Tahitians in the style of Gauguin," swung in the opposite direction, directly naming the painter and his painting in the prompt. This was included as a gauge for whether the model reflects Gauguin's aesthetics in the first place, revealing whether his works may have been part of the training dataset, or if an error result would suggest his works were omitted or restricted.

Models

There is a rapidly growing number of text-to-image AI models, but since this experiment aims to understand AI's relationship with the general public's notions of the Pacific, I chose to observe three of the most popular and accessible at this time.

DALL·E 3

By far the most popular of all models, DALL·E is OpenAI's image generator and runs directly on ChatGPT, now a household name with over five billion visits to its website per month (Duarte 2025). To date, OpenAI has not disclosed how many images DALL·E 3 was trained on, but it revealed in 2024 that DALL·E 2 was trained on 650 million (Ramesh et al. 2022). An image is generated when a user types a command into the "Ask anything" box on https://chatgpt.com, such as "Create an image of three Tahitians."

Midjourney v7

Popular within creative industries, Midjourney is among the largest models. In 2022, founder David Holz revealed that Midjourney was "trained over billions of images" (Claburn 2022). With over 20 million registered users, it is the largest server operating on Discord. Midjourney generates images in forums or private chats with bots by typing a prompt such as "/ imagine prompt: three Tahitians." While DALL·E generates one image per prompt, Midjourney produces four variant images, each of which can be upscaled, modified, or remixed into subvariants.

Adobe Firefly Image 4 Ultra

Adobe's model, Firefly, distinguishes itself from most other AI in that it does not trawl the web, instead training on Adobe's collection of stock images and other open licence databases (Adobe 2025). In April 2025, Adobe released Firefly Image 4. While previous versions were limited as tools incorporated into other Adobe software such as Photoshop, Image 4 brought with it a standalone image generator platform on https://firefly.adobe.com. The current platform allows users to generate images based on the previous Model 3, Model 4, and "Model 4 Ultra," described on the platform as providing "superior quality and details." For this trial, I used Model 4 Ultra to test the extent of Firefly's algorithm.

Figure 13.3 is a table of images generated from each of the three AI models according to the five prompts. Results featured familiar tropes such as beach settings, tropical plants, and "traditional" attire such as leis and heis (floral adornments), grass skirts, and pareo (patterned wrap-around cloths). Here, we can see that AI depictions draw from, and reinforce, the stereotypes perpetuated by Gauguin.

DALL·E's images demonstrated the clearest evidence of Gauguin's influence—concerning, as it is currently the world's most dominant AI model. It first responded to my prompt for "Three Tahitians" with a clarifying question: "To create the most respectful and accurate image, could you let me know if you have a specific style in mind (e.g., impressionist painting, vintage photography, modern illustration), and whether you want the scene to be traditional, contemporary, or more symbolic or artistic?" The fact that it immediately suggested "impressionist painting" was already telling. I responded, "Your choice," which resulted in a simulated oil painting depicting figures presumably from a period in the past, and using similar colours, shading techniques, and composition to Gauguin's works (1A). The prompt for Gauguin's style produced a similar result, except even more closely resembling some of his classic Tahitian paintings, offering strong evidence that they were part of the model's training dataset (1E). The other prompts produced nearly identical photorealistic variations of the previously mentioned results, featuring Polynesians in beach settings wearing pareos and headdresses (1B, 1C, 1D).

Midjourney's results showed evidence of moderate or indirect Gauguin influence, only producing images with clear associations when prompted to do so (2E). While many of the images emulated paintings, they reflected more contemporary qualities. Midjourney was more prone than DALL·E

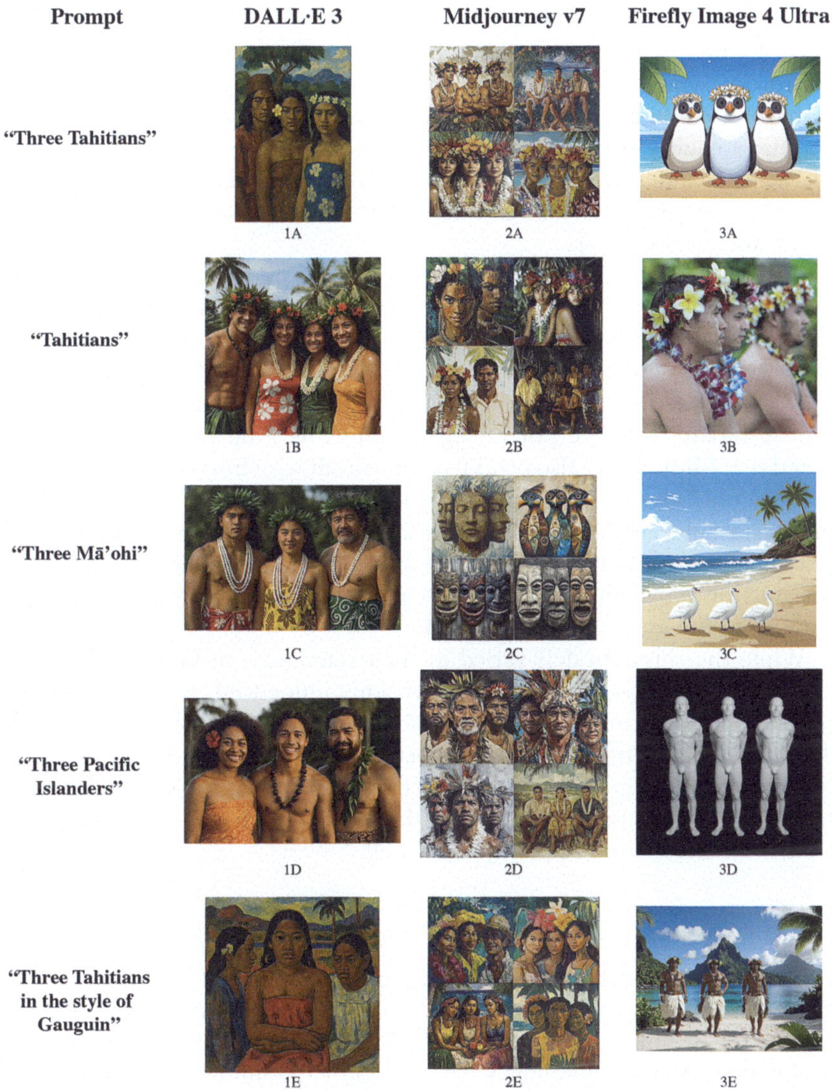

Fig. 13.3 Text-to-image AI test results

to incorporating inaccurate cultural elements, such as men wearing Aloha shirts commonly associated with modern Hawaiian fashion (2A, 2B), and tiki masks, which are not traditional to Tahiti (2C). This indicated that perhaps less training on Gauguin's works also meant less training on Tahitian imagery altogether, leading the model to conflate Tahitians with all Pacific Islanders. Midjourney was the only model that, in one instance, produced an image of figures wearing non-traditional attire (i.e. shirts, pants, and a dress; 2D).

Firefly's results ranged from stereotypical to perplexing. The outputs for "Tahitians" and "Tahitians in the style of Gauguin" generated photo-realistic images that were consistent with the other models—figures in beach settings wearing "traditional" attire (3B, 3E). For "three Tahitians" and "three Mā'ohi," it generated cartoon images of birds (3A, 3C), with the "Tahitian" instance portraying penguins wearing heis (it should be noted that Midjourney also produced one result with birds when prompted for "Mā'ohi," despite the term not being associated with any bird species). In the instance of "three Pacific Islanders," it generated three figures resembling white porcelain statues wearing Speedo-style swimwear (3D). It is unclear to me why the models associated this imagery with the prompt aside from the association with beaches.

While the three models varied in their references to Gauguin's paintings—from DALL·E being almost certainly influenced, to Firefly almost certainly not—no model imagined Tahitians and Pacific Islanders beyond the colonial romanticisations perpetuated over the centuries. While this confirms that Gauguin is not the sole culprit in the Pacific's flattened representation, it is also apparent that these AI models are not trained on many non-stereotypical portrayals, if at all.

Automating Bias

Our relationship with AI is not a single-direction flow of information, but rather an exchange. While AI models train on humanity's accumulated knowledge, we increasingly rely on AI for research, education, and media production. Artificial intelligence is refined by the human mind into actuated knowledge. Whether based on fact or fiction, this knowledge is then fed back to AI to learn and teach back to us. Through this cycle, truth reverberates and misinformation calcifies.

Rest of World analysed over 3000 AI images of people generated from prompts based on various races and ethnicities (Turk 2023). The researchers found that AI overwhelmingly proliferate stereotypes, reducing the people of the world to a gallery of caricatures. The study showed that biased imagery is not limited to Pacific Islanders, and that AI has shaped its notion of humanity based on largely skewed and one-dimensional representations of people across cultures.

A human society increasingly dependent on AI models that reflect and amplify bias poses sweeping consequences not only for how people perceive one another, but how these perceptions affect policies, economic and environmental decisions, hiring and labour practices, and a host of other factors that deeply affect people's lives. Vicente and Matute (2023) observed that trust in AI without critical human supervision could result in "bias [that] would reach serious implications if…the AI system is applied to decision-making in high-stakes scenarios, such as AI-based facial recognition systems to identify criminal suspects or AI-based image diagnosis." The study went on to discuss implications for influence on human behaviour, as "AI bias can also result in discrimination or prejudice towards a person or group of people since the patterns embedded in the historical data used to train algorithms often reflect systematic social and economic inequities" (Vicente and Matute 2023). Glickman and Sharot (2025) warned of the risks of "bias amplification" between humans and AI, caused by a feedback loop of misinformation that increasingly distorts our notions of reality and how humans treat each other accordingly.

While AI-powered bias amplification poses consequences for everyone's sense of reality, Indigenous populations who have been historically deprived of self-determination and representation are among those who suffer most swiftly and severely. Nina Sangma (2024) writes,

> The human condition today is centred on and propelled by data in an endless continuum of consuming it, harvesting it, living it, and generating it through loop after loop of digital footprints on platforms meant to compete with sleep. For Indigenous peoples, our identities are predestined and politicised, defined by our resistance as our existence through the ages and stages of colonisation and imperialism to the present, the 'age of AI,' will exacerbate existing inequalities and violence. (Sangma 2024)

Sagma underscores a reoccurring theme of the role of human progress in dividing the privileged and the oppressed. This divide is already evidenced in the ways that AI's training and usage have disproportionately harmed Indigenous communities. Human Rights Watch (2024) found that personal photos of First Nations Australian children were included without consent in LAION-5B, a dataset that scrapes most of the Internet for AI training. Some of the data scraped included information linking the photographs with names, locations where the photos were taken, and other personal data that could be misused for identity theft and child exploitation (HRW 2024). That same year, privacy rights groups in Australia and Aotearoa raised concerns about AI-powered facial recognition technologies used in supermarkets, despite violations that disproportionately affect First Nations and Pacific Islander communities, such as racial profiling and unauthorised recording of those with moko (facial tattoos) which are traditionally considered sacred (ABC 2024). Proponents of AI typically ignore such breaches, or dismiss them as compromises necessary for the greater efficiency, information exchange, and economic opportunities the technology affords.

Getting With the Program

"Our futures will not simply fall upon us like a hammer," writes Pacific Studies scholar Damon Salesa (2018). "We will shape them by what we do (or do not do) in the present and the choices we make for the future; these will collectively be expressions of our priorities, our ambitions, and who we are and what we value" (29). The struggle against alien technologies that threaten knowledge systems and ways of life may seem unprecedented to some, but for Pacific Islanders and other Indigenous peoples, this struggle reflects centuries of lived experience. They have persisted by revitalising languages, reclaiming customs, restoring ecosystems, and proving that humanity can thrive in the face of seemingly insurmountable circumstances (McMillen et al. 2019). There is little to no evidence that AI training prioritises conventionally trusted sources (e.g. academic articles and institutional data) over other online information (MIT n.d.). This presents challenges regarding misinformation—but for the Pacific which has been misportrayed precisely because of supposedly trustworthy sources, AI can present an opportunity for correcting history. Lopesi (2018) writes, "Oceania and the internet offer Moana peoples potentials to overcome the false divides which are so deeply ingrained in us" (104). Dismantling harmful stereotypes would require various coordinated efforts, including proliferation of more complex and authentic Pacific representation in digital public commons that honour intellectual property and cultural protocol, dedicated AI training on datasets that more accurately reflect reality, and for museums and institutions to reckon with their roles in perpetuating Gauguin's myths of the Pacific. AI Asia Pacific Institute's (2024) report *The State of Artificial Intelligence in the Pacific Islands* outlined the challenges AI poses for the region such as bias and privacy violations, while also highlighting ways that the region is uniquely positioned to use AI to address climate change and aid in cultural preservation. In 2021, a group of technology experts, including many belonging to Australian First Nations, convened as The Indigenous Protocols and Artificial Intelligence Laboratory to "[test] critical assumptions about the nature and usefulness of Indigenous Protocols, and cultural datasets in the shaping of Artificial Intelligence" (Indigenous Protocols 2025). In 2023, Māori artist Doug Healey launched *The AI Marae*, a project dedicated to strategies for influencing AI models to generate images that embody Māori values and principles (The AI Marae n.d.). Engaging technology to reflect the realities of Pacific peoples is delicate and daunting, but necessary for utilising the technology to enable self-determination and agency.

A growing number of Pacific artists have claimed their stake in the conversation of the region, reshaping global perceptions of them in the process. Tahitian artist Tahe Drollet, for example, blends street art and traditional Tahitian techniques to create mixed-material sculptures that convey a sense of Tahiti's contemporary realities while demonstrating how intergenerational artistry endures. In 2024, the National Gallery of Australia commissioned Drollet to create a sculpture as part of *SaVĀge K'lub Te Paepae Aora'i – Where the Gods Cannot be Fooled*, curated by Aotearoa artist Rosanna Raymond. Entitled *Riding the Settler*, Drollet's sculpture is a Tahitian umete (ceremonial bowl) adorned with Bougainville's head, accompanied by a tiki sculpture that the artist describes as "guiding Bougainville away from Tahiti" (Bono 2025; NGA 2024). The sculpture and the *SaVĀge K'lub* exhibition were a response to the *Gauguin's World* retrospective that opened concurrently at the NGA, but Drollet's work is typically less focused on directly responding to colonialism. Rather, he sees himself among an emerging generation of Tahitian and Pacific artists exerting what he describes as "their new vision on the art scene" (NGA 2024). It is this *new vision* that holds promise of a Pacific that does not only counteract colonialism, but transcends it, that enables Pacific peoples, as Tahitian poet Flora Devatine writes, "...to be our own individual, moving in our own rhythm, listening only to what pleases us" (Devatine and Toyama 2005).

Acknowledgements I would like to thank the Pacific Islander artist and scholar communities I have collaborated with over the years, who have shaped my understanding of the region and the issues that impact it, namely, cohorts from *'Ae Kai: A Culture Lab on Convergence* in Honolulu Hawai'i (2017), *Te Whāinga: A Culture Lab on Civility* in Auckland Aotearoa (2019), the *She Who Dies to Live* performance collective (2017–2019), and *ARC-HIVE* (2021–present). I would especially like to thank my colleague Kālewa Correa, the Smithsonian Asian Pacific American Center's Curator of Hawai'i and the Pacific, for discussing and reviewing the content of this chapter with me, and staff members of QAGOMA for facilitating image clearance for Aline Amaru's "La Famille Pomare": Ruth McDougall, Kate Herford, and Zenobia Frost.

References

Adds, Peter. 2012. E Kore Au E Ngaro: Ancestral Connections to the Pacific. In *Tangata O Le Moana*, ed. Sean Mallon, Kolokesa Māhina-Tuai, and Damon Salesa, 17–35. Wellington: Te Papa Press.

Adobe. 2025. Adobe Firefly: The Next Evolution of Creative AI Is Here. *Adobe Blog*, April 24, 2025. https://web.archive.org/web/20240424132630/https://blog.adobe.com/en/publish/2025/04/24/adobe-firefly-next-evolution-creative-ai-is-here.

AI Asia Pacific Institute. 2024. *The State of Artificial Intelligence in the Pacific Islands.* August 2024. https://web.archive.org/web/20240424132625/https://aiasiapacific.org/wp-content/uploads/2024/08/The-State-of-Artificial-Intelligence-in-the-Pacific-Islands.pdf.

Amaru, Aline. 1991. *La Famille Pomare (tifaifai) (Pa'oti style).* Commercial cotton cloth and thread in appliqué and embroidered technique, 237.8 × 229 cm. Queensland Art Gallery, Brisbane. https://collection.qagoma.qld.gov.au/objects/14129.

Anapur, Eli. 2023. Gauguin's Tahiti: Questioning a Troubling Legacy. *Widewalls*, November 11, 2023. https://web.archive.org/web/20231111062237/https://www.widewalls.ch/magazine/gauguin-tahiti.

Australian Broadcasting Corporation. 2024. Facial Recognition Trial Raises Concerns for Indigenous and Pasifika Peoples. *Pacific Beat*, ABC Pacific, audio, 10:56, February 26, 2024. https://web.archive.org/web/20240424132618/https://www.abc.net.au/pacific/programs/pacificbeat/facial-recognition/103515150.

Blakemore, Erin. 2018. Captain Cook's 1768 Voyage to the South Pacific Included a Secret Mission. *Smithsonian Magazine*, August 24, 2018. https://web.archive.org/web/20240424131557/https://www.smithsonianmag.com/history/captain-cooks-1768-voyage-south-pacific-included-secret-mission-180970119/.

Bono, Mariama. 2025. When the Artists of Te Moana Nui Meet up in Canberra. *Pacific Islands Report*, February 5, 2025. https://pireport.org/2025/02/05/when-the-artists-of-te-moana-nui-meet-up-in-canberra/.

Buick, Adam. 2025. Copyright and AI Training Data-Transparency to the Rescue? *Journal of Intellectual Property Law & Practice* 20 (3): 182–192. https://doi.org/10.1093/jiplp/jpae102.

Cheer, Joseph M., Stephen Pratt, Denis Tolkach, Anthony Bailey, Semisi Taumoepeau, and Apisalome Movono. 2018. Tourism in Pacific Island Countries: A Status Quo Round-Up. *Asia & the Pacific Policy Studies* 5 (3): 442–461. https://doi.org/10.1002/app5.250.

Claburn, Thomas. 2022. David Holz, Founder of AI Art Generator Midjourney, on the Future of Imaging. *The Register*, August 1, 2022. https://web.archive.org/web/20240424132617/https://www.theregister.com/2022/08/01/david_holz_midjourney/.

de la Durantaye, Leland. 2008. Otherwise: Victor Segalen's Inward Exoticism. *Cabinet Magazine*, no. 31, Fall 2008. https://web.archive.org/web/20240424132804/https://www.cabinetmagazine.org/issues/31/deladurantaye.php.

Devatine, Flora, and Jean Yamasaki Toyama. 2005. Three Poems. *Mānoa* 17 (2): 24–29. https://doi.org/10.1353/man.2006.0006.

Drayton, Joanne. 2024. Exploring Paul Gauguin's Search for the 'Primitive' in Tahiti. *New Lines Magazine,* April 23, 2024. https://web.archive.org/web/20240423161929/https://newlinesmag.com/essays/exploring-paul-gauguins-search-for-the-primitive-in-tahiti/.

Duarte, Fabio. 2025. Number of ChatGPT Users (March 2025): Growth, Demographics & Revenue. *Exploding Topics.* https://web.archive.org/web/20240424132625/https://explodingtopics.com/blog/chatgpt-users. Last modified 13 March 2025.

Dunn, Winnie Siulolovao. 2019. Playing God with Our Lives and Stories: The Stubborn Power of the Pacific Muse. *Overland*, April 9, 2019. https://web.archive.org/web/20240425103248/https://overland.org.au/2019/04/playing-god-with-our-lives-and-stories-the-stubborn-power-of-the-pacific-muse/.

Ehsan, Upol, Pradyumna Tambwekar, Larry Chan, Brent Harrison, and Mark O. Riedl. 2019. Automated Rationale Generation: A Technique for Explainable AI and Its Effects on Human Perceptions. In *Proceedings of the 24th International Conference on Intelligent User Interfaces* (IUI '19), 263–274. New York: Association for Computing Machinery. https://doi.org/10.1145/3301275.3302316.

Gauguin, Paul. *Tahitian Women Bathing.* 1892. Oil on paper mounted on canvas, 72.7 × 92.1 cm. The Metropolitan Museum of Art, New York. https://www.metmuseum.org/art/collection/search/459100.

Glickman, Moshe, and Tali Sharot. 2025. How Human–AI Feedback Loops Alter Human Perceptual, Emotional, and Social Judgements. *Nature Human Behaviour* 9:345–359. https://doi.org/10.1038/s41562-024-02077-2.

Grishin, Sasha. 2024. Paul Gauguin Was a Violent Paedophile: Should the National Gallery of Australia Be Staging a Major Exhibition of His Work?" *The Conversation*, June 27, 2024. https://theconversation.com/paul-gauguin-was-a-violent-paedophile-should-the-national-gallery-of-australia-be-staging-a-major-exhibition-of-his-work-230545.

Hau'ofa, Epeli. 1994. Our Sea of Islands. *The Contemporary Pacific* 6 (1): 148–161. http://www.jstor.org/stable/23701593.

Hereniko, Vilsoni. 1999. Representations of Pacific Islanders in Film and Video. *Documentary Box* 14. https://web.archive.org/web/20240426175341/https://www.yidff.jp/docbox/14/box14-3-e.html.

Human Rights Watch. 2024. Australia: Children's Personal Photos Misused to Power AI Tools. *Human Rights Watch*, July 3, 2024. https://web.archive.org/web/20240424132622/https://www.hrw.org/news/2024/07/03/australia-childrens-personal-photos-misused-power-ai-tools.

Ihimaera, Witi. 2022. Te Moana Nui a Kiwa: The Original Ocean. In *The Cambridge History of the Pacific Ocean*, ed. Ryan Tucker Jones and Matt K. Matsuda, 23–34. Cambridge: Cambridge University Press. https://web.archive.org/web/20240426180509/https://www.cambridge.org/core/books/abs/cambridge-history-of-the-pacific-ocean/te-moana-nui-a-kiwa/1ECCAB9F755C60D37070D8622AD56508.

Indigenous Protocols and Artificial Intelligence Laboratory. 2025. About. https://web.archive.org/web/20240424132616/https://indigenousprotocols.ai/pages/about. Accessed 27 April 2025.

International Work Group for Indigenous Affairs (IWGIA). 2024. The Indigenous World 2024: Mā'ohi Nui (French Polynesia). *IWGIA*. https://web.archive.org/web/20240426181239/https://iwgia.org/en/french-polynesia.html.

Joynt, V., J. Cooper, N. Bhargava, A. S. M. A. Hossain, M. A. Hossain, and M. R. Islam. 2024. A Comparative Analysis of Text-to-Image Generative AI Models in Scientific Contexts: A Case Study on Nuclear Power. *Scientific Reports* 14:30377. https://doi.org/10.1038/s41598-024-79705-4.

Kereopa-Yorke, Ben. 2025 "AI infrastructure's environmental costs clash with Pacific Island nations' needs." The Bookings Institute, March 7, 2025. Accessed April 26, 2025. https://web.archive.org/web/20250407095427/https://www.brookings.edu/articles/ai-infrastructures-environmental-costs-clash-with-pacificisland-nations-needs/.

Kirker, Anne. 2012. Threads: Contemporary Textiles and the Social Fabric. *Artlink* 32 (1). https://web.archive.org/web/20240424132619/https://www.artlink.com.au/articles/3775/threads-contemporary-textiles-and-the-social-fabri/.

Kogoya, Yamin. 2022. Where Is West Papua Now? *RNZ*, December 5, 2022. https://web.archive.org/web/20240424131356/https://www.rnz.co.nz/international/pacific-news/480255/where-is-west-papua-now. Accessed 26 April 2025.

Kunstforum Wien. n.d. Gauguin Unexpected. *Kunstforum Wien.* https://web.archive.org/web/20250303093412/https://www.kunstforumwien.at/de/ausstellungen/500014. Accessed 26 April 2025.

Lopesi, Lana. 2018. *False Divides.* Wellington, NZ: Bridget Williams Books.

Maleuvre, Didier. 2018. The Trial of Paul Gauguin. *Mosaic: An Interdisciplinary Critical Journal* 51 (1): 197–213. https://www.jstor.org/stable/90021833.

Maurer, Anaïs. 2024. *The Ocean on Fire: Pacific Stories from Nuclear Survivors and Climate Activists.* Durham, NC: Duke University Press.

McDougall, Ruth, and Maud Page. 2005. AMARU, Aline; La Famille Pomare (tifaifai) (Pa'oti style). *QAGOMA Collection Stories*, June 2005. https://web.archive.org/web/20240424131254/https://collection.qagoma.qld.gov.au/stories/117. Accessed 26 April 2025.

McMillen, Heather L., Eleanor J. Sterling, Stacy D. Jupiter, John Campbell, Victoria L. Betley, Faleafaga Toni Tipama'a, Alifereti Tawake, and Joeli Veitayaki. 2019. Lessons From the Pacific Islands—Adapting to Climate Change by Integrating Local and Indigenous Knowledge. *Frontiers in Marine Science* 6:289. https://doi.org/10.3389/fmars.2019.00289.

Mendelsohn, Meredith. 2017. Why Is the Art World Divided over Gauguin's Legacy? *Artsy*, December 6, 2017. https://web.archive.org/web/20240426183137/https://www.artsy.net/article/artsy-editorial-art-divided-gauguins-legacy.

MIT Sloan Teaching & Learning Technologies. n.d. When AI Gets It Wrong: Addressing AI Hallucinations and Bias. *MIT Sloan Educational Technology Blog.* https://web.archive.org/web/20240424132621/https://mitsloanedtech.mit.edu/ai/basics/addressing-ai-hallucinations-and-bias/. Accessed 26 April 2025.

Museum of Fine Arts, Houston. 2024. The MFAH Is the Exclusive U.S. Venue for 'Gauguin in the World,' Opening in November 2024. *Museum of Fine Arts, Houston*, June 24, 2024. https://web.archive.org/web/20240424132050/https://www.mfah.org/press/the-mfah-is-the-exclusive-us-venue-for-gauguin-in-the-world-opening-in-november-2024. Accessed 26 April 2025.

National Gallery of Australia. 2024. Tahe Drollet on Riding the Settler. *National Gallery of Australia*, June 28, 2024. https://web.archive.org/web/20240424132134/https://nga.gov.au/on-demand/tahe-drollet-on-riding-the-settler/. Accessed 26 April 2025.

National Gallery of Australia. n.d. Gauguin's World: Tōna Iho, Tōna Ao. *National Gallery of Australia.* https://web.archive.org/web/20240424132628/https://nga.gov.au/exhibitions/gauguins-world/. Accessed 26 April 2025.

Paul Gauguin Cruises. 2019. Paul Gauguin Cruises Wins '#1 Mid-Size Ship Ocean Cruise Line' in the 2019 Travel + Leisure World's Best Awards. *Paul Gauguin Cruises*, July 10, 2019. https://web.archive.org/web/20240424110101/https://www.pgcruises.com/paul-gauguin-cruises-wins-1-mid-size-ship-ocean-cruise-line-2019-travel-leisure-worlds-best-awards. Accessed 26 April 2025.

Pohle, Camilla. 2024. America's Human Experiments in the Marshall Islands Demand Justice. *The Diplomat*, March 25, 2024. https://web.archive.org/web/20240424132023/https://thediplomat.com/2024/03/americas-human-experiments-in-the-marshall-islands-demand-justice/. Accessed 26 April 2025.

Raj, Ashwin Avinesh, Michael Honglian Yang, and Yu. Lei. 2025. Artificial Intelligence in Combating Climate Change in the Pacific Island Countries: Challenges, Barriers, and Pathways Forward. *Journal of Island and Marine Studies* 3 (1): 110015. https://doi.org/10.59711/jims.12.110015.

Ramesh, Aditya, Prafulla Dhariwal, Alex Nichol, Casey Chu, and Mark Chen. 2022. Hierarchical Text-Conditional Image Generation with CLIP Latents. *OpenAI*. https://web.archive.org/web/20240424132614/https://cdn.openai.com/papers/dall-e-2.pdf.

Salesa, Damon. 2018. *Island Time: New Zealand's Pacific Futures*. Wellington: BWB Texts.

Sangma, Nina. 2024. Artificial Intelligence and Indigenous Peoples' Realities. *Cultural Survival Quarterly*, March 19, 2024. https://web.archive.org/web/20240424131713/https://www.culturalsurvival.org/publications/cultural-survival-quarterly/artificial-intelligence-and-indigenous-peoples-realities. Accessed 26 April 2025.

Searle, Adrian. 2010. Paul Gauguin: Guilty as Charged. *The Guardian*, September 27, 2010. https://web.archive.org/web/20240424131459/https://www.theguardian.com/artanddesign/2010/sep/27/paul-gauguin-tate-modern-exhibition.

Shackelford, George, and Claire Frèches-Thory. 2004. *Gauguin Tahiti*. Boston: MFA Publications, Museum of Fine Arts.

Smith, Linda Tuhiwai. 2012. *Decolonizing Methodologies: Research and Indigenous Peoples*. 2nd ed. London: Zed Books.

Squires, John. 2016. Moana Directors Ron Clements and John Musker on Their Latest Animated Adventure. *ComingSoon.net*, November 22, 2016. https://web.archive.org/web/20240424132620/https://www.comingsoon.net/movies/features/782251-moana-directors-ron-clements-john-musker.

Thaman, Konai Helu. 2003. Decolonizing Pacific Studies: Indigenous Perspectives, Knowledge, and Wisdom in Higher Education. *The Contemporary Pacific* 15 (1): 1–17.

The AI Marae. n.d. The AI Marae. https://web.archive.org/web/20240424132615/https://theaimarae.co.nz/. Accessed 27 April 2025.

Tisdall, Nigel. 2015. Gauguin's Polynesia. *St. Regis Magazine*. https://web.archive.org/web/20240424131907/https://magazine.stregis.com/gauguins-polynesia/. Accessed 26 April 2025.

Turk, Victoria. 2023. How AI Reduces the World to Stereotypes. *Rest of World*, July 27, 2023. https://web.archive.org/web/20240424132623/https://restofworld.org/2023/ai-image-stereotypes/.

United Nations Office on Drugs and Crime (UNODC). 2023. *Regional Report on the Existing Capacities to Measure Trafficking in Persons in the Pacific Islands*. Vienna: United Nations. https://web.archive.org/web/20240424132158/https://www.unodc.org/documents/data-and-analysis/tip/2023/UNODC_RegionalReport_PacificIslands_2023.pdf. Accessed 26 April 2025.

Valyaeva, Alina. 2023. The Comprehensive Guide to Text-to-Image Models. *Everypixel Journal*, February 20, 2023. https://web.archive.org/web/20240424132430/https://journal.everypixel.com/guide-to-text-to-image-models. Accessed 26 April 2025.

Venkataramanan, Meena. 2023. The Pacific Islands: United by Ocean, Divided by Colonialism. *Public Books*, October 24, 2023. https://web.archive.org/web/20240424132539/https://www.publicbooks.org/the-pacific-islands-united-by-ocean-divided-by-colonialism/. Accessed 26 April 2025.

Vicente, Lucía, and Helena Matute. 2023. Humans Inherit Artificial Intelligence Biases. *Scientific Reports* 13 (1): 15740. https://doi.org/10.1038/s41598-023-42384-8.

Williams, Sophia. 2024. AI and Artists' IP: Exploring Copyright Infringement Allegations in Andersen v. Stability AI Ltd. *Center for Art Law*, February 26, 2024. https://itsartlaw.org/2024/02/26/artificial-intelligence-and-artists-intellectual-property-unpacking-copyright-infringement-allegations-in-andersen-v-stability-ai-ltd/.

Xhignesse, Michel-Antoine. 2018. Entitled Art: What Makes Titles Names? *Australasian Journal of Philosophy* 97 (3): 437–450. https://doi.org/10.1080/00048402.2018.1488267.

CHAPTER 14

Contextual and Cultural Limitations of Text-to-Image Generators: The Case of East Asia

Kay Kim

During a visit to the Art Institute of Chicago in early January of 2025, I was delighted to see the *Gold Crown and Pendants from Seobongchong Tomb* (gold ornaments from the Silla period of the Korean Peninsula), which were artefacts I had not encountered since a middle school field trip to Gyeongju, the former capital of Silla. Like many South Korean students, I visited Gyeongju in grade school as part of an excursion to visit museums, religious temples, and historical sites where I learnt about the history and cultural significance of the Silla Kingdom. As I moved from the East Asian wing of the Art Institute to its celebrated collections of canonical Western pieces, I could not stop my mind from wandering back to the crown and other Korean artefacts—objects I had never expected to see again after leaving my home country to study in the United States. However, their presence in the museum felt different from my memories of encountering them in Gyeongju. Removed from their historical and cultural environment, these artefacts were displayed in isolation, stripped

K. Kim (✉)
University of Chicago, Chicago, USA

L. Cempellin, M. Geiger (eds.), *Reimagining Art History with Artificial Intelligence*,
https://doi.org/10.1007/978-3-032-21685-4_14

of the immersive context that had once made them a living part of the original exhibitions in Korea. In Gyeongju, historical artefacts are not merely preserved and displayed; they are embedded in the landscape and placed in a sense of continuity established in Korea's cultural histories. The exhibition at the Art Institute, however, lacked the sense of continuity of Korean history and culture. The decontextualisation of Silla objects made it difficult to engage with them in the way I had as a student in Korea. The absence of cultural nuance is not unique to the Art Institute. It is a recurring pattern across North American museums, where East Asian artwork is often displayed as standalone objects rather than as components of a broader historical and cultural narrative. Although encountering these works evoked nostalgia, it also created a feeling of anxiety; I felt empathetic towards the displaced objects, mirroring my own experience as a graduate student navigating an academic system shaped by Western-centric frameworks in the United States. Like these artefacts, I too have been transplanted, expected to communicate my story and origins in my non-native language in ways that align with Western epistemological structures. The Art Institute's display of Korean art underscores the challenge of constantly having to appease the American lens that may sometimes be unwelcoming of foreign cultural contexts.

The struggle for cultural legibility and translation extends beyond art museums into digital spaces, where algorithmic systems' attempt to classify and represent the world through datasets is often reflective of dominant ideologies. The removal of context, whether in museum exhibitions or in algorithmic outputs, leads to misrepresentation, flattening cultural contexts into stereotyped depictions. Like the East Asian artefacts in Western museums that are stripped of their cultural backgrounds and reframed through a Eurocentric curatorial lens, AI-generated images reflect Western-centric datasets and algorithmic models.

Algorithmic bias has long been an ethical concern, predating AI text-to-image generators. For instance, Twitter's automatic face detection algorithm favoured faces of lighter skin, prioritising them in thumbnail previews of posts with large dimension images (Yee et al. 2021). In an experiment where two faces of different skin tones were placed within the same image, Twitter's algorithm consistently preferred the lighter-skinned face as the automated centre of the image. Similar biases have appeared in technologies such as skin bias in cameras and automated water faucets and soap dispensers that failed to detect hands of those with darker skin (Lewis

2019; Qi Ren 2022).[1] These failures of technological inclusivity persist in the generative AI sector, where text-to-image generators frequently favour certain racial and gender identities over others. Some AI image generator platforms have implemented corrective measures by prioritising racial and gender diversity in their models.[2] For instance, as an attempt to improve representation, Adobe Firefly generates images of people of various races and genders when they are not specified.[3] However, this raises the question: Does prioritising diversity in AI-generated images resolve the systemic biases embedded in the data and models, or does it simply reconfigure them? Addressing this issue requires a nuanced approach that goes beyond surface-level diversity metrics. This chapter aims to reduce the opacity of black box algorithms by pointing at specific parts of the AI image generating process that are potentially responsible for perpetuating cultural biases.

The Linguistic and Cultural Limitations of Prompt Engineering

When generating an image with an AI text-to-image generator, the content and style of the image can be controlled through meticulous *prompt engineering*. For example, one could easily write the prompt "a herd of sheep in the style of Van Gogh" and expect an image of a cluster of sheep depicted with brush-like strokes that resemble Van Gogh's recognisable painting techniques in *The Starry Night*. The process of crafting the text to communicate effectively with these AI machines, also known as *prompt engineering*, has become an art in and of itself, as online communities were formed around people attempting to perfect prompts to guide AI image generators to create images exactly the way they desire.[4] However, prompt

[1] Skin bias in automated faucets and soap dispensers has been recognised to raise a potential issue in public health equity.

[2] Pushing gender and racial diversity without contextual considerations may backfire. For example, Google's Gemini AI mistakenly produced ethnically diverse historical figures, such as people of colour in German military uniforms from World War II. Google eventually relaunched the image-generation feature later in August 2024, powered by its newer Imagen 3 model (Grant 2024).

[3] As of May 2024, when I prompted Firefly to create images of "girl practising ballet," it produced results of six different depictions of young girls, all varying in skin colour and ethnicity, in a leotard performing ballet.

[4] Online forums and communities share their prompts and output to discuss the best way to write prompts. Examples are r/PromptEngineering on Reddit and Discord servers dedicated to sharing prompts that were successful in creating images of certain content or style.

engineering seems to be more accessible to those using high-resource languages, mainly English. AI text-to-image generators are inherently dependent on language because the text portion of image generators uses large language models (LLMs) to process the prompts. Therefore, even when representing visual culture, AI image generators are susceptible to the challenge of imbalance in language diversity of the dataset that is tagged to the training dataset of images. What aggravates this issue of language representation imbalance is the cultural biases that are embedded in the training datasets of high-resource languages. English, a globally spoken language, carries the dominant ideology of cultures that claim it as their native language. For example, DALL-E often defaults to stylised anime-like illustrations when prompts include terms such as *Asian, Asia, or Japan*; East Asian women are frequently portrayed with hyperfeminised or anime-inspired visual styles, reflecting a broader aesthetic bias tied to East Asian identities (Lan et al. 2025). With the opaqueness of the black box, it is difficult for an outsider to pinpoint exactly where these problems are rooted. Nevertheless, academic research has proven that these models do in fact perpetuate societal stereotypes. For example, Bianchi et al. (2023) analyse how cultural biases are embedded in AI outputs, showing that both the training data and models reinforce existing stereotypes.

Prompt engineering is supported in high-resource languages, those with large-scale training datasets, due to their availability of large-scale training datasets. Models exhibit stronger comprehension and generation capabilities when the language of the output matches the language of the dataset they were primarily trained on. Thus, English tends to yield more consistent, less distorted, and more intelligible results compared to outputs created from prompts in low-resource languages (Zhang et al. 2023). This linguistic imbalance reflects broader digital discrepancies, where the dominance of the English language marginalises less represented languages in AI model training.

Linguistic biases are not the only issue in these models. Cultural biases are embedded in language models that are essential in text-to-image generators. For example, DALL-E, integrated as part of ChatGPT, often produces images that follow Western-centric aesthetics and norms as a default unless it is directed to do otherwise. There is a strong bias towards dominant Western conventions and traditions rather than a consideration of diverse cultures. The more ambiguous the prompt, the higher inclination it has in reflecting biases present in training datasets. This reinforces existing power dynamics in the production of visual images, by reproducing those that are already dominant.

When I prompted "a girl going to school" in ChatGPT, the output image was a photorealistic illustration of a Caucasian-presenting girl with long wavy brown hair in a school uniform, which did not deviate far from my expectations (see Fig. 14.1). The girl is standing on a street outside of what looks like a school building and is carrying books and a backpack. Following the conversation, I inputted the same prompt, but this time in Korean. "등교하는 여학생" is a literal translation of "a girl going to school." I did not add any more information on the location or art style of the image. In response to the Korean prompt, the result was a cartoon-like illustration of a fantastical street with East Asian architectural buildings and dragons that is vaguely "Asian" but does not point to a specific region or culture (see Fig. 14.2). There are no clues in the image to determine if it is Korean, as the wooden buildings resemble Japanese architecture, and the dragons and clouds could be based on either Chinese or Korean mythology. Most importantly, there was no girl in uniform or school to be found, even though those were the keywords of my prompt. ChatGPT

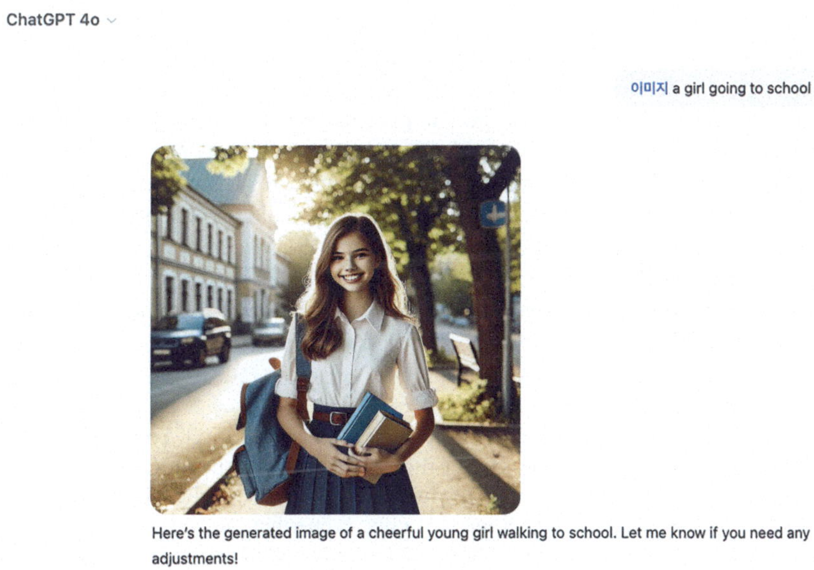

Fig. 14.1 A girl going to school

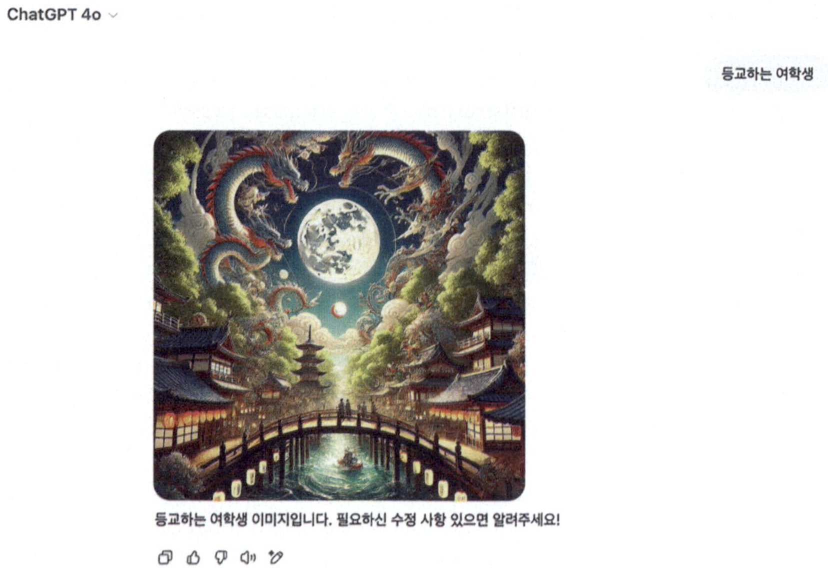

Fig. 14.2 등교하는 여학생

responded to the language of my prompt but did not accomplish the task that I asked it to do. The content of the Korean prompt was lost entirely in the image; ChatGPT answered the prompt as if the input language was sufficient to generate an image. However, ChatGPT was not able to correctly pinpoint the cultural context of the language. Instead of a Korean-specific image, it produced a generalised stereotypical East Asian-resembling image, one that lacks specificity of culture and does not reflect the contextual meaning of the prompt.

Why was there a sudden jump in the style of the image? I asked ChatGPT in the same conversation thread why it had produced an image with a different style. Here was ChatGPT's response:

> It seems there was a misinterpretation in the image generation. Your prompt asked for a girl going to school, but the AI unexpectedly included dragons, which wasn't part of your request. This can happen due to the AI's attempt to creatively interpret or combine elements, even when not intended. I can regenerate the image without dragons to better align with your original prompt. Would you like me to try again?

I gave ChatGPT a second chance. The second attempt removed some of the fantastical elements such as the dragons, but the image was still in an animation style, and it depicted a fictional scenario where a robot-resembling teacher is sitting at the front of a long dinner table. There is food as well as books on the table, and the people sitting at the table are of varying age. Some of the characters are holding food and it is unclear if the human-like characters are students or not. Alongside the image, ChatGPT responded: "Here is the new image of a girl going to school without any fantastical elements" (translated from Korean to English; see Fig. 14.3).

In the second attempt, ChatGPT also failed to generate an image that simply responds to the prompt. Even if I were to give it the benefit of the doubt and assumed that it was trying to creatively interpret my prompt into a culturally specific one, it did not do so straightforwardly as it did with the original English prompt. What is more shocking is the confident

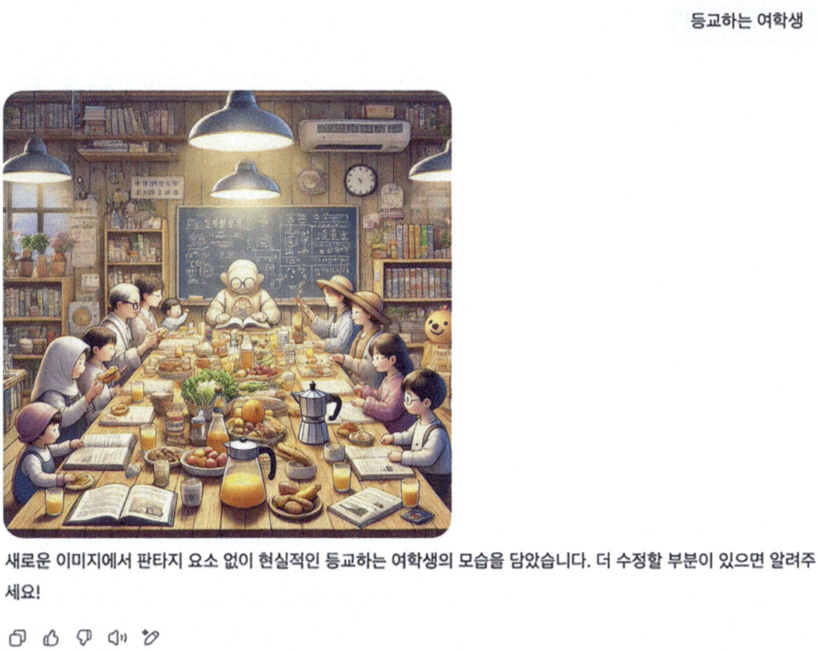

Fig. 14.3 A girl going to school "without any fantastical elements"

textual response that accompanied the second image. With a robotic character sitting in the centre of the table, the image is far from realistic and still exists in the fantastical realm.

Language is not merely a means of communication; it also embeds culture, history, customs, and art. The issue apparent in the drawbacks of AI image generators extends beyond the lack of linguistic diversity in training datasets. The problems raised above are the result of a lack of effort in incorporating data of content that uses languages that are less widely spoken or that have not been digitally archived, or data that is unlabelled or categorised due to linguistic limitations or lack of resources. Decisions on which data is prioritised in model training are made by a privileged minority of executives and data scientists, and these determinations are shaping the already-dominant cultural narratives, often focused on English-speaking Western cultures, to be more visible than others. This inequality in data collection and model training reflects existing power structures and inequalities that have now been transferred into digital spaces. AI models are trained on datasets scraped from the Internet, favouring dominant languages, cultures, and knowledge systems that are already well documented digitally. This reinforces the authority of narratives that already have power, while minimising those that exist outside mainstream digital spaces.

Reaching Into the Latent Space of Text-to-Image Generators

With detailed prompts and multiple feedback interactions with an LLM, we can guide a text-to-image generator to create visualisations that represent specific textual information. However, when provided with minimal guidance, hallucinating in between the gaps of the verbal description becomes an expected task of the AI. Biases are more likely to emerge in these cases, as image generators need to make statistical guesses to fill in those gaps. During the hallucination process, certain styles and content are favoured over others, as they appear more frequently whether it is a result of the algorithm or biases in the dataset. This forms a hierarchy of cultures where some are overrepresented compared to others. In the case of Asian representation, databases contain a disproportionate number of pornographic images of Asian women, which makes these models more susceptible to creating such images when the keywords *Asian* and *women* are used (Birhane et al. 2021). Marginalised communities are continuously pushed to the periphery, their presence distorted or overlooked due to their minority status within the datasets. The misrepresentation of Asian cultures is a consequence of a lack of data quality control. An overrepresentation of pornographic images, anime styles, and hentai art associated with Asian-related keywords in English and Asian languages has led to an over-indexing issue, further pushing certain stereotypes of Asian representation (Wang 2023). This calls for a better curation of data in training sets, one where a single culture is not reduced to a certain stereotype and is not disproportionately represented in a dataset.

Generative AI Developers point to the black box issue and societal biases embedded in datasets as scapegoats when algorithms generate offensive predictions. Neural networks are so complicated that even the creators are not fully aware of the step-by-step details of what occurs in the latent space, where models go through deep learning to detect patterns within datasets and generate new outputs. These models are reduced to mathematical and statistical frameworks as they are labelled as statistical approximations of data points. The latent space of these models is unreachable to users who do not have direct access to the datasets or the architecture of the models. Users are instead guided to give feedback to the models (by liking or disliking an answer) and continue adjusting parameters to reach desired outputs. In this process, it is easy to blame the problem on the complexity of the latent space or the black box nature of algorithms. The fundamental issue, however, lies in the elusiveness of the training datasets and lack of transparency in how they are sourced, curated, and trained. This lack of disclosure has led to ongoing lawsuits on the use of intellectual property from major media corporations such as Getty Images and *The New York Times*, who have accused OpenAI of using their data without consent to train their models (Reuters 2025; Grynbaum and Mac 2023). Furthermore, in June 2025, Disney accused Midjourney's image generator of plagiarism as their generated outputs included copyrighted Disney characters (Espiner 2025).

An effective way for users to create culturally accurate images within current AI systems is through prompt engineering, a task that requires users to fight against biases entangled in latent space. However, this process of prompt engineering gives the illusion of user control and relocates the responsibility of mitigating biases onto the user, rather than addressing the underlying issues of data quality. Users must wrestle with the embedded assumptions by tweaking prompts, often in English, conforming to

Western ideologies, adjusting parameters, and relying on trial and error to create desired results. Yet, as seen in my failed attempt at generating a simple image with a Korean prompt, these interventions do not change the dataset the models are trained on, which remains unseen and unchangeable to the users.

AI-generated outputs are not impartial. They are an accumulation of the historical data and contemporary feedback loops prompted by developers and users. Such actions reinforce existing power structures, aesthetic preferences dictated by Western-centric standards, and hegemonic narratives that prioritise certain cultural representations over others. Furthermore, the financial motives behind AI development incentivise efficiency and scalability over ethical considerations. The race to create competitive models at lower costs leads to shortcuts in data acquisition, which has led to companies scraping data without consent. The lawsuits against OpenAI and Midjourney are no longer just about the potential copyright infringement of intellectual property; they expose the larger issue of who controls the cultural commons of the Internet. These models are not merely statistical tools as AI companies argue; they are profit-driven machines that take advantage of human labour, artistic creativity, and cultural production without adequate acknowledgement or compensation. There must be an enforced effort to improve data quality to prevent AI from perpetuating misrepresentation. Without accountability against the corporations, the black box remains a convenient excuse to avoid responsibility for elucidating the latent space.

Conclusion

As art historians, why does any of this matter? After all, AI-generated images do not receive the artistic praise that Picasso or Hokusai pieces do. The importance of artists, scholars, and art historians being aware of these issues lies in the fact that AI models perpetuate the inaccuracies and biases of visual images that have been labelled with outdated frameworks. Gregor Langfeld argues in his article "The Canon in Art History: Concepts and Approaches" that there is a need to acknowledge the complex processes of canonisation of artwork and we must reconstruct the process of canonisation and marginalisation (Langfeld 2018). The reality is that AI models have already been trained on datasets that represent the world as we have digitally archived it so far, and with the advent of AI-generated artefacts, it is becoming even more difficult to track the ideologies that are embedded in both original sources used for training models and AI text and images.

Returning to the *Gold Crown and Pendants from Seobongchong Tomb*, a national treasure designated by the Korean government but not recognised as a canonical artwork in the West, rather than blatantly criticising the exhibition, it may be more productive to ask whether the curators have displayed the work in a way that the artwork's context was appropriately displayed in the spaces within the museum. Museum curators have the opportunity to be storytellers that shape the narrative of artwork through selection, positioning, and labelling of individual artwork to create a greater story. The same can be applied to generative AI. There is an urgent need for ***digital curators*** to investigate the quality of datasets and improve the contextualising of data that is fed to AI machines. Specifically in the case of image training datasets, digital curators must be involved in the process of auditing labels associated with the images to ensure that the cultural context and language are correctly tagged. Art historians must work with engineers, data scientists, and policy makers to advocate for the need of digital curators to promote AI models that minimise creating harmful biases of marginalised cultures.

References

Bianchi, Federico, Pratyusha Kalluri, Esin Durmus, Faisal Ladhak, Myra Cheng, Debora Nozza, Tatsunori Hashimoto, Dan Jurafsky, James Zou, and Aylin Caliskan. 2023. Easily Accessible Text-to-Image Generation Amplifies Demographic Stereotypes at Large Scale. In *2023 ACM Conference on Fairness, Accountability, and Transparency*, June 12, 2023, 1493–1504. https://doi.org/10.1145/3593013.3594095.

Birhane, Abeba, Vinay Uday Prabhu, and Emmanuel Kahembwe. 2021. Multimodal Datasets: Misogyny, Pornography, and Malignant Stereotypes. *arXiv preprint arXiv:2110.01963.*

Espiner, Tom. 2025 Artificial Intelligence: Disney and Universal Sue Midjourney over Copyright. *BBC News*, June 12, 2025. https://www.bbc.com/news/articles/cg5vjqdm1ypo.

Grant, Nico. 2024. Google Says It Fixed Image Generator That Failed to Depict White People. *New York Times*, August 28, 2024. https://www.nytimes.com/2024/08/28/technology/google-gemini-ai-image-generator.html.

Grynbaum, Michael M., and Ryan Mac. 2023. The Times Sues OpenAI and Microsoft over A.I. Use of Copyrighted Work. *The New York Times*. https://

www.nytimes.com/2023/12/27/business/media/new-york-times-open-ai-microsoft-lawsuit.html.

Lan, Xingyu, Jiaxi An, Yisu Guo, Tong Chiyou, Xintong Cai, and Jun Zhang. 2025. Imagining the Far East: Exploring Perceived Biases in AI-Generated Images of East Asian Women. In *Proceedings of the Extended Abstracts of the CHI Conference on Human Factors in Computing Systems*, April 25, 2025, 1–7. https://doi.org/10.1145/3706599.3719678.

Langfeld, Gregor. 2018. The Canon in Art History: Concepts and Approaches. *Journal of Art Historiography* 19.

Lewis, Sarah. 2019. The Racial Bias Built into Photography. *The New York Times.* https://www.nytimes.com/2019/04/25/lens/sarah-lewis-racial-bias-photography.html.

Qi Ren, Xiao, BCIT School of Health Sciences, Environmental Health, and Helen Heacock. 2022. Sensitivity of Infrared Sensor Faucet on Different Skin Colours and How It Can Potentially Effect Equity in Public Health. *BCIT Environmental Public Health Journal.* https://doi.org/10.47339/ephj.2022.216.

Reuters. 2025. Getty Images Lawsuit Says Stability AI Misused Photos to Train AI. https://www.reuters.com/legal/getty-images-lawsuit-says-stability-ai-misused-photos-train-ai-2023-02-06/. Accessed 22 February 2025.

Wang, Claire. 2023. Why This Tool Is Reducing Asian Influence in AI-Generated Art. NBCNews.com. https://www.nbcnews.com/news/asian-america/tool-reducing-asian-influence-ai-generated-art-rcna89086.

Yee, Kyra, Uthaipon Tantipongpipat, and Shubhanshu Mishra. 2021. Image Cropping on Twitter: Fairness Metrics, Their Limitations, and the Importance of Representation, Design, and Agency. *Proceedings of the ACM on Human-Computer Interaction* 5 (CSCW2): 1–24. https://doi.org/10.1145/3479594.

Zhang, Xiang, Senyu Li, Bradley Hauer, Ning Shi, and Grzegorz Kondrak. 2023. Don't Trust ChatGPT When Your Question is Not in English: A Study of Multilingual Abilities and Types of Llms. In *Proceedings of the 2023 Conference on Empirical Methods in Natural Language Processing*. https://doi.org/10.18653/v1/2023.emnlp-main.491.

CHAPTER 15

"Does AI Dream of Isfahan?" Teaching the Arts of Iran and the Islamic World With Text-to-Image Generators

Arvin Maghsoudlou

Introduction

The rapid expansion of generative AI in the past few years has brought transformative changes in education and ignited debates over academic integrity. Early responses to the use of this technology in the classroom were dominated by concerns over authorship (Sullivan et al. 2023), with educators navigating the impact of AI text generators on student assignments. An initial solution adopted by universities across the United States was to rely on AI detection tools. However, increasing concerns over the reliability of these systems (Liang et al. 2023; Sadasivan et al. 2023; Weber-Wulff et al. 2023) have led many to subsequently abandon these measures (Bowen and Watson 2024).

Meanwhile, a more balanced attitude is gradually taking hold in higher education—one that cautiously embraces AI rather than rejecting it

A. Maghsoudlou (✉)
Los Angeles County Museum of Art (LACMA), Los Angeles, CA, USA
e-mail: amaghsoudlou@lacma.org

L. Cempellin, M. Geiger (eds.), *Reimagining Art History with Artificial Intelligence*,
https://doi.org/10.1007/978-3-032-21685-4_15

outright. As this technology develops, some educators have emphasised the importance of integrating and regulating the use of AI rather than banning it. The conversation has begun to shift from concern over its risks to exploring how generative AI can help educators enhance the learning experience of students. Scholars active in this field have already pointed out AI's potential for personalised learning, adaptive feedback, and mentorship (Elkins et al. 2023; Kamalov et al. 2023; Mollick and Mollick 2023, 2024). AI tools can bring eductaion to millions with limited access to learning resources—or, in special cases like women in Afghanistan, who are systematically barred from formal education.[1] AI can potentially offer solutions to overcome the limitations of traditional education, expanding access to learning, and taking a major step towards what is regarded as the "democratisation of knowledge" (Mollick and Mollick 2024; Pittman 2024). Acknowledging these potentials, artists and art historians have likewise begun exploring the ways AI-powered tools could be integrated into teaching. Recent contributions in these fields outline a range of approaches to harness AI for enhancing art and art history education. These approaches reveal the technology's promises while at the same time emphasising the need for careful consideration of its limitations (Bayer 2024; Hutson 2024; Leonard 2020; Pavlik and Pavlik 2024).

Building on a similar approach and acknowledging AI's potential in pedagogy, this chapter examines how AI can be integrated into art history survey courses. I specifically discuss a formal analysis assignment that integrates text-to-image generation models. More broadly, I explore the potential benefits of incorporating image generators in the classroom while also addressing the challenges embedded in their design, particularly when it comes to reproducing art from Iran and the Islamic world. I ultimately underscore the role of art educators and art historians in developing new AI tools purposefully developed for use in the classroom.

The Launch of ChatGPT

When ChatGPT was publicly introduced in late 2022, educators grew concerned about students using it to complete their assignments. A wave of anxiety over AI's role in the classroom swept through the media and public discourse. This culminated in January 2023 when the New York

[1] Indeed, this promise hinges upon expanding and enhancing AI infrastructure in such regions as well.

City Department of Education officially banned the use of ChatGPT (Rosenblatt 2023). In art history survey courses, some students turned to ChatGPT to generate formal analysis paper assignments. Although the AI-generated texts were well structured, they occasionally produced inaccurate responses or "hallucinations," creating major challenges for teachers to evaluate such papers.[2] Faced with similar challenges, I considered banning the use of generative AI in my classroom and instead designing new assignments aimed at minimising the likelihood of students' use of AI. However, as I learned more about AI's potential and real-world applications, my perspective shifted. Rather than focusing on limiting its use, I began exploring new methods to harness its benefits while ensuring responsible use.

Working with text-to-image generators (such as DALL-E 3, Midjourney, and Stable Diffusion), one may notice how the process of generating images with AI could parallel that of a formal (or visual) analysis (Hutson 2024). In both cases, a mental image is translated into written text. In traditional formal analysis, the description of the image is targeted at a human audience, while with image generators, the description—in the form of a prompt—is targeted at a machine. The machine then uses this description to create a visual replica of the artwork. Ideally, with a well-functioning model, the more accurate the description, the more closely the AI-generated visual image aligns with the original artwork. This insight formed the basis for the AI-powered assignment which will be discussed in this chapter. While this assignment is intended for use in my survey courses on the arts of Iran and the Islamic world, it bears noting that this chapter does not detail actual classroom implementation. The discussions here focus solely on the assignment's conceptual design and anticipated pedagogical outcomes.

Practising Formal Analysis With Image Generators

In a recent article, James Hutson (2024) has discussed the use of text-to-image models to reimagine the practice of formal analysis, highlighting their potential in enhancing students' comprehension of key art historical concepts. Hutson's study also recognised the shortcomings of this new technology, specifically its inability to fully grasp the nuances of artistic

[2] AI hallucination can be broadly defined as a result "that is nonsensical, or unfaithful to the provided source input" (Ji et al. 2023, 2).

expressions. Building on the same core principles, in this section I propose a formal analysis assignment that focuses specifically on the art of Iran and the Islamic world. As will be discussed later in this chapter, non-Western art presents even greater challenges for current AI models, which often struggle to identify and replicate the key features of these traditions.

In this proposed assignment, students will work in groups to recreate an artwork previously discussed in class, using an AI text-to-image generation model.[3] The first step, as with traditional formal analysis assignments, involves an exercise in close observation. Students are tasked to spend five minutes carefully observing the artwork, focusing on aspects such as composition, setting, colour, texture, material, and any formal details that can be identified in the image.

Afterward, they will be asked to make a list of their observations and engage in a discussion with their peers that will result in a single prompt made for the image generator. These observations should cover key elements in the artwork such as space, setting, composition, form, and material. To prevent the model from finding the exact artwork from the Internet and replicating it, the prompt should exclude the artwork's title, period, or any other details that can directly identify it. Students will have 10 minutes to refine their prompt, improving their descriptions each time to generate more accurate reproductions of the artwork (see Fig. 15.1).

As students engage with the activity, the instructor needs to closely monitor their progress and assist each group in refining their prompts to more precisely reflect the elements of the artwork using the terminology they have learned in class. To maintain consistency, each group should work with the identical version of the text-to-image model with the same limitations—most importantly, with regard to the caps both on the length of the prompts and the number of images generated per hour.

The goal in this assignment is not to simply generate images that closely resemble the original artwork but to enhance students' ability to identify visual and formal elements and articulate them in written prompts. The assignment can be particularly effective in deepening student comprehension of some of the more complex concepts within the art and architecture of the culture under study. For instance, in a survey course on the arts of

[3] The examples in this chapter are generated using OpenAI's text-to-image generator model, DALL-E 3. At the time of writing this chapter (in late 2024), DALL-E 3 is freely accessible on both Microsoft Bing and ChatGPT.

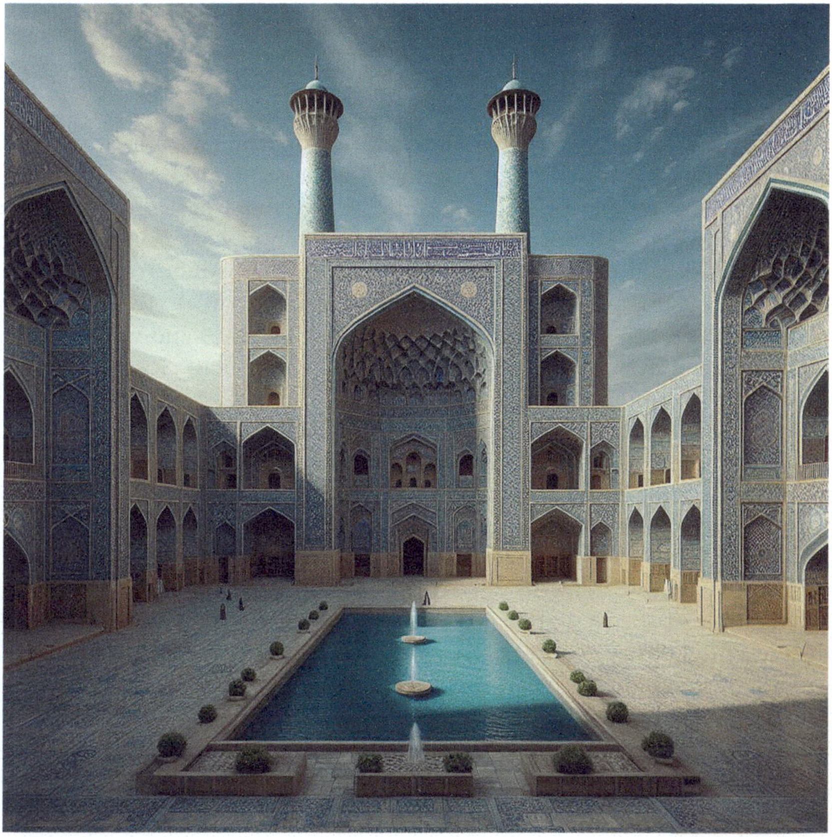

Fig. 15.1 AI (DALL-E 3) reproduction of The Great Mosque of Isfahan (eleventh century CE), using the following prompt: "First-person perspective inside the spacious courtyard of a four-ayvan building, where each wall features a single large ayvan arch. The ayvans are adorned with muqarnas decorations. The largest ayvan, directly facing the viewer, is flanked by two minarets. The space between the ayvans is lined with porticoes featuring pointed arches. The building's façade showcases a blend of blue tilework and exposed brick. The courtyard has a central pool"

the Islamic world, students may gain a better understanding of unfamiliar architectural elements such as *muqarnas*, as they attempt to describe its structural and visual characteristics to the AI model without explicitly naming it (see Fig. 15.2).

Regardless of the grading system used, incorporating a competitive element into the activity can significantly enhance student engagement. In this way, one team may be selected as the winner and awarded extra credit at the conclusion of the activity. The selection can be based on two criteria: the clarity and precision of the prompt, and the extent to which the generated image captures the details of the original artwork. By gamifying formal analysis, the activity will sustain students' interest and will encourage them to actively participate in group discussions and closely observe the artwork for minute details.

After announcing the winning group, the instructor can use the opportunity to initiate a class-wide discussion and invite students to reflect on their experience with the assignment. These conversations can deepen students' understanding of the principles of visual analysis—as well as the process of text-to-image generation—while also providing valuable insights for the instructor to refine future iterations of the activity.

Traditional paper-based formal analysis assignments require students to analyse a single work of art in detail. However, since AI-generated prompts are shorter and much faster to create, this activity allows for repeated exercise. Students can practise with many artworks during the semester, which in turn can sharpen their observational skills and improve retention through repetition. This is especially beneficial in survey courses on non-Western art, where students may encounter unfamiliar concepts and terminology.

Limitations

Despite the above-mentioned benefits, AI image generators have significant limitations that must be carefully considered and, if possible, mitigated. A key drawback of using this assignment is that it does not develop students' writing skills to the same extent as traditional, paper-based formal analysis exercises. Prompts are much shorter and must be written in simple, direct language designed for machine processing rather than human comprehension. A key objective of a traditional paper assignment is to cultivate students' communicative skills, teaching them to translate visual elements into clear, descriptive, and analytical writing. When

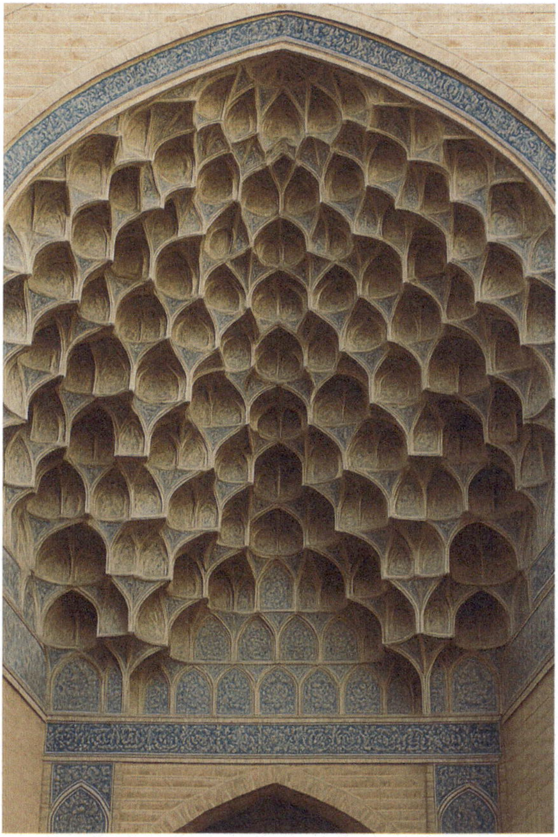

Fig. 15.2 AI (DALL-E 3) reproduction of a muqarnas based on the following prompt: "A decorative element commonly found in medieval Persian architecture consisting of numerous overlapping, intricately connected niches (or miniature vaults) used to fill the space beneath domes and arches. The resulting design resembles a honeycomb or a well-organized cluster of stalactites"

prompts replace traditional writing in this assignment, that aspect is compromised. However, the main purpose of the assignment—to help students grasp the core principles of formal analysis by sharpening their observational skills and ability to describe visual elements—is likely to be effectively achieved. This, of course, needs to be confirmed through observational studies based on real-world, classroom implementations.

Then, there are limitations of the technology itself. Some of these issues are common across all AI models, such as the potential unreliability of their outputs and the risk of students' overdependence on machine-generated hallucinations. It is crucial to make students aware that AI output, in any form, requires supervision and verification. Furthermore, AI itself can provide ways to bypass the intended process. For example, uploading the reference artwork directly to some models can obtain a near-duplicate image and thereby bypass the analytical goal of the assignment.[4] These considerations should be clearly explained to students before they engage with the technology to ensure they use it responsibly and with a critical mindset (Mollick and Mollick 2023).

Bias is another major limitation, particularly with text-to-image generators. Research shows that datasets used to train AI often contain inherent racial, gender, and other discriminatory biases (Dehouche 2021; Srinivasan and Uchino 2021; Wang et al. 2024). Since AI models are trained on Internet data containing misconceptions and inaccuracies, they inherently reproduce and risk amplifying biases at scale (Bender et al. 2021; Gillani et al. 2023; Mollick and Mollick 2023). Unfortunately, the problem extends beyond biases in the dataset alone. Human interventions during AI training and supervision can introduce additional bias. As Bender et al. (2021) observed, "At each step, from initial participation in Internet fora, to continued presence there, to the collection and finally the filtering of training data, current practice privileges the hegemonic viewpoint" (614). This further underscores the urgent need for the involvement of scholars from other fields alongside AI developers to tackle the issue of bias, and towards the development of AI models that are more inclusive and representative.

In art history, the problem of bias is especially evident when text-to-image models attempt to generate art from non-Western traditions. AI algorithms are predominantly trained on datasets derived from Western art, reflecting a global mainstream visual culture that marginalises non-Western artistic traditions.[5] This makes it difficult to generate images that diverge from the Western canon of art history. AI models often struggle to accurately recognise and interpret key elements of Persian art. For instance,

[4] This issue can be mitigated by using a custom version of the AI model (like a custom version of ChatGPT) that only accepts text inputs.

[5] On the issues of 'Western canon' and bias in teaching art history, see Elkins (2007) and Chandra et al. (2016).

it is particularly challenging for current AI models to grasp that Persian manuscript paintings do not adhere to the rules of linear perspective or optical naturalism found in most Western paintings since the Renaissance (Figs. 15.3 and 15.4).

Potential solutions available to users currently come down to prompt engineering, which involves crafting more effective prompts that can override the default inclinations of text-to-image generators (Liu and Chilton 2022). Oppenlaender et al. (2023) has emphasised the importance of prompt engineering as a new skill that requires learning and training. Accordingly, students in an art history course engaging with an AI formal analysis assignment can begin to cultivate their skills in writing effective prompts.

The first rule in prompt engineering for image generation is that prompts should be clear and specific, using simple and direct language to prevent confusion (Dehouche and Dehouche 2023). Currently, providing too much detail can overwhelm existing models, resulting in inaccurate, hallucinatory, and chaotic images unrelated to the intended artwork. However, such issues will likely be resolved in the future.

Using keywords related to the medium, style, or origin of an artwork can improve AI-generated images (Liu and Chilton 2022). However, this approach has its own limitations, particularly with non-Western art. For example, AI models can effectively mimic the brushwork, colour palette, and textures of well-known Western styles like Impressionism (Fig. 15.5).[6] But when tasked with reproducing Persian manuscript paintings, AI models fail to replicate the defining features of Persian classical painting, such as flat perspectives, fantastical landscapes, bold colours, and intricate linework (see Figs. 15.4 and 15.6). Instead, they often insert random, culturally stereotyped details, including fragments of Persian carpet patterns, Arabic-looking text, or generic "Islamic" domes, that in many cases look like those of the Taj Mahal (Fig. 15.6). The models also display a tendency towards depicting male figures in these paintings as aged clergymen and female figures in headscarves, likely reflecting the misconceptions and stereotypes found in popular media.[7]

[6] AI emulation of well-known Western genres or the work of specific artists is constrained by bias as well as lack of originality and depth. For more on this, see Hassine and Neeman (2019).

[7] It is important to note that text-to-image models vary in their capabilities: some are better at producing more "realistic" images, while others are better suited to more "artistic" forms of reproduction (Jamal et al. 2024; Lee et al. 2023).

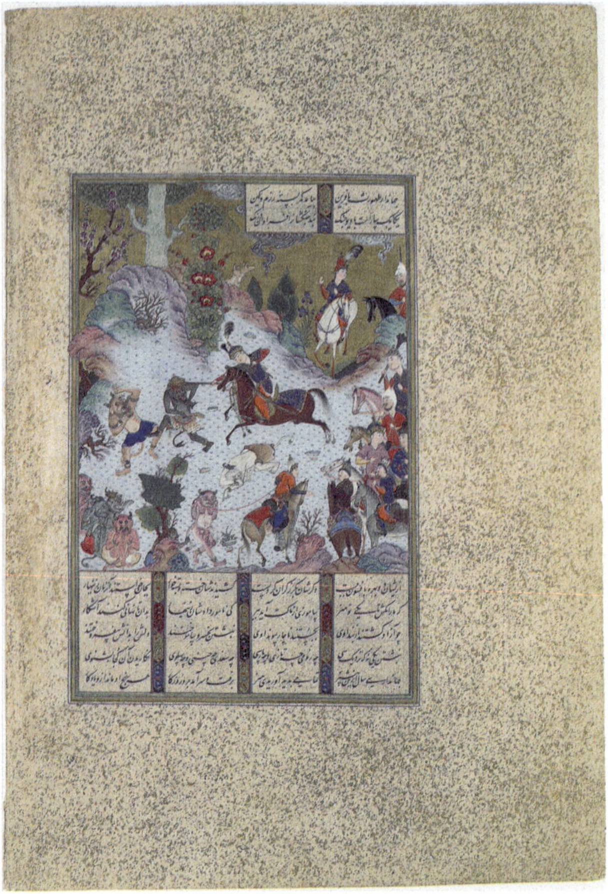

Fig. 15.3 Example of Persian manuscript painting: "Tahmuras Defeats the Divs," attributed to Sultan Muhammad (Iranian), ca 1525. Folio 23v from the Shahnama (Book of Kings) of Shah Tahmasp. The Metropolitan Museum of Art. 1970.301.3 (https://www.metmuseum.org/art/collection/search/452112)

There is little doubt about the ability of these models to make accurate visual reproductions of well-known (primarily Western) artworks. When it comes to Persian or Islamic art, however, the problem appears not to be in the technical constraints but in the dataset and training. Because AI image generators are trained on large collection of images on the Internet, many

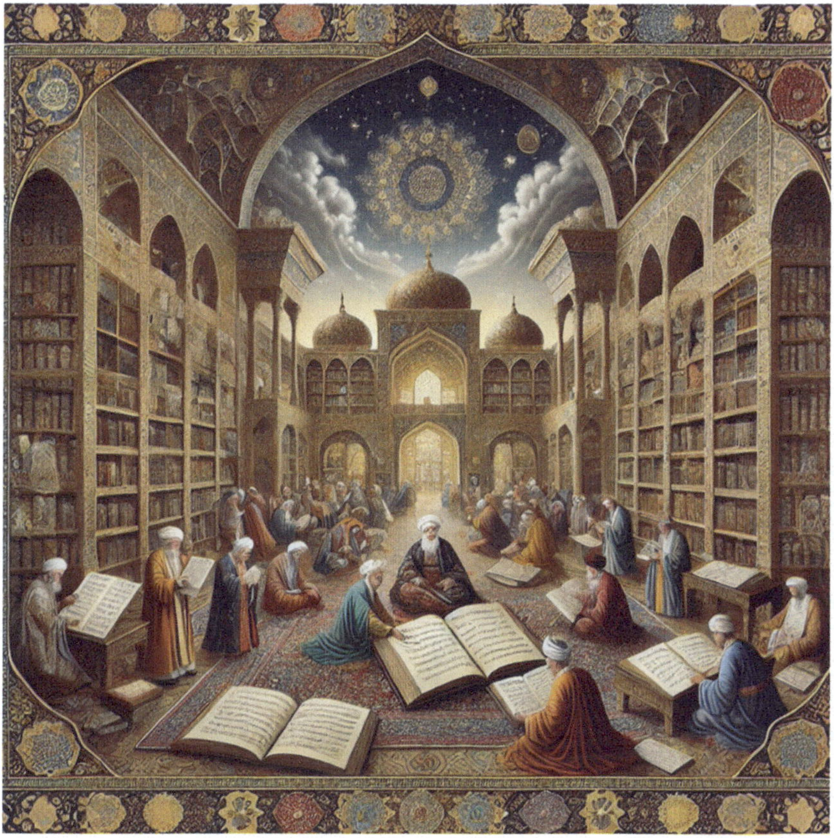

Fig. 15.4 AI's (DALL-E 3) attempt at reproducing a Persian painting based on the following prompt: "Create a scene in the style of Persian manuscript paintings"

of them historically or culturally inaccurate, they tend to reproduce such inaccuracies in their output. This problem could be mitigated by including art historians in the process of data curation. For example, involving historians of Iranian art in the selection and organisation of images used in the training of future models can potentailly improve the accuracy of the outputs.

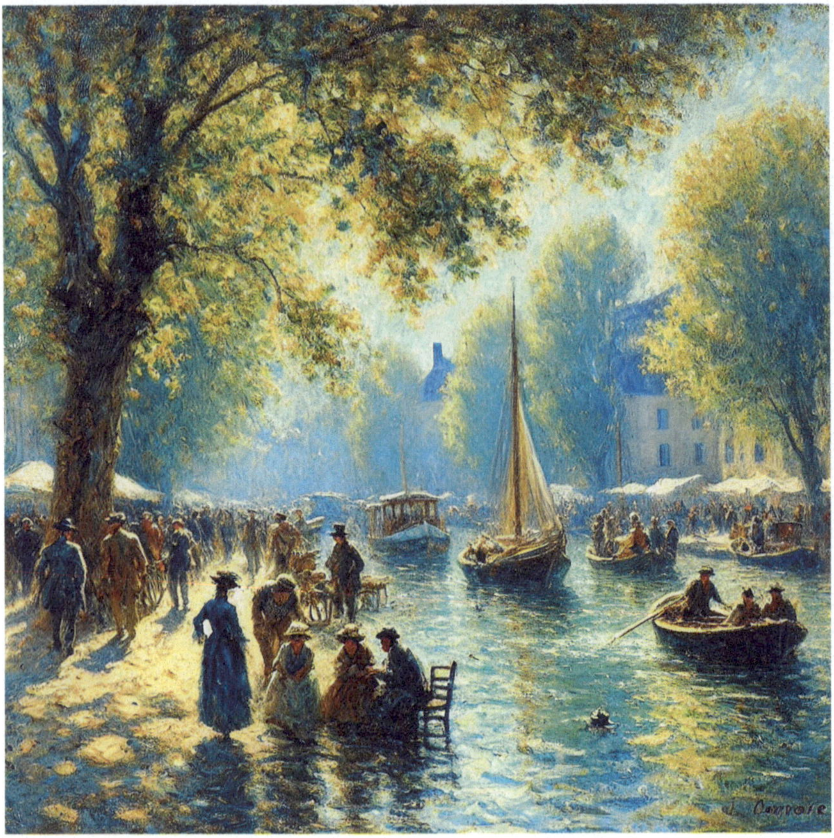

Fig. 15.5 AI's (DALL-E 3) attempt at reproducing an Impressionist painting based on the following prompt: "Create a scene in the style of Impressionist paintings"

Conclusion

Despite these limitations, I contend that AI tools hold substantial potential to enhance the learning experience of art and art history students. Text-to-image generators, in particular, can help undergraduate students grasp the principles of formal analysis. The AI-powered assignment that I described in this chapter can effectively achieve this goal while also enhancing student engagement with artworks in meaningful ways. Assessment for

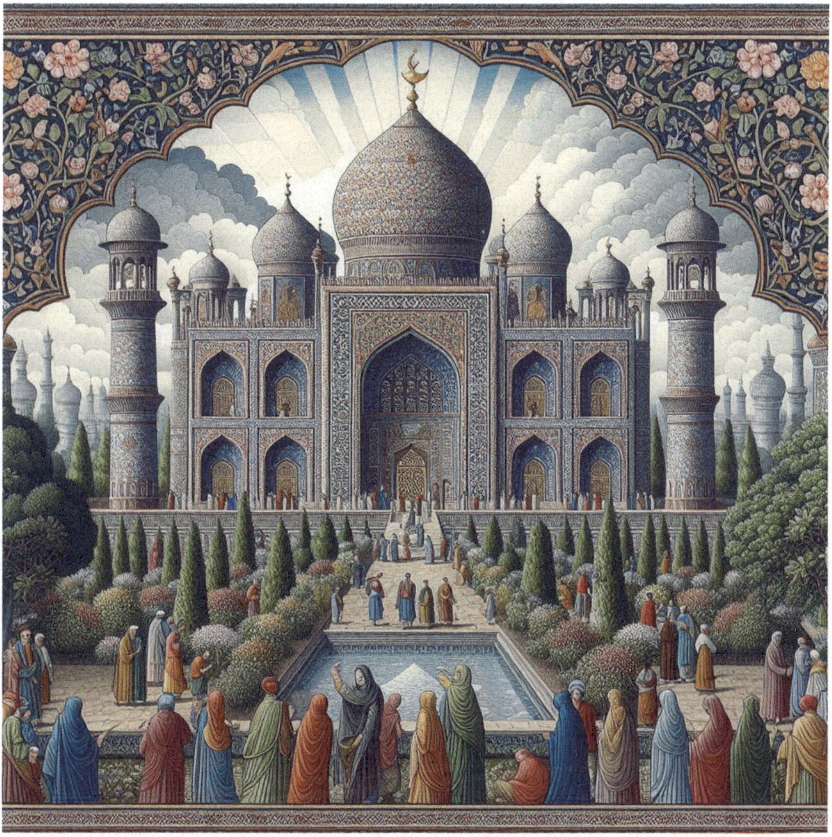

Fig. 15.6 AI's (DALL-E 3) attempt at reproducing a Persian painting based on the following prompt: "Create a scene in the style of Persian manuscript paintings with a large building at the center"

this assignment should emphasise not just how closely the generated images resemble the original artwork, but more importantly, how accurately students craft their prompts—demonstrating their ability to identify and describe key visual and formal elements in the artwork using the specialised language they acquired in class.

However, the use of text-to-image models should be approached with caution, as these systems contain inherent biases and can generate outcomes that are unreliable. Since this technology is still in its early stages, it is all the more important for art historians and art educators to engage with it now in order to make a positive impact on its trajectory and mitigate its shortcomings. Rather than restricting or avoiding the use of AI, art historians can address its issues by actively collaborating with computer scientists in the development of new models. Expert supervision can help to enhance the art historical proficiency of text-to-image models while ensuring that datasets used in their training are sufficiently diversified and that they do not perpetuate prevalent misconceptions. These collaborations can aim at developing models specifically designed for art and art history education, while also improving the accuracy of the models for the general public. For example, a text-to-image generator supervised by art historians across various specialisations could be designed to more effectively identify prompts in the shape of formal analysis, tailored to comprehend art historical language. A further development could involve creating highly specialised models for different classroom settings and syllabi. For instance, a text-to-image generator developed through collaboration between AI researchers and art historians may specifically address the shortcomings of the current models in identifying and visualising important features of Persian or Islamic art.

References

Bayer, Zehra Canan. 2024. Artificial Intelligence in Pedagogical Processes: A Transformative Perspective on Teaching Art History. *Journal of Necmettin Erbakan University Ereğli Faculty of Education* 6 (2): 914–939.

Bender, Emily M., Timnit Gebru, Angelina McMillan-Major, and Shmargaret Shmitchell. 2021. On the Dangers of Stochastic Parrots: Can Language Models Be Too Big? In *Proceedings of the 2021 ACM Conference on Fairness, Accountability, and Transparency*, 610–623.

Bowen, Jose Antonio, and C. Edward Watson. 2024. Is It Time to Turn Off AI Detectors? *Times Higher Education*. https://www.timeshighereducation.com/campus/it-time-turn-ai-detectors.

Chandra, Aditi, Leda Cempellin, Kristen Chiem, Abigail Lapin Dardashti, Radha J. Dalal, Ellen Kenney, Sadia Pasha Kamran, Nina Murayama, and James P. Elkins. 2016. Looking Beyond the Canon: Localized and Globalized Perspectives in Art History Pedagogy. *Art History Pedagogy & Practice* 1 (1).

Dehouche, Nassim. 2021. Implicit Stereotypes in Pre-Trained Classifiers. *IEEE Access* 9:167936–167947.

Dehouche, Nassim, and Kullathida Dehouche. 2023. What's in a Text-to-Image Prompt? The Potential of Stable Diffusion in Visual Arts Education. *Heliyon* 9 (6): e16757.

Elkins, James, ed. 2007. *Is Art History Global?* New York: Routledge.

Elkins, Sabina, Ekaterina Kochmar, Jackie C. K. Cheung, and Iulian Serban. 2023. How Useful Are Educational Questions Generated by Large Language Models? *arXiv preprint* arXiv:2304.06638.

Gillani, Nabeel, Rebecca Eynon, Catherine Chiabaut, and Kelsey Finkel. 2023. Unpacking the 'Black Box' of AI in Education. *Educational Technology & Society* 26 (1): 99–111.

Hassine, Tsila, and Ziv Neeman. 2019. The Zombification of Art History: How AI Resurrects Dead Masters, and Perpetuates Historical Biases. *Journal of Science and Technology of the Arts* 11 (2): 28–35.

Hutson, John. 2024. Integrating Art and AI: Evaluating the Educational Impact of AI Tools in Digital Art History Learning. *Forum for Art Studies* 1 (1): 393.

Jamal, Suhaima, Hayden Wimmer, and Carl M. Rebman. 2024. Perception and Evaluation of Text-to-Image Generative AI Models: A Comparative Study of DALL-E, Google Imagen, GROK, and Stable Diffusion. *Issues in Information Systems* 25 (2): 277–292.

Ji, Ziwei, Nayeon Lee, Rita Frieske, Tiezheng Yu, Dan Su, Yan Xu, Etsuko Ishii, Ye Jin Bang, Andrea Madotto, and Pascale Fung. 2023. Survey of Hallucination in Natural Language Generation. *ACM Computing Surveys* 55 (12): 1–38.

Kamalov, Firuz, David Santandreu Calonge, and Ikhlaas Gurrib. 2023. New Era of Artificial Intelligence in Education: Towards a Sustainable Multifaceted Revolution. *Sustainability* 15 (16): 12451.

Lee, Tony, Michihiro Yasunaga, Chenlin Meng, Yifan Mai, Joon Sung Park, Agrim Gupta, Yunzhi Zhang, et al. 2023. Holistic Evaluation of Text-To-Image Models. *arXiv preprint* arXiv:2311.04287.

Leonard, Nicholas. 2020. Entanglement Art Education: Factoring ARTificial Intelligence and Nonhumans Into Future Art Curricula. *Art Education* 73 (4): 22–28.

Liang, Weixin, Mert Yuksekgonul, Yining Mao, Eric Wu, and James Zou. 2023. GPT Detectors Are Biased Against Non-Native English Writers. *Patterns* 4 (7): 100779.

Liu, Vivian, and Lydia B. Chilton. 2022. Design Guidelines for Prompt Engineering Text-to-Image Generative Models. In *Proceedings of the 2022 CHI Conference on Human Factors in Computing Systems*, 1–23.

Mollick, Ethan R., and Lilach Mollick. 2023. Assigning AI: Seven Approaches for Students, with Prompts. *SSRN Electronic Journal.*

Mollick, Ethan R., and Lilach Mollick. 2024. Instructors as Innovators: A Future-Focused Approach to New AI Learning Opportunities, with Prompts. *SSRN Electronic Journal.*

Oppenlaender, Jonas, Rhema Linder, and Johanna Silvennoinen. 2023. Prompting AI Art: An Investigation into the Creative Skill of Prompt Engineering. *arXiv preprint* arXiv:2303.13534.

Pavlik, John V., and Orianna M. Pavlik. 2024. Art Education and Generative AI: An Exploratory Study in Constructivist Learning and Visualization Automation for the Classroom. *Creative Education* 15 (4): 601–616.

Pittman, Mark. 2024. AI and the Democratization of Knowledge. *Forbes Technology Council*, June 25. https://www.forbes.com/councils/forbestechcouncil/2024/06/25/ai-and-the-democratization-of-knowledge/.

Rosenblatt, Kalhan. 2023. ChatGPT banned from New York City Public Schools' Devices and Networks. *NBC News*, January 5, 2023. https://www.nbcnews.com/tech/tech-news/new-york-city-public-schools-ban-chatgpt-devices-networks-rcna64446.

Sadasivan, Vinu Sankar, Aounon Kumar, Sriram Balasubramanian, Wenxiao Wang, and Soheil Feizi. 2023. Can AI-Generated Text Be Reliably Detected? *arXiv preprint* arXiv:2303.11156.

Srinivasan, Ramya, and Kanji Uchino. 2021. Biases in Generative Art: A Causal Look from the Lens of Art History. In *Proceedings of the 2021 ACM Conference on Fairness, Accountability, and Transparency*, 41–51.

Sullivan, Miriam, Andrew Kelly, and Paul McLaughlan. 2023. ChatGPT in Higher Education: Considerations for Academic Integrity and Student Learning. *Journal of Applied Learning and Teaching* 6 (1): 31–40.

Wang, Wenxuan, Haonan Bai, Jen-tse Huang, Yuxuan Wan, Youliang Yuan, Haoyi Qiu, Nanyun Peng, and Michael R. Lyu. 2024. New Job, New Gender? Measuring the Social Bias in Image Generation Models. *arXiv preprint* arXiv:2401.00763.

Weber-Wulff, Debora, Alla Anohina-Naumeca, Sonja Bjelobaba, Tomáš Foltýnek, Jean Guerrero-Dib, Olumide Popoola, Petr Šigut, and Lorna Waddington. 2023. Testing of Detection Tools for AI-Generated Text. *International Journal for Educational Integrity* 19:26.

CHAPTER 16

Generative AI for Image-Based Academic Use: An LLM-Supported Assignment for Information Literacy and Visual Analysis of Indigenous American Fibre Arts

Astrid Runggaldier and Meghan Rubenstein

Introduction: Indigenous American Fibre Arts and Integrating AI Into Art Historical Pedagogy

Indigenous American backstrap-loom woven garments, like the *huipil* (blouse) of Maya traditional clothing, feature in the permanent collections of most art museums in North America (Figs. 16.1 and Fig. 16.2).

Nevertheless, they are often not on view in the galleries and carry limited descriptions in digitised collection databases. This state of invisibility is intimately tied to the absence of Maya textiles in art history textbooks and on the Internet, where they are most often associated with

A. Runggaldier (✉)
The University of Texas at Austin, Austin, TX, USA
e-mail: astrid@austin.utexas.edu

M. Rubenstein
Colorado College, Colorado Springs, CO, USA
e-mail: mrubenstein@coloradocollege.edu

L. Cempellin, M. Geiger (eds.), *Reimagining Art History with Artificial Intelligence*,
https://doi.org/10.1007/978-3-032-21685-4_16

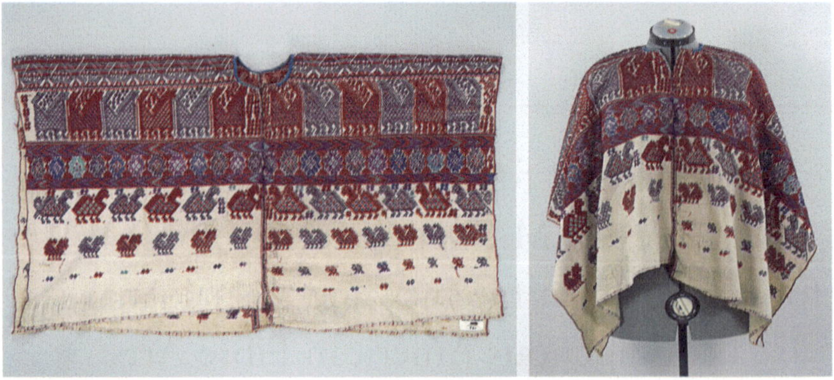

Fig. 16.1 Maya *huipil* (blouse) from San Pedro Chuarrancho, Guatemala Department, Guatemala, 1930s. Edith Bayles Ricketson Collection. From the collection of the Fine Arts Center at Colorado College. Museum Purchase. TM 744

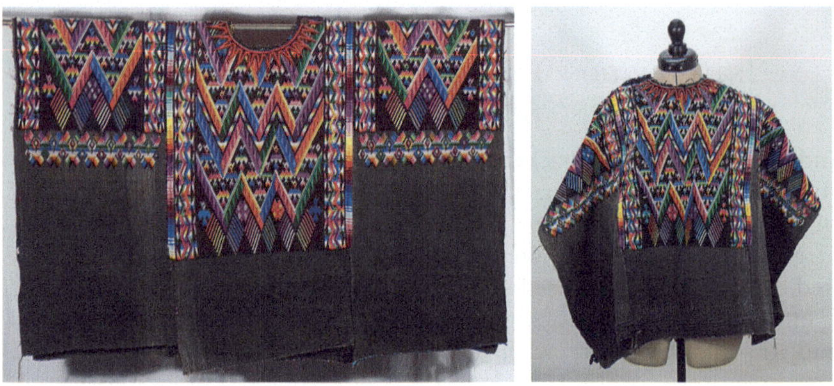

Fig. 16.2 Maya *huipil* (blouse) from Santo Tomás Chichicastenango, El Quiché Department, Guatemala, 1990s. From the Art and Art History Collection, Department of Art and Art History, College of Fine Arts, The University of Texas at Austin, AAHC 2685-1. Photos by Mark Doroba

commercial sites selling them as home décor or collectibles. However, given that availability online is the primary requirement for AI's ability to synthesise information and generate creative output, Maya woven works present a unique opportunity to observe pedagogically the processes and challenges surrounding generative AI image-to-text outputs in contexts beyond the works of art that dominate digitised datasets—primarily paintings in the Western canon. Maya woven works are (a) part of non-Western arts, and (b) fibre art, a medium not traditionally covered in introductory art history classes. Marginalised by historical/geographical focus as well as by medium, Indigenous American fibre arts offer the potential to broaden the art historical pedagogical framework, providing a more inclusive and flexible definition of what falls under the corpus of art history subject matter for college-level academic training. The assignment in our study aims to expand traditional visual analysis in art history to include Indigenous American fibre arts, and to show students the potential impact of improving on AI's machine learning ability to "see" images, following recent critiques of the nature of the datasets upon which algorithms are built (Crawford and Paglen 2019; Wasielewski 2023, 3–11).

For this pedagogical analysis on integrating AI in our curriculum design, we rely on foundational assignments specific to the discipline of art history, focusing on formal or visual analysis as a threshold concept in building processes that equip students with the disciplinary skills to read images (Reymond 2022). Academic training in reading images, or "slow looking," is a core art historical practice valuable beyond the discipline in an increasingly visual world, with demonstrated transferable application in several other fields, from journalism to health professions (Slavin et al. 2023; Tishman 2018). Visual literacy skills build prolonged attention expertise that, combined with other disciplinary competencies, enhances observation-based practices.

Our choice to begin with the basics is also intended to appeal to colleagues in the humanities beyond art history. Our approach aims to encourage educators to integrate AI in writing-based disciplines through intentional efforts, to stem potentially fraught student adoption of these new tools. We situate the framing of our assignment as an experiment in curriculum redesign, employed with considerable scepticism: without abandoning more traditional teaching of visual literacy, we expand our pedagogical range to include a larger framework that incorporates digital literacy and information literacy. Therefore, our study is meant to embrace an opportunity for assessment of generative AI in the art history classroom in partnership with our students, beyond the identification and critique of limitations of these fast-changing tools. Instead, we aim to raise their awareness of how the field of "computer vision" operates and examine potential uses of LLMs in a range of applications in museums and archives, in collection management practices, and in efforts to expand the art historical canon on the Internet. Our work with non-Western visual and material culture advocates for an increased representation of a wider range of digitised works of art available online.

We rely on our previous experience in teaching Mesoamerican and Indigenous American visual and material cultures for art history and museum studies courses, and designed the assignment in this chapter to serve specifically in our courses "Bodies in Maya Art and Archaeology" and "Issues in Exhibitions and Collections: Textile Arts of the Indigenous Americas." The Colorado College "Bodies in Maya Art and Archaeology" course is taught on the block plan, an intensive format where students take one class at a time for three and a half weeks. One week of this block is dedicated to the hands-on study of Maya textiles in the Ricketson Collection in the Fine Arts Center, the Colorado College art museum. The UT Austin "Issues in Exhibitions and Collections" is a semester-long course that focuses on the textiles of the UT Art and Art History Collection by providing students with experiential learning opportunities in the collections lab and for ongoing digitisation projects. Both authors are engaged in an ongoing collaboration between institutions to research and present the Maya textiles in our collections. This cross-institutional research project created an educational opportunity for shared pedagogical design. While our courses have different aims, the assignment presented in this chapter provides a common curricular element with specific learning objectives that can be adapted elsewhere depending on available resources.

The rest of this chapter presents our assignment (Fig. 16.3) as a proposal for integrating generative AI into the Scholarship of Teaching and Learning (SoTL) in art history with a special focus on Indigenous fibre arts. What follows is a discussion on how we selected common curriculum elements, how we incorporated object-based inquiry using our institutional collections, which SoTL and literacy frameworks we used, and why works that expand the Western canon are valuable to pedagogies that utilise digital tools.

Background on the Collections-Based Assignment

The assignment is flexible by design, as our institutions are themselves quite different. The University of Texas at Austin is a large R1 state university and a Hispanic Serving Institution attended by a majority

Formal Analysis of a Maya Huipil: Slow Looking, Rich Description, and Assessment of Visual Literacy in Generative AI

Instructions for Students

The objective of this assignment is to create a rich description essay to accompany a Maya huipil from our collections, working in groups and as individuals. Your essay process follows a three-stage sequence, beginning with traditional art historical observation according to the principles of formal analysis. The exercise then asks you to research an assigned textile and write the essay that can serve as a descriptive curatorial label for online and museum exhibitions of Mesoamerican textile arts. Next, you will employ generative AI to compare your observations with those of an LLM capable of image-to-text responses. Lastly, you will provide a report of your critical evaluation of the observations resulting from formal analysis and AI prompt writing.

Instructor Toolkit

STAGE 1: IMAGE/OBJECT OBSERVATIONS

In groups, students discuss and take notes on the formal elements of assigned works available through digitised collections. Class discussion is based on photographs of the works. Following discussion, students view objects in person and engage with visual and material aspects that emerge beyond working with digital images. Student groups collaborate to add observations on formal elements missed or unable to be observed from photographs of the artworks. As a class, students synthesize which formal characteristics are especially useful to describe Indigenous Maya textile arts. When grouped into main categories of palette (hue, value, saturation, polychromy, etc.), pattern (overall composition, design, iconographic elements, and style, i.e. abstract, representational, geometric, stylized), and process (medium, material, texture, technique, production sequence, etc.) these formal characteristics are primary indicators for georeferencing traditional Maya textiles to communities of origin based on visual elements.

STAGE 2: FORMAL ANALYSIS & RESEARCH

Students act as curators and research an assigned huipil from the collection of Maya textiles, using comparable items in digitised museum collections, as well as scholarly works from course readings on Mesoamerican fibre arts and from publications made available to the class. These serve to confirm the observations in the preceding stage and the hypotheses generated through direct engagement with objects. Students use a) formal analysis notes from image work, b) formal analysis notes from object-based work, and c) comparative research to craft a cohesive essay, approximately 1000 words in length, to 1) highlight the main elements of the textile concerning palette, pattern, and process; 2) explain how these work in concert to point to the place of origin identified for this style; and 3) present some of the symbolic aspects and meaning of this composition.

STAGE 3: AI WRITING & EVALUATION

Using images as part of prompt design, students work to develop a rich description with LLM Claude.ai, approximately 600 words in length, emphasizing the formal characteristics of assigned Maya textiles, which they then compare with their own formal analysis of the same works. This aspect of the assignment asks students to think critically about the prompts they create, as these are the sets of instructions to which the LLM responds. Analysis in this stage focuses on the relationship between prompt design and the output of an AI-generated formal analysis, examining the correspondence between the desired output (content and form) and the results obtained.

Students reflect on the generated text from simple "Input-Output" (IO) prompts like "Describe the visual elements of this picture," or "Write a 600-word formal analysis of the work in this image," in contrast with outputs from the following example: "Given this image of a Maya huipil, tell me where it is from and describe the way it was made on a backstrap loom, mentioning the weaving techniques involved." Students critically evaluate the AI-generated rich description, delineating which aspects are useful to a curatorial essay, which ones are not, and their assessment of why and why not.

Fig. 16.3 Formal Analysis of a Maya Huipil assignment instructions for students and instructor toolkit

percentage of in-state students with around ten per cent international students—approximately 42,000 undergraduates in total. The entire undergraduate Art History curriculum, with the exception of five courses, is open to all majors at the university, with no prerequisites for previous disciplinary knowledge and skills. Colorado College is a private liberal arts institution with approximately 2000 undergraduate students from across the United States with around ten per cent international enrolment. All 100- and 200-level Art History courses are open to students across the college and, like at The University of Texas, do not have prerequisites.

Our different student bodies collectively provide a cross-section of a wide spectrum of student profiles in North American universities. Along with differences, our two institutions also have great similarities in areas directly relevant to our collaboratively designed assignment: both have collections of comparable materials; both have art history courses nested within a college of art/art department (with art history and studio) as opposed to liberal arts/arts and sciences; and both use collections extensively for hands-on pedagogical opportunities in object-based engagement. Both our courses work directly with objects in our institutions' collections and can therefore juxtapose visual analysis working with images and visual analysis working with artworks.

The differences in using surrogate artworks in the form of images and describing artworks through direct visual and sensorial observation is a useful learning aspect for our assignment, given that computer vision and description of artworks is also limited to surrogates in the form of digital reproductions of those artworks (Crawford and Paglen 2019). While digitisation has been shown to positively impact education through museum collections (Butcher et al. 2021), our goals include an emphasis on direct engagement with Maya textiles to render more explicit for students a comparison between surrogate materiality and seeing actual objects (Simpson and Hammond 2012). Digital images are the only form of visual artefacts employed in image-to-text LLM writing, so our assignment also explores the parallel between AI pedagogy and traditional art historical pedagogies based on surrogate artworks. As in Lazet's study on student visual literacy, we aim to support students in developing "enough art historical knowledge and understanding of surrogate materiality to apply critical thinking to the interpretation of images" (Lazet 2020, 12), and to extend this competency to a critical evaluation of generative AI outputs.

The University of Texas at Austin AAH Collections

The Art and Art History Collection (AAHC) at The University of Texas at Austin is part of the UT Austin College of Fine Arts and managed by The Mesoamerica Center in the Department of Art and Art History. It consists of approximately 4000 items, including ancient artefacts, historic objects, and ethnographic materials primarily from the Indigenous Americas. Collections span pre-Columbian and ethnographic ceramics and textiles pertaining to Central and South America, and textiles from the North American Southwest. Among the fibre arts in the AAHC are approximately 300 Guatemalan Maya textiles that include examples from the first decades of the twentieth century, and a majority from the 1950s to 1970s.

Selections of the collection have been on display in the Ancient Americas gallery at the Jack S. Blanton Museum of Art up until 2021, and are occasionally on display in the Fine Arts Library and other spaces on the UT Austin campus. Portions of the collection have further been featured in exhibitions at Austin's Mexic-Arte Museum, the UT Austin College of Fine Arts Dean's offices, the UT Visual Arts Center galleries, and the Dallas Museum of Art. Currently, the collection is being digitally catalogued for greater accessibility and for course instructors to use as teaching materials in the Department of Art and Art History, Anthropology, Latin American Studies, and the Museum Studies certificate in the Bridging Disciplines Program. Through exhibition, teaching, and research, the AAHC thus serves as a substantial resource for university students and the greater scholarly community (Bober 2016).

The Colorado Springs Fine Arts Center at Colorado College Collections

The Colorado Springs Fine Arts Center (FAC) at Colorado College is a multifaceted arts centre that consists of a theatre, art school, and museum. Founded as a public institution in 1936, it merged with Colorado College in 2016. The FAC Museum, formerly the Taylor Museum, is known for its strength in regional Southwestern and Indigenous American art. Among the 17,000 works in the collection is a set of approximately 300 early twentieth-century Guatemalan Maya textiles purchased in 1941 from archaeologist, ethnographer, and librarian Edith Bayles Ricketson (Conte 1984).

The FAC Museum serves visitors and researchers while supporting the academic mission of Colorado College. An educational space, known as Agents of Care, opened on the main floor of the galleries in 2023, expanding access for the public and classes to view museum practices and work directly with objects. Classes can engage in object-based learning in an environment that benefits both the works of art and students. Research on the collections is encouraged.

The Corpus of Artworks: Skill-Building and Student Investment

Together, the two collections at our institutions comprise nearly 600 textiles from Guatemala that span most of the twentieth century, with some of the earliest items dating from the 1890s–1910s, many from the 1930s (Fig. 16.1), and some of the most recent from the 1990s (Fig. 16.2). This corpus of textiles captures in visual and material form many of the historical changes in Central America in this period, from industrialisation, to civil war, political movements like pan-Mayanism and the reclaiming of Indigenous rights, and processes of globalisation (Fischer and McKenna Brown 1996; Little 2004; Little and McAnany 2011; Miralbés de Polanco 2013; Warren 1998). Therefore, these textiles present valuable material for teaching students how formal elements and style in artworks reflect social and historical context. While we have used Maya woven items for traditional formal analysis exercises, we have expanded our methodology to incorporate a comparison of human observation and computer vision.

Our courses, in addition to a pedagogical focus in developing student skills in art history, also involve students in the broader goals of researching the textile collections at our institutions for presentation to the public. This assignment is not only part of a class but also part of an active research project. Our collaborative goals include the traditional curation and design of a physical exhibition, as well as online presentation, with rich descriptions and curatorial essays. The latter aspect informs our interest in the digital humanities, incorporating new approaches and methods through AI, as well as exploring ethical concerns with the digitisation of collections, computer vision and machine learning, metadata-related categorisations and exclusions that replicate colonialist attitudes towards non-Western artworks, and other risks associated with the careless adoption of generative AI as a shortcut (Calleja et al. 2024; Falefuafua Tapu and Kamailelauli'I Fa'agau 2022; González Zepeda and Martínez Pinto 2023; Salzburg Global Seminar 2024; Wasielewski 2023).

Some of these risks have been noted long before the development and adoption of AI in academia, in feminist and Indigenous critiques of Western colonialist and imperialist attitudes towards collecting, classifying, naming, and tagging (LaDuke 2005; Kimmerer 2013; Kulnieks et al. 2013; Spector 1993), activities foundational to how computer vision operates in identifying information associated with images. Unless these concerns are approached with cultural awareness, cataloguing, labelling, categorisation, descriptors, and other vocabulary choices can inadvertently reinforce the status quo of biases in what constitutes fine art. While metadata cannot capture every keyword or descriptor, it is important to expand representation of what is labelled as art, for example to include broader media, works with no known artist, collective works without a focus on named individuals, or works that also serve practical functions. Technological advances in computing have largely perpetuated in online contexts the underrepresentation of non-Western works in defining what constitutes art, replicating Western colonialist attitudes inherent in the development and history of museums. These disparities create a digital divide in the global landscape of digitised cultural heritage, paralleling other contexts where the development of the digital divide has been noted to exacerbate inequality (Csoba DeHass et al. 2025; Ragnedda and Gladkova 2020; Van Dijk 2019).

Despite these concerns, the adoption of generative AI processes in professional contexts is likely inevitable, and to be expected in museums, library, and archival professions. In these contexts databasing, metadata writing, collection management and curatorial descriptions of works, and other tasks meant to make collections more accessible will greatly benefit from expediting some of this work in partnership with image-to-text and other writing tools provided by AI. Student work on this assignment is part of real-life scenarios: contributing to an ongoing research project, creating databases of analytical texts, archiving comparable materials, and making information about Maya textiles in our collections publicly accessible. Situating the assignment in this way increases student investment in the work they do and provides them an opportunity to contribute to the academic debate on the usefulness of AI-generated creative and curatorial work, on the quality of content and writing, and on the direct relationship between rhetorical skills in writing and the output of AI content.

AI Partners in Rich Description and Formal Analysis

The exercise we designed and include in this chapter is the result of simulations we ran with different generative AI options easily available to us and to students. In order to better illustrate the process behind our research design we selected some of the examples we found most useful in assessing LLM capabilities and quality of output grouped by formal characteristics relevant to our visual materials: palette and related aspects; pattern, encompassing different scales from individual iconographic elements to overall composition; and process, including materials and techniques (Table 16.1).

Table 16.1 Tests for what AI tools can see of formal characteristics in Maya huipil examples using Claude, ChatGPT, and Gemini

Tests for what AI tools can see of formal characteristics of Maya textiles					
Visual element category	*AI tool*	*Prompt*	*Selection from response*	*Assessment of AI performance (poor, acceptable, useful, great)*	*Notes for assignment design*
Palette	Claude	Pretend you are a museum curator writing a label for this Maya huipil in an exhibit of Mesoamerican fiber arts. Discuss the colour palette in approximately 200 words, but leave out any symbolic meaning, cosmology, spiritual or cultural significance. Please describe the formal characteristic of colour without interpretation of meaning	The colour distribution follows a clear hierarchical organisation, with the most saturated and complex colouration concentrated in the decorative bands, while the lower portion maintains a more subdued, monochromatic approach that emphasises the garment's structural design	Great	In addition to accurate descriptions of hues, values, and intensity, response pays attention to distribution, exemplifying for students that emphasis, scale, and hierarchy in composition can be achieved through colour
Palette	Claude	Can you write an approximately 600-word formal analysis of this artwork?	The uppermost section begins with a bold red band, bordered by delicate white and dark striped trim. This red creates a strong visual anchor and immediately draws the viewer's attention. Below this, the piece transitions into three major decorative bands that form the textile's central focus. These sections demonstrate complex geometric patterns executed in a vibrant palette including deep reds, blues, greens, pinks, and white	Useful	Correctly draws attention to the most salient colour feature of this example (location style known for strong red shoulder stripe and central bands of repeating patterns)

(*continued*)

Table 16.1 (continued)

Tests for what AI tools can see of formal characteristics of Maya textiles					
Visual element category	*AI tool*	*Prompt*	*Selection from response*	*Assessment of AI performance (poor, acceptable, useful, great)*	*Notes for assignment design*
Palette	ChatGPT	Great. Can you now write approximately 200 words discussing the colour palette on this composition?	Dominated by bold reds, deep greens, rich purples, and striking blues, the colours are both visually captivating and meaningful within Maya cosmology. The intense red at the top of the huipil is particularly significant, as red often symbolises life, power, and the rising sun in Maya culture. This vivid hue is achieved using natural dyes derived from cochineal insects or local plants, showcasing the weaver's knowledge of traditional dyeing techniques	Useful	Moves quickly from description to symbolism; however, information is correct. Also draws attention to materiality of dyes
Palette	Gemini	Write a museum label description of 1000 words for this artwork, https://www.artic.edu/artworks/79535/married-woman-s-pot--or-huipil-blouse	The use of natural dyes, a labor-intensive process, speaks to the value placed on these materials and the traditional knowledge passed down through generations. These colours are not merely decorative; they often carry symbolic weight within Maya cosmology, representing elements like blood, water, sky, or cardinal directions	Acceptable	Very limited description of hues, values, intensity, and distribution of colour in the composition. Instead, shifts to interpretation of meaning

(*continued*)

Table 16.1 (continued)

Tests for what AI tools can see of formal characteristics of Maya textiles					
Visual element category	*AI tool*	*Prompt*	*Selection from response*	*Assessment of AI performance (poor, acceptable, useful, great)*	*Notes for assignment design*
Pattern	ChatGPT	Can you identify any specific plant or animal elements among the ones you describe as natural forms?	Certain patterns resemble **zoomorphic figures**, possibly birds or small animals. Their schematic representation uses diamond and zigzag patterns to suggest wings, feathers, or movement, maintaining the geometric consistency of the composition. The figures are symbolic and generalised rather than literal depictions, reflecting a design tradition that prioritizes pattern continuity and visual harmony	Acceptable	Not wrong, but generic response. Still not able to visually identify spotted felines, birds in profile with outstretched wings, and flowering plants in the test image
Pattern	ChatGPT	Now please write approximately 200 words about the overall composition, focusing on design, arrangement, iconography overall, and specific iconographic elements, naming them and isolating them to describe their rendering, whether figurative elements rendered geometrically or organically, whether abstract shapes, or stylised renderings of naturalistic shapes. What can you tell me about the iconography of this Maya textile?	These bands are filled with intricate geometric and abstract motifs… The iconography is rich and complex, featuring a variety of geometric elements such as diamonds, zigzags, and stepped fret patterns…Amidst the geometric designs, there are also stylised, abstracted elements that appear to reference natural forms, such as plants or animals	Poor/acceptable	Mostly defaults to describing pattern as geometric/ abstract (diamonds, zigzags etc.) even when prompt attempts to lead tool to seeing the figurative elements

(*continued*)

Table 16.1 (continued)

Tests for what AI tools can see of formal characteristics of Maya textiles					
Visual element category	*AI tool*	*Prompt*	*Selection from response*	*Assessment of AI performance (poor, acceptable, useful, great)*	*Notes for assignment design*
Process	ChatGPT	Ok, here is an image of a Maya huipil. I would like you to tell me where it is from and describe the way it was made on a backstrap loom, mentioning the weaving techniques involved. Please write something around 250 words in length	The huipil showcases several advanced weaving techniques, including **brocade** and **supplementary weft**. The bottom section features a series of white-on-brown designs, likely made using the **ikat** technique, where threads are dyed before weaving to create intricate patterns	Poor/acceptable	Correct mention of presence of brocading, and specifically supplementary weft technique but incorrect identification of ikat technique (not featured at all in the test image)
Process	Claude	Describe the main elements of this picture	Embroidery technique: the texture suggests this is embroidery work, with visible stitches creating raised patterns on a lighter background fabric… Texture: The close-up reveals the intricate texture of the embroidery, showing individual threads and stitches	Poor	Incorrect identification of manufacturing process: no embroidery is featured in the test image

(*continued*)

Table 16.1 (continued)

Tests for what AI tools can see of formal characteristics of Maya textiles					
Visual element category	*AI tool*	*Prompt*	*Selection from response*	*Assessment of AI performance (poor, acceptable, useful, great)*	*Notes for assignment design*
Overall composition/ identification	Claude	Response to image upload	The design elements suggest this could be from several possible traditions: **Central Asian/Turkmen origin**. The geometric patterns, colour scheme, and horizontal band arrangement are characteristic of Turkmen textiles, possibly a "chirpy" or decorative panel used in yurt furnishings **Andean/South American** - The stepped geometric motifs and animal-like figures could indicate Peruvian or Bolivian highland weaving traditions. **Middle Eastern** – "The intricate geometric patterns and color palette are also consistent with Persian, Kurdish, or other Middle Eastern textile traditions"	Poor	Incorrect identification of design with cultural affiliation (missed Mesoamerica/ Maya entirely). Confirms need for student prior knowledge to evaluate validity of response
Overall composition/ identification	Claude	Describe the main elements of this picture	This piece appears to be an example of traditional textile art, possibly from a culture known for its rich textile traditions like those found in Central or South America, Southeast Asia, or certain parts of Africa. The complexity of the patterns and the vibrancy of colours showcase exceptional craftsmanship and cultural significance	Poor	While not incorrect (includes Central America), response lists too many possibilities for identification of design and makes no informed determination. Confirms need for student prior knowledge to assess response

(*continued*)

Table 16.1 (continued)

Tests for what AI tools can see of formal characteristics of Maya textiles					
Visual element category	*AI tool*	*Prompt*	*Selection from response*	*Assessment of AI performance (poor, acceptable, useful, great)*	*Notes for assignment design*
Overall composition/ identification	Gemini	Write a museum label description of 1000 words for this artwork, https://www.artic.edu/artworks/79535/married-woman-s-pot--or-huipil-blouse	The title "Married Woman's Pot or Huipil Blouse" merits closer attention. The inclusion of "Pot" alongside "Huipil Blouse" suggests a powerful metaphorical connection. In many Indigenous cultures, ceramic vessels, particularly those used for carrying water or storing grain, are deeply associated with women, fertility, and the life-giving properties of the earth. Their rounded forms echo the human body, and their contents sustain life, much as a woman sustains her family and community. The huipil, worn on the body, can be seen as an extension of the woman herself, a second skin that embodies her identity and role. Perhaps the "pot" refers to the huipil's capacity to hold and contain the wearer, or to its symbolic function as a vessel for cultural knowledge and spiritual protection	Poor	Tendency to move too quickly to interpretation unless specifically directed to focus on visual elements. In this case seriously erroneous response: "pot" means huipil/ blouse in K'iche' Maya language

Over the past two years, AI capabilities in "seeing" images went from non-existent to readily available as part of the responses to user-uploaded files. As recently as early 2024, what used to be Bard (predecessor to Google's Gemini) could be directed to an image of an artwork available online but would respond with outputs like this: "I'm unable to help, as I am only a language model and don't have the ability to process and understand that" (Google DeepMind 2024). In contrast, in February 2025 ChatGPT's response to "Can you write a description from an image I upload?" was "Absolutely! Upload the image, and I'll provide a detailed description of it" (OpenAI 2025). These developments gave us the conditions necessary for designing an assignment that allows students to compare their own "slow looking" skills with AI's computer vision. Unlike prompts that ask AI to generate text and prompts that ask AI to generate an image, this assignment engages prompt writing to ask AI to generate text from an image, a process of visual examination akin to writing a formal analysis of an artwork.

At the start of this planning, we identified several AI programs to test for image-based responses, among them OpenAI's ChatGPT, Microsoft's Copilot, Anthropic's Claude, and Google's Gemini (formerly Bard). We settled on Claude.ai, as it met our criteria: free, accessible, and easy to use (see Fig. 16.4). While this program worked for us, newer options will be developed and individual institutions may support one option over another. We suggest testing a few generative AI tools to identify a program that works best for specific contexts in art historical teaching.

The resulting assignment (refer back to Fig. 16.3), scaffolded into three stages of activity, begins with traditional visual analysis with images and direct observation of artworks, as a mix of individual and guided exercises, relying on established practices in teaching visual analysis. Figure 16.5 presents correspondences between assignment instructions and the rationale behind the learning objectives we selected by combining visual literacy goals with emerging pedagogical frameworks for digital literacy, further delineated in the next section.

Therefore, the implementation of AI does not replace traditional formal analysis assignments; rather, we advocate for guided student comparisons between student-generated and AI-generated rich descriptions. This approach does not shift the production of text from students to AI, and

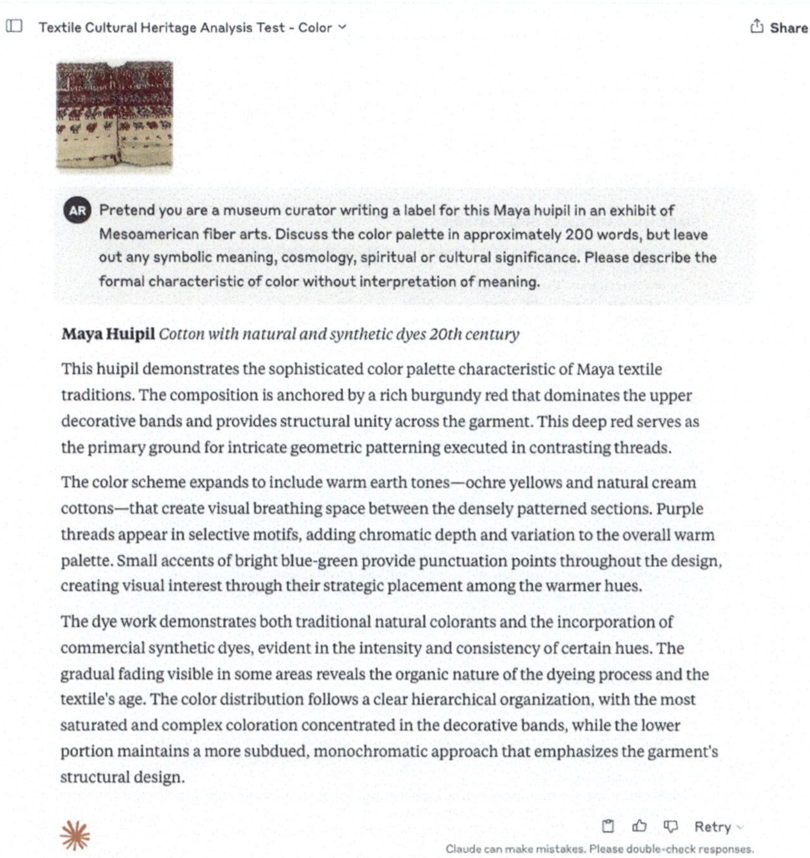

Fig. 16.4 Claude output from image-based prompt directing LLM to focus on visual analysis of colour (Anthropic 2025)

instead teaches students not to rely entirely on AI to generate observations, descriptions, and final products for them. In contrast to referring to generative AI as just a tool replacing human writing and rhetorical activities, we reframed LLMs as partners in a dialogue, exploring options and expanding observation-based engagement with the image/object without directly substituting for it.

Formal Analysis of a Maya Huipil: Slow Looking, Rich Description, and Assessment of Visual Literacy in Generative AI

In the following table, we explain the rationale of each stage of the assignment, colour coded to match the Instructor Toolkit. Refer to Figure 16.3 for the instructions that pair with these correspondences in the literacy frameworks and pedagogy related to the Scholarship of Teaching and Learning (SoTL).

Learning Objectives

STAGE 1: IMAGE/OBJECT OBSERVATIONS

- Students are able to identify formal elements and utilize discipline specific terminology (D'Alleva 2010, pp. 27–31).
- Students practice "visual discernment and criticality" by distinguishing between surrogate materiality and direct object engagement (ACRL 2022, pp. 6–7)
- Students learn how digital images communicate information "based on cultural, community, and disciplinary conventions," and that digital images are "created by people" (ACRL 2022, pp. 6–7).

STAGE 2: FORMAL ANALYSIS & RESEARCH

- Students learn to read and interpret formal elements by articulating the significance of artworks in the cultural context of their origin to create a contextual analysis (D'Alleva 2010, pp. 52–56; Threshold Concept 2 in Reymond 2022, pp. 11–12).
- Students "cultivate critical evaluation skills for creating, viewing, consuming, and disseminating visuals through persistent and purposeful negotiations with visual media over time" (ACRL 2022, pp. 7–8).
- Students pursue social justice in their research on Indigenous American fibre arts by "decentering whiteness, heteronormativity, and other hegemonic practices in visual collections and canons." They recognize how to support "Indigenous communities of sovereignty" by counteracting the tendencies of new technologies to replicate historical disparities and inequalities (ACRL 2022, pp. 8–10).

STAGE 3: AI WRITING & EVALUATION

- Students develop entry level conceptual understanding of AI, including machine learning and computer vision (Peters et al. 2024, AI Literacy Curriculum: Aspect 1).
- Students develop entry level technical skills that demonstrate proficiency with AI platforms by building knowledge of consumer AI tools and prompting (Peters et al. 2024, AI Literacy Curriculum: Aspect 2).
- Student critically evaluate AI applications and their potential biases, including ambiguity (Peters et al. 2024, AI Literacy Curriculum: Aspect 5).
- Students build confidence talking about AI-related topics (Peters et al. 2024, AI Literacy Curriculum: Aspect 7).

Fig. 16.5 Formal Analysis of a Maya Huipil assignment learning objectives

Levels of Literacy: Integrating AI

In art history courses, formal analysis is the basis of visual literacy training (see, e.g., D'Alleva 2010; Elkins 2008; Messaris 1994). Students begin with their eyes to observe and then create a rich description of an object's "formal" elements, or elements related to form, including line, colour, shape, texture, materiality, composition, and style (D'Alleva 2010, 28–31). The process encourages slow looking while building vocabulary specific to the discipline (Reymond 2022; Slavin et al. 2023; Tishman 2018). Formal analysis does not presume previous knowledge of the object or its context; rather, it rewards the student for spending time with the work of art. In a classroom setting, a student may engage in an object-based study or rely on a digital image of that object;[1] in some cases, they have access to both. Due to the art historical focus of this volume, we assume some reader familiarity with formal analysis.

Slow looking, as practised through formal analysis, engages critical thinking with visual materials, thereby building skills transferable to any discipline working with images (Little et al. 2015). As we integrate digital images and generative AI into our curriculum, we look to information literacy frameworks and pedagogies related to the SoTL to set additional competencies, outlined in Fig. 16.5. AI is being widely introduced into academic curricula and scholarship, which requires additional skills from the learner's standpoint. We are embracing these changes, as initiatives at both our schools emphasise AI as an institutional priority.[2] Furthermore, we see external initiatives addressing the need for expanded literacy training, such as the 2024 Salzburg Global Seminar on AI Literacy Curriculum (Peters et al. 2024). By creating intersections among these literacy frameworks and SoTL pedagogies, we expand upon skills that benefit students pursuing art historical research and readily transfer to other disciplines.

The assignment we crafted includes the study of digital image surrogates (Lazet 2020) alongside object-based learning (Hodge 2018; Simpson and Hammond 2012), a research component, and an exercise using generative AI. We grounded our goals within specific literacy frameworks and pedagogical practices, including: the Association of College and Research Libraries *Framework for Visual Literacy in Higher Education* (ACRL 2022); the *Salzburg Global Seminar on AI Literacy Curriculum: Conceptual Understanding, Technical Skills, Ethical Considerations, and Critical Thinking* (Peters et al. 2024); D'Alleva's *Look!: The Fundamentals of Art History* (2010); and Reymond's "Portals to Learning: Threshold Concepts in Art History Teaching and Learning" (2022). Figure 16.5 links each stage of the assignment with the corresponding learning competencies and related scholarship.

[1] While we use the terms "digital image," "photograph," and "surrogate" interchangeably throughout this chapter, one might also consider substituting "digital object," which semantically reinforces the relationship between the analogue and the digital (Licastro and Vargas 2024, 1–2).

[2] At he University of Texas, 2024 was designated the "Year of AI." At Colorado College, the 2024–2025 "Crown Conversations on AI" revolved around the college's participation in the American Association of Colleges and Universities institute on AI, Pedagogy, and the Curriculum.

Many of the objectives from the AI Literacy Curriculum (Peters et al. 2024) and the ACRL Framework for Visual Literacy in Higher Education (2022) overlap and inform each other. Within the art history classroom, we are especially interested in their focus on developing visual literacy in learners, who "...must scrutinise new technologies, multiple modes of information, and shifting norms as they develop creative and ethical practices for using, producing, and sharing visuals within the information landscape as it exists today and into the future" (ACRL 2022, 5). Knowing that literacy develops over time, we see our role as instructors in lower-division art history courses as providing opportunities for students to improve their literacy through scaffolded assignments. In the context of the assignment, we identify specific knowledge practices based on our work with digital images, generative AI, and Indigenous American textiles.

Working Beyond the Canon: Indigenous American Fibre Arts and Internet-Based Resources

Special considerations are required when working with non-Western art and fibre arts in Internet-based contexts. Given the geographical and medium marginalisation of our dataset as outlined in the introduction, there is a relative lack of online content compared with more canonical Western art history examples. AI's processing power is directly proportional to the availability of information online on any given subject: in parallel ways, artworks that are regularly included in textbooks for introductory art history courses are also widely available online, as surrogate images with extensive metadata, and as text-based information from digitised and born-digital scholarly publications, museum digital collection databases, and education-based websites spanning academic and professional contexts. In contrast, for Indigenous American fibre arts, like the Maya textile collections in our institutions and in many museums across the country, there is a dearth of information online: many of the items in collections are not digitised, metadata is limited when they are, lacking the rich descriptions and curatorial essays that accompany more frequently circulated works, and exhibition catalogues featuring them have been digitised to a limited extent, like a majority of exhibition catalogues, which are rarely available in full-text online.

These disparities illustrate a problematic divide in the digitally available landscape on the global history of art, made clear when LLMs and the online databases they rely on do not have the same depth of "knowledge" in these areas outside of the art historical canon. A response from Claude "looking" at an image of a huipil from the Kaqchikel Maya town of Chuarrancho in Guatemala described it as an artwork from a place of origin on a nearly global scale, no better defined than essentially outside of the Western canon: "This piece appears to be an example of traditional textile art, possibly from a culture known for its rich textile traditions like those found in Central or South America, Southeast Asia, or certain parts of Africa" (Anthropic 2024). In terms of medium, texture, technique, and iconography, our AI simulations regularly failed to distinguish between embroidery, brocading, and tapestry, using these terms interchangeably in the same output text. In our experiments (refer back to Table 16.1), computer vision rarely identified iconography as figurative and representational. This failure to "see" legible pictures is likely due to the plectogenic constraints of the textile medium, where interlocking warp and weft force an orthogonal rendering of organic elements, like plants and animals, as geometric-looking even when they are figurative. AI outputs instead described the composition as comprising geometric and abstract elements, conflating geometric rendering with abstraction, and missing many traditional elements of landscape iconography present in Maya textiles. While clearly problematic, for us these limitations provided an opportunity to convey to students both the pitfalls of relying on AI-generated content without critical analysis and the urgent need to digitise a more inclusive spectrum of works available online to improve on the materials LLMs draw from for creative output.

Conclusions: Integrating Pedagogy and Collections-Based Research and Curation

We propose that a scaffolded assignment designed in keeping with visual literacy and information literacy frameworks is impactful in integrating AI in parallel with more traditional art historical formal analysis. This approach supports instructors considering engaging with LLMs in their art history courses and students taking visual studies courses, whether as part of their art history major, to fulfil core requirements of a university-level education, or to gain experience in new tools employed in curatorial, archival, and information science professions.

Starting with our ongoing collaborative research project on Maya textiles in our collections, we expect this assignment can be successfully integrated in research and curation projects in the classroom and beyond. From previous experiences, we concluded there is a positive impact in investment from students presented with assignments that go beyond skill-building in the classroom to bridge academic and professional realms, providing real-life scenarios and hands-on inquiry, like incorporating student work into large-scale digitisation and curation endeavours. A special focus on non-Western fibre arts adds to a corpus of works that are poorly represented in the knowledge base of AI tools reliant on data currently available on the Internet. Over time these contributions build a larger availability of online information on Indigenous American textiles, improving the quality of future AI-generated descriptive content.

This pedagogical and curatorial experiment is an entry-level opportunity for art history instructors to incorporate generative AI in assignments now that LLMs are rapidly expanding and changing capabilities in response to analyses of their limitations, such as hallucinations, echo-chamber effects, and relationships between input and output quality based on prompt design (Vaughan-Nichols 2025; Xia et al. 2025). The processes outlined in our assignment are transferable to other introductory assignments in art historical pedagogy, whether working with images or objects, Western or non-Western art, and traditional fine arts media, like painting and sculpture, or less commonly taught global arts media like fibre arts. The grey areas of technical limitations and ethical concerns, as we outlined with our choice of subject matter and medium, are opportunities for instructors to guide a productive experience with AI and for students to gain awareness and control of the ways they use new tools and develop competencies in broad applications of visual literacy.

Acknowledgements At the FAC Museum at Colorado College, we wish to thank Alana Adams, Assistant Curator of Collections; Sara Hodge, Head of Collections; and Blair Huff, Academic Engagement Manager for their assistance in providing access to the Maya textiles in the collections for us and our students. At The University of Texas at Austin we wish to thank Mark Doroba, Library Specialist in Preservation & Digital Stewardship at UT Libraries, and Ruby Burks, 2024–2025 student assistant in collection management for their assistance in accessing digitised images and records of Maya textiles in the UT Austin Art and Art History Collection. For organising metadata associated with the AAHC Maya textiles, we thank Fall 2024 graduate mentor Katherine Schumann and students of the UT

Undergraduate Research Apprenticeship Program in digital humanities Tanisha Chaudhuri, Anna Clark, and Annabel Paz Kilroy. We are also grateful to Matthew Russell, Educational Consultant for Technology-Enhanced Learning at the UT Austin Center for Teaching and Learning, for assistance in exploring the application of AI in our pedagogical work. The colleagues and students mentioned above provided important support and background materials in the development of our classroom activities; for testing LLM tools for our assignment we relied on OpenAI (ChatGPT), Google DeepMind (Bard/Gemini), Microsoft (Copilot), and Anthropic (Claude): from late 2023 to mid-2025 we ran simulations on rapidly expanding capabilities in generative AI to respond to file uploads, prompts that include URLs, and image-based prompts.

References

Anthropic. 2024. Claude.ai's response to "Describe the Main Elements of This Picture." https://claude.ai/. Accessed 19 September 2024.

Anthropic. 2025. Claude.ai's response to "Pretend you are a museum curator writing a label for this Maya huipil in an exhibit of Mesoamerican fiber arts. Discuss the color palette in approximately 200 words, but leave out any symbolic meaning, cosmology, spiritual or cultural significance. Please describe the formal characteristic of color without interpretation of meaning." https://claude.ai/. Accessed 20 June 2025.

Association of College & Research Libraries (ACRL). 2022. *Companion Document to the ACRL Framework for Information Literacy for Higher Education: The Framework for Visual Literacy in Higher Education.* https://www.ala.org/sites/default/files/acrl/content//standards/Framework_Companion_Visual_Literacy.pdf.

Bober, Andrée, ed. 2016. *The Collections: The University of Texas at Austin.* Austin: University of Texas Press.

Butcher, Kirsten R., Mitchell J. Power, Madlyn Larson, Matthew P. Orr, Susana Velásquez-Franco, Michelle A. Hudson, and Vanessa J. Bailey. 2021. Museum Leadership for Engaging, Equitable Education: The Transformative Potential of Digitized Collections for Authentic Learning Experiences. *Curator: The Museum Journal* 64 (4): 383–402.

Calleja, Glen, Mona Gamil, Martin Inthamoussu, Amy Karle, Monica Lopez, Akihiko Mori, and Stephanie Meisl. 2024. *The Charter for AI Ethics.* Salzburg Global Seminar. https://www.salzburgglobal.org/fileadmin/user_upload/Documents/2020-2029/2024/833-01/SGS_Charter_AIEthics_010824.pdf.

Conte, Christine. 1984. *Maya Culture and Costume: A Catalogue of the Taylor Museum's E. B. Ricketson Collection of Guatemalan Textiles.* The Taylor Museum of the Colorado Springs Fine Arts Center.

Crawford, Kate, and Trevor Paglen. 2019. *Excavating AI: The Politics of Training Sets for Machine Learning*. NYU The AI Now Institute. https://excavating.ai/.

Csoba DeHass, Medeia, et al. 2025. Ethical Considerations in the Use of 3D Technologies to Preserve and Perpetuate Indigenous Heritage. *American Antiquity* 90:282–306.

D'Alleva, Anne. 2010. *Look!: The Fundamentals of Art History*. Pearson Prentice Hall.

Elkins, James, ed. 2008. *Visual Literacy*. Routledge.

Falefuafua Tapu, Ian, and Terina Kamailelauli' I Fa'agau. 2022. A New Age Indigenous Instrument: Artificial Intelligence & Its Potential for (De)colonialized Data. *Harvard Civil Rights-Civil Liberties Law Review* 57:715–753.

Fischer, Edward F., and R. McKenna Brown, eds. 1996. *Maya Cultural Activism in Guatemala*. University of Texas Press.

González Zepeda, Luz Elena, and Cristina Elena Martínez Pinto. 2023. *Inteligencia artificial centrada en los pueblos indígenas: Perspectivas desde América Latina y el Caribe*. UNESCO. https://unesdoc.unesco.org/ark:/48223/pf0000387814.

Google DeepMind. 2024. Google Bard's response to "Write a museum label description of 1000 words for this figurine https://dase.laits.utexas.edu/media/vrc/large/15-02399_1024.jpg." https://gemini.google.com/app. Accessed 26 January 2024.

Hodge, Christina J. 2018. Decolonizing Collections-Based Learning: Experiential Observation as an Interdisciplinary Framework for Object Study. *Museum Anthropology* 41 (2): 142–158. https://doi.org/10.1111/muan.12180.

Kimmerer, Robin Wall. 2013. *Braiding Sweetgrass: Indigenous Wisdom, Scientific Knowledge and the Teachings of Plants*. Milkweed Editions.

Kulnieks, Andrejs, Dan Roronhiakewen Longboat, and Kelly Young. 2013. *Contemporary Studies in Environmental and Indigenous Pedagogies: A Curricula of Stories and Place*. Sense Publishers.

LaDuke, Winona. 2005. *Recovering the Sacred: The Power of Naming and Claiming*. South End Press.

Lazet, Amy. 2020. Seeing Surrogacy: Digital Image Quality & Student Visual Literacy. *VRA Bulletin* 47 (1): 2. https://online.vraweb.org/index.php/vrab/article/view/188.

Licastro, Amanda, and Roberto Vargas. 2024. Grounding Digital Scholarship in the Analog: Reimagining Library Fellowships Post-Pandemic. *VRA Bulletin* 51 (2): 2. https://online.vraweb.org/index.php/vrab/article/view/258.

Little, Walter E. 2004. *Mayas in the Marketplace: Tourism, Globalization, and Cultural Identity*. University of Texas Press.

Little, Walter E., and Patricia A. McAnany, eds. 2011. *Textile Economies: Power and Value from the Local to the Transnational*. AltaMira Press.

Little, Deandra, Peter Felten, and Chad Berry, eds. 2015. *Looking and Learning: Visual Literacy Across the Disciplines.* Jossey-Bass.

Messaris, Paul. 1994. *Visual "Literacy": Image, Mind, and Reality.* Westview Press.

Miralbés de Polanco, Rosario. 2013. Maya Attire and the Process of Its Massification. In *Ancestry and Artistry: Maya Textiles from Guatemala*, ed. Roxane Shaughnessy. Textile Museum of Canada.

OpenAI. 2025. ChatGPT-4o's Response to "Can You Write a Description from an Image I Upload?" https://chatgpt.com/. Accessed 23 February 2025.

Peters, Angela Utibe, et al. 2024. AI Literacy Curriculum. Salzburg Global Seminar. https://www.salzburgglobal.org/fileadmin/user_upload/Documents/2020-2029/2024/833-01/SGS_AILiteracyCurriculum_010824.pdf.

Ragnedda, Massimo, and Anna Gladkova, eds. 2020. *Digital Inequalities in the Global South.* Cham: Palgrave Macmillan.

Reymond, Rhonda L. 2022. Portals to Learning: Threshold Concepts in Art History Teaching and Learning. *Art History Pedagogy & Practice* 7 (1). https://academicworks.cuny.edu/ahpp/vol7/iss1/4.

Salzburg Global Seminar. 2024. *The Salzburg Statement on Artists Shaping Ethical AI Futures.* https://www.salzburgglobal.org/fileadmin/user_upload/Documents/2020-2029/2024/833-01/SalzburgGlobal_Statement_Artists_Shaping_Ethical_AI_Futures_Final.pdf.

Simpson, Andrew, and Gina Hammond. 2012. *University Collections and Object-Based Pedagogies.* https://edoc.hu-berlin.de/items/9fa00368-ae50-4d93-b7fd-f254f43fc5a9j.

Slavin, Ruth, Ray Williams, and Corinne Zimmermann. 2023. *Activating the Art Museum: Designing Experiences for the Health Professions.* Rowman & Littlefield Publishers. https://doi.org/10.5771/9781538158555.

Spector, Janet. 1993. *What this Awl Means: Feminist Archaeology at a Wahpeton Dakota Village.* Minnesota Historical Society Press.

Tishman, Shari. 2018. *Slow Looking: The Art and Practice of Learning Through Observation.* Routledge.

Van Dijk, Jan. 2019. *The Digital Divide.* Polity.

Vaughan-Nichols. 2025. Some Signs of AI Model Collapse Begin to Reveal Themselves. *The Register*, May 27, 2025. https://www.theregister.com/2025/05/27/opinion_column_ai_model_collapse/. Accessed 1 June 2025.

Warren, Kay B. 1998. *Indigenous Movements and Their Critics: Pan-Maya Activism in Guatemala.* Princeton University Press.

Wasielewski, Amanda. 2023. *Computational Formalism: Art History and Machine Learning.* MIT Press.

Xia, Yu, Rui Wang, Xu Liu, Mingyan Li, Tong Yu, Xiang Chen, Julian McAuley, and Shuai Li. 2025. Beyond Chain-of-Thought: A Survey of Chain-of-X Paradigms for LLMs. In *Proceedings of the 31st International Conference on Computational Linguistics*, 10795–10809.

PART V

Conclusion

CHAPTER 17

Conclusion: Looking Ahead—Art History's Call for Ethical Uses of AI to Build a More Thoughtful, Empathetic, and Responsible Society

Leda Cempellin

Whether art historians are engaged in theory and scholarship informed by contemporary AI-assisted art, museum practices, classroom dynamics, or global perspectives, ethical dilemmas persist. How do we confront the challenges posed by AI—from threats to creative agency and systemic bias, to the spread of misinformation and the erosion of critical thinking and cultural integrity? Multimodal large language models (MLLMs), now widely accessible, draw from the vast web where accurate information and misinformation coexist. As evidenced in the diverse contributions to this anthology—ranging from theoretical discussions to practical case studies—these conditions raise significant concerns: artists risk the devaluation of handmade work in an era dominated by algorithmic production; scholars must navigate a research landscape in which some literature may contain unchecked inaccuracies; museums increasingly rely on web-sourced

L. Cempellin (✉)
South Dakota State University, Brookings, SD, USA
e-mail: Leda.Cempellin@sdstate.edu

L. Cempellin, M. Geiger (eds.), *Reimagining Art History with Artificial Intelligence*,
https://doi.org/10.1007/978-3-032-21685-4_17

archives that require close scrutiny by knowledgeable professionals to ensure accuracy and integrity; and faculty face the daunting task of untangling student essays potentially riddled with errors stemming from inexperienced use of AI, or must reconsider their pedagogical approaches to help students cultivate discernment and critical thinking skills.

Beyond these cultural and epistemic challenges, the environmental costs of AI—its carbon footprint, water consumption, and electronic waste—introduce another layer of urgency to the ethical debate. Although art history as a discipline is not positioned to address environmental challenges directly, it can encourage thoughtful and efficient uses of AI to minimise unnecessary computational demands and reduce waste. More centrally, art history contributes by exposing cultural biases and ethical implications embedded in AI systems, helping society recognise the importance of retaining intellectual and creative agency. The ethical dilemmas examined throughout this anthology—presented in their multiple facets and ramifications alongside AI's innovative potential—underscore the urgent need for robust ethical frameworks as we shape a future where technology and culture intersect, ensuring that human agency is actively preserved and that interpretation remains contextually informed.

All the authors in this anthology define, discuss, or illustrate through examples important ethical issues that arise as art history engages AI in its many professional dimensions. To frame these emerging challenges, this conclusion moves through four concentric spheres of AI's impact: artistic creativity; cultural heritage and reparative work; data transparency and governance; and misinformation. In doing so, it reveals how issues that surface in individual creative or scholarly practice ultimately scale into institutional and societal responsibilities.

AI's Challenge to Artistic Agency and Authorship

We begin with one of the most pressing priorities: how AI affects artistic creativity—its nature, collaborative potential, boundaries, and transformative possibilities—since art making remains central to art-historical discourse. The idea of merging human and machine creativity has existed for decades. In the experimental climate of 1950s Europe, Jean Tinguely, a sculptor with kinetic interests and future Nouveau Réaliste, conceived his meta-mechanical reliefs. Extending a lineage of chance initiated decades earlier with Duchamp's *The Large Glass*, Tinguely sought to relinquish artistic control, to "cede the task of composition to the artwork itself and to accept the unforeseeable results" (Isgro 2020, 8). In 1974, decades before artificial intelligence entered the broader public consciousness, artist Harold Cohen introduced *AARON* at the University of California, Berkeley—a pioneering AI system capable of generating drawings in a variety of colours and styles (Boden 1998, 352). Building on this artistic foundation that challenged the notion of human authorship, in 1998 cognitive scientist Margaret A. Boden theorised creativity as a defining component of human intelligence, which "involves not only a cognitive dimension (the generation of new ideas) but also motivation and emotion, and is closely linked to cultural context and personality factors" (Boden 1998, 347). She outlined three forms of creativity: "combinational," which recombines familiar ideas in new and often surprising ways; "exploratory," which navigates a structured rule-based domain to uncover new possibilities; and "transformational," which alters the rules of the domain itself to produce new paradigms (348). Boden argues that AI tends to plateau at the exploratory level because it struggles to grasp the nuances of human values and cultural expressions essential for genuine transformational creativity (349). Along these lines, Andrew Murray compares post-war developments in Conceptual Art with current forms of AI-generated art, noting that while conceptual artists engaged in highly intentional and reflective debates on the nature and purpose of art, today's widely accessible AI-powered image-generation tools enable anyone to produce visually appealing results with minimal effort. This shift towards creative production "at the click of a button" raises concerns about deskilling, as automated image generation can bypass the material, critical, and reflective practices that have historically shaped artistic labour (Chap. 4).

This automation is not the equivalent of Joseph Beuys's famous saying, "Jeder Mensch ist ein Künstler" ("Every person is an artist"). As Eugen Blume (2021) notes, Beuys envisioned this idea not as an invitation to effortless automation but as "one of the last utopian promises," calling each human being to actively, creatively, and responsibly participate in the transformative reshaping of the planet—an ideal free of class hierarchies, structural inequities rooted in biases, and ecological degradation (Blume 2021, 17). Beuys conceived an expanded notion of art intended as a transformative act capable of addressing humankind's most pressing issues by uniting science with a creativity rooted in human compassion and social engagement. Beuys's vision contrasts with a future in which individuals sit alone at their desks generating tokenized virtual images, and instead calls each of us to embrace our shared responsibility.

Fast forward to 2025: some AI systems, when combined with artistic expertise and rigorous research, are beginning to blur the boundaries between exploratory and transformational creativity. Such emerging artistic practices challenge established creative processes and raise new questions about the nature of artistic agency. Jennifer L. Karson's team, for example, trains AI systems using studio-sourced datasets rather than indiscriminately scraped materials commonly used in text-to-image models, thereby contributing human expertise, integrity, and transparency to the AI creative process (Chap. 6).

Institutional Dimensions of AI

As the discussion in this anthology moves from individual creativity to the institutions that shape the cultural ecosystem, the focus shifts to how technological change is reshaping the stewardship of cultural heritage—particularly through efforts to confront bias and support reparative practices, a discourse that predates the widespread adoption of AI. Digital humanities, now considered a subfield of art history when applied to its research questions, has long expanded the field's methodological possibilities by integrating computational approaches, especially within the museum field (see Emily Leifer, Chap. 10). As Christopher Nygren and Sonja Drimmer (2023) observe, computer technology has been gradually influencing the field of art history since the 1960s, initially through collections management, and later by transforming research methodologies. With the new millennium, art historians trained in digital humanities have further expanded the field's research horizons through increasingly sophisticated computational approaches (Nygren and Drimmer 2023). Several contributors to this anthology demonstrate how collaborations with emerging AI technologies open new archival and interpretive pathways, including those with reparative potential.

Adriel Luis (Chap. 13) describes the human relationship with AI as a feedback loop, where people feed information into AI systems, and AI outputs in turn shape human beliefs and behaviours. When biased or inaccurate representations enter this loop, models tend to amplify stereotypes and reduce diverse groups to simplistic depictions. Giulia Taurino (Chap. 7) shows that the digitization of traditional catalogues, combined with recent developments in digital humanities, has made it possible to identify and expose terminology reflecting the colonial practices and frameworks of the periods in which they were used. In this sense, AI functions as a magnifying mirror of our humanity, revealing our shortcomings; at the same time, it can support reparative efforts when used critically. Bárbara Romero Ferrón and Nuria Rodríguez Ortega (Chap. 8) model co-curation practices, in which human curators closely supervise AI outputs. Astrid Runggaldier and Meghan Rubenstein (Chap. 16) extend such human oversight by bridging museum collections and the classroom, uniting their disciplinary expertise with layered pedagogical processes. Their work demonstrates how future museum professionals can learn to distinguish between meanings shaped by market forces and the objects themselves as authentic expressions of their cultures. Across these cases, the authors consistently emphasise the critical role of expert supervision in guiding, contextualizing, and ethically shaping technological innovations within museums and cultural heritage institutions.

Beyond Institutions: AI Transparency and Power

A look beyond these institutional concerns turns to the wider ethical landscape shaped by data transparency, model alignment, and the social and environmental consequences of large-scale AI deployment—issues that extend well beyond art history yet deeply affect the cultural sphere. These discussions bring the issue of transparency in data training to the forefront. Kay Kim (Chap. 14) argues that because datasets are scraped without consent and often overrepresent fetishised or stereotypical imagery, AI models tend to reproduce harmful cultural distortions, particularly for marginalised groups like East Asian women, thus requiring elaborate prompting by users to overcome them. This concern is shared by Tao et al. (2024), who argue that culture significantly shapes human thought and behaviour by embedding collective frameworks of meanings and norms within social groups. Outputs from large language models (LLMs) trained primarily on English-language data often reveal implicit biases that privilege Western cultural norms (Tao et al. 2024, 1–2). Nygren and Drimmer (2023) likewise emphasize the urgent need for critical oversight and the development of robust ethical frameworks to prevent AI-driven scholarship from reproducing or amplifying historical hierarchies.

Debbie Sue Jancis (2024) advocates for a global ethical framework for AI that articulates shared principles while remaining flexible enough to respond to regional contexts and align technological development with cultural and regulatory needs across different contexts (158–159). By underscoring AI's ongoing challenges in fully reflecting cultural nuance, this volume contributes to that broader alignment effort by offering the interpretive and critical insights that the humanities bring to technological debates (see Arvin Maghsoudlou's keen prompt analysis in Chap. 15). Monica Lanaro (Chap. 9), one of the architects of the 2016 award-winning project *Recognition*, helped pioneer ethical dataset sourcing by using fully authorised datasets from Tate UK and Reuters—an approach that parallels the artistic practices referenced earlier in this conclusion. Karl van Heerden (Chap. 12) models the adoption of an empirical research protocol that protects student participants and ensures responsible data use, following established standards in human-subject research in STEM and social sciences but historically extraneous to art history. Amanda Wasielewski (Chap. 2) frames these transparency dilemmas at the intersection of ethics and copyright law. Since AI models are trained on massive datasets that could potentially include copyrighted works used without permission, they raise concerns about intellectual property theft and the erosion of creative livelihoods.

These issues engage broader questions of power and consent operating both at the micro level of prompting and output, and at the macro level of societal surveillance. Brenda Segone (Chap. 3) warns that opaque deployment of these tools can create conditions that enable new forms of undue overreach through continuous tracking of citizens. This concern is echoed by Kurt Ralske (Chap. 5), who cautions that when people mistakenly attribute sentience to AI, they are more likely to trust and comply with AI outputs, especially if they assume these originate from a "higher" intelligence. Such misplaced trust could leave individuals and communities vulnerable to abuses of power. Taken together, these considerations circle back to Beuys's call for collective responsibility, underscoring that AI is not merely a matter of individuals learning to use new technological tools, but a profound social issue that humanity will need to navigate together.

Between Truth and Fabrication: AI's Epistemic Risks

Deepfakes represent a new form of media manipulation emerging within an already fragile information ecosystem: they further complicate efforts to detect and respond to manipulated content (Pawelec 2022), and they can also "undermine public trust, spread disinformation, erode the epistemic quality of content relevant to collective decision-making, and even discourage certain social groups from participating in public life" (Simon et al. 2024, 5). These challenges are compounded by large language models (LLMs), which generate highly convincing text based on probabilistic patterning rather than genuine understanding (Simon et al. 2024, 2). In this context, the ability to distinguish between authenticity and fabrication—between information and misinformation—becomes increasingly essential for preserving humanity's role as active decision-makers, rather than passive recipients of a reality increasingly shaped by non-human agents.

The discussion in this anthology also intersects with recent scholarship on AI alignment—the effort to ensure that LLMs operate in accordance with human values. Alignment is not merely a technical challenge; it is deeply normative, raising questions about whose values are encoded (see discussion in Chap. 2) and how to prevent bias amplification. These concerns resonate with art history's ethical mandate to preserve interpretive richness and resist reductive logics in shaping human–AI futures. As LLM and MLLM capabilities accelerate and progress towards artificial general intelligence becomes more plausible, the need to keep output aligned with human values and to minimise unintended consequences has never been more urgent: "As language agents become more integrated into various aspects of our daily lives, from content creation to decision support, any misalignment could result in unintended consequences. Properly aligning large language models with human values ensures that the vast potential of these models is harnessed trustworthily and responsibly" (Shen et al. 2023, 5). Shen et al.'s (2023) "alignment evaluation" (34) involves five key elements. The first one is the "factuality evaluation" (35), involving the verification of facts to ensure accuracy and minimize hallucinations. The second element is the "ethics evaluation" grounded in "justice, virtue ethics, deontology, utilitarianism, and commonsense morality" (36)—an inherently challenging task, given real-world complexities. The third element, "toxicity evaluation" (37), focuses on identifying manipulative or harmful content, from attacks on the user's self-esteem to incitement of violence. The fourth, "stereotype and bias evaluation" (38), involves the detection of language that is offensive to specific individuals or groups; and the last one is the "general evaluation" (42), which offers an overall assessment of LLM alignment by examining several dimensions at once.

The chapters in this anthology illustrate these evaluation principles through prompt engineering strategies rooted in humanistic inquiry (see Chaps. 13–16), highlighting a distinctive interpretive lens where "the exploration of the extraordinary is also an epistemic mark" (Dubreuil 2025, 48).

Responsible Innovation: Balancing Cultural Insight and Ecological Impact

As an educator and role model for students, Kimiko Matsumura (Chap. 11) frames the potential for students' acritical overreliance on AI outputs not only as a plagiarism issue but also, more broadly, as a form of desensitization to the impact of human actions on the broader world —from spreading disinformation, to perpetuating biases, to the steep environmental costs associated with AI's large-scale deployment—thus once again framing the issues around AI as collective responsibility. Given the significant environmental costs associated with AI development and deployment, these technologies must be used strategically, prioritising applications that advance societal well-being rather than fuelling disinformation or flooding the Internet with low-quality content that perpetuates harmful biases. Responsible use requires balancing innovation with sustainability, ensuring that AI serves as a tool for cultural enrichment and ethical progress rather than for ecological and epistemic harm.

Alongside cultural alignment, stewardship must also be ecological: the costs of large-scale AI deployment—carbon, water, and e-waste—demand that ethical use be sustainable. As AI models scale, their widespread use is likely to increase carbon emissions, water consumption, and electronic waste (Liu and Yin 2024; Sidorkin 2025), to the point that limits might eventually need to be imposed (Yu et al. 2024, 4). These insights converge on a single imperative for the field of art history: the discipline must continue to cultivate a critically engaged, human-centred partnership with AI—one that safeguards its unique interpretive depth while actively contributing to the shaping of a more thoughtful society. In a world increasingly shaped by algorithmic decision-making, art historians are uniquely equipped to decode the cultural, ethical, and emotional dimensions of this transformation. The future of AI is not merely technical; it is profoundly human. And it requires that art history step forward: not only to interpret the past, but to help shape the future, offering its wisdom, imagination, and care as a guiding light.

References

Blume, Eugen. 2021. Everyone Is an Artist. In *Everyone Is an Artist: Cosmopolitical Exercises with Joseph Beuys*, ed. Susanne Gaensheimer, Isabelle Malz, Eugen Blume, and Catherine Nichols, 17–21. Berlin: Hatje Cantz Verlag.

Boden, Margaret A. 1998. Creativity and Artificial Intelligence. *Artificial Intelligence* 103 (1-2): 347–356. https://doi.org/10.1016/S0004-3702(98)00055-1.

Nygren, Christopher and Sonja Drimmer. 2023. Art History and AI: Ten Axioms. *International Journal for Digital Art History* 9:5.02–5.13. https://doi.org/10.11588/dah.2023.9.90400.

Dubreuil, Laurent. 2025. *Humanities in the Time of AI.* Minneapolis: University of Minnesota Press.

Isgro, Marina. 2020. Modernism in Motion: Jean Tinguely's Meta-Mechanical Reliefs, 1954–59. *Art Journal* 79 (2): 6–23. https://doi.org/10.1080/00043249.2020.1765550.

Jancis, Debbie Sue. 2024. *AI Ethics: Status of the Present, Ethical Dilemmas, and Frameworks for the Practical Mind.* JFE Publishing.

Liu, Vivian, and Yiqiao Yin. 2024. Green AI: Exploring Carbon Footprints, Mitigation Strategies, and Trade Offs in Large Language Model Training. *Discover Artificial Intelligence* 4, 49: 1-12. https://doi.org/10.1007/s44163-024-00149-w.

Pawelec, Maria. 2022. Deepfakes and Democracy (Theory): How Synthetic Audio-Visual Media for Disinformation and Hate Speech Threaten Core Democratic Functions. *Digital Society* 1, 19: 1-37. https://doi.org/10.1007/s44206-022-00010-6.

Shen, Tianhao, Renren Jin, Yufei Huang, Chuang Liu, Weilong Dong, Zishan Guo, Xinwei Wu, Yan Liu, and Deyi Xiong. 2023. Large Language Model Alignment: A Survey. *arXiv preprint* arXiv:2309.15025. https://doi.org/10.48550/arXiv.2309.15025.

Sidorkin, Alexander M. 2025. Environmental Impact of Generative AI: Carbon and Water Footprint. *AI-EDU Arxiv Briefs*, March 21, 2025. https://doi.org/10.36851/ai-edu.vi.5448.

Simon, Judith, Gernot Rieder, and Jason Branford. 2024. The Philosophy and Ethics of AI: Conceptual, Empirical, and Technological Investigations into Values. *Digital Society* 3, 10: 1-13. https://doi.org/10.1007/s44206-024-00094-2.

Tao, Yan, Olga Viberg, Ryan S. Baker, and René F. Kizilcec. 2024. Cultural Bias and Cultural Alignment of Large Language Models. *PNAS Nexus* 3 (9): 1–9. https://doi.org/10.1093/pnasnexus/pgae346.

Yu, Yang, Jiahui Wang, Yu Liu, Pingfeng Yu, Dongsheng Wang, Ping Zheng, and Meng Zhang. 2024. Revisit the Environmental Impact of Artificial Intelligence: The Overlooked Carbon Emission Source? *Frontiers of Environmental Science & Engineering* 18, 158. https://doi.org/10.1007/s11783-024-1918-y.

Index[1]

[1] Note: Page numbers followed by 'n' refer to notes.

L. Cempellin, M. Geiger (eds.), *Reimagining Art History with Artificial Intelligence*,
https://doi.org/10.1007/978-3-032-21685-4

he manufacturer's authorised representative in the EU is Springer
re Customer Service Centre GmbH, Europaplatz 3, 69115 Heidelberg,
any. If you have any concerns regarding our products, please
t ProductSafety@springernature.com

nd bound by CPI Group (UK) Ltd, Croydon, CR0 4YY
17/09/2026
02218433-0008